The 100 Best Honeymoon Resorts of the World

100 BEST RESORTS SERIES

The 100 Best Honeymoon Resorts of the World

by
Katharine D. Dyson

A Voyager Book

The Globe Pequot Press

Old Saybrook, Connecticut

Photo credits: p. x: courtesy Little Palm Island; p. 3: courtesy Curtain Bluff; pp. 5, 277: courtesy Turtle Island; p. 24: courtesy Tashiro Marketing & Advertising, Inc.; p. 30: copyright © 1995 The Walt Disney Company; p. 52: courtesy Sheila Donnelly & Associates; p. 70: courtesy The Equinox; pp. 79, 122, 130, 237: photo by J. Dyson; p. 84: courtesy La Pinsonnière; p. 158: courtesy Sans Souci Lido; p. 161: courtesy Swept Away Resort; p. 198: photo by J.B. Weir; p. 209: courtesy La Casa que Canta; p. 215: courtesy Las Hadas; p. 222: courtesy ITT Sheraton Corporation; p. 242: photo by J. Jerrik; p. 254: courtesy Hotel Danieli; p. 257: Foto Vasconi; p. 263: copyright © Nick Passmore 1992, all rights reserved; p. 268: courtesy Bedarra Bay Resort; p. 286: courtesy Hotel Bora Bora. All others by the author.

Cover photo credits, from top to bottom: courtesy Sheila Donnelly & Associates (for Kona Village Resort); courtesy La Pinsonnière; courtest Turtle Island.

Library of Congress Cataloging-in-Publication Data
Dyson, Katharine D.
    100 best honeymoon resorts of the world / by Katharine D. Dyson. -- 1st ed.
        p. cm. — (The 100 best resorts series)
    "A Voyager book."
    Includes index.
    ISBN 1-56440-765-9
    1. Hotels—Guidebooks.   2. Resorts—Guidebooks.   3. Honeymoon.
    I. Title. II. Series.
TX907.D97   1996
647.94'025—dc20   95–44145
                                                          CIP

Manufactured in the United States of America
First Edition/First Printing

To my husband, John, with my heartfelt thanks and appreciation for cheerfully enduring my long hours at the computer, late meals, and piles of paper all over the house. With much love for making our life—at home or on the road—a continual honeymoon.

Contents

Author's Thanks

Since the quality of a resort can change dramatically in a short period of time, I have made sure that each place comes with a firsthand, recent recommendation. However, because of time and distance constraints involved in researching and writing such a book, it was physically impossible for me to personally revisit each of the 100 resorts within the allotted time frame and still get the material to the publisher on deadline. Thus I am indebted to many fellow travel writers and others who have generously helped me put together an accurate, up-to-date account of these 100 most romantic resorts around the globe.

My deepest appreciation to the following people:

Risa Weinreb, for her many contributions, particularly on resorts in Hawaii, Tahiti, Morocco, and California; Jerry Mekler, who scouted out some of the Florida properties; Lea Lane, Roberta Graff, and Sara Southworth, who shared their experiences and wrote about recent visits to several resorts; Jean Rae for her Bermuda input; Christopher Pinckney for Hyatt Regency Aruba; Georgina Kassatly for Hyatt Regency Grand Cayman and Merrie Murray for Four Seasons Maui. Also Frank "Poncho" Shiell for all his help in Ixtapa/Zihuatanejo; Bob Burrichter and Rose Abello of Karen Weiner Escalera Associates; Deborah Bernstein of Hyatt Hotels; Cheryl Andrews of Cheryl Andrews Marketing; Marcella Martinez of Marcella Martinez Associates; Teresa Delaney of Relais & Châteaux; Karen Preston of Leading Hotels of the World; Mary Homi of Mary Homi International Public Relations; Megan Sumner of Burson-Marsteller; Donna Attra and Clif Cooke of *Jax Fax Travel Marketing Magazine;* Geri Bain of *Modern Bride;* as well as Virgin Atlantic Airways, Air Aruba, and American Airlines.

My thanks also to the following who took time to meet with me and share their resort experiences: Jack and Jeanne Klinge, June Lurey, Doris Forest, Reenie and Roy Makowsky, Ruth Gold, Betsy and Joel Russell, Barbara Riley and Audrey Harper.

Also my deep appreciation to my editor, Laura Strom, at Globe Pequot Press.

Little Palm Island, Florida

Introduction

Selecting the "100 Best Honeymoon Resorts in the World" is much like tapping an iceberg: The more you chip away, the more you discover. With this first edition I have described a wide and diverse selection of wonderfully romantic resorts to consider for your honeymoon.

Each of the 100 Best has unique, special qualities—some are even a bit quirky. In my travels and research I came across some marvelous places that perhaps didn't quite fit the definition of a full-service resort. Nonetheless, because they are especially romantic and may be just what you're looking for, they are in the book.

All of the 100 Best have a number of characteristics in common. These include:

1. Romantic setting
2. Best in category/region for overall quality
3. Primarily caters to vacationers seeking recreation, entertainment, and escape from the "real world"
4. Easy to reach
5. Safe location
6. Excellent, friendly service
7. One or more restaurants on the property
8. Spiffy clean and superbly maintained
9. Appeals to couples in love
10. Offers good value

Romantic setting. This is very subjective: Some might love a deserted beach with coconut palms, others a window view of an early morning "moon set" over a river in Africa, or perhaps a cabin in the woods with a crackling fire. I have written these profiles so that you can grasp the unique character and essence of each resort. It's up to you to choose what turns you on.

Best in category. It might have made my job easier if I had simply gone for the most expensive and exclusive places in each regional area. Expense doesn't necessarily add up to value, though, and since many honeymooners are just starting out, I've included a number of reasonably priced resorts as well as the pricier hotels to give you a range of choices—all which represent the best in their price category for ambience and quality.

Recreation, entertainment, and escape. These resorts are more than just a place to overnight. Most have pools and/or beaches for swimming, tennis courts, and fitness facilities. Recreation might mean skiing, hiking, horseback riding, windsurfing, or croquet; entertainment could be anything from soft piano music to disco. The bottom line is that these resorts cater to travelers who are on vacation, rather than on a business trip. The 100 Best exist for fun and romance.

Easy to reach. After all the excitement of the wedding festivities is over and you find yourself on your way to your honeymoon destination, if you are like most newlyweds, you'll suddenly realize you are both quite exhausted. It would help if your trip to your resort is a quick and easy one. The majority of the resorts in this book are within reasonable traveling distance of North America, I have included some in exotic faraway places, however, for those who feel adventurous and have the time and money to go farther. If you do decide on a long journey, I would suggest you spend a night or two at a lovely inn close by and give yourselves time to unwind before boarding a plane bound for Fiji or Africa.

Safe location. It's your honeymoon. You want to feel safe and secure. Going to an iffy area with a history of turbulence is not a good idea if you want to relax and simply enjoy each other. The 100 Best are what are considered to be located in safe, stable areas (at press time), but remember that no matter where you go, you should always take necessary precautions such as putting your money in travelers checks and stowing cash in two or three different places. Carry all the "must have" items with you on the plane (don't check them with your luggage) and put your valuable items in the hotel safe. Better yet, leave expensive jewelry at home, and you won't have to worry about it.

Excellent, friendly service. When you order room service at 3:00 A.M., you'd like to get your order before the sun rises. When your waiter greets you at the table, it would be nice to see a smile. All these things help make your resort experience a fine one.

Choice of restaurants. It's good to have two or more places to eat, ranging from gourmet/formal to casual. A range of prices, ambience, and kinds of cuisine is also important.

Clean and superbly maintained. There's nothing like a leaky faucet dripping in the middle of the night or a dust ball behind a chair to turn the romance level down a notch or two. The 100 Best get high ratings in the cleanliness and maintenance departments.

Appeals to couples in love. Now here's where it gets tricky. I discovered some great resorts that had all my other criteria except this one. Perhaps the youngest guest was the thirty-seven-year-old third wife of a seventy-five-year-old baron. Or the kids took over the pool most of the day. Or the resort was just too exclusive, geared to the hopelessly well off and out of reach to all but 2 percent of our readers (who probably already know

Curtain Bluff, Antigua

where they are jetting off to and don't need anyone to tell them where to go). Resorts like these didn't make it.

Good value. This is very important. I tried to eliminate any place that was unreasonable or doing the "big rip-off." If prices are steep to begin with and you know it, you can budget for it. If rates at first sound reasonable and then the cash register starts ringing up every time you climb on a windsurfer, play an hour of tennis, or walk into the nightclub, your good deal starts to devalue. Whenever possible, I have listed romance packages and other plans that give you the biggest bang for your buck. Even if a package is not listed in the book, ask the resort if they offer any special plans, such as ones for tennis, scuba diving, or golf. Many do; they just may not promote them.

One of the best bets for budget-minded honeymooners is the all-inclusive resort, where one price pays for everything, including drinks, meals, and sports activities. No surprises here at checkout time.

Helpful Tips for Using This Book

Each resort profile in this guide begins with a complete description of the resort, including its special features, ambience, decor, cuisine, and activities offered. Following the description is a section of at-a-glance information about the resort—types of accommodations, rates, sports and facilities available, and so on. Most of this information is self-explanatory, but the following clarification of a few items should help you utilize this book to the fullest as you plan your honeymoon.

Rates: Each resort has its own unique way of putting together its rate schedule. Although I have tried to give you the rates in as consistent a manner as possible, you will see several variations on such details as seasons—some have none, others several—and items that are included in a package. I have given you my best shot in describing these rates so you can understand what is and is not offered.

Following are some terms used throughout the book in reference to rates.

> *Rack Rates:* Published rates—usually the top retail price without any discounts.
>
> *MAP:* Modified American Plan; includes accommodations, breakfast, and dinner
>
> *AP:* American Plan; includes accommodations, breakfast, lunch, and dinner
>
> *EP:* European Plan; includes just the accommodations

Package Rates: Promotional packages that are discounted and/or geared to specific-interest groups such as honeymooners; these include a number of extra features, such as champagne and room upgrade.

All-Inclusive: Usually this means that the rate includes accommodations, all meals, sports, and other activities. A truly all-inclusive rate will include all beverages, including name-brand liquors; some even include the wedding ceremony. I have found, however, resorts that advertise an all-inclusive rate but require you to pay for your beverages. Read the fine print and make sure you know what you're buying.

Room Upgrade: This means getting a better room than you paid for. It is dependent on whether or not one is available and is usually not guaranteed.

Seasonal Rates: Prices are geared to the time of year and can vary widely from hotel to hotel. The high season is the most expensive and is the time when the resort is the busiest. In the Caribbean this means the colder months; in Europe it's usually spring, summer, and fall; in New England it is often fall foliage season. Christmastime is also considered high season by many places. Low season rates are the least expensive and are available when the resort is not in such great demand. Some resorts do not use season designations but instead give you a schedule of periods during the year with their corresponding rates. Some offer just one year-round rate. ("Shoulder" season rates are those between high and low.)

Deposit: Deposit and refund policies vary greatly with each hotel. Some

Turtle Island, Fiji

require only a guarantee with a credit card. Typically you get your money back if you cancel within a particular period. Check with the hotel and be sure you understand their policy

Exchange Rates: You'll find that some of the rates in this book are in U.S. dollars, others in local currency. Often when a hotel has a U.S. representative, you'll find rates quoted in U.S. dollars. Some hotels, however, only quote in their local money. To convert to U.S. dollars, look up the exchange rate in the daily paper (usually in the business section).

Arrival/Departure: Transfers mentioned under this item refer to the resort's arrangements for getting you from and to the airport, i.e., by bus, van, private car, or otherwise.

Weddings: If you want to get married at your honeymoon destination, make sure you inquire well ahead of time as to residency requirements, documents required, etc. Your travel agent, resort, and/or country tourism office representative in the United States can help you with this.

A note about electricity: Dual-voltage appliances such as hair dryers often have a special switch that allows you to convert to either 110 or 220 volts. You will also, however, need a special plug for your appliances when traveling to many places out of the country. Hardware stores generally sell these plugs in sets.

Tips on planning your honeymoon

Attention to the following details can make the difference between having an OK honeymoon and a great one.

1. Book a late flight the morning after the wedding when possible.
2. Know what your budget is and work within these limits. If money is tight, look into an all-inclusive resort, where you know ahead of time what you'll spend. Many resorts sound reasonably priced until you add up all the extra charges. Checkout time can be a mind-blower.
3. Book the best room you can afford. Complaints from returning honeymooners tend to focus on the quality of their accommodations.
4. Ask about bed size. In some parts of the world, double beds may be smaller than what you'd expect. In Europe, you'll find a lot of twin-bedded rooms, so if you're Europe-bound, you might want to ask for a "matrimonial bed."
5. Both the bride and groom should take part in deciding where to go and how much to spend.
6. Unless you want to keep your honeymoon a secret, let the hotel know ahead of time that you are newly married (your travel agent can do this for you). Honeymooners often enjoy special perks, such as champagne and breakfast in bed.
7. It is often helpful to be in the travel agent's office while your room is being booked so that you can answer any special questions the hotel might have.
8. If being directly on the beach overlooking the water is very important to you, make sure the hotel and the room you book is just that. Sometimes properties advertised as "beachfront hotels" are in reality not right on the beach, but close by. Rooms may also have a view of the garden instead of the water.
9. Ask about the best way to get from the airport to your resort. Are you being met? Do you need to look for someone in particular? How much is a taxi or van service?
10. If you are renting a car, find out ahead of time about insurance requirements. Check with your credit card company to see if you are covered by collision damage waiver.
11. Check what travel documentation you will need and get everything in order.
12. On international travel, it is good to fax the hotels a few days before your arrival date to reconfirm your arrangements. This is particularly important when the booking was made well in advance. This is one vacation you want to make sure runs like clockwork. Your travel agent should do this for you, but be sure to request that it be done.

13. I highly recommend purchasing trip cancellation insurance. If you have to cancel for any reason (heaven forbid), you'll get your deposit back. Ask your travel agent about this.

14. If you are traveling to a place such as Africa or the South Pacific, check with your doctor or local health authority to find out if you need any special inoculations or medicines to take either prior to or during your trip. In some areas you must show proof that you are up to date on certain disease-preventing immunizations (for example, yellow fever and malaria) in order to enter the country.

15. If you are not leaving for your vacation destination until a day or two after your wedding, you may want to stay at a relaxing, romantic inn on your first night. Most couples find they are quite exhausted after the festivities and need some time to unwind.

16. Book your airline seats at the same time you make plane reservations. This is also the time to order special meals if you have any dietary restrictions.

Honeymoon Countdown

Don't wait until the last minute to plan your honeymoon. Good groundwork can really pay off when it comes to lining up the perfect romantic holiday. Here are some guidelines.

• *Five months before your wedding:* Select a travel agent, read up on destinations, and nail down your budget. Be sure to include spending money in your calculations.

• *Four months:* Decide where you're going and book your reservations with your travel agent.

• *Three months:* Get your travel documents together. Allow up to six weeks to process the paperwork for a new passport. Applications are available at the main branch of your local post office and at U.S. government passport agencies.

• *Two months:* Get your confirmation numbers for hotel, airlines, rental cars, etc.

• *One month to one week:* Purchase film for your camera. Check to make sure your camera batteries are working. Get out the converter plugs for your hair dryer, etc., or purchase them from a hardware store. Confirm your reservations and get your traveler's checks.

This book offers a wide range of resorts to choose from. You and your partner should look through it individually and select a few establishments that appeal to each of your tastes. Then compare notes and narrow down the list to the ones that sound wonderful to both of you. The next step is to contact your travel agent for brochures and more information.

My hope is your honeymoon will be far more romantic than you ever dreamed; that you'll get the opportunity to get off the beaten track and create memories that will last a lifetime as you discover what is unique and special about a place, its people, and its traditions.

I welcome your comments on the resorts included in this book and would appreciate any suggestions for other resorts that should be considered for the next edition. Please address all comments to K. Dyson, 15 Nutmeg Ridge, Ridgefield, CT 06877.

The prices and rates listed in this guidebook were confirmed at press time. We recommend, however, that you call the resorts before traveling to obtain current information.

The United States and Canada

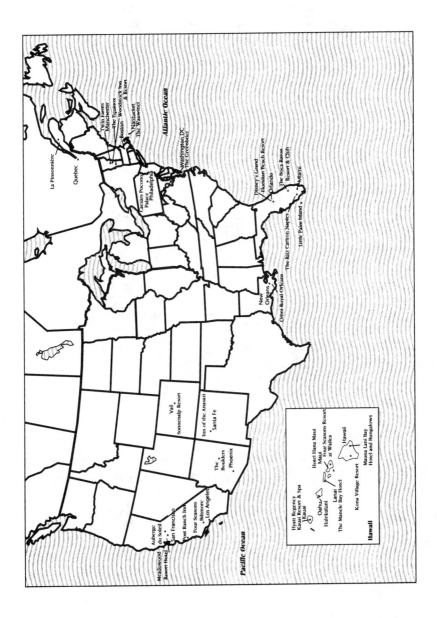

Arizona

The Boulders, Arizona

The Boulders

Location: Nestled in the high Sonoran Desert northeast of Phoenix and Scottsdale, Arizona, on 1,300 acres.
Romantic Features: Vast beauty of the desert setting; fireplace in your private casita; hikes on the magnificent grounds; balloon rides over the desert.

As you approach the resort and round a corner, you see just ahead some huge, reddish boulders. At first you don't see the resort itself—it blends so well into its environment. Individual casitas are molded into the terrain; the wall around the pool is interrupted here and there by boulders that were never moved, but rather incorporated into the design.

You know you are in the desert. In the evening you may hear the cries of a coyote. The days are sunny and warm; nights, cool. Giant fingers of the saguaro cactus, several times as tall as you are, stick up out of the desert foliage; one even sits smack in the center of a rather formidable sand trap. It was there when the golf course was built, so the trap was simply constructed around it to preserve the 300-year-old "desert monument."

Granite boulders, their edges rounded and smoothed by millions of years of wear, sit one atop another in a bit of a hodgepodge, just as they have lain for centuries, as silent sentries watching over the desert. Tucked in the crevices and cracks and rooted in the land are the flowers and plants of this rich desert environment, for the Sonoran is home to more than 2,500 species of plant life and more than 600 species of birds. From its inception, those who carved The Boulders into the desert did it with great ecological sensitivity. The 160 casitas made of earth-tone adobe were hand molded and rubbed to follow the contours of the rocks and land, and like the ancient boulders themselves, hard edges were softened and rounded.

Each individual casita has a sitting area and fireplace, balcony, large tiled bath, and comfortable chairs and sofas upholstered in earthy fabrics reflecting the rich colors and patterns of the desert and the arts of its people. Stone floors, hand-hewn ceiling beams, area rugs, baskets, clay pots, and regional art objects and paintings add to the southwestern ambience. You'll find many of the Indian weavings and paintings hanging on the walls are for sale. Just ask.

Life at The Boulders revolves around the main lodge, where you'll find most of the restaurants. Thanks to their emphasis on healthy eating, you can enjoy food such as mesquite-grilled meats and fish, roast range chicken, anchiote-basted veal chop with sun-dried tomato orzo, grilled salmon and quesadilla with Anaheim chiles. Through the large windows,the indoor Latilla restaurant affords marvelous views of the Sonoran landscape and a softly lit waterfall. The Palo Verde restaurant invites you to dine outside, where the "walls" are massive cacti and flowering plants.

Enjoy breakfast on your balcony while you gaze across the desert to the mountains and hills. Or get cozy in front of your fireplace, with a wood fire blazing away.

At the Boulders golf course restaurant, you can eat lunch and dinner on the terrace overlooking the fairways and mountain foothills. The Discovery Lounge, in the main lodge, features live entertainment most evenings.

There are two great golf courses at The Boulders, which, like the rest of the resort, have been integrated into the landscape. A special kind of grass that needs much less water than traditional fairway grasses is used. Named by *Golf Magazine* as one of the nation's top twelve golf resorts, The Boulders treats its players to stunning vistas from elevated tees—on one hole you actually tee off from the top of a boulder.

In addition to the two golf courses, The Boulders Club, a private country club reserved exclusively for resort guests and club members, includes the Tennis Center, with six courts and a pro shop. Clinics and private lessons are offered daily. And if this isn't enough, you'll find two pools at your disposal.

The $3.7 million Fitness Center offers programs such as aerobics, hiking, biking, and flexibility exercises. The new $1.8 million Sonoran Spa features a number of special treatments, such as reflexology, Swedish and sports massages, and special body treatments utilizing the natural healing properties of desert herbs—not a bad way to wind up the day if you've been playing golf or tennis.

You can explore the area on horseback or hike on the Apache Trail, which passes by lakes, volcanic rock formations, and awesome buttes. A colorful market area, el Pedregal, contains more than forty boutiques, restaurants, art galleries, and an amphitheater where dance concerts and theatrical performances are scheduled.

No great resort can stand on its physical beauty and facilities alone, and The Boulders goes to the top of the class for its friendly and solicitous staff. You are greeted warmly on your arrival, and if you come back for more visits (and you will), you are remembered and catered to. And who wouldn't want to return? This is one super place.

Address/Phone: P.O. Box 2090, 34631 North Tom Darlington Drive, Carefree, AZ 85377;(602) 488–9009; fax: (602) 488–4118

Reservations: (800) 553–1717

Owner/Manager: William J. Nassikas, president; Kenneth Humes, general manager

Arrival/Departure: Pickup at either the Scottsdale or Phoenix airports can be arranged; with prior permission, private planes may land at the Carefree Airport. A helicopter landing pad is also located on-site.

Distance from Scottsdale Airport: 13 miles (30 minutes); 33 miles from Phoenix Sky Harbor Airport

Distance from Phoenix: 16 miles

Accommodations: 160 adobe guest casitas

Best Rooms/Suites: If you like water views, try one of the casitas near the end overlooking the pond.

Amenities: Air-conditioning, ceiling fan, wood-burning fireplace, wet bar, large dressing area, TV, toiletries, telephone, room service

Electricity: 110 volts

Sports and Facilities: 2 championship 18-hole golf courses; tennis park featuring 6 plexi-cushioned courts and a pro shop; Fitness Center with Aerobic Studio, weight room, heated outdoor lap pool, hiking program; desert jeep tours, hot-air ballooning, horseback riding; spa

Dress Code: Casually smart

Weddings: Can be arranged

Rates/Packages: $295–$495 per couple per night, including breakfast and dinner. Honeymoon package, $1,735–$2,175 per couple, includes 5 nights in private casita, breakfasts and dinners, champagne, 1-hour horseback ride, 2½-hour sunset jeep tour, unlimited use of Fitness Center, spa and swimming pools. Golf and sports packages available.

Payment/Credit Cards: Most major

Deposit: 2-night deposit or half the package rate to be applied to first and last night's stay. Cancel 3 weeks in advance of arrival date for full refund.

Gov't Taxes: 10.25 percent tax on accommodations; 6.7 percent tax on food and beverage charges

Service Charges: $15 per night in lieu of cash gratuities for all resort personnel, excluding those serving food and beverages

Closed: Late June to early September

California

Auberge du Soleil

Location: Thirty-three-acre olive grove in the Mayacama foothills.

Romantic Features: Knockout views of Napa Valley's most illustrious vineyards (each room has a private deck and fireplace); ½-mile nature trail studded with more than fifty sculptures.

Location, location, location is yours to savor at this luxury resort in the heart of Napa Valley wine country. Snuggled in an olive grove in the eastern Mayacama foothills, Auberge du Soleil overlooks a tapestry of vineyards, stone wineries, and the rugged ridge of the Mayacamas Mountains. A Relais & Chateaux property, it's the perfect hideaway for couples wanting to sample the best of the wine country lifestyle—tasting rooms and fine restaurants, smart boutiques and antiques stores, hot-air ballooning and bicycling.

Auberge cossets guests in tranquil beauty from the moment they enter the lobby, with its oversize floral display placed on a massive cast-stone table. The grounds are spectacular, with gardens and courtyards cached in nooks and crannies accented by pergolas, fountains, and gigantic pots overflowing with ivy geranium.

Accommodations are tucked into one-story villas, stuccoed in warm earth tones. Inside, the decor is class, not flash, embellished with cool Mexican tile floors and rawhide chairs. Recently redecorated, the guest rooms now percolate in vibrant (and maybe a tad strident) hues of hot pink and yellow. Everything encourages you to relax, from the two chaise longues poised on the terrace, to the king-size bed primped with a medley of oversize pillows. Flowers are everywhere, either arranged in vases or floating languidly in glass bowls.

Even more impressive is how every need seems to have been anticipated. Logs are laid in your fireplace, candles and bath salts wait by the side of the tub (some units have Jacuzzis), even the extra roll of toilet paper comes "giftwrapped" with a bow. Both drawer and closet spaces are ample, and the wet bar includes a refrigerator stocked with regional wines and cheeses.

In fine weather (almost a certainty here in Northern California), you'll enjoy basking by the lovely swimming pool, heated to a comfy 85 degrees year-round. Broad wooden decks provide plenty of space for sunning, while a flotilla of white market umbrellas seem to mirror the resort's contours all the way to distant mountain peaks. Tennis players can hone their strokes on three hard courts. While the workout room, equipped with exercise bike, stair machine, and free weights, is small, it features incredible valley views. You'll also enjoy strolling through the inn's new sculpture garden, displaying a collection of sixty works by well-known artists. Set in a four-acre olive grove, it provides a unique venue for appreciating works alfresco.

For wining and dining, there's the Auberge du Soleil restaurant, with meals served either indoors in a French country dining room or outdoors on a rough-hewn wooden deck with awesome views of the valley. Actually, our only quibbles about the resort concern the restaurant, which for the past few years has strayed into serving unimpressive wine-country cuisine at exorbitant prices. Service can also get a bit high-handed. Recently one diner, not all that hungry, ordered just a salad and appetizer. "Is that all you're having?" the waiter asked condescendingly.

While menu descriptions sound inviting enough—pan-seared natural veal chop with green-onion risotto—the result on your plate does not justify the $30 price tag. With some of America's best restaurants just a few miles away, including the French Laundry, Mustards, Tra Vigne, and Catahoula's, it seems a shame to shell out top dollar for a mediocre meal. You might be wise to forgo the restaurant entirely and instead dine on the bar terrace: same wonderful views, similar competent food—at about one-half the price. Time your reservation so you can catch the last glow of sunset flaming behind the mountains. By dessert, the stars will be twinkling goodnight.

All this nit-picking really reflects a desire to see the restaurant do better. Auberge du Soleil is so good, we'd love to see it reach perfection.

Address/Phone: P.O. Drawer B, 180 Rutherford Hill Road, Rutherford, CA 94573, (707) 963–1211; fax: (707) 963–8764

Reservations: (800) 348–5406; Relais & Chateaux, (800) RELAIS 8

Owner/Manager: George A. Goeggel, general manager

Arrival/Departure: Car rentals available at airport

Distance from San Francisco International Airport: 65 miles north (1½ hours)

Distance from Rutherford: 5 minutes

Accommodations: 50 one-, two-, and three-room suites, each with valley views and fireplaces

Best Rooms/Suites: The Upper Suites are the most spectacular, with huge patios and large living rooms.

Amenities: Air-conditioning, fireplace, refrigerator stocked with wine and cheese, TV, VCR, coffeemaker, basket of snacks; toiletries, skylight in bath, double sink, some baths with Jacuzzi, hair dryer; valet, 24-hour room service, down comforter, bathrobes, slippers, twice-daily maid service; full-service beauty salon

Electricity: 110 volts

Sports and Facilities: Swimming pool; massage, whirlpool, steam rooms, and small workout room; 3 tennis courts (instruction available). Golf, horseback riding, bicycling, and jogging nearby.

Dress Code: Casually smart

Weddings: Can be arranged

Rates/Packages: $175–$475 per couple per night for a room; $375–$800 for a suite. Romance package, $525 per couple per night, includes 1 night in a one-bedroom suite with fireplace and private terrace; wine, flowers, and Napa Valley guidebook upon arrival; dinner and breakfast for two; and one choice from a variety of options, such as a 3-hour winery tour in a town car. Available Sunday through Thursday only, holidays excluded.

Payment/Credit Cards: Most major

Deposit: Your reservation will be confirmed in writing upon receipt of full payment. Prepayment is required at the time of booking to secure your

reservations. Reservations must be cancelled 14 days prior to scheduled arrival date to receive a refund.
Government Taxes: 10.5 percent
Service Charges: Not included

Four Seasons Biltmore

Location: Across the street from Butterfly Beach, in the exclusive Montecito enclave.
Romantic Features: Beachfront setting, Roaring Twenties panache (the hotel opened in 1927), glamorous public areas.

The Four Seasons Biltmore reigns as the red tile–roofed queen of Santa Barbara. You can't beat the vintage 1920s style or the California dream setting, with the deep-blue Pacific glimmering just across the way.

The resort glows with the burnished patina of a classic. It opened in 1927 as part of the original Biltmore chain; the property became a Four Seasons resort in 1987. Over the years, the clientele has included everyone from Douglas Fairbanks to Michael Douglas and President Ronald Reagan. (The Reagan ranch is located in the nearby Santa Ynez foothills.)

Set on nineteen acres, the Spanish-Mediterranean resort is composed of a main building plus separate wings and cottages. Public areas resemble the castle of a Spanish grandee, with high, coffered ceilings, thick, red tile floors, and hand-painted tiles adorning the corridors and stairways. Red tile or flagstone walkways ramble past bright green lawns and impeccable flower borders. Giant blue gum trees, broad Monterey cypress, and spreading camphor trees shade the grounds.

Accommodations all differ in layout and view; there are also separate cottages poised along the back ridge of the property in a lush garden setting. Furnishings reflect classic good taste (although they're a little bit bland), decorated in a palette of soothing tones of sage, sand, and peach. You can slide open the white plantation shutters for an airy country cottage feel (rooms are not air-conditioned, but the oceanside setting practically always keeps temperatures comfortable). Extremely well laid out, the white-marble bathrooms are replete with nice touches such as Chinese ceramic containers to hold cotton balls. Some rooms have fireplaces, balconies, or private patios.

The new executive chef, Eric Brennan, who had garnered top notices while at the Four Seasons Boston, now presides over the Biltmore's superb four restaurants. Dining in The Patio is like eating in a country garden—

there's even a glass roof with retractable panels to open or close to fit the weather's moods. The nightly Mediterranean buffet earns raves, and Sunday brunch is a Santa Barbara tradition, with huge platters of fresh seafood, a stir-fry table, omelette and Belgian waffle stations, and lots more. Afternoon tea is served in the Sala Lounge, an elegant drawing room beautified with a high, open-beamed ceiling and a fireplace. La Marina is known for romantic dining, with flowers, candlelight, and arched windows framing the seaward view. In addition to a la carte selections, Chef Brennan presents a four-course tasting menu, where choices might include squab with scallion polenta and mission figs, followed by roast tenderloin of veal. Heading to a polo match or into Santa Barbara wine country? The hotel can customize a picnic basket for you.

Guests enjoy preferred tee-time privileges at Sandpiper Golf Course, one of the top-rated public golf layouts in the country. For tennis players, there are three lighted courts. On the property, you'll also find an eighteen-hole putting green, croquet, and shuffleboard; the concierge can make arrangements for sportfishing, horseback riding, and sailing.

The recently refurbished workout room comes with an ocean view, along with treadmill, bikes, free weights, and stair machines, and lolling by the Olympic-size swimming pool on the edge of the Pacific makes life luxuriously wonderful. But the biggest treats of all may just be the guest privileges at the Art Deco–era Coral Casino, a private club that has been the center of Santa Barbara social life for over half a century.

Address/Phone: 1260 Channel Drive, Santa Barbara, CA 93108; (805) 969–2261; fax: (805) 969–4682
Reservations: (800) 332–3442
Owners/Managers: Managed by the Four Seasons Hotels & Resort
Arrival/Departure: Transfers can be arranged; car rentals available at airport
Distance from Santa Barbara Airport: 12 miles
Distance from downtown Santa Barbara: 2 miles (5 minutes)
Accommodations: 234 rooms and suites, many with balconies or private patios and fireplaces
Best Rooms/Suites: Cottage suites; Odell Cottage suite is top of the heap.
Amenities: Air-conditioning, ceiling fan, hair dryer, 3 phones, VCR, TV, in-room safe, minibar, bathrobes, AM/FM clock/radio, toiletries; in-room spa treatments available, 24-hour room service, twice-daily maid service, shoe shine
Electricity: 110 volts
Sports and Facilities: 3 tennis courts, 2 swimming pools, bicycles; golf and whale watching expeditions nearby (February to mid-April)

Dress Code: Casually elegant
Weddings: Can be arranged
Rates/Packages: $199–$360 per couple per night for a room; $650 for a suite. Romance package (3 days, 2 nights): $540–$660 per couple. Includes welcome bottle of champagne, dinner for two at La Marina restaurant.
Payment/Credit Cards: Most major
Deposit: Deposits are required within 14 days of making reservation. Cancellations are accepted with a full refund up to 72 hours prior to the expected arrival date.
Government Taxes: 10 percent
Service Charges: Not included

Meadowood Resort Hotel

Location: In the heart of the Napa Valley wine region, just outside the charming town of St. Helena.
Romantic Features: Wood-burning fireplaces; private cottages hidden up a long, winding lane; great spa facilities (a well-kept secret).

You'll be treated like Napa Valley landed gentry while staying at this luxury resort located in the area's most prestigious country club. The Meadowood Resort Hotel is a picture perfect property tucked into a 250-acre vale off the Silverado Trail. A member of the Relais & Chateaux group, this elegant hideaway is surrounded by vineyards and trees.

You'll feel as if you've stepped back in time when you enter the turn-of-the-century farmhouse-style lobby, with its huge fireplace, bowls of apples ready for the taking, and glass-fronted cabinets filled with books and knickknacks. For Meadowood's casual, clubby atmosphere reflects hominess and coziness, not glitz; it's conducive to doing nothing—yet it offers all the facilities of a full service luxury resort.

Over the years, the property served as a Christmas tree farm and rice paddy, before being groomed into the area's preeminent golf course and country club in the 1960s. The resort itself opened in 1984, and today guests rub shoulders with the "who's who" of Napa Valley, especially during the many top social events that are held here, including the annual Napa Valley Wine Auction in June.

Guests dwell in grey clapboard cottages, which look part Martha's Vineyard, part California wine country, with gables, white trim, cathedral ceilings, and stone fireplaces. There is more than a little romance in these gracious abodes nestled into the woods of tall California oaks and conifers. What a place to go and hide out—with the scent of pine permeating the airy rooms, a fine Chardonnay resting in an ice bucket next to two flutes, plush down comforters, and piles of fat pillows stacked on the queen-size bed; and in the cooler months, a cozy fire crackling in your fireplace. With room service available, who needs to go anywhere?

One of the best features of the cottages are the wraparound porches, each with an oh-so-private sitting area furnished with rockers. In your room you'll find rattan furniture, a writing desk and minibar and tasteful decor. Bathrooms are spacious and come with all the modern comforts. Some cottages have kitchenettes.

Meadowood offers a tantalizing array of choices for the sports-minded. In addition to miles of hiking and walking trails, where it would not be unusual for a deer or two to cross your path; you can swim in two pools and play croquet on the primped and clipped croquet lawns, which are trimmed as meticulously as a golf green and have wickets just the thickness of a nickel wider than the ball.

You can shake out your golf game on the resort's nine-hole course, play tennis, explore the area by bike, or be pampered with a variety of soothing treatments at the new (1993) health spa. The aerobics room provides a setting for classes ranging from a thirty-minute abs intensive to yoga, and the air-conditioned exercise room features Cybex equipment, bikes, stair machines, and more. The masseur will even do treatments in your room—one of life's great happinesses.

Want to check out Napa Valley and the grapes? You can get an overview of more than one hundred vineyards from a lofty perch in a hot air balloon, or you can hop in a car and explore the area. Pick up a loaf of sourdough bread (a specialty in the region), a bottle of wine, and some good cheese and have a picnic on the way. Meadowood can help you with directions and suggestions for visiting not only the vineyards but the scores of art galleries and boutiques in the vicinity.

The Restaurant at Meadowood offers the most extensive wine list in the valley, with more than 600 selections. Practically every vineyard in the valley is represented, and bottles are all fairly priced. Overlooking gnarled oaks and the golf course, the dining room makes an especially pretty picture at night, with floral displays, table lamps, spotlighted watercolors, and music from the bar's player piano in the background. The menu tempts you with seared diver scallops with white truffles and bacon butter; crisp salmon with ratatouille and red-beet vinaigrette; lightly smoked Maine lobster with caramelized potatoes; or roast rabbit with foie gras. Desserts are hard to resist, but the flourless chocolate cake is rich enough to satisfy the most audacious of chocoholics. All this, of course, is accompanied by a fine wine—would you expect anything less here!

Breakfast, lunch, and dinner are served in the casual Napa Valley Bistro, and snacks are available during the summer months at the poolside cafe. The food and other services are delivered by a caring, attentive staff in a friendly, unobtrusive manner.

Meadowood is a peaceful and unspoiled sanctuary in the midst of one of the nation's most interesting areas. Little more than an hour's drive from San Francisco, it is an exceptional retreat that has great charm and style. With its woodsy privacy it can help you put the outside world on hold.

Address/Phone: 900 Meadowood Lane, St. Helena, CA 94574; (707) 963–3646; fax: (707) 963–3532

Reservations: (800) 458–8080; Relais & Chateaux, (800) RELAIS 8;

Owner/Manager: Jorg Lippuner, managing director; H. William Harlan, managing partner

Arrival/Departure: Limousine service available from airport

Distance from San Francisco Airport: 70 miles; Santa Rosa Airport, 20 miles; Oakland Airport, 60 miles

Distance from downtown San Francisco: 70 miles

Accommodations: 55 rooms and 44 apartment/suites are scattered over 256 acres. All rooms have a private entrance and porch; some are located in the woods overlooking the pool, others by the tennis courts and golf course fairways, and 13 are located in the Croquet Cottage. All have queen-size beds; most have fireplaces.

Best Rooms/Suites: The Hillside Terrace cottages, set deep in the woods, with huge porches, stone hearths, and plenty of privacy

Amenities: Air-conditioning, TV, minibar, toaster, coffeemaker, hair dryer, terry robes, toiletries, duvets, fireplaces in most rooms; fresh fruit basket, newspaper, room service

Electricity: 110 volts

Sports and Facilities: 7 championship tennis courts, 2 regulation croquet lawns, 2 pools (1 is a heated, 25-yard pool and is open year-round), 9-hole golf course, bicycling, hiking trails; full service health spa with sauna, Jacuzzi, classes, quality equipment, and massage treatments

Dress Code: Informal; jacket requested for dinner at the main restaurant.

Weddings: Can be arranged

Rates/Packages: $280–$690 per couple per night (winter); $305–$710 (summer); Escape to Romance Package, $450 per couple per night, includes luxury accommodations, champagne, dinner and breakfast for two, use of health spa. Sport and Spa packages also available.

Payment/Credit Cards: Most major

Deposit: Guarantee with 1-night deposit (use a credit card); cancel 7 days

prior to arrival for refund
Government Taxes: 10.5 percent
Service Charges: Not included

Post Ranch Inn

Location: On ninety-eight acres amid the seaside cliffs of Big Sur.

Romantic Features: Endless views of the Pacific from the villas' ridge top perches; outdoor hot tubs lighted at night; guided nature hikes and pioneer history walks; on-staff tarot reader and astrologer; star-gazing through a 10-inch Meade electronic tracking telescope.

They sometimes have problems with deer grazing on the roofs. That challenge reflects the uniqueness of Post Ranch Inn, a magnificent new resort located in one of the most majestic spots on earth—Big Sur. Opened in 1992, Post Ranch was the first new hotel in nearly twenty years to debut along this untamed, almost mythological coastline, which over the decades has attracted avant-garde writers and actors such as Henry Miller, Jack Kerouac, and Orson Welles. Big Sur was one of America's last frontiers, a place where roads did not arrive until the 1930s, electricity until the 1950s.

To win the approval of development-abhorring locals and legislators, the resort had to meet stringent environmental standards. In part, the property was planned by Bill Post III, whose great-grandfather had homesteaded the land (he paid $4.00 an acre for 160 acres) some 130 years previously. The resultant enclave manages to feel both rustic and futuristic—Star Wars meets the Old West.

Planked with redwood, the accommodations seem more like private houses than hotel rooms. Although rooms vary in layout and view, all offer the same amenities and square footage and make extensive use of gold-grey rajah slate, quarried by hand in India, for the floors. Railings and doors in Cor-Ten steel weather to the same brown-red tone of the neighboring oaks and madrone trees. Furnishings are comfortable, with features such as curvilinear sofas or window seats. Color schemes of blue, green, and earth tones soothe the spirit. Bathrooms are embellished with slate and granite; many have tubs next to windows positioned so no one can see you, but you can enjoy a 100-mile view. Bath towels are thick, the down comforters plump.

Tree Houses live up to their name, built on stilts so as not to disturb the adjoining redwoods. Walls are angled to maximize views and privacy. Personal favorites are the Ocean Houses, which hunker into the ridgeline—

the terrain rising from the back to form the sod-covered roofs, the aforementioned salad bar for perambulating deer. Out front, views of the Pacific surge to the horizon. The fireplace is arranged so that you can view it from both the living room and the bathroom.

Because Michael Freed and Myles Williams, Post Ranch's creators, wanted to spotlight the splendor of nature rather than the playthings of man, distractions are kept to a minimum. Rooms have no TVs (though they do come with pretty nifty stereo/CD systems), and there are no tennis courts or golf courses. What you have are miles of big-country hiking trails through redwood forests into the valleys snaking hillward behind Highway 1. Some guided hikes are offered, including nature treks and a pioneer history walk. The lap pool awaits, a warm 80 degrees all year-round. A new fitness room opened in 1995, complete with step machine, free weights, and exercise machines; yoga classes are held poolside in the morning. Dramatic seascapes can be enjoyed at Pfeiffer and Andrew Molera beaches, both less than 5 miles to the north.

Rates include an elaborate continental breakfast, served in your room or in the restaurant. Choices generally include fresh fruits, home-baked breads, granola, and quiche. Floor-to-ceiling glass windows (each of which took nine men to carry into position during construction) of the Sierra Mar restaurant afford cliff-hanging views of the water. So as not to compete with the vistas, decor is simple, with slate floors and a big fireplace.

Superintended by executive chef Wendy Little, the Californian menu dallies with flavors from around the world. Entrees might feature a grilled venison chop with fermented black beans or John Dory (a fish that is like sole) with lemongrass, papaya, chili, and roasted peanuts. Prices run $50 per person for the four-course, prix-fixe dinner. The wine list is phenomenal, encompassing 2,000 different wines.

Not much is known about the Ohlone Indians, the original inhabitants of the Northern California coast. From their celebrations, only a line from a song remains, "dancing on the brink of the world." From your cliff-side perch at Post Ranch Inn, you'll probably experience a similar feeling of joy.

Address/Phone: P.O. Box 219, Highway 1, Big Sur, CA 93920; (408) 667–2200, fax: (408) 667–2824
Reservations: (800) 527–2200
Owner/Manager: Michael Freed and Myles Williams, general partners; Larry Callahan, general manager
Arrival/Departure: Easily accessible by car
Distance from Monterey Airport: 35 miles south; 90 miles south of San Jose Airport; 150 miles south of San Francisco International Airport
Distance from Carmel: Approximately 30 miles south; 150 miles south of

San Francisco

Accommodations: 30 villas, each with ocean or mountain views, in four styles: 5 Ocean Houses recessed into ridge with sod roofs, 7 Tree Houses on stilts, 10 Coast Houses, 2 Mountain Houses, and 6 guest accommodations in three-level Butterfly House

Best Rooms/Suites: Top-of-the-line Ocean Houses hang on the brink of the cliff and feature private, slate-floored terraces. These often book up way in advance.

Amenities: Wood-burning fireplace, bathtub/Jacuzzi, stereo/CD music system, in-room massage table; coffeemaker, minibar, toiletries, terry-cloth robes, hair dryer

Electricity: 110 volts

Sports and Facilities: 2 swimming pools, including a "basking pool" and lap pool; new fitness center and spa; hiking and walking trails

Dress Code: Casually smart

Weddings: Can be arranged

Rates/Packages: $265–$525 per couple per night

Payment/Credit Cards: Most major

Deposit: Reservations require guarantee or deposit in advance. Cancellations must be made 7 days in advance.

Government Taxes: 10 percent

Service Charges: Not included

Colorado

Sonnenalp Resort

Location: Three separate houses set in the center of Vail near the covered bridge; within walking distance of just about everything.

Romantic Features: Sitting by a blazing fire in your suite while the snow falls softly just outside; sleeping under fluffy down duvets; moonlight sleigh ride; European ambience.

You don't have to go all the way to Austria to find the archetypal European ski and mountain resort. Just grab your skies and head to Vail, where the Fässler family has created a resort that fairly sings with charms of the Old World. The Sonnenalp is actually three separate inns within easy walking distance of each other. Each has its own restaurants and personality, yet the facilities of all are open to Sonnenalp's guests.

Sonnenalp Resort, Colorado

The Austria Haus, located next to Vail's covered bridge, is the smallest and coziest. It has the Stüberl Restaurant and bar, a Jacuzzi, sauna, on-site ski storage, and an intimate lobby with a large fireplace. Many of the thirty-seven rooms, with their antique brick and barn-board walls and washed pine furniture, overlook picturesque Gore Creek. At the Stüberl Restaurant, you'll enjoy trying various regional dishes as the menu highlights a different country's cuisine each night.

The new Bavaria Haus, winner of *Snow Country Magazine's* National Design Award for ski area lodges and hotels, consists of the elegant Ludwig's Restaurant, the more casual Bully Ranch Restaurant, and the King's Club Lounge, with its piano bar and library.

The light, airy 5,000-square-foot spa features a 1,200-square-foot indoor/outdoor pool, indoor and outdoor Jacuzzis, a sauna, steam rooms, and an exercise room with the latest in exercise and weight-lifting equipment. You can also pamper yourself with various massages, seaweed wraps, and other soothing treatments. The spa has lots of windows affording great views of the beautiful mountain world just outside.

The largest and most luxurious of the three inns, Bavaria Haus has eighty-eight suites decorated with handcrafted woodwork, gas fireplaces, cozy sitting areas, European fixtures, and warm, natural wood furniture. Bathrooms have heated marble floors, double sinks, and large tubs just right for soaking out kinks acquired on the ski slopes.

With its white exterior trimmed with wooden balconies and stone arches and a roofline that swoops over towers and gables, Bavaria Haus reminds one of a lovely palace chalet. Covered with snow, it's a picture postcard. Send this one to your friends, and they won't believe it's not somewhere in the Alps.

At the Swiss Haus, just half a block away from Bavaria Haus, you'll find a European treatment spa offering aromatherapy and massage and body treatments as well as facials, manicures, and other pampering services. The spa also has an indoor Jacuzzi, outdoor heated pool, cold plunge pool, fitness room, Finnish saunas, Turkish steam rooms, and a juice bar as well as a full bar serving beverages and light meals.

The fifty-seven rooms and two suites at the Swiss Haus feature pine armoires and beds, attractive Alpine decor, and views of the creek or the village. Be sure to try the fondue and raclette, specialties at the Swiss Chalet Restaurant.

The Cosmetique Boutique and the new Sonnenalp Shop, located in Swiss Haus, feature a tempting array of items including jewelry, accessories, perfumes, and unique gifts.

During the summer months, Sonnenalp is a wonderful base for those who love hiking, biking, swimming, horseback riding, tennis, golf, and exploring this lovely mountain area. Prices go down at this time of the year, too.

If you've got Europe on your mind but want to leave your passports at home, Sonnenalp is highly recommended.

Address/Phone: 20 Vail Road, Vail, CO 81657; (303) 476–5656; fax: (303) 476–1639

Reservations: (800) 654–8312; fax: (970) 476–8066

Owner/Manager: Owned and operated by the Fässler Family

Arrival/Departure: Colorado Mountain Express shuttle service available at $48 per person, one way.

Distance from Denver International Airport: 2 hours; Eagle County Airport is only 35 miles to the west.

Distance from Denver: 100 miles west

Accommodations: 92 guest rooms and 94 suites

Best Rooms/Suites: Suites in Bavaria House; spacious Bald Mountain Suite overlooks creek and comes with a separate bedroom; large living room with fireplace and minibar and a great bathroom with separate shower, double sinks, and soaking tub. Lodgepole Suite also roomy and luxurious with fireplace, soaking tub, separate sitting area, minibar, and view of Vail Village or Gore Creek. Creekside Room in Austria House has view of mountain and creek and is cozy and less expensive.

Amenities: Hair dryer, bathrobes, iron and ironing board, toiletries, telephone, TV, VCR, down duvet, minibar, air-conditioning (Bavaria House only). Suites have fireplaces, minibar, double vanity, soaking tub, balcony, separate living room and loft.

Electricity: 110 volts

Sports and Facilities: Vail Ski area has 4,000 skiable acres serviced by 25 lifts; in addition to Alpine and cross-country skiing you can go snowboarding, snowshoeing, bobsledding, paragliding, dog sledding, snowmobiling, and ice skating; 18-hole golf course with pro shop, pool, and clubhouse; outdoor Jacuzzi, indoor and outdoor heated pools; 2 European spas; 4 tennis courts

Dress Code: Casual; jacket and tie requested for Ludwig's restaurant only.

Weddings: Can be arranged

Rates/Packages: Per couple per night with full breakfast: $253–$283 for a room, $358–$1,206 for a suite (winter season); $85–$162 for a room, $187–$694 for a suite (summer season)

Payment/Credit Cards: Most major

Deposit: 1 night's lodging due within 10 days of booking; full payment due 30 days (60 during holiday period) prior to arrival. Cancellations made 30 days (60 for holiday period) or more prior to arrival, forfeit $50 per room. Cancellations made less than 30 days, forfeit all monies held on account.

Government Taxes: 8 percent

Service Charges: Not included

Florida

The Boca Raton Resort & Club

Location: On a 356-acre estate on Florida's Gold Coast, in Palm Beach County.

Romantic Features: Private beach; Sunday Brunch in the Cloister; the view at sunset from the Tower.

Dreamers, risk-takers, moguls, and millionaires all contributed to the mystique of Florida's Boca Raton Resort & Club, beginning with Ponce de Leon, who sailed along these shores looking for the "Fountain of Youth" in 1513. He was followed by Spanish conquistadors and pirates.

In the early 1920s, the famed architect Adison Mizner bought 17,500 acres here to create a great resort, and proceeded to do so in grand style. In 1926 The Cloister Inn was the most expensive one-hundred-room hotel ever built up to that time. Today it is the fantasy centerpiece for the Boca Raton Resort & Club, still a superb resort. In 1993 it underwent a $70 million renovation program, further enhancing its guest rooms and public areas, and since 1990, about $10 million has been spent annually on property upgrades and maintenance. The physical beauty of the setting and buildings, combined with the sports facilities and top-notch staff, all add up to one great honeymoon resort.

This imposing complex on Florida's Gold Coast offers something for every taste. The most dramatic and romantic section is the original six-story Cloister, redolent of Florida in the 1920s, displaying Moorish, Mediterranean, and even gothic touches. Modeled after a Spanish castle, the Cloister is a harmonious blend of Venice and Palm Beach, with a dash of ancient Greece and Rome thrown in for extra flavor. Flower-filled tropical courtyards, hidden gardens, barrel-tile roofs, and dusky archways all contribute to the mystique of this creamy pink palace. The fountain in the center of the courtyard is a sculpture of an alluring nude woman said to be modeled after a mistress of the architect.

The Cloister lobby is filled with columns, mosaics, and beamed ceilings of ornate pecky cypress. Furnishings feature Mizner's rare antiques from old churches and universities in Spain and Central America. At the far end, a little museum highlights the resort's history.

Other sections of the sprawling resort, which hugs the Atlantic, the inland waterways, and rolling golf links, are connected by free water taxi and shuttle service. They include the twenty-six-story Tower, Boca Beach Club, Palm Court Club, and the Golf Villas, all with lovely accommodations and all with a different focus.

There are Mediterranean-style or modern, terraces over the water or twinkling high-rise views, Jacuzzis or kitchens, balconies or patios. The Boca Beach Club, which is casual and quiet, is steps from the water. Golf Villa Apartments, located on the fairways, are spacious, private, and secluded. Tower rooms have panoramic windows with sweeping views of the coast—very sophisticated. And the quiet, Mediterranean-type Cloister boasts the Palm Court Club, a floor with a private concierge and special amenities. Depending on your interests and whether you prefer the dreamily historic, the pounding surf, or the convenience of rolling out of bed and onto the greens, the choice is yours. You could even spend some nights in more than one section, as the resort aims to please in any way possible.

Everything here is pristine and delightful, and reflects the good life. Walkways are lush with flowers, the sand is sparkling, the shops are brimming with stylish goods, the well-prepared food is presented with snap. Even the tropical birds in the Cloister have spotless cages and gourmet fruit.

A perfect day in Boca might start with breakfast in the grand old Palm Court, a water taxi ride over to the ½-mile of private beach, and a leisurely lunch at the open-air poolside bar. In the afternoon you might bike or play croquet, swing a racquet, or play eighteen holes. Or maybe board a private charter for some deep-sea fishing off Boca's famous reefs—now free of pirates.

Most of the sports activities require a fee so budget accordingly. For example, bike rentals are $9 for a half day, $15 a full day. Windsurfing is $25 per hour and snorkeling is $8 per hour. Greens fees are $44 during the week and $74 on weekends, cart rentals are $20. If you are into a particular sport in a big way, you should ask about the special packages, such as golf or tennis plans, which might be your best deals.

The dine-around plan is a good way to enjoy any of the resort's several indoor and outdoor restaurants. Dinner might be Florida stone crabs at Nick's Fishmarket at the Beach Club, or fresh pasta at The Italian Restaurant on the twenty-seventh floor of The Tower, with far-reaching views from Palm Beach to Miami Beach. You might want to end the evening at Malone's Magic Bar, one of the resort's several nightclubs and lounges with live entertainment.

And then, of course, there's always a walk under the streaming bougainvillea and magic moon. Perhaps the Fountain of Youth was discovered around here, after all.

Address/Phone: 501 E. Camino Real, P.O. Box 5025, Boca Raton, FL 33431–0825; (407) 447–3038; fax: (407) 391–3183

Reservations: (800) 327–0101

Owner/Manager: Michael F. Glennie, president; David Feder, vice president and manager

Arrival/Departure: Taxis available at airports

Distance from Ft. Lauderdale Airport: 24 miles; Palm Beach Airport, 28 miles; Miami International Airport, 45 miles

Distance from Palm Beach: 22 miles

Accommodations: 963 rooms and suites in four areas: The Cloister, The Tower, the Golf Villa Apartments, and Boca Beach Club

Best Rooms/Suites: Boca Beach Club rooms with ocean views

Amenities: Air-conditioning, hair dryer, ceiling fans, minibar, safe, TV, telephone, bathrobes, toiletries, marble baths, magnifying makeup mirror; room service

Electricity: 110 volts

Sports and Facilities: 34 clay tennis courts, 4 racquetball courts, fitness

center, two 18-hole golf courses by Joe Lee, driving range, putting green, private beach, 5 pools, 23-slip marina, most water sports, private beach club, deep-sea fishing, sailing, scuba diving, snorkeling, windsurfing, Waverunners, bicycling
Dress Code: Casually elegant
Weddings: Can be arranged
Rates/Packages: Per couple, per night $130–$265 (summer); $205–$400 (spring and fall); $265–$430 (winter); Romance packages: 3 nights, $499 per couple (summer); $754 (spring and fall), $899 (winter), 7 nights, $978 (summer), $1,573 (spring and fall), $1,888 (winter), including accommodations, champagne, dinner for two, round of golf, 1-day tennis fees, 1 hour rental of beach water-sports equipment, 1 day use of beach cabana, 2-hour catamaran cruise, cocktails, logo sport shirts. Golf and tennis packages available.
Payment/Credit Cards: Most major
Deposit: 1 night's deposit for rooms, $250 for packages; cancel 24 hours to 21 days prior to arrival date for refund, depending on time of year.
Government Taxes: Not included
Service Charges: $9.00

Disney's Grand Floridian Beach Resort

Location: On 40 acres in the heart of Walt Disney World on the west side of Seven Seas Lagoon, between the Magic Kingdom and the Polynesian Resort.
Romantic Features: The whole of Walt Disney World at your doorstep; opulent Victorian-style accommodations.

If you thought Walt Disney World was just for kids, think again. This area, with all its various attractions, is one of the top honeymoon destinations in the world. And within this complex of fun and games, the Grand Floridian Beach Resort is just about the most romantic of the places you can stay. Special honeymoon suites overlook the palm-shaded pool and lazy lagoon of this Victorian-style hotel that rests like an oasis right in the heart of all the action just beyond its entrance.

Designed in the grand manner of the Victorian era and reminiscent of the setting for *The Great Gatsby,* the Floridian, with its sprawling white facade, accented by gabled roofs, intricate latticework, and ornate balustrades, is set amid gardens and lawns planted with canary palms, magnolias, hibiscus, and other lush tropical flora. This grand hotel boasts wide

Grand Floridian Beach Resort, Florida

verandas with wicker rockers, more than 120 miles of decorative scroll-work, white towers, and a red-shingle roof.

A curious touch in the lofty, five-story atrium lobby is an open-cage elevator that whisks guests up and down. Look up and admire the lobby's ceiling, with its three illuminated stained-glass domes, ornate chandeliers, and metal scrolls.

Rooms carry out the early 1920s mood, though the colors used are softer and lighter. Applied with flair are printed wall coverings coordinated with fabrics, light woods, marble-topped sinks (but with old fashioned–looking fittings) and Victorian woodwork. Most rooms have two queen-size beds; some have kings. Suites include a parlor plus one or more bedrooms.

The mood may hark back to the turn of the century and the days of John D. Rockefeller and Thomas Edison, but the amenities are pure twentieth-century modern, with monorail service and air-conditioning—the monorail stops right beside the Grand Lobby. The resort has five restaurants, two lounges, two snack bars, four shops, a pool, health club, marina, and children's facilities.

The opportunities for fun and romance are seemingly unlimited. You can visit the cultures and entertainment worlds of many countries at Epcot; thrill at the sharks and tropical fish at The Living Seas; and ride the spine-tingling Thunder Mountain. Or rent a boat from the marina and explore the lagoon; whiz down the 120-foot-high Summit Plummet from the top of Mt.

Gushmore at the new 66-acre Blizzard Beach water park; thrill to an alien encounter in Tomorrowland; and dodge (imaginary) flying objects at the new 3-D exhibit, "Honey, I Shrunk the Audience." Later you can dine by candlelight in the privacy of your room, and enjoy a moonlit walk on the white sand beach.

You can go nightclub hopping at Pleasure Island (yes, that man's eyes in the portrait at the Adventurers Club really do follow you), laugh at the comedians at the Comedy Warehouse, and dance up a storm at the Mannequins Dance Palace. See how films are made and special effects created at MGM Studios and shop at the many, many stores.

There are six restaurants, ranging from the formal Victoria and Albert's to the hamburgers and hot dogs of Gasparilla Grill. At V & A's the menu changes daily, and what you get depends on what is available in the local market that day. Selections include fresh fish and seafood and meat. A nice touch is the red rose you are given when you arrive. For northern Italian dishes, try Flagler's, and for southern specialties head for the Grand Floridian Cafe. Nineteen Hundred Park Fare serves breakfast and features a dinner buffet; Narcoosee's features a variety of seafood. All serve baked goods prepared in the hotel bakery.

At the close of the evening, the night sky lights up with a spectacular display of fireworks during IllumiNations, a laser and water spectacular—it's guaranteed you'll see stars!

Address/Phone: Walt Disney World, FL 32830–1000; (407) 934–7639; fax: (407) 352–3202

Reservations: (407) W–DISNEY; (800) 327–2996

Owner/Manager: John Hallowell, general manager

Arrival/Departure: Transfers included in the Grand Honeymoon package

Distance from Orlando International Airport: 26 miles

Distance from Orlando: 25 miles southwest

Accommodations: 901 rooms and suites, including Standard, Concierge, and Lodge

Best Rooms/Suites: Honeymoon rooms have all the amenities included in the Concierge rooms, with a few differences. Some are octagonal; some have balconies; some Jacuzzis. Lodge suites located in a separate building enjoy special amenities such as afternoon tea, complimentary continental breakfast, and hors d'oeuvres and wine. For high rollers, try the Roosevelt Suite, which has three rooms, five private balconies, two bedrooms with king-size canopy beds, and oversized bathrooms, including a Jacuzzi in the master bath. The living room has a complete entertainment center with a stereo system, CD player, VCR, and a 52-inch wide-screen TV.

Amenities: Air-conditioning, ceiling fans, hair dryer, telephones, minibar, in-room safe, bathrobes, turndown service, room service, iron and ironing board (on request), and toiletries. Concierge rooms and suites also include special shampoos and lotions, slippers, VCR, continental breakfast, tea, hors d'oeuvres, and late-night dessert and cordials. Down pillows, refrigerator, and microwave can be requested.

Electricity: 110 volts

Sports and Facilities:: A 275,000-gallon swimming pool, beach, marina, water sports, health club, exercise room, saunas, massage room; also in the Disney complex are 5 championship golf courses, tennis courts, jogging paths, horseback riding, ponds and pools for swimming and boating.

Dress Code: Casual; dressier if you want to dine at Victoria and Albert's

Weddings: Disney plays fairy godmother to more than 1,000 couples who come to tie the knot here. The new, glass-enclosed Wedding Pavilion, set on an island in the Seven Seas Lagoon, offers a magical site for the ceremony. You can also arrange with Disney's wedding department for a wedding and Cinderella reception at the Grand Floridian or a Sunset Beach wedding. Call (407) 828-3400 for wedding details.

Rates/Packages: Nightly rates per couple for Honeymoon rooms are $485 (high season), and $465 (low season). The 4-night Grand Honeymoon package, priced from $3,023 per couple, includes accommodations, 5 days unlimited admission to Disney World attractions; unlimited use of bicycles; canoes; sail, pedal, and rowboats; use of Disney's transportation facilities; breakfast, lunch, and dinner at a variety of locations (gratuities included); private in-room dining with a personal chef; private golf and tennis lessons; use of health club; VIP amenities such as flowers and fruit, use of rental VHS video camera, honeymoon photo session, keepsake album, and a guide to the area. The Honeymoon Enchantment 4-night plan, priced from $2,179 per couple, includes accommodations, 5-day Disney passes, meals, photos, and a guide. There is also the Honeymoon Escape, $869 per couple, for 4 nights, passes, 1 breakfast, and special treats.

Payment/Credit Cards: Most major

Deposit: 2 night-deposit at time of booking to cover first and last night's accommodations; refundable if cancelled up to 15 days prior to arrival.

Government Taxes: 11 percent sales tax on rooms; 6 percent on food

Service Charges: Some gratuities are included in honeymoon packages.

Little Palm Island

Location: Off the tip of Little Torch Key, 120 miles southwest of Miami and 28 miles east of Key West.

Romantic Features: Your own thatched cottage—it's like being in the South Pacific, only you don't have to knock yourself out getting there.

It used to be a rustic fishing retreat for America's presidents and high-profile stars. It still attracts people like Mario Andretti, Robert Wagner, Jill St. John, and Ivana Trump, but Little Palm Island is no longer rustic. The South Seas–style thatched bungalows, which stand on stilts amid the more than 250 coconut palm trees, tropical foliage and gardens of this idyllic island Shangri-la, just 3 miles offshore in the Lower Florida Keys, come with air-conditioning, whirlpool baths, king-size beds, and fully stocked minibars. Little Palm Island, which opened as a public resort in 1988, succeeds in combining the best of both worlds.

Once your boat pulls into the pier—and that's the only way you get here—you leave behind things like TVs, cars, alarm clocks, and telephones. There's one public phone located in a former outhouse (used by Truman, they say), but that's it. So look around, stroll along the gravel paths that link the cottages to the pool area and beach, find a hammock, settle in, and relax. Since young children are not allowed here, you'll have the pool and the beach all to yourself.

You share the island, maintained as a nature preserve, with a variety of species of birds and animals, including herons, parrots, manatees, Key deer, and loggerhead turtles, which lay their eggs each year on the beach.

The sugar-white sand beach runs in a thin strip around the five-acre island and broadens out at one end, where you'll find a vast tidal flat, home to a fascinating number of birds and other creatures, which are best seen in the early morning or evening. During the day, from your lounge on the beach, you need only plant your pink flag in the sand to summon a member of the ever-watchful staff, who will be quick to take your drink or snack order.

Sunsets are special here. Look carefully, and you can see the green flash just as the sun drops below the horizon. Walk completely around the island in the early evening and watch the colors brighten and mellow.

Your suite has a soaring pitched ceiling of thatch and bamboo, a ceiling fan, king-size bed draped with a filmy white net canopy, really comfortable Guatemalan lounger, sitting area, wraparound sundecks, dressing area, and bathroom decorated with Mexican tile.

Although each bathroom comes with a whirlpool tub, the most popular way to freshen up is to use your outdoor shower, which is enclosed by bamboo walls and is totally private. On Little Palm's list of ways to conserve natural resources is the suggestion to "shower with a friend."

Louvered wood walls (with screens) open to let the sea breezes in— you rarely need to turn on your air-conditioning; some never do. Your sitting area has natural wicker and rattan chairs and sofas with cushions in brightly hued tropical fabric. Linens are changed daily by the staff unless requested by guests not to do so.

Of course, you'll have to make major decisions, like whether to go snorkeling or try out one of the canoes, whether to loll at the lagoonlike pool or head to the spa for a massage. Since the water off the beach is usually too shallow to swim in, you'll need the pool for your lap work. Nearby are superb dive sites for scuba enthusiasts. Just 3 miles away, Looe Key, a long reef protected by the National Park Service stretches for miles and is home to myriad multicolored fish and other sea creatures.

There is a small library with a good selection of books to borrow, and nearby are hammocks strung in the trees. You also have a hammock on your deck—at Little Palm, hammocks are in. And if you really can't stand all this serenity and good living, you can sneak down to the Quarter Deck, which is located on the dock, and rent a TV/VCR.

You can dine indoors in the main restaurant, located in the Great House, or outside on the terrace. You can also dine at the casual, literally on the beach, restaurant where your dining chairs and table sit on wood "island" platforms set right on the sand. And the food prepared by chef Michel Reymond is as good as it looks—a trendy blend of French, American, and Caribbean with flavors from the Pacific rim. Magnifique!

Especially tasty is the fresh dolphin, grouper, tuna, grilled salmon, rack of lamb, and homemade soups and pastas. Fresh herbs and seasonings are just right, sauces splendid, desserts impossible to resist. On Thursdays you really get a chance to test your eating capacity with the seven-course Gourmet Night, and on Sundays it's brunch time. Everything's accompanied by a bottle of red or white from Little Palm's impressive wine cellar.

Physically Little Palm Island is fifteen minutes from shore; psychologically it's another world, where cares wash away, and romance blooms.

Address/Phone: 28500 Overseas Highway, Little Torch Key, FL 33042; (305) 872-2524; fax: (305) 872-4843

Reservations: (800) 3–GET LOST; Relais & Chateaux, (800) RELAIS 8

Owner/Manager: Ben Woodson, managing general partner

Arrival/Departure: Transfer and van service to the Little Torch Key Shore Station (mile marker 28.5) is available from both Key West and Marathon Airports. Little Palm's shuttle service will meet you and take you to their shore station, where you will board a boat for the 3-mile, 15-minute ride to the island. Limousine service can also be arranged from Miami International for the 2½-hour drive through the Florida Keys to the station. Seaplane and helicopter service available from Miami. Advance notice is required for all of these services.

Distance from Miami International Airport: 120 miles; Key West International Airport, 28 miles

Distance from Key West: 120 miles

Accommodations: 28 one-bedroom suites are located in 14 thatched-cottage bungalows, and 1 additional suite is located in the resort's Great House.

Best Rooms/Suites: Although all rooms have a view of the sea, those directly facing the open ocean are tops.

Amenities: Air-conditioning, minibar, wet bar, coffee bar, whirlpool bath, outdoor shower, ceiling fans, bathrobes (TVs, telephones, and alarm clocks are "banned" from the island. There is one public phone, located in the former outhouse, which takes credit cards only).

Electricity: 110 volts

Sports and Facilities: Pool, beach, spa, exercise room; windsurfing, sailing, kayaking, canoeing, fishing, snorkeling; pontoon boats and Sun-Kat motorized lounge chairs can be rented; deep-sea fishing, scuba diving, guided nature tours can be arranged.

Dress Code: Casual elegance

Weddings: Can be arranged

Rates/Packages: $465–$495 per couple, per night (winter); $330–$465 (spring); $290–$385 (summer through mid-December). For full American plan (3 meals a day) add $95 per person, per day; for Modified American Plan (breakfast and dinner), add $75 per person, per day; A 6-day/5-night honeymoon package, $3,280–$3,913.25 (depending on the season), includes accommodations, all meals, Thursday Night Special Gourmet Night with seven courses and champagne, two massages, sunset sail, two snorkeling trips to Looe Key Reef, use of windsurfers, canoes, day sailers, kayaks, fishing gear, snorkeling gear, exercise room, and sauna.

Payment/Credit Cards: Most major

Deposit: First and last night's lodging at time of booking, refundable if cancelled no later than 14 days prior to arrival date; $25 service charge applies. If cancelled during the 14 days, 1 night's deposit will be retained.

Government Taxes: 7 percent

Service Charges: 15 percent

The Ritz Carlton Naples

Location: In Naples, on the west coast of Florida.
Romantic Features: Luxurious rooms with views of the sea; Old World elegance.

The internationally acclaimed Ritz Carlton name conjures up all sorts of romantic notions: elegantly appointed rooms, marble baths with oversized tubs and Jacuzzis, king-size beds that seem even larger, thick terry bathrobes, exquisite cuisine, and, of course, twenty-four-hour room service—all you have to do is place a quick call and your order will be fulfilled at a moment's notice.

The Ritz Carlton Naples does not disappoint. Built in 1983 on twenty acres of waterfront property on the famed Gold Coast in Naples, the hotel evokes Old World Mediterranean grandeur with its classic arches, stone fountains, and manicured gardens with unexpected vistas at every turn.

A huge veranda dotted with Southern-style rocking chairs overlooks the gardens and swimming pool. Tall Palladian windows frame views of the Gulf of Mexico and flower-bedecked courtyards. Garden benches are strategically placed near fountains amid flowers. And if one distinction of a grand hotel is a palatial lobby, then the creators of the Ritz Carlton score a ten. It's a beauty. And set off against a quiet color scheme of rose and green are some 250 magnificent pieces of antique furniture and art.

For afternoon relaxation, you can head to the lobby lounge, which hosts a tea every afternoon, complete with Devonshire cream and scones, or if something more potent tempts you, you can order cocktails while seated in cozy armchairs and sofas.

Rooms and suites are beautifully furnished with armoires, writing desk, club chairs, and fine art. All rooms have a separate dressing area with vanity and a marble bath with an oversize tub. There are twenty-eight suites, including twenty-two gulf-view one-bedroom suites, four two-bedroom suites with extended parlor, and two Presidential suites.

For those who like their creature comforts orchestrated to the highest possible level, the Ritz has its Club, a lofty place in more ways than one: It's located on the top two floors and is accessible only by private elevator (you get a special key). Here you enjoy the services of a private concierge devoted exclusively to your needs. Continuous food and beverage services, complimentary cocktails, newspapers, magazines, ice service, and more goodies are all provided in the lounge's warm, living room atmosphere.

When it comes to accolades for cuisine, the Ritz is no slouch either. Its restaurants (seven in all) have garnered more awards than any hotel in the state of Florida and are right up there with the best in the world. And at the Ritz, there is sure to be a dining facility that fits your mood, whether it be formal or very casual.

The main dining room is devoted to classic cuisine in the grand hotel tradition—elegant, sophisticated, and very romantic. Silks, chandeliers, French doors, oil paintings, piano music, and all that good stuff set the mood. On the more casual side, the Beach Pavilion, an open-air cottage-style restaurant located directly on the gulf beach, is open for breakfast and lunch.

Three miles of pure white sand beach on the warm, calm gulf offer up a variety of water activities, including sailing and catamaran cruising, and there is a super pool for the serious lapper. Tennis enthusiasts have a choice of hard or clay surfaces on six lighted courts, and there is a pro shop, a beverage bar, and professional instruction available. Golfers can head out to more than forty-five courses that are close by, including Pelican's West, a Tom Fazio–designed course recognized as Naples's finest. The Ritz golf coordinator will set it all up for you.

The romantic pièce de résistance is the hotel's fleet of personal limousines, which are available for transportation to and from the airport and for shopping sprees.

Address/Phone: 280 Vanderbilt Beach Road, Naples, FL 33963; (813) 598–3300; fax: (813) 598–6667

Reservations: (800) 241–3333

Owner/Manager: Jorge Gonzalez, general manager

Arrival/Departure: Taxis available at Ft. Myers Airport; transfers can be arranged

Distance from Southwest Florida International Airport (Ft. Myers Airport): 15 miles (30 minutes)

Distance from Naples: 10 miles from center of town

Accommodations: 463 rooms and suites with views of the Gulf of Mexico

Best Rooms/Suites: Ocean-view Club rooms

Amenities: Hair dryer; air-conditioning; toiletries; bathrobes; telephone, some with fax and computer hookups; separate dressing area with vanity; minibar; remote-controlled TV; personal wall safe; twice-daily maid service; 24-hour room service; afternoon ice delivery

Electricity: 110 volts

Sports and Facilities: Heated pool, fitness center, 6 tennis courts, water sports, billiard room, bicycles, golf nearby

Dress Code: Two of the restaurants require gentlemen to wear jackets and ties. Others are casual.

Weddings: Can be arranged. The Ritz has a full-time wedding coordinator.

Rates/Packages: From $135 per couple per night for a room, from $570 for a suite (summer); $305–$850 (winter); Presidential Suites (good if you're an oil sheik) $3,000. Honeymoon Package, $250–$460 per couple per night, including deluxe or suite accommodations, breakfast for two, champagne, chocolate-dipped strawberries, valet parking, use of fitness center
Payment/Credit Cards: Most major
Deposit: First and last nights' room rate and tax; cancel 7 days prior to arrival date for refund
Government Taxes: 8 percent sales tax
Service Charges: Not included

Hawaii

Fours Seasons Resort Maui at Wailea

Location: On fifteen waterfront acres between the slopes of the Haleakala Crater and the Pacific shore in Wailea, along Maui's southwestern coast.
Romantic Features: Total pampering in magnificent garden setting; breathtaking views of the rugged volcanic coast and moonlit surf; huge marble bath with separate soaking tub; the ultimate romantic dinner for two on a grassy knoll, high above the sea; limo picnic lunch with champagne.

Everything about the Four Seasons Resort Maui at Wailea, rated Five Diamonds each year by AAA (American Automobile Association) since the resort opened in 1990, is as it should be—geared for the pleasure of its guests. Most would agree that chilled towels, ice water, and Evian mist brought to your poolside cabana throughout the day are not necessities. But boy are they appreciated! The Four Seasons' propensity for pampering and attention to detail have helped it earn the distinction of ranking among the top hotels in the world.

The young, energetic staff look more like winners from central casting for a new California surfing movie than their real-life roles as dispensers of good will, frosty drinks, and fluffy towels. Four Seasons in Maui has managed to put together a great package, combining exquisite facilities with superb personnel.

A study of elegance and style, the property has the look and feel of a plantation home settled in perfect harmony with its seaside surroundings. The lofty, open design integrates the vibrant blues of the Pacific with pastel-colored walls, floor-to-ceiling wooden shutters, ceiling fans, and plump-cushioned rattan couches. Gentle trade winds keep a profusion of white orchids in constant motion. Scattered throughout the lobby and other (un)common areas are pieces of art and period furniture.

Measuring a generous 600 square feet, the guest rooms are both elegant and comfortable and are decorated in a decidedly tropical mode. The in-room safe is simple to use, the light in the closet, a welcome touch, and sitting on your bedside table is a tiny book with excerpts from James Michener's *Hawaii*, complete with an attached reading light.

Catering to the diversity of its many guests, the Four Seasons maintains the delicate balance between too much activity and not enough, and successfully separates activities geared for children and adults. With two pools, water sports galore, a health club, jogging trail, aerobics, and more, there is no lack of things to do. Sea kayaks and water scooters are available at the dive shop.

At the heart of the resort, royal palms define the borders of a large swimming pool, which boasts an adjacent computer-controlled fountain; it's programmed to react to the whims of the trade winds so its spray keeps within defined boundaries. Two Jacuzzis spill into the pool; one is for adults only. Hundreds of flowers follow a sweeping stairway from the upper lobby to the pool area and beyond. Beneath the stairway, two tropical birds greet visitors as they pass. A manicured lawn between the pool and Wailea Beach provides an additional lounging area, and wide, semicircular grass steps add a pleasing touch.

Nearby, a waterfall cools guests as they swim in the smaller, second pool, effectively hidden by tropical plants. The resort also has tennis courts; cold, wet towels are provided.

Dining options abound and range from casual to elegant *haute cuisine*. Seasons, the resort's signature restaurant, is a treat for even the most assiduous gourmet. The offerings are varied and exceptional: island seafood with upcountry Maui greens; tropical fruit charlotte and papaya coulis, for example. All are presented with pride in a pleasing, open setting with wonderful ocean views. After dinner, you can sway to the music of a local band.

Soft breezes and a breathtaking view also factor in at the Pacific Grill, where guests can enjoy a sumptuous buffet breakfast, lunch, and/or dinner. For more casual dining, the Cabana Cafe by the pool attracts honeymooners as well as family groups.

A car isn't necessary, as other dining options, shops, and golf are just a short walk away along Wailea's 2-mile ocean pathway. A complimentary shuttle is also available. However, if you want to go off on your own and go exploring, you will probably want to rent a car for a couple of days. There is a lot to see and do in Maui. You can get up early in the morning, be driven up to the top of the volcano, and then ride back down the mountain on a bike, and you can visit some of the small nearby villages and browse in the shops. Or you can stay just where you are on your lounge and wait for someone to come by and refresh you with a light mist of cool water.

Address/Phone: 3900 Wailea Alanui, Wailea, Maui, HI 96753; (800) 334–6284, (808) 874–8000; fax: (808) 874–2222

Reservations: (800) 332–3442 or (800) 334–6284

Owner/Manager: Shimizu Corporation, owner; Randy Morton, general manager

Arrival/Departure: Airport limousine transfers; Avis rental cars; motor coach minibus and van service can be arranged.

Distance from Kahului Airport: 17 miles

Distance from Kihei: 4 miles

Accommodations: 380 spacious rooms and suites, all with one or more lanais (porches); 85 percent have ocean views

Best Rooms/Suites: Ocean-view or executive suite

Amenities: Air-conditioning, ceiling fans, hair dryer, bathrobes, room safe, double vanity as well as separate vanity, built-in refrigerator bar, separate soaking tub, TV, cosmetic mirror, toiletries, spacious lighted closet; complimentary morning coffee, twice-daily maid service, valet parking

Electricity: 110 volts

Sports and Facilities: 2 pools, 2 Jacuzzis, beach, use of 3 golf courses at Wailea Golf Club, tennis at the 14-court Wailea Tennis Center (including 3 grass courts), 2 on-site tennis courts lighted for night play, health club with exercise machines and steam room; running paths, snorkeling, scuba diving, sailing instruction, aerobics, aqua exercise, power walking

Dress Code: Casual elegance

Weddings: The resort offers a number of wedding packages ranging from $995 for the Plumeria Wedding, with ceremony, leis, solo musician, and a bottle of champagne, to the Lokelani Wedding, priced at $1,775, a more elaborate affair with wedding cake, private limousine transfers to and from the airport, more flowers, champagne glasses, and all of the things included in the Plumeria package. Popular sites for the ceremony include the Seasons Garden, the Luau Grounds, the Sculpture Gardens, and a grassy knoll above the ocean. There are a number of other options available in addition to the basic wedding packages, including the Ultimate Dinner for Two.

Rates/Packages: $320 per couple per night for a room with a garden view; $515–$655 for an executive suite; $560–$775 for a room or suite on the

Club floor; $710–$2,400 for a bedroom suite. Romance for All Seasons package, priced at $3,940 per couple, gives you limo transfers from airport, champagne, bathrobes, dinner for two, limo picnic with champagne, and either 3 nights in a one-bedroom ocean-front suite and a Lincoln town car or convertible rental, or you can choose 7 nights in an ocean-view room and the use of a convertible. The 3-night Romantic Interlude package, with convertible rental car, champagne, and dinner for two, is $1,400–$1,644 per couple.

Payment/Credit Cards: Most major
Deposit: 1-night deposit plus tax; refund if cancelled 3 days prior to arrival.
Government Taxes: 10.17 percent
Service Charges: Not included

Halekulani

Location: On five oceanfront acres on Waikiki Beach, Oahu.
Romantic Features: At twilight sounds of Hawaiian music float up to your balcony overlooking the sea; candlelit dinner on your own private lanai (porch); moonlit walks on the beach.

It's smack in the middle of Waikiki Beach, yet worlds away from the hustle and bustle of Honolulu's resort glitz just outside the gates. Consistently named as one of the most romantic resorts in the world, including kudos from *Lifestyles of the Rich and Famous,* Halekulani is a first-rate luxury resort. From the time you check in and receive your gift of Halekulani chocolates and champagne and step outside on your lanai to see the white sand beach, which stretches all the way to Diamond Head, you know you're in for a vacation to remember.

Originally a private, oceanfront estate, the Halekulani has been welcoming guests since 1917. Over the years ownership has changed and buildings have been built and demolished and built again. What remains of the original hotel is a 1930s building (now called the main building), which has been incorporated into the overall design of the five interconnected structures. Throughout the resort, you'll find that lots of marble, Italian terrazzo, and fine woods have been used in creating this Hawaiian oasis.

From your languorous lanai, you see the exquisite oval pool and beyond that, the beach and sea. *Halekulani,* which means "house befitting heaven," has everything you require to make it your own personal paradise. Wraparound lanais with nonstop views of the sunsets, sea, and Diamond Head are only the beginning. Decorated in soft whites, beiges, greys, and blues, rooms are furnished with rattan and upholstered furniture, glass-top tables, king-size beds, wall-to-wall carpeting, marble baths, and large, glass-walled showers. Rooms are quietly elegant. You'll not find any Hawaiian clichés lurking in the decorating schemes of these rooms.

Your opportunities for dining are no less impressive. Orchids, an oceanside indoor/outdoor restaurant open for all meals, specializes in contemporary American cuisine. Living up to its name, it is decorated with live orchids, placed throughout this three-tiered restaurant.

House Without a Key, another indoor/outdoor restaurant, serves breakfast, lunch, and sunset cocktails with Hawaiian entertainment and dancing under the stars each night. Watch Kanoe Miller dance the hula. Arrive in time to watch the sun go down—House Without a Key is one of the best seats in town for this nightly spectacle.

French-inspired meals are served at La Mer, an elegant indoor restaurant in the main building with great ocean views (and high accolades from those who rate). You'll find several Hawaiian-produced items on the menu, such as Kahuku prawns, Kula tomatoes, and Lanai venison. Plates appear at your elbow like a series of gifts. Even the names of your dishes, like fine wines, need to be rolled across the tongue: Poached Onaga with Wilted Greens and a Three-Caviar Sauce, Broiled Opakapaka on Stewed Leeks, Baked Long-Tailed Red Snapper in Salt Crust La Mer, and Ginger Carrots *Fondantes* with a Fumé Blanc Watercress Sauce.

Tea is served every afternoon in the living room in the main building, and cocktails hold center stage in Lewers Lounge afternoons and evenings.

Halekulani offers a full range of water sports as well as aerobics classes, jogging sessions, and sight-seeing programs. A giant orchid made of glass mosaic tiles is set into the bottom of the huge pool, which overlooks the sea and the beach. It really takes your breath away, and only gets more beautiful as night falls.

Staying at Halekulani may not be at the low end of the budget scale, but for your vacation of a lifetime, it's worth going the extra mile.

Address/Phone: 2199 Kalia Road, Honolulu, HI 96815–1988; (808) 923–2311; fax: (808) 926–8004

Reservations: (800) 367–2343

Owner/Manager: Patricia Tam, general manager

Arrival/Departure: Taxis available at airport—one-way is approximately $25; limousine service is $80; city bus 60 cents; complimentary limousine service is provided for those staying in the Presidential and Royal Suites.

Distance from Honolulu Airport: 11 miles (25 minutes)

Distance from Honolulu : You're in the center of the Waikiki action;

downtown Honolulu is 4 miles (15 minutes) away.

Accommodations: 456 rooms and suites located in five low-density buildings, ranging in height from two to seventeen stories; 95 percent have ocean views.

Best Rooms/Suites: Corner ocean-view suites with 1,620 square feet, have a separate bedroom, bathroom, powder room, living room, wet bar, and dining area. Diamond Head ocean-view suites are also very roomy and overlook the famous Diamond Head; Club ocean-view suites are 720 square feet and come with two lanais, bedroom/sitting area, bathroom, wet bar, and cozy bay window.

Amenities: Air-conditioning, hair dryer; remote-control cable TV, mini refrigerator with overhead cabinet and bar accessories, 3 telephones, adjustable reading lamps, TV audio in bathroom, in-room safe, separate glassed-in shower with thermostat control, makeup mirror, bathrobes, wooden coat and satin dress hangers, private label toiletries, 24-hour room service, twice-daily turndown service

Electricity: 110 volts

Sports and Facilities: Large 46-by-82-foot pool; beach center, where you can arrange outrigger canoes, surfing, snorkeling, deep-sea fishing, windsurfing; golf and tennis lessons; fitness room with scheduled workouts and classes as well as massages

Dress Code: Tropical elegance

Weddings: The Halekulani does a lot of weddings, each one personalized. The resort has its own floral shop, and bridal gown rental shops are within walking distance. Usually a marriage license and minister can be arranged within 24 hours; gazebo on the grounds is a popular wedding site.

Rates/Packages: $275–$440 per couple per night for a room; $595–$1,200 for a suite; Table d'hôte meal rates: breakfast $19, lunch $27, dinner $47. Heaven on Waikiki honeymoon package: 8 days/7 nights $2,929, 4 days/3 nights $1,429; includes guaranteed ocean-view accommodations with private balcony, breakfast on your private lanai, special welcome gift, flowers and French champagne on arrival, memento gift of his and her cotton bathrobes, use of beach, fitness room, aerobics classes, personalized check-in; additional nights at $375 per night.

Payment/Credit Cards: Most major

Deposit: $375 required 14 days after confirmation, with full prepayment required 7 days prior to arrival. Reservations must be made at least 7 days in advance, with full prepayment. Full refund if cancellation received at least 72 hours prior to arrival. Cost of 1 night's lodging will be withheld for all late cancellations and no-show reservations.

Government Taxes: 4.17 percent for package; additional nights at 10.17

percent (room only)
Service Charges: Not included

Hotel Hana Maui

Location: Eastern end of the island, in Maui's back pocket.
Romantic Features: Quiet, secluded area recalls old Hawaii; private Jacuzzis on bungalow decks overlooking Pacific.

Geography has played a key role in making Hotel Hana Maui one of the most romantic resorts in Hawaii. Located on the eastern end of Maui, which was formed when the volcano Haleakala erupted, Hana is isolated from the more developed touristy areas by deep valleys and ravines dividing this part of the island from areas around Kahana and Kaanapali, which lie in the shadow of another volcano. In order to reach Hana, you embark on a breathtaking journey along the Hana Highway, called one of the most beautiful roads in the world.

Around many of the 617 bends of the road, which twists and wiggles along the rugged coastline, waterfalls bubble and gush, falling into deep pools of clear mountain water—bring your bathing suit and take a dip in these clean, cool mountain "Jacuzzis." Jungle vegetation, lush and dense, cloaks the hills in a rich, dark green blanket damp with moisture and glistening in the sun, which filters through during the fickle mood shifts in the weather. If you're driving a convertible, you'll find you may be raising and lowering your roof several times during the 50 or so miles of your ride, which takes about three hours. The sea is seldom out of view, and the scenery is spectacular. Watch out for parked vehicles—photo opportunities are enticing, and cars stop frequently along the route.

Finally, after crossing about fifty-four bridges along the Hana Highway (from Kahului), you come to the small town of Hana. There's not much here except for a couple of small stores, a bank, post office, a gas station, and restaurant. And Hotel Hana Maui. Sitting prettily on the very end of the island, below the rainy slopes of Haleakala, this hideaway resort is located on twenty-three acres of rolling, landscaped grounds.

This land was once devoted to the production of sugarcane and later, to raising cattle. In the early fifties, Hotel Hana Ranch was created by Paul Fagen, the owner of the 14,000-acre Puu O Hoku cattle ranch, specifically to accommodate Fagen's wealthy friends. There are still several thousand head of cattle on the property, but the hub of activity for most who find their way here is the hotel itself. It's not very flashy, nor does it have a

Hotel Hana Maui, Hawaii

long, sandy beach. It doesn't even have much of a golf course—just a three-hole practice field.

But once you check in and stroll around the gardens and lawns, richly planted with heliconias, exotic palms, and a wide variety of flowering shrubs, and walk to the top of the hill overlooking the coast, where waves crash against jagged black rocks, the spell of Hana will soon captivate. Whether you stay in one of the garden cottages or in the traditionally styled ranch bungalows, you'll appreciate the appointments and details that make this place so special. Live orchids growing out of ceramic containers and baskets, original Hawaiian arts and crafts, four-poster bamboo beds, quilt bedspreads, rattan furniture, and beautiful tiled baths designed so that you don't need a curtain or door, lend an air of low-key elegance. Even the extra roll of toilet tissue is "gift wrapped."

Bleached hardwood floors, stone countertops and carpets of split bamboo, along with muted natural colors of whites, tans, and soft browns, appeal to those who love things that are natural, not overdone. Soaps come in the shapes of shells, and among the items in your toiletries basket is a pearl-like giant fish scale, the Hawaiians' answer to a nail file. Towels are thick and thirsty, as are the terry bathrobes.

Your view from your trellised patio or deck could be a fragrant garden or the sea. The one-story cottage suites are quite different from the ranch bungalows. Cottages are nestled into the gardens, and the views from the patios are of flowers and palms and towering trees. You'll find it hard to resist scooping up the petals from the plumaria trees, which drop their fragrant blossoms along the walkways. All cottages have been recently renovated and redecorated.

The ranch bungalows, designed in the manner of traditional Hawaiian houses, have spacious decks, and some come with private Jacuzzis that overlook the sea. Louvered window walls allow the sea breezes to cool the rooms, which are comfortable, quiet, and very private.

Hana has a number of recreational facilities on the grounds or nearby. A 1932 Packard sedan takes you on a five-minute ride to a silver-black sand volcanic beach right down the road, a beach James Michener has called the most perfect crescent beach in the Pacific. The beach is public but never crowded, and the hotel has its own changing and refreshment house, where you can get fresh towels and a snack. You can also ask the hotel to pack a picnic lunch for you.

Early risers may want to join the morning walk, followed by breakfast cooked on the beach. You can also go horseback riding along the sea or follow the trails up the lower slopes of Haleakala, where you can see exotic birds and plants in the rainforest. An excursion to Ulaino brings you to lovely waterfalls and a stream you can swim in as well as an idyllic pond called the Blue Pond. Very private and romantic.

You can also go bicycle riding; play tennis, croquet, and sand volleyball; or practice your golf on the three-hole course, where tees are marked by coconuts. Take a nature hike into the forest, or head to the Hana Health and Fitness Center, located near the pool at the top of a grassy hill above the sea, where you'll find the latest in fitness equipment. Aerobics classes are offered daily; massages are also available.

Every week a luau is held at the garden pool pavilion and is one of the best ones around. The staff puts it on and invites you to be a part of the ceremonies. A Hawaiian show, imu ceremony, and tropical feast are all part of the festivities.

The dining room, with its beautiful garden view and dramatic 35-foot open-beamed ceiling, is located in the Plantation House. It overlooks the gardens and features a range of Hawaiian specialties along with Polynesian, American, and Oriental cuisine. The chef uses lots of local produce, such as herbs, vegetables, taro, coconut, mango, and bananas. A "wellness" menu meets the needs of guests who prefer a low-cal, low-fat meal. The Paniolo Bar, on the covered lanai overlooking the Bay, is the place to go for those who want to relax after dinner. The more casual Hana Ranch Restaurant is open daily for breakfast and lunch and on Friday and Saturday for dinner. Wednesday is pizza night, always popular with guests and local residents.

The marvelous Hana Coast Gallery and the library are also located in the Plantation House. The gallery features the finest in genuine Hawaiian art and master crafts, including paintings, pottery, sculpture, wooden bowls, and rare antique floral prints.

You'll find the staff extremely friendly and helpful. Most live in the village and walk to work. Some have been employed at the hotel since its opening in 1946!

At Hotel Hana Maui, you won't find a TV or even a clock in your room. You won't be able to track down a disco or a jet ski. What you will find here is a quiet beauty and people who genuinely care about pleasing you.

The Hotel Hana Maui casts its spell with exquisite subtlety. Serene and lovely, it's a resort romantics must discover at some point in their lifetimes. A honeymoon is a good place to start.

Author's note: Recently Hana Maui was purchased by a new investor group, which plans to bring in Amanresorts as the operator to take over from ITT Sheraton. Knowing what the founder of the company, Adrian Zecha, has created with his other thirteen small, upscale properties (most located in Asia and some profiled in this book), I have every confidence that Hana's assets will only be enhanced. Zecha is passionate about preserving the idyllic nature and character of those properties he builds and/or operates.

Address/Phone: P.O. Box 8, Hana, Maui, HI 96713–9989; (808) 248–8211; fax: (808) 248–7202

Reservations: (800) 321–4262

Owner/Manager: Gerald Bahouth, general manager

Arrival/Departure: By car from Kahului Airport: A 56-mile drive along the scenic (and winding) Hana Highway. If you're going to rent a car, make arrangements before you leave, and rent the car in Kahului. You'll pay more if you rent in Hana, and only Dollar has an office there. By air: A 15-minute flight to Hana from Kahului Airport by Air Molokai or Aloha Island Air. You can also fly from Honolulu to Hana via Aloha Island Air (90 minutes) or take a private charter or private helicopter. The hotel's open jitney picks up guests at all flights coming into Hana Airport and transports them to the property, a 10-minute ride.

Distance from Kahului Airport: 54 miles

Distance from Hana: Located in town; 50 miles from Kahului

Accommodations: 94 rooms and suites, including garden lanais and sea ranch cottages on the ground sloping to the seacoast on the Pacific side.

Best Rooms/Suites: Ranch cottages with private Jacuzzis

Amenities: Coffee bar with coffeemaker, grinder, and selection of Kona coffee beans; hair dryer, toiletries; ceiling fans and refrigerator with ice maker

Electricity: 110 volts

Sports and Facilities: Beach, tennis court, pool, three-hole practice golf course; hiking, horseback riding, snorkeling, croquet, volleyball

Dress Code: Casual by day; dressier during evening

Weddings: The wide veranda of the Plantation House and the beautiful lawn and gardens are popular sites.

Rates/Packages: $325–$795 per couple per day, including tennis, bicycles, snorkeling, and beach equipment; $85 per person per day for breakfast, lunch, and dinner; $65 for breakfast and dinner. Honeymooners get 25 percent off rack rates as well as dinner one evening, champagne, and a massage for two.

Payment/Credit Cards: Most major

Deposit: 1 night, guaranteed with credit card

Government Taxes: 10.17 percent

Service Charges: 10 percent

Hyatt Regency Kauai Resort & Spa

Location: On fifty acres in the Poipu resort area on Kauai's south shore, the sunniest side of this island.

Romantic Features: Lovely oceanfront setting on Shipwreck Beach, a prime surfing strand; five acres of saltwater lagoons plus a water slide; unique "Discover Kauai" adventure expeditions.

Something old, something new—that's what you'll find at the Hyatt Regency Kauai. Although the resort first opened in 1990, it has the classic warmth and romance of hotels built on the islands in the 1920s and '30s, a time when bands serenaded luxury ocean liners as they arrived in port, and songs like "Little Grass Shack" topped the mainland Hit Parade.

The design and decor pay tribute to this golden era. With its double-pitched, green-tiled roofs and wide verandas, the low-rise architecture recalls the Hawaiian plantation period. Entering the open-air lobby, you have to be impressed by the vaulted ceilings with exposed beams, splendid glass chandelier, and huge floral displays. Before development the property had been a sugarcane plantation, so a cane motif has been incorporated in the grillwork, lamps, and masonry. Koa wood—the lustrous Hawaiian mahogany—is used throughout the hotel. Corridors are lined with Hawaiian photos, artfully displayed quilts, superb collections of rare shell leis, and calabashes (wooden bowls).

The hotel snuggles at the top of a gentle slope, and the grounds undulate to the water's edge, leaving plenty of room for waterfalls, palm trees, and teak-wood bridges. The Hyatt is located on Shipwreck Beach, which has 3- to 5-foot waves that make it a favorite of surfers and boogie boarders. Since swimming is tricky in this booming surf, the hotel has created five acres of swimming lagoons down by the beach. The lagoons are actually part of an advanced energy recycling system: Heat generated by the air-conditioning system is used to warm the pools as well as guest showers and laundry. In the sprawling, meandering pool with its small "ponds" and grottos, a current gently carries you along at about 3 miles per hour. If this is too slow for you, there is a twisting water slide that will zip you from the top level to the bottom in seconds.

Most accommodations have ocean views. The rooms immediately make you feel at home with their old Hawaiian warmth; they're furnished with rattan and wicker armchairs, a mahogany armoire that hides a TV and snack bar, commodious dresser, and ceiling fan. For reading, there's a comfortable armchair and hassock. The rooms also feature a most user-friendly bath with plenty of shelves to stow articles and an attractive 1930s-design floor made of white and celadon ceramic tile. Orchids appear everywhere—tucked into towels or the edge of a soap dish, for example.

At the Hyatt, you can choose from four restaurants, all excellent. For elegant Italian dining, there's Dondero's, accented by a striking wall mural inset with bronzed shells. The best place for sunset cocktails is on the terrace at Stevenson's Bar, with views of meandering greenery, palm trees, and lighted tiki torches. Inside, the splendid bar, which features broad panels of koa wood accented by carved pineapples, specializes in unusual ports and single-malt scotch.

The resort is surrounded by the Poipu Bay Resort Golf Course, a challenging eighteen-hole layout designed by Robert Trent Jones II set on 210 acres. Four tennis courts and a pro shop await racquet players. And save some time for the Anara Spa, one of the most beautiful and pampering in the islands. The exercise equipment includes six Lifecycles, four Stairmasters, and four treadmills. Or swim in the beautiful lap pool set in a semicircular courtyard. After your workout, reward yourself with one of the open-air showers surrounded by lava rock. Then indulge in a massage or facial—treatment rooms are open to gardens and you can opt to have your session outdoors. The house specialty is the Royal Hawaiian facial, which uses dozens of different products, including the Hawaiian essences, seaweed and papaya. Special spa packages are available for honeymooners.

Kauai is considered by many to be the loveliest of the Hawaiian Islands. To help people explore its little-known treasures, the Hyatt has launched a "Discover Kauai" program, with options ranging from "talking story" sessions about island legends to archaeology walks to Pictured Ledge, petroglyphs located right near the hotel. For adventure enthusiasts, expeditions include kayaking on the Hanalei River and helicopter flights to the "Forbidden Island" of Niihau, once accessible only to people of Hawaiian descent. Any of these adventures are sure to make your honeymoon in Kauai even more memorable.

Address/Phone: 1571 Poipu Road, Koloa, Kauai, HI 96756; (808) 742-1234; fax: (808) 742-1557

Reservations: (800) 233-1234

Owner/Manager: Operated by Hyatt Hotels Corporation; Rick Riess, general manager

Arrival/Departure: Taxis and car rentals at airport

Distance from Lihue Airport: 16 miles (20 minutes)

Distance from Koloa: 3 miles (5 minutes)

Accommodations: 600 rooms and suites, 70 percent with ocean views; each has separate sitting area

Best Rooms/Suites: Opt for a Regency Club Ocean Room, where perks include services of a concierge, complimentary continental breakfast, and hors d'oeuvres as well as a five-star view of the Pacific.

Amenities: Air-conditioning, ceiling fan, toiletries, remote-control TV, private servi-bar, in-room safe; double marble sinks; twice-daily maid service

Electricity: 110 volts

Sports and Facilities: 2 swimming pools—a "quiet" pool and an "action" pool with waterfalls, slides, and water volleyball; 4 tennis courts with pro shop and tennis professional; golf on an 18-hole course and driving range designed by Robert Trent Jones II; horseback riding (stables on property). Water sports on the property include snorkeling and sea kayaking; scuba diving and snorkel day trips can be arranged; kayak excursions are available nearby.

Dress Code: Casually elegant

Weddings: About 200 couples a year say their "I do's" at the Hyatt Regency Kauai. The resort has a wedding department that can handle all the details. They can even arrange for a replica of an award-winning Hawaiian wedding gown (holoku) for the bride. A variety of wedding packages are available, ranging from $750 to $1,500, Many include island touches such as flower leis, a conch-shell blower, and Hawaiian music.

Rates/Packages: $275–$465 per couple per night for a room; $550–$2,500 for a suite, "Tropical Romance" package (4 days/3 nights), $715 per couple, includes luxury accommodations, a subcompact rental car, welcome gift, flower lei greeting, champagne upon arrival, one breakfast in bed for two, "his and her" matching kimonos, dinner for two in the resort's northern Italian restaurant, a ½-hour Swedish massage for two, complimentary use of the spa, discounts on spa treatments and services.
Payment/Credit Cards: Most major
Deposit: 2-night deposit within 14 days of booking; cancel 72 hours prior to arrival date for refund.
Government Taxes: 10.17 percent
Service Charges: Not included

Kona Village Resort

Location: Natural black-and-white beach on Kahuwai Bay.
Romantic Features: Luxury hales (cottages), each designed in a different Polynesian style, such as Tahitian, Fijian, and Samoan; natural black-and-white beach on Kahuwai Bay; privacy protected when you place coconut at door.

Native grass shacks were never like the luxurious hales that loll along the crystal-blue bay at Kona Village Resort, a hideaway strung around peaceful lagoons and blessed by a natural black-and-white speckled beach. The setting is something of a miracle—a small oasis of coco palms and beach that was left untouched by a fiery lava flow in 1801. Today, Kona Village remains a lush, eighty-two-acre paradise of emerald lawns and mirror-still ponds. It's a quiet retreat for simple pleasures: watching a coconut drift in with the tide or stopping to watch the nightly "water ballet" by the resident manta rays, who softly swirl near shore.

Located at the site of an ancient Hawaiian fishing community, the resort resembles an old Hawaiian village. Its paths are edged by fragrant pikake and plumeria blossoms, and bungalows are thatched with coconut fronds and planted on stilts beside the ocean and lagoons or on lava fields. The resort is, in fact, the largest group of thatched buildings in the state of Hawaii. Local materials, such as coral, stone, koa and ohia woods, are used extensively.

Inside, however, twentieth-century accoutrements include king-size beds in most accommodations, a refrigerator stocked with juices and soft

Kona Village Resort, Hawaii

drinks, modern bathrooms, and dressing rooms. The designs of the hales reflect nine different Polynesian cultures. The Hawaiian accommodations, for example, have steeply pitched thatched roofs, while the Maori feature boldly patterned fronts and carved figures on the rooflines. Interiors are panelled with wood, and ceilings are lined with lauhala matting. Furnishings might include rattan chairs and tropical-print spreads. The hales are also notable for what they don't have—in-room telephones, radios, or television. Instead of air-conditioners, ceiling fans enhance nature's cooling trade winds. A coconut placed in front of your hale's door alerts the staff to leave you alone.

Every mealtime is special, from the macadamia-nut pancakes with coconut syrup at breakfast to duck breast with taro leaves and mango coulis at dinner. Friday and Monday nights, the resort hosts a traditional luau, one of the most authentic in the islands—many Big Island residents drop by to enjoy the feast. Kailua pig is roasted in the *imu* (underground oven), accompanied by other delicacies such as *lau lau* (pork and fish in taro leaves) and lomi salmon.

Afterward, a Polynesian revue showcases Pacific Island dances, including the Samoan fire dance and hip-quivering Tahitian tamure. Another favorite is the paniolo steak cookout, with ukulele music to accompany the kiawe-grilled steaks.

A bevy of water sports activities are available for guests, including outrigger canoeing and glass-bottom boat excursions. In addition to the crescent-shaped swimming beach, the property offers two freshwater pools and a whirlpool. The resort has three lighted outdoor Plexi-pave tennis courts, all recently resurfaced. You can take advantage of the complimentary adult clinic, or sign on for the round-robin series for practice and fun.

The grounds also include many Hawaiian archaeological sites, including fish ponds, house sites, and shelter caves. You can learn more about Hawaiian culture on several different excursions, including historical walks, tide pool explorations, and petroglyph tours highlighting the powerful depictions of turtles, fish, dogs, and humans.

About half of the guests at Kona Village have stayed at the resort previously. You'll probably want to add your names to the roster of returnees soon.

Owner/Manager: Fred Duerr, general manager
Address/Phone: P.O. Box 1299, Kailua-Kona, HI 96745; (808) 325–5555; fax: (808) 325–5124
Reservations: (800) 367–5290 or (800) 423–5450 (in Hawaii)
Arrival/Departure: Transfers included in honeymoon package
Distance from Keahole-Kona Airport: 6 miles
Distance from Kailua-Kona: 15 miles
Accommodations: 125 thatched hales (cottages) in nine architectural styles
Best Rooms/Suites: The luxurious Lava Tahitians are set out on the lava rock along the ocean, away from other hales. The Sand Marquesans are also very luxurious and are located on the water, with lots of greenery to provide privacy.
Amenities: Ceiling fans, hair dryer, toiletries, king-size bed, dressing room, refrigerator stocked with juices and soft drinks, coffeemaker (with fresh Kona beans)
Electricity: 110 volts
Sports and Facilities: Sunfish sailboats, outrigger canoes, snorkeling, and 3 lighted tennis courts all available on premises. Nearby activities include five 18-hole championship golf courses, horseback riding, deep-sea fishing
Dress Code: Tropically casual
Weddings: The resort's wedding coordinator sees to everything from ministers to marriage licenses. Wedding packages are available.
Rates/Packages: $395–$680 per couple per night, including breakfast, lunch, and dinner daily. Prices also cover most resort activities, including tennis, kayaking, Sunfish sailing, historical and petroglyph tours, airport transfers in the Big Island, and more. The Honeymoon Hideaway package costs $2,315 per couple for four nights; $3,935 for seven

nights. It includes all meals, superior accommodations, and a line-art reproduction of your honeymoon hale. Couples can also choose one optional activity: a snorkel/sail, body massage, tennis lesson, or one-tank scuba dive (certification required).

Payment/Credit Cards: Most major
Deposit: 1 night's lodging; guarantee with credit card
Government Taxes: 10.17 percent
Service Charges: Not included

The Manele Bay Hotel

Location: Southeastern coast of Lanai.
Romantic Features: White-sand Hulopoe Beach; serene courtyard gardens; two hotels for the price of one—stay at Mahele Bay and enjoy facilities at the upcountry Lodge at Koele.

A decade ago, the island of Lanai was about a twenty-five-minute flight from—and about fifty years behind—Honolulu. With 98 percent of the land owned by Dole Food, Lanai was called the Pineapple Island, a laid-back world with one funky hotel and a one-room airport.

All that changed in the early 1990s with the debut of two elegant new sister resorts, among the most luxurious in Hawaii. In the short time they have been open, the hotels have wowed rich and famous guests such as Kevin Costner and Billy Crystal, and hosted major sporting events such as the Merrill Lynch Senior Shoot-Out on the PGA tour.

Playful spinner dolphins often visit Hulopoe Bay, Lanai's best beach and the setting for the Manele Bay Hotel, which opened in May 1991. Architecturally, the resort combines both Hawaiian and Mediterranean detailing, with arcaded loggias and sloping roofs. White walls and a sea-green tile roof harmonize with plush lawns and ochre pathways. To maintain an intimate feeling, individual wings surround garden courtyards, each with a different theme, such as Hawaiian, Japanese, or bromeliad.

In the lobby, murals by John Wullbrandt depict the legend of Kaululaau, said to have chased evil spirits from the island. Honoring Lanai's pineapple-plantation heritage, bronze chandeliers incorporate leaves and fruit in their design; vintage Hawaiian prints line the corridors.

As you stroll through the lush grounds, you'll encounter staff members diligently pursuing perfection—perhaps a wizened gardener raking imaginary leaves from an immaculate lawn, or a housekeeper polishing a bronze urn until it's mirror bright.

Rooms are very large and decorated in chinoiserie chic, with bamboo-framed chairs, porcelains poised on the armoire, and a four-poster bed. Spacious bathrooms sparkle with marble floors, counters, and a separate glass stall shower. In addition to the usual shampoos and soaps, the lavish toiletries basket also includes hairspray, a miniloofah, and prethreaded needles. The lanai (terrace) is designed to be enjoyed and is furnished with a plump-cushioned chaise longue and two comfy armchairs. About half of the rooms have ocean views.

A diamond-bright crescent, Hulopoe is one of the loveliest beaches in the islands. When conditions are calm, there's good snorkeling along the rocks at the left (as you face the ocean). Among the hotel's facilities, the only downside is the health club, which is tiny and stuffed down a side corridor (the entry looks like a broom closet).

Through the hotel, guests can arrange various excursions, including a snorkel cruise aboard the Trilogy trimaran. They can also sign on for an ocean rafting trip along Lanai's coast, which is lined by 1,000-foot cliffs and secret coves.

For dining-with-a-view, you can't top the outside terrace of the Hulopoe Court, with sound effects courtesy of the rustling palm fronds and wash of surf. The menu centers on Hawaiian regional cuisine. Accented by crystal chandeliers and murals, the Ihilani formal dining room re-creates the splendor of the Hawaiian monarchy and serves a French Mediterranean cuisine. Save room for one of the chocolate desserts, made with Hawaiian-grown cocoa beans.

The Lodge at Koele, Manele's Bay's sister property, is also extremely Hawaiian—but in a way mainlanders rarely imagine Hawaii to be. The upland setting—a cool 1,700-foot elevation where hills often wear clouds like misty halos—resembles more a scene from *The Sound of Music* than *South Pacific*. Styled after a turn-of-the-century plantation estate, the resort features high beamed ceilings, twin 30-foot stone fireplaces in the Great Hall, and spacious verandas arranged with phalanxes of wicker armchairs.

Although Koele feels as if it has purred along in Grand Hotel perfection for at least a century or two, it only opened in April 1990. Connoisseurs can happily browse among rarities, ranging from a Burmese elephant howdah in the foyer to the eighth-century Persian painting in the music room. At the same time, the ambience is friendly, thanks to interior designer Joszi Meskan's sprightly touches, such as monkeys cavorting among the 8-foot-tall chandeliers.

Coddling remains the byword here, from the butter-soft suede armchairs in the library to the real down pillows on your bed. Rooms encourage relaxing, with a lavishly cushioned window seat, two wicker armchairs, and a four-poster bed crowned with pineapples. Bathrooms feature exotic blue-marble countertops paired with Italian tile floors and hand-painted cups from Portugal. Look carefully at the walls—they're painstakingly hand-painted, not papered.

Lanai is golfers' heaven, with two spectacular eighteen-hole layouts. Designed by Jack Nicklaus, the championship Challenge at Manele opened in December 1993 to immediate acclaim. Every hole on the course offers an unobstructed ocean vista. Upland, the Experience at Koele, designed by Greg Norman and Ted Robinson, boasts panoramic views and several dramatic elevation drops from tees to greens.

It all adds up to the perfect choice for couples who love outdoor adventures by day, and sumptuous accommodations at night.

Address/Phone: P.O. Box L, Lanai City, HI 96763; (808) 565–7700; fax: (808) 565–2483

Reservations: (800) 321–4666

Owner/Manager: Dole Food Company, Inc., owner; Lanai Resort Partners, operator; Matt Bailey, general manager

Arrival/Departure: Complimentary airport and island shuttle transportation included

Distance from Lanai Airport: 9 miles (15 minutes)

Distance from Koele: 7 miles (12 minutes)

Accommodations: 250 rooms and suites

Best Rooms/Suites: If you want to splurge, ask for one of the suites that includes butler service (e.g., the midpriced Mauka Mini Suite); deluxe oceanfront rooms are also very romantic.

Amenities: Air-conditioning, ceiling fans, hair dryer, minibar, toiletries, TV, radio, clock; coffee/tea service; 24-hour room service. Some suites have butler service.

Electricity: 110 volts

Sports and Facilities: 36 holes of championship golf, 6 tennis courts, 1 swimming pool, snorkeling, free introductory scuba-diving course. The hotel can arrange scuba diving and snorkel sails.

Dress Code: Casually elegant

Weddings: Can be arranged

Rates/Packages: $250–$495 per couple per night for a room; $700 for a suite. Lanai for Lovers package: $1,206–$1,566 per couple for 4 nights; additional nights, $282–$373. Includes lei greeting upon arrival, a welcome bottle of champagne and island chocolates, gourmet picnic in the country, his and her massage.

Payment/Credit Cards: Most major

Deposit: 2-night deposit required within 14 days of the reservation request. Deposits will be refunded in full when cancellations are received at

least 14 days prior to arrival.
Government Taxes: 10.17 percent
Service Charges: Not included

Mauna Lani Bay Hotel and Bungalows

Location: On twenty-nine oceanfront acres at Kalahuipua'a, on the Big Island's Kohala Coast.

Romantic Features: Two white-sand beaches; fifteen acres of ancient, spring-fed Hawaiian fishponds plus pools teeming with tropical fish; fine restaurants.

Its name means "mountain reaching heaven," a perfect visual for honeymooners, who will feel like they've come close to finding paradise at the Mauna Lani Bay Resort. Located on the sunny, dry (only 7 inches of rain annually) Kohala Coast, this six-story hotel presents a bold, contemporary design. Shaped like an arrowhead thrust seaward toward Makaiwa Bay, Mauna Lani Bay is a true-blue haven fringed by pearl-white beaches. The lobby reflects a spare elegance, with koi ponds and banks of orchids, torch ginger, and birds of paradise flanking the atrium. Jet-weary travelers are immediately soothed by the whoosh of waterfalls, view of the sapphire-blue Pacific, and friendly ministrations of the concierge, who checks you in.

The resort is built around fifteen acres of ancient fishponds, once *kapu* (forbidden) to all but Hawaiian royalty. They're stocked with mullet, awa, and lemon butterflies, whose brilliant colors swirl like an aquatic kaleidoscope. Paths encourage peaceful wanderings.

Decorated in serene tones of white and sand, each of the accommodations measures more than 550 square feet and has a private lanai. Ceiling fans, polished teak furnishings, and live orchids complement the tropical oasis decor. Top-of-the-line accommodations are the five bungalows—private houses, really, encompassing more than 4,000 square feet. Each has a private swimming pool and whirlpool spa and is served by a butler who can handle everything from unpacking your bags to grilling mahi-mahi on the barbecue. Steven Spielberg and Roseanne are among the celebrities who have roosted amid the sumptuous decor, accented by koa wood, marble, and crystal.

The signature restaurant is the celebrated Canoe House, which has won accolades in magazines such as *Bon Appétit*. Poised on the brink of the ocean, it offers diners ringside views of the polychromatic Kohala Coast sunsets. The Pacific Rim menu highlights choices such as wok-fried *lilikoi* (passion fruit), shrimp, and lemongrass–crusted ono (a fish). A new club is open for late-night music and dancing. In all, Mauna Lani has three restaurants.

Carved from a sixteenth-century lava flow, the two championship golf courses (home to the annual Senior Skins golf tournament) present dramatic juxtapositions between stark black lava rock, smooth emerald turf, and an ever-changing sea. Meanwhile, *Tennis Magazine* has included the ten Plexi-pave tennis courts on its list of top fifty U.S. resort facilities. The roster of activities also includes aerobics classes, hula and lei-making lessons, beach picnics, and more. At the Mauna Lani Health Spa, options range from low-impact aerobics classes at water's edge to lomi lomi, a Hawaiian-style massage.

For relaxing and sunning, Mauna Lani's two beaches are regarded as some of the finest on the Big Island. Try to snare one of the private cabanas, and lie back on the two-person lounge chairs shaded by a cabriolet roof. One of Hawaii's best scuba-diving locales, the waters off the Kohala Coast are stippled with lava tubes, archways, caves, canyons, and coral heads. Favorite sites include Turtles Reef, a cleaning station for Hawaiian green sea turtles. Dive packages are available.

According to Hawaiians, Mauna Lani Bay is set on sacred ground. Perhaps that explains the tremendous feeling of *mana* (spiritual power) that the resort exerts over all those who visit.

Address/Phone: 68–1400 Mauna Lani Drive, Kohala Coast, HI 96743; (808) 885–6622, fax: (808) 885–1484

Reservations: (800) 327–8585; (800) 367–2323; (808) 885–6622; (800) 992-7987 (in Hawaii)

Owner/Manager: Don Dickhens, general manager

Arrival/Departure: Taxis available at airport; transfers can be arranged.

Distance from Keahole-Kona Airport: 25 miles north

Distance from Kona: 34 miles north

Accommodations: 345 rooms; 5 bungalows with private swimming pools and 24-hour butler service; 23 ocean villas. Over 92 percent of the accommodations have ocean views.

Best Rooms/Suites: Bungalows with pools; ocean villas

Amenities: Oversize TV (with cable), VCR, honor bar, electronic safe, refrigerator, makeup mirror, toiletries, hair dryer, robes; concierge service

Electricity: 110 volts

Sports and Facilities: 36 holes of golf, 10 tennis courts, heated swimming pool, health club; sailing, snorkeling, windsurfing, boogie boarding, and surfing. Scuba diving and deep-sea fishing can be arranged.

Dress Code: Casually elegant

Weddings: The director of guest services can arrange all the details, from formal weddings to nuptials in a helicopter. A favorite site is a little island in one of the fishponds.

Rates/Packages: $260–$795 per couple per night for a room; $795 for a suite; $395 for a one-bedroom villa; $3,025–$3,850 for a bungalow. Honeymoon package (3 nights): $1,025 per couple for an ocean-view room; $1,295 for ocean-front accommodations. Additional nights, $395 and $465 respectively. Includes a bottle of champagne and fresh fruit basket upon arrival. Couples can also custom-design their own romance package, with options ranging from limousine service to a private dinner accompanied by a violin serenade.

Payment/Credit Cards: Most major
Deposit: 2-night deposit required to guarantee reservation.
Government Taxes: 10.17 percent
Service Charges: Not included

Louisiana

Omni Royal Orleans

Location: In heart of historic French Quarter of New Orleans.
Romantic Features: Rooftop terrace overlooking historic New Orleans and Mississippi River; Jacuzzi suites.

In 1842, the rates at the hotel were $2.50 per day. That was the good news. The bad news was that gentlemen could dine from 3 P.M. until 5 P.M.; ladies, at 5 P.M.—hardly conducive to a romantic rendezvous. Fortunately for couples in love, this has all changed at the fashionable Omni Royal Orleans. Today those who are New Orleans–bound will find this historic old hotel a memorable place to stay. It is an especially good choice if you want to be in the middle of the nightlife in the Bourbon Street area.

Just two blocks from the front entrance is the French Market, and kitty-corner, across the street, is the popular Preservation Jazz Hall. Also in the neighborhood are Arnauds Restaurant, the Hard Rock Cafe, Brennan's, and the Musée Conte Wax Museum. There are also numerous antiques shops, boutiques, and cafes throughout the area.

Located in the midst of the famous area known as the French Quarter, the Royal Orleans has been known as a mecca for the rich and powerful,

Omni Royal Orleans, Louisiana

who have come here over the years to dine and overnight. Today the renowned Rib Room is the "in" place for power lunches.

Although the actual structure went through some dramatic changes due to a devastating hurricane in 1915, which did a real number on the building, the elegance and grace of the property was restored; the original exterior arches were saved and are part of the lovely facade today. Like other charming buildings in the quarter, the Royal Orleans has its share of ornate wrought iron grillwork balconies, hanging lanterns, and garden courtyards. At night, when the lights are shining from the multipaned windows through the arches and grillwork, the hotel is really beautiful. Take a stroll down the street and see for yourself.

After a day of sight-seeing or browsing in the local shops, you can head to the seventh floor to the rooftop garden terrace. Here you'll find a lovely pool, which is heated during the cooler months and cooled during the hotter season—a wonderful haven for relaxing after a day on the town. Also on this level is a bar and La Riviera restaurant as well as a health club equipped with the latest in exercise equipment. La Riviera serves breakfast and light lunches.

The rooms, which were furnished with English chintz, have recently been redecorated using colors such as peach and light blue, giving them a lighter, more southern flair. They're comfortable and come with all the amenities you will need. Many have king-size beds, and you'll find the linens are exceptionally fine. Some suites come with a Jacuzzi right in the room, along with a cozy sitting area. There are also balcony rooms overlooking St. Louis and Royal Streets—they're fun but can be noisy. The Rib Room Restaurant is well worth a visit. If you want to live dangerously, try the Washbucket Martini, a specialty of the house. This lethal brew comes in a brandy snifter kind of glass with a spout, along with a king's ransom in gin or vodka on the rocks, with just a whiff of vermouth. As you'd expect, the ribs are great. So are the other dishes, such as spit-roasted flounder, salmon, turtle soup, and chocolate mousse.

If you like southern hospitality, you'll find it in spades at the Omni Royal Orleans, where you'll be treated royally. The staff is great.

Address: 621 St. Louis Street, New Orleans, LA 70140; (504) 529–5333; fax: (504) 529–7089
Reservations: (800) THE OMNI or (504) 529–5333; fax: (504) 529–7089
Owner/Manager: Gary Froeba, general manager
Arrival/Departure: Taxi or shuttle from airport
Distance from New Orleans International Airport: 12 miles
Distance from New Orleans: Right in the center of it
Accommodations: 351 rooms: 16 suites; 5 Jacuzzi Suites; 1 Royal Suite; 1 Penthouse Suite
Best Rooms/Suites: Jacuzzi Suites (these are quieter than the balcony rooms, which are located on a main street)
Amenities: Hair dryer, toiletries, air-conditioning, remote-control TV, telephones with message alert; in-room movies, balconies (some rooms); nonsmoking rooms; laundry and valet service, 24-hour room service, concierge, covered valet parking, in-room safes
Electricity: 110 volts
Sports and Facilities: Swimming in rooftop pool; fitness center
Dress Code: Informal for daytime; dressier for Rib Room at night
Weddings: Can be arranged
Rates/Packages: $135–$240 per couple per night for room with queen- or king-size bed; $310 for room with balcony and king-size bed; $310 for Petit Suites; $350 for Jacuzzi Suites. Ask about a honeymoon package (it was in the works at press time).
Payment/Credit Cards: Most major
Deposit: 1-night deposit; cancel 2 days prior to arrival for refund.
Government Taxes: 11 percent room tax plus $2.00 occupancy tax
Service Charges: 9½ percent food and beverage

Massachusetts

The Wauwinet

Location: On the northeastern end of the island of Nantucket.
Romantic Features: Walks on windswept beaches; bike rides; picnics in a secluded cove.

The weathered clapboard houses and tucked-away gardens brimming over with hollyhocks, black-eyed Susans, and cascades of roses tumbling over white picket fences are all part of Nantucket's inescapable charm. At the heart of it all is one of the oldest inns on the island, The Wauwinet. Located just about as far away as you can get from the noise and complexities of everyday life, The Wauwinet stands firmly planted on its grassy carpet, a bastion of peace and tranquility.

Its traditions reach back to the mid-1800s, when the inn was a restaurant, known as Wauwinet House, that served shore dinners to guests arriving by boat. In 1876 it became an inn and soon emerged as not only a Nantucket social center but a hot spot for Northeasterners to head for their vacation. It went through a period of decline until 1986, when Bostonians Stephen and Jill Karp purchased the property, restoring it to the tune of $3 million. A more recent facelift has resulted in new wall treatments, upholstery, furniture, and artwork.

Flanked by Nantucket Bay on one side and the Atlantic Ocean on the other, The Wauwinet is New England at its best. Its gables, porches, and lawns invite guests to sit back in the comfortable wicker chaises and white lawn chairs to gaze out at magnificent, endless ocean views, gentle dunes, and wispy gardens of wildflowers and roses all around. Sandy paths cut through the low-lying shrubs lead to the sea and to private, buff-colored beaches.

Rooms are individually decorated, many with an eclectic mix of English-style period pieces, country antiques, and casual wicker. Chintz and stenciling add to the warmth of the decor; headboards are iron or upholstered. Around the rooms you'll find special touches such as baskets, hatboxes, books, and woodcarvings.

You have all the amenities you could wish for to assure that you will be sublimely comfortable—extra things like Egyptian cotton bathrobes; armoires with soft, scented hangers; eyelet-trimmed linens; bottled water beside your bed; and fresh flowers. Windows are large, letting in lots of fresh air and light; ceilings are high.

Topper's, one of the best known and most respected restaurants on Nantucket, is located right at The Wauwinet. Topper's award-winning cuisine and wines continually garner rave reviews. You can dine alfresco on the umbrella-shaded Bayview Terrace or eat inside in two indoor dining rooms. The executive chef, Peter Wallace, uses local produce, such as bushberries and cranberries, as well as fresh fish and seafood to prepare his American cuisine with a light touch. Service is polished and gracious; wines, superb.

The inn's jitney is available to take you into Nantucket town, always an interesting excursion. (You can also bicycle in.) Once the largest whaling center in the world, Nantucket has a fascinating museum that details the history of the whaling industry. The town's streets are lined by more than 800 homes built between 1740 and 1840, many owned by whaling captains. You can spend hours browsing through the countless small shops, cozy restaurants, and art galleries. And take time to check out the harbor, where there are many lovely yachts riding at anchor or tied to the wharfs.

For a more intimate outing, ask the staff to prepare a gourmet basket lunch and take the *Topper, Too* launch to a secluded beach for a lazy afternoon of sunning and swimming.

Activities and sports at The Wauwinet are centered on Nantucket's natural assets. You can swim; go out in the inn's many boats and sailing craft; hike, bike, and jog through the trails that wind through the area; or play tennis, croquet, or beach chess. Golf can be arranged nearby.

During the crisper months, which some feel are the very best, after a walk through the dunes, you can head to the cozy library, sit before the fire, and sip sherry or port.

Once you've stayed there, when you define the word "bliss," you'll naturally think Wauwinet.

Address/Phone: P.O. Box 2580, Wauwinet Road, Nantucket, MA 02584; (508) 228–0145; fax: (508) 228–6712

Reservations: (800) 426–8718

Owner/Manager: Stephen and Jill Karp, owners; Russ and Debbie Cleveland, innkeepers

Arrival/Departure: If you want to get there in a hurry, you can fly from Hyannis via Island Air for about $40 one-way (800–698–1109) or take Nantucket Air (800–635–8787). Cape Air also goes from New Bedford to the island (800–352–0714). Or you can take the ferries from Hyannis operated either by the Steamship Authority (508–540–2022), or Hy-Line Cruises (508–778–2602); the trip ranges from 1 hour 50 minutes to 2 hours, 10 minutes. Fares are about the same (approximately $22 round-trip) for both lines, but the Hy-Line ships are 20 minutes faster. For about $10 more, you can enjoy first-class service on the Hy-Line's run: you sit in a comfortable lounge set up with couches. If you plan on taking your car, make your ferry reservations well ahead of time, especially during the peak summer season. Rental cars are available in town. Complimentary transportation to The Wauwinet from the Steamship Authority dock only (Hy-Line's dock is right down the street).

Distance from Nantucket Airport: 9 miles

Distance from Nantucket town: 9 miles

Accommodations: 30 rooms; 25 located in the inn, 5 in private guest cottages

Best Rooms/Suites: The inn's rooms have warmth and character; the guest cottages are more private; deluxe rooms have king-size beds

Amenities: Air-conditioning, ceiling fans, hair dryer, TV, VCR, cotton bathrobes, irons and ironing boards, bottled water at bedside, telephone, Crabtree & Evelyn toiletries, scented hangers; evening turndown service

Electricity: 110 volts

Sports and Facilities: 2 Har-Tru clay tennis courts, jogging, hiking, and walking trails; swimming at 2 private beaches, Sunfish sailing, windsurfing, rowboats; jeep safaris, croquet, bocce, BeetleCat, mountain bikes, fishing, golf; racquetball and squash can be arranged

Dress Code: Smart casual; jackets with or without ties or dress sweaters and slacks are requested for gentlemen dining at Topper's.

Weddings: Can be arranged

Rates/Packages: Per couple per night rates include room, breakfasts, cheese, port and wine, tennis, use of bikes, boating, natural history excursions, jitney service into town: $190–$1,170 (spring/fall); $290–$1,400 (summer). A romance package, The Wauwinet Interlude, is priced from $1,400 per couple and includes a bay-view guest room for 3 nights, champagne, gourmet fruit and cheese basket, candlelight dinner in Topper's, 2 logo champagne flutes, a dozen long-stemmed red roses, and a box of chocolates.

Payment/Credit Cards: Most major

Deposit: Prepayment required. Cancellation penalties apply; must cancel 14 days (or more) prior to arrival date for refund less $35 cancellation fee.

Government Taxes: 9.75 percent room tax

Service Charges: Not included

Closed: October 30 to mid-May

New Mexico

Inn of the Anasazi

Location: In the center of Santa Fe.
Romantic Features: Seductive desert colors; private kiva fireplace; four-poster bed.

It's only been open since 1990, but its spirit stretches back over 700 years ago to a time when the creative Anasazi Indians lived in cliffs in the southwestern hills. The Indians, who were artistic and in tune with their surroundings, left a heritage of beautiful geometric designs that were found in everyday items such as pottery and weavings.

When the Inn of the Anasazi was built, the creators successfully captured the essence of the culture of this ancient people throughout the inn without imposing any of the clichés often found in such tourism-related endeavors. This place feels as if it has sat here in the heart of historic Santa Fe for many, many years.

Its romantic appeal is in both the low-key, classy way the inn has been designed and the warmth of the people who run it. Each room has its own private kiva fireplace, king-size bed (most rooms) with a fluffy duvet, fine, 100 percent cotton sheets, down pillows, and colors that carry you out to the desert.

Lie back on your bed and look up at the ceiling, which is made of authentic *vigas* and *latillas,* a traditional wooden beam and pole construction. Really interesting and indicative of the kind of thought that went into the inn's design.

The decor is pure Southwestern: massive hand-hewn furniture, Indian blankets, mellow brown leather chairs, stone-top tables; terra-cotta pots filled with cactus, original artwork and crafts by Native American artists, and antique Indian rugs. Baskets woven in Anasazi-style patterns, unpainted sandstone and adobe walls (hand plastered), wide plank floors, a palette of desert earth tones, and handmade tile baths all add to a mood that is soft and seductive.

The ninety-six-seat restaurant, winner of the AAA (American Automobile Association) Four Diamonds award, serves a lot of fresh, organically grown food purchased from local farmers. The menu is contemporary Southwestern fare: grilled corn tortilla soup with ginger pork; Anasazi flatbread with fire-roasted sweet peppers; peanut-and-coconut-grilled prawns with watermelon salsa, fresh herb-and-lime marinated rack of lamb. It's delicious.

Santa Fe has a lot going for it, and you're just steps away from it all. Right outside Anasazi's bold timbered entrance, you can stroll to the market stands of the Pueblo Indians who sell turquoise and silver jewelry and belts, and you can visit the many art galleries that feature wonderful, hand-crafted pots, baskets, and paintings. The inn can arrange for you to visit the ancient Anasazi ruins of Chaco Canyon and see some of the northern pueblos that are in the area. You can also go hiking, white-water rafting, and fishing. In the winter months, you can head to the ski slopes not too far away.

Steeped in the earthy world of the Southwest, The Inn of the Anasazi will enchant those romantics who love the culture and spirit of the West. This place is really well done.

Address/Phone: 113 Washington Avenue, Santa Fe, NM 87501; (505) 988–3030; fax: (505) 988–3277

Reservations: (800) 688–8100

Owner/Manager: Merry Stephen, general manager

Arrival/Departure: By rail: Amtrak leaves passengers at Lamy, 17 miles from Santa Fe. Shuttle service is available into town by calling (505) 982–8829. By air: Shuttle service, via Shuttlejack, to downtown Santa Fe available at Albuquerque International Airport. Mesa Airlines operates a daily schedule of flights between Albuquerque and Santa Fe Municipal Airport. Transportation can be arranged to hotel. Taxis also available.

Distance from Albuquerque International Airport: 60 miles

Distance from Santa Fe: In the center of town

Accommodations: 59 rooms: Standard rooms are fairly small; Superior rooms are larger, and Deluxe rooms, the largest, have small sitting areas. 51 rooms have king-size beds; 8 have two twins.

Best Rooms/Suites: Deluxe or superior rooms

Amenities: Hair dryer, air-conditioning, toiletries with organic bath oils, shampoo and soaps, minibar, bathrobe, TV, VCR, stereo, coffeemaker, safe, two-line phones, 100 percent cotton sheets, duvet, down pillows, stationary bike for use in room on request; room service 7 A.M. to 11 P.M.

Electricity: 110 volts

Sports and Facilities: Massage therapist; white-water rafting and horseback riding can be arranged.

Dress Code: Southwestern casual

Weddings: Can be arranged

Rates/Packages: $235–$395 per couple per night (April 1–October 31), $199–$345 (November 1–March 31). Romance packages available. $10 parking fee.

Payment/Credit Cards: Most major
Deposit: 1 night deposit; cancel 72 hours prior to arrival for full refund
Government Taxes: 10.25 percent
Service Charges: Not included

Pennsylvania

Caesars Pocono Palace

Location: Tucked in the northeastern corner of Pennsylvania, in the heart of the Pocono Mountains.
Romantic Features: Heart-shaped tubs; private, en suite swimming pools; starry ceilings, and round beds; sleigh rides; tons of activities, all included in price.

Anchored in the northeastern part of Pennsylvania, the Pocono Mountains have been wooing honeymooners since the 1940s. Then there were only a few rustic cabins, where brides made their own beds and couples washed dishes together. They came here to enjoy the fresh mountain air, the crystal-clear lakes, and the scenic, forested hills. In 1959 *Life Magazine*'s photo of a heart-shaped tub in a Pocono resort sparked a keen interest in this area for those seeking a romantic haven. And they've been coming here ever since.

Nowhere in the world are rooms designed more tenaciously to be seductive. Caesars Pocono Resorts has four different properties, including Cove Haven, the flagship of the group and the oldest and largest; Paradise Stream; Brookdale; and Pocono Palace. If you're looking for a lot of activity with big-name entertainers like Jerry Seinfeld and Dana Carvey, Cove Haven might be a good choice. But for sheer fantasy, the brand new Roman Tower Suites at the Pocono Palace are something else.

Here in your multilevel plushly carpeted suite, you have your own heart-shaped pool, sauna, exercise room, two-story champagne-glass whirlpool tub, fireplace, fantastic king-size round bed, and everything else you could possibly think of to set the mood. Tiny white lights sparkle against the dark ceiling. The decor is pure glitz—contemporary art, tall white columns, open balconies, plants, wraparound windows overlooking the mountains, and strategically placed mirrors.

You'll find a generous amount of bubble bath in your suite. Pour some of this sweet-smelling stuff into your whirlpool, climb into the "tub," and watch as the bubbles mound into a high froth. It's great fun.

Breakfast is served until 11 A.M., and couples often arrive late and linger until noon. Or they can order breakfast in bed. Hors d'oeuvres are served at 5 P.M., followed by dinner and entertainment. Every day there is a different menu, with selections such as chicken cordon bleu, shrimp scampi, and roast prime rib.

During the day, a resort news bulletin tells you about all that's going on at Pocono Palace as well as the other three Caesars resorts. Since your package gives you complimentary privileges to use the facilities at the other Caesars, you have a mind-boggling choice of things to do. Hike on the many trails and discover paths that lead to romantic, secluded spots. Take a box lunch and head for Mauch Chunk Lake or Lake Harmony for a picnic. Participate in the Ping-Pong tournament; roller-skate in the arena; go cross-country skiing, waterskiing, or join in the resort's version of the Newlywed Game. Play tennis, golf, racquetball, or catch some sun at the pool. And if you're still in high gear, nearby there is white-water rafting, horseback riding, auto racing, mountain sliding, and plenty of shopping.

Need some help in deciding what to do? No problem. The resort's social directors are always on hand to help you out. They are proficient in knowing just who needs a gentle nudge of encouragement to join in the fun—be it a mini–golf tournament or freeze-dance contest. They also know when you'd rather be left alone to do your own thing. In the evening there is dancing and entertainment into the wee hours.

Just about everything is included in your package price. Only lunch is on your own, and should you feel the need for a midday meal, you can head to the snack bar, where you can get things like hamburgers, sandwiches, soups, and salads at reasonable, fast-food prices.

Address/Phone: Route 209, Marshalls Creek, PA 18335; (717) 226–2101; fax: (717) 226–4697

Reservations: (800) 233–4141; for fly-in rates, call (800) 432–9932.

Owner/Manager: Phil Tumminello, general manager

Arrival/Departure: Transfers are included for those booking a fly-in package. New York City is 1½ hours; Philadelphia is 2 hours; Baltimore is 3¾ hours; and Washington D.C. is 5 hours.

Distance from Allentown Airport: 40 miles (45 minutes); 80 miles (1¼ hours) from Newark International Airport

Distance from Stroudsburg: 10 miles (about 15 minutes)

Accommodations: 189 multilevel rooms and suites all with king-size round beds; 20 Roman Towers (new suites) with champagne-glass whirlpool, heart-shaped pool, fireplace, steam shower, sauna, massage table, two TVs, VCR; 40 Champagne Towers suites with champagne-glass whirlpool, heart-shaped pool, fireplace, massage table, sauna; 32 Fantasy Apples with fireplace, balcony, sauna, round heated pool, heart-shaped whirlpool; 24 Garden of Eden Apples with private pool, fireplace, sauna, heart-shaped whirlpool bath; 16 Lakeside Chalets with heart-shaped whirlpool, fireplace, picture windows overlooking Echo Lake; 43 Fairway Suites with fireplace, heart-shaped whirlpool, and views of golf course; 7 Club Lodge Suites overlooking golf course with living room, whirlpool; and 7 Club Lodge Rooms by the lake

Best Rooms/Suites: Roman Tower or Champagne Tower suites

Amenities: Refrigerator, air-conditioning, round king-size bed, steam shower, mirror headboard, TV, telephone, radio, toiletries; some with heart-shaped whirlpool tub, heart-shaped pool, patio, balcony, in-room sauna and gym, massage table, AM/FM stereo system, fireplace, champagne-glass whirlpool, CD player, VCR, celestial ceiling.

Electricity: 110 volts

Payment/Credit Cards: Most major

Sports and Facilities: Tennis (indoor and outdoor), waterskiing, paddleboats, kayaks, rowboats, sailing, golf, motorboating, snowmobiling, cross-country skiing, racquetball, use of health spa and pools, roller skating, hiking, billiards, Ping-Pong, archery, ice skating, bicycling, basketball, volleyball, miniature golf, softball, and fishing

Dress Code: Casual

Weddings: Wedding Package: $325 for ceremony, champagne, photo album, cake, and choice of setting for those honeymooning at Caesars.

Rates/Packages: Per couple rates include accommodations, breakfast and dinner daily, hors d'oeuvres, late-night snacks, all sports activities—just about everything except lunches; 2 nights, $380–$700; 5-nights, $832–$1,635; 7 nights $1,112–$2,235 (other multinight packages available).

Payment/Credit Cards: Most major

Deposit: $100; cancellation must be made at least 14 days prior to arrival. A credit will be issued if cancelled at least 48 hours prior to arrival. Cancellation within less than 48 hours will result in forfeit of deposit.

Government Taxes: 6 percent

Service Charges: 15 percent

Vermont

The Equinox, Vermont

The Equinox

Location: In the center of Manchester Village, in southern Vermont's Green Mountains.

Romantic Features: Sleigh rides; late evening nightcaps in the cozy Marsh Tavern; en suite Jacuzzis and fireplaces.

The allure of Vermont's Green Mountains beckons to those who love the outdoors. From your base at The Equinox, a charming country inn resort that holds center stage in the small village of Manchester, you can hike; go horseback riding in the surrounding hills; play golf on a picturesque, par 71, 6,423-yard championship course; swim, fish, and ski.

Close to the ski areas of Bromley and Stratton Mountains, the stately Equinox has a long history of welcoming guests. It started life in 1869 as the Marsh Tavern (now one of the hotel's restaurants), and by the mid-1800s the hotel had put Manchester Village on the map as one of America's finest year-round destinations. In 1972 the resort was added to the National Register of Historic Places, and in 1991 The Equinox underwent an ambitious renovation program, including the restoration of all public areas and guest rooms as well as the golf course.

Anyone driving through the center of Manchester Village could not possibly miss it. The Equinox, which faces the village green, is simply the most impressive structure in town. It boasts an imposing, white pillared facade with a long porch set up with green rocking chairs and two wings that create an interior garden courtyard. Just across the street from the front entrance are a number of classy clothing and gift shops—fun to browse through, but bring lots of cash if you intend to buy. Also located here are a number of 200-year-old buildings, including the Congregational church and Bennington County Courthouse.

You'll find the rooms at The Equinox very comfortable. Furnished in a traditional style in muted New England colors, there are king-size beds, washed pine armoires, desks, wing chairs, rich drapes and bedspreads, and marble tiled baths.

Next door is the newest Equinox addition, the Charles Orvis Inn. Dating back to 1833, this house was originally used to accommodate guests during the winter months, when the main hotel was closed. Today it has been totally rebuilt and houses nine, one- and two-bedroom deluxe suites, each with its own working fireplace, living room, dining room, full kitchen, and super appointments. Check in here and you'll have your own private en suite Jacuzzi and the use of an intimate bar and billiard room.

If you're into golf, perhaps one of the best parts of staying here is that you can easily walk from the hotel to the first tee of one of the loveliest golf courses in New England. The Gleneagles course, originally designed by the legendary Walter Travis, has been improved and updated by the well-known golf course designer, Rees Jones. The course's ups and downs will very likely do the same to your score card. It's hilly, challenging, and breathtaking in its beauty. As you hit your ball from the tee on the eighth hole, your ball will soar into the sky against a backdrop of dense green mountains and deep blue skies. Straight ahead is the white spire of a quintessential New England church, nestled at the base of a mountain. On the fifth hole, you'll have to wait for those ahead of you to ring a bell before hitting over the blind hill. This is one course you can play again and again without getting bored—there are new challenges around every bend.

Equinox also has a great fitness spa, located at the back of the hotel's courtyard, as well as three clay tennis courts, a 75-foot heated swimming pool outdoors, and a 47-foot heated indoor pool. You can rent bikes and cycle out to the many trails in the area, and hikers will also have a good selection of wooded mountain trails to explore.

Canoeing trips on the Battenkill River can be arranged, and if you ever wanted to try your hand at fly fishing or shooting, the Orvis Fly Fishing School, the oldest of its kind in the country, and the Orvis Shooting School are located right in Manchester Village.

You can eat breakfast, lunch, and dinner at the Marsh Tavern, a darkish, cozy place that dates back to 1769. You can also enjoy cocktails on the tavern's terrace during July and August. For a more elegant dining experience, head to the grand Colonnade, which features fine continental cuisine and wines and is open for dinner June to October on Wednesday through Sunday evenings and November to May on Friday and Saturday evenings.

Some nights there is entertainment in the Marsh Tavern, and during the summer months, a number of local performing art centers offer an assortment of concerts and theater productions. Come here if you love New England and all it offers. Your accommodations at The Equinox will be supremely comfortable; your choice of activities plentiful if you love exploring the countryside and participating in traditional sports.

Think of any name-brand clothing or sporting goods company, and you'll find it in the outlet stores, which line the roads leading into town. The stores are housed in attractive New England-style buildings of weathered wood and clapboard, in harmony with the surrounding countryside. If you have some wedding money you want to spend, you can easily fill the backseat of your car with bags full of bargains from Anne Klein, Liz Claiborne, Ralph Lauren, London Fog, Armani, Dexter, and Donna Karan, to name a few.

Address/Phone: Historic Route 7A, Manchester Village, VT 05254; (802) 362–4700; fax: (802) 362–1595

Reservations: (800) 362–4747

Owner/Manager: S. Lee Bowden, vice president and general manager

Arrival/Departure: Transfers via private car can be arranged at $85 per car, one-way, plus 15 percent gratuity.

Distance from Albany Airport: 64 miles; about 1½ hours

Distance from Manchester Village: In heart of town

Accommodations: 163 rooms and suites plus 9 new suites in the Charles Orvis Inn, next door. Most rooms are oversize and offer a choice of garden, village, or mountain views.

Best Rooms/Suites: Try one of the new one-bedroom suites in the Charles Orvis Inn. Main building suites also good.

Amenities: Toiletries, air-conditioning, telephones, clock/radio, ironing facilities, cable TV, in-room movies, bathrobes, fireplaces (some),

Jacuzzis (some); concierge services; room service; valet parking

Electricity: 110 volts

Sports: Tennis (3 clay courts), swimming (indoor and outdoor pools), fishing, shooting range, golf, fitness spa with aerobics classes, gym, saunas, downhill skiing nearby at Bromley and Stratton Mountains; cross-country skiing on grounds; biking (rentals available at hotel); nearby hiking trails, horseback riding, and canoeing

Dress Code: Casual in Marsh Tavern; jackets required in The Colonnade

Weddings: Can be arranged

Rates/Packages: $140–$500 per couple per night; add $55 per person for breakfast and dinner or $75 for breakfast, lunch, and dinner; Honeymoon Package, $355 per person, includes three nights in deluxe accommodations (upgrade to suite, if available), flowers, champagne, use of Fitness Spa and mountain bikes. A Fireside Package, at $409 per person, gives you 2 nights in a one-bedroom townhouse suite with fireplace, bottle of wine, Equinox tartan throw, breakfast and dinner daily, and use of the Fitness Spa. Ski and spa packages also available.

Payment/Credit Cards: Most major

Deposit: 1-night deposit required to confirm reservation and will be applied to last night of visit. Refunds will be issued only if cancellation is received 2 weeks before your scheduled arrival date. Cancellations are subject to a $20 processing fee.

Government Taxes: 7 percent Vermont rooms and meals tax

Service Charges: $2 per room per night housekeeping gratuity

Twin Farms

Location: Just north of Woodstock, on 235 acres.

Romantic Features: Fireplaces and featherbeds; lunch in a meadow; sleigh rides.

Twin Farms, in Barnard, Vermont, could just be the finest small resort in the world—and probably one of the most expensive. But if the comments in the guest book are any indication, guests feel it is worth every penny of the 70,000 to 150,000 cents they shell out for a night's stay.

Its history is filled with romance. In 1928, the Nobel Prize–winning writer Sinclair Lewis gave this 235-acre estate to his wife, Dorothy Thompson, as a wedding present. During the time they lived there, the property was the scene of many a gala party between 1928 and the late 1940s.

Today, what was once two farms is now a place where you can go to escape from the real world, for when the electronic front gate guarding this estate lifts, you enter the ultimate in sybaritic pleasure. The stratospheric tariff covers absolutely everything at your disposal, including an open bar. You can easily feel like you are personal guests of some unseen philanthropist who has opened his private retreat to you and a few lucky others, providing you with staff, food and drink, and the run of the place. You'll find Twin Farms' young staff eager to make you feel like a real VIP.

The main farmhouse has been reconstructed and is now the guests' meeting area and dining room, with soaring spaces, a mix and match of antique and new, and a fortune in artwork. Represented in the collection are works by Roy Lichtenstein, Frank Stella, Milton Avery, and many others. It's no wonder that Twin Farms insists on a good security system.

In addition to the main house, where some of the suites are located, eight new cottages are scattered throughout the grounds. Vistas are superb in all seasons: wildflowers carpeting the valley, gnarled apple orchards, perennial gardens against old stone walls, a new miniature covered bridge over a pond, and even a waterfall.

As for the cuisine, you name it, you've got it. You can visit the award-winning chef, Neil Wigglesworth, and state your preference. Normal fare is contemporary American, one exquisite presentation at each meal, aside from special requests. A typical winter meal might be seared scallops with crisp celeriac; a port sorbet; roast squab atop a mound of potatoes puréed with black truffles, leeks, and cabbage; and a gingered pear mousse. Many of the vegetables and herbs served come directly from the inn's gardens (in season); all is accompanied by fine wines (or beer from a local microbrewery). Coffee is freshly ground Kona from Hawaii.

Meals can be served wherever you want—in the baronial dining room, which is furnished with bentwood chairs and unique antler cutlery; on your cottage porch; in a meadow; in front of a big-screen TV in the pub; or even in the wine cellar. A low-key cocktail hour on the porch precedes dinner and is hosted by the charming young managers.

The cheerful activities director can arrange and instruct in hiking, tennis, croquet, golf, and riding. The large pond is a great place to head for a refreshing dip, and you can try your skills at fly-fishing, boating, and ice skating. Mountain bikes provide a thrilling downhill ride to Woodstock, and a pickup will drive you back on the uphill run, unless you feel up to the return trip on your wheels. Five miles of trails on the property provide good paths for hikers and skiers.

In winter, a poma lift to six trails, named after Lewis's novels, may serve only one couple a day on slopes a few hundred yards away from Twin Farms. And for after ski relaxing, there is a fully equipped fitness center and a Japanese faro (soaking pool).

Spacious accommodations, whether in the main house or in the cottages, are all designed around separate, dazzling themes, such as Treehouse, which is perched on stilts and features a bark-covered armoire, or Dorothy's Room (in honor of Lewis's wife, a journalist who was known for her controversial radical views), which is done up as a Russian dacha with decidedly capitalistic appointments, such as expensive leather couches. There is also Perch Cottage, which hovers right over a stream.

All rooms are exquisitely decorated with the finest materials, art, and antiques and have fireplaces and king-size featherbeds. Huge, lavish baths have heated floors and deep copper or claw-footed tubs. Fireplaces are already supplied with wood; you need only touch a match to the kindling.

This is your chance to indulge in special fantasies, such as a picnic in the meadow, where your meal arrives in a Morris Minor car, is laid out for you on elegant china and crystal, and served with attention. Or perhaps you visualize pouring a Cognac and gazing at the valley as the sun sets or just the two of you taking off on skies for a run down a private mountain. It's all possible at Twin Farms, the place where dreams come true.

Address/Phone: Barnard, VT 05031; (802) 234-9999; fax (802) 234-9990
Reservations: (800) 894-6327
Owner/Manager: Beverley and Shaun Matthews, managing directors
Arrival/Departure: You are picked up at the local airport (Lebanon); arrangements can be made for pickup at other airports as well.
Distance from Hartford's Bradley Airport: 2½ hours; from Boston's Logan Airport, 3 hours
Distance from Boston: 3 hours; 10 miles from Woodstock
Accommodations: 13 suites and cottages
Best Rooms/Suites: One of the cottages sits in a meadow and is a fanciful interpretation of a Moroccan minipalace, with the living and bedroom ceilings plastered to look like tents.
Amenities: Fireplace, featherbeds, air-conditioning, robes, tea tray, sherry and cheese tray, minibar, telephone, toiletries, TV, fax capacity, clock/radio, CD/tape deck, VCR, hair dryer, wood for fireplace, small serving bar
Electricity: 110 volts
Sports and Facilities: Swimming in the pond, cross-country and downhill skiing, mountain biking, 2 tennis courts, golf nearby, hiking, boating, canoeing, fitness center, billiards, massages, gym, Japanese soaking pool, croquet
Dress Code: Casually smart
Weddings: Can be arranged; a wedding reception using the whole prop-

erty can accommodate up to 150 people.

Rates/Packages: From $700 per couple per night; includes breakfast, lunch, dinner, tea, beverages, sports, and whatever else you can think of.

Closed: Month of April

Payment/Credit Cards: Most major

Deposit: $100 per night; during foliage season (September/October), for refund cancel 3 months before arrival date with $50 fee; otherwise cancel 1 month before arrival. Within less than cancellation period, full refund (less $50) will be made if room is resold.

Government Taxes: 23 percent

Service Charges: 15 percent

Woodstock Inn & Resort

Location: Centrally located in Vermont near the New Hampshire border.
Romantic Features: En suite fireplaces; New England village setting.

If you are dreaming of a honeymoon in New England, with warm fires crackling, and snow falling on the mountains, or brilliant fall foliage shading a village green lined by pristine clapboard houses, or perhaps lazy summer days strolling on woodland trails, your fantasies will turn into reality when you arrive in Woodstock, Vermont. At the heart of this beautiful little town of only about 2,500 people lies the stately Woodstock Inn & Resort, a lovely inn built by Laurance S. Rockefeller in 1969 on the site of the original inn and tavern, which dated back to 1793.

It's a resort you can enjoy all by itself. The impressive facilities include a putting green located in the courtyard of the inn; the Woodstock Country Club, with its superb golf course, Sports Center, Ski Touring Center; the nearby Suicide Six ski area; and many planned activities. But just outside your door is the delightful village of Woodstock, with all its eighteenth- and nineteenth-century homes, interesting shops, covered bridges, and historic places, like the Billings Farm & Museum, an active historical museum and working dairy farm depicting what farm life was like in the nineteenth century.

Furnished in colonial style, with soft reds, greens, and blues, the rooms are bright and cheery, many opening onto a central courtyard, where the putting green is located. Many have fireplaces—just ask, and the staff will lay the logs for you. Beds are covered with hand-made quilts and hand-loomed coverlets, bookshelves are filled with hardbacks and paperbacks;

and built-in cupboards and bureaus give you plenty of storage space. You also have white louvered blinds that you can close when you wish privacy, as well as modern tile and marble baths.

The lobby area is most inviting, especially on a cold day, when the massive, 10-foot fireplace is blazing away. Exceptional original artwork in various styles ranging from primitive to contemporary is located throughout the inn along with antique fixtures, lamps, and furniture.

You can dine in the main dining room at tables elegantly appointed with fine linen and gas lamps or enjoy a more casual meal in the Eagle Cafe. Particularly appealing is Richardson's Tavern, where you can settle into a comfortable sofa in front of the fireplace and sip a Cognac before heading to your room. The cozy bar area is a popular gathering place.

Just a five-minute walk down South Street from the inn is the Wood-stock Country Club. Here you'll find the 6,001-yard, eighteen-hole, Robert Trent Jones–designed golf course. It's narrow and lined with more than eighty bunkers and has some nasty water hazards guaranteed to give wild hitters more than a few nightmares—the Kedron Brook comes into play on all but six of the eighteen holes. (You might want to leave your driver in the car.) It's also one of the most interesting little courses you'll find in New England. A real gem.

The 40,000-square-foot Woodstock Sports Center, located adjacent to the club, has two indoor tennis courts, two squash courts, two racquetball courts, a 30-by-60-foot lap pool, whirlpool, gym, massage room, croquet court, and the Courtside Restaurant. Tennis buffs can enjoy ten outside tennis courts.

In the winter the golf operations turn into the Woodstock Touring Center. Ski trails lace the golf course and beyond, and equipment for sale or rent occupy the space where in the summer, you find golf bags, balls, and accessories.

The personal, user-friendly Suicide Six ski area, which opened in 1937, has nineteen trails in addition to the Face, which is served by two chair lifts and a beginner area with a J-bar. Although the more advanced skiers may prefer to head to nearby Killington, Suicide Six is still a good choice for skiers of all levels who want a pleasant, challenging ski experience. Here you'll find a ski school, ski shop, cafeteria, and lounge-restaurant in the Base Lodge.

Other activities at your fingertips include hiking, biking, horseback riding, fishing, and cultural performances (Dartmouth College's Hopkins Center for the Performing Arts is just a half-hour's drive away). There are also complimentary evening movies at the inn, morning coffee, and afternoon tea and cookies in the Wicker Lounge, a greenhouselike lounge.

Your best bet, if you want to play golf or ski, is to look into a package that includes these activities. Otherwise you will be charged for the use of many of the sports facilities. For example, greens fees are $49 to $56 per person; tennis is $7.00 to $8.50 per person, per hour, and inn guests pay $7.00 per person for the use of the racquetball or squash courts. The use of the pool, sauna, steam room, whirlpool, exercise room, and croquet court is complimentary for Woodstock Inn guests.

The Woodstock Inn & Resort is a comfortable, friendly hotel boasting a staff that is eager to see to it you have everything you need. It has just enough spit and polish to make it a top-rated property, yet happily is not pretentious or stuffy. It's a place you'll want to come back to on your first anniversary.

Address/Phone: Fourteen the Green, Woodstock, VT 05091–1298; (802) 457–1100; fax: (802) 457–6699

Reservations: (800) 448–7900

Owner/Manager: Chet Williamson, president and general manager; Jim Promo, resident manager; Chuck Vanderstreet, sports center/country club/ski area manager

Arrival/Departure: Daily air service from New York, Hartford, and Boston is available to Lebanon, New Hampshire. Taxi and car rentals available at Lebanon Airport.

Distance from Lebanon Airport: 15 miles; 138 miles from Albany; 148 miles from Boston

Distance from Woodstock: In heart of town

Accommodations: 143 rooms and suites, 21 with fireplaces

Best Rooms/Suites: The fireplace rooms or Suites 304 and 349

Amenities: Toiletries, air-conditioning, telephones, clock/radio, ironing facilities, cable TV, VCR, bathrobes; fireplace (some); concierge services; room service; valet parking

Electricity: 110 volts

Sports and Facilities: Putting green, outdoor pool, 12 tennis courts (2 indoor, 6 clay, 4 all-weather); 18-hole golf course, practice green, pro shop, practice range; 2 squash courts, two racquetball courts; lap pool; whirlpool; 10-station Nautilus Room; Aerobics Room; steam baths, saunas; croquet court; ski trails, Alpine ski center; horseback riding; biking; hiking; fishing

Dress Code: Casual; jackets required in dining room; blue jeans, T-shirts, and swimming shorts not permitted on golf course or tennis courts

Weddings: Can be arranged

Rates/Packages: $139–$265 per couple; add $46 per person per day for MAP (breakfast and dinner); honeymoon package at $850 per couple includes three nights' accommodations, breakfast and dinner daily, two days of complimentary sports in season, champagne, and special gift. Tennis, golf, and ski packages available.

Payment/Credit Cards: Most major

Deposit: Two-night deposit required to confirm reservation and will be applied to first and last nights of visit. Refunds will be issued only if cancellation is received one week before your scheduled arrival date. Cancellations are subject to a $15 processing fee.

Government Taxes: 7 percent Vermont rooms and meals tax

Service Charges: Not included

West Virginia

The Greenbrier, West Virginia

The Greenbrier

Location: On a 6,500-acre estate in the Allegheny Mountains, in White Sulphur Springs, West Virginia.

Romantic Features: Victorian carriage ride followed by private lunch in gazebo; sleigh rides in the Allegheny foothills; fireplaces.

The Greenbrier, a venerable bastion of southern gentility and great golf, is a destination in itself—a place to come for golf, tennis, hiking in the great outdoors, and for other gracious pleasures, such as afternoon tea, carriage rides, late-night hot chocolate, croquet, and horseback riding. Mineral baths, an array of spa treatments, good food, and dancing in the cocktail lounge are all part of the scene here.

Grooms will have to pack their ties and jackets and brides will get to wear their favorite fancies. At The Greenbrier, tradition reigns, and dressy attire is required for dinner at three of the resort's six restaurants. Black tie is also acceptable.

When the rich and famous travelled here in the mid-1800s to revive themselves in the famous mineral waters and socialize with their peers, they told their friends they were going to the "Old White." The guest book of this stately grande dame includes historical greats such as Dolley Madison, Andrew Jackson, Thomas Edison, and John F. Kennedy. At least twenty-three presidents have come here to take in the fresh mountain air and southern hospitality.

The original 400-foot-long building is gone, but in its place a majestic Georgian-style structure with pillars and rows of windows sits like a great European castle in the midst of a sea of green pine. Most impressive.

This is not exactly a place you'd describe as intimate or cozy. Any resort that claims to sit on 6,500 acres is major stuff. However, accommodations such as the cottages and suites give you all the privacy you want along with a generous dash of luxury.

The public and private rooms are truly grand. The designer Carleton Varney orchestrates all the interior decoration, including the creation of new fabric and wallpaper designs every year. Each of the hotel's 672 rooms and suites has its own unique decor. Yards and yards of brightly flowered fabric, richly swagged and draped around the high windows; bed canopies, pillows; upholstered chairs and chaises; and bedspreads create surprising riots of fresh color against walls and carpets of reds, emerald greens, and yellows. No faint-hearted application of color here! Furnishings are a combination of traditional period antiques and antique reproductions, along with gilt-framed mirrors, paintings, and oriental carpets.

In the lofty lounge, in spite of the dramatic black-and-white marble floor and high columns, chairs and tables have been arranged in intimate, inviting groupings conducive to a quiet chat, a game of backgammon, or enjoying afternoon tea to the accompaniment of chamber music.

If you want to hide away in your own cottage, ask for accommodations in one of the guest houses, which are located on the property. The cottages are airy and roomy, and each has its own porch, fireplace, oversize tub, wet bar or kitchen, separate parlor, and dressing room.

With the staff of 1,600 outnumbering the guests, you can be totally decadent and do nothing but allow yourself to be pampered. If your journey here has been a long one, perhaps the first place you should visit is the Spa. In addition to a Greek-inspired Olympic-size pool ringed with pillars and patterned tile work, you'll find whirlpool baths, saunas, herbal wraps, and massages—over eighteen different treatments.

For the more energetic there are aerobics classes, exercise equipment, and other instruments designed for hard labor. There are guided hiking excursions along the miles of mapped and unmapped trails on The Greenbrier grounds and on nearby Kate's Mountain and plenty of tennis courts, indoors and outdoors, along with three great golf courses. Winding through the rolling countryside at the base of the starkly beautiful Allegheny Mountains, these courses give golfers a visual gift as well as a challenge. Newer golfers may prefer the picturesque, gentle-on-your-score Lakeside course. The more competent links mavens can tee off on the championship Nicklaus layout or the Old White, a traditional favorite.

Golf packages are one of the better deals here, giving you unlimited golf, use of a practice range, a professional clinic, and daily club cleaning and storage as well as breakfast and dinner. It is quite a bargain, as the cost to a nonguest for just playing the course is over $100 with cart.

For a special romantic day, Greenbrier's Romantic Rendezvous takes you on a Victorian carriage ride on the grounds and ends at their gazebo, where a waiter is there to serve you lunch. The cost for this treat is $175 per couple.

When it comes time to eat, you have a lot of choices. The main dining room, the largest of the eateries, is an elegant affair with chandeliers, pillars, and ornate plasterwork. Meals, featuring Continental and American cuisine, are served with a flourish. The presentation is a work of art. Be sure to save room for the chocolate truffles.

The Drapers Cafe is fun, colorful, and informal. Here you can get breakfast, lunch, and dessert and good things from the soda fountain. For a cozy, intimate meal, try the Tavern Room, which specializes in American food, seafood, and rotisserie selections. (Although rates include breakfast and dinner, you'll pay a surcharge to eat here.)

If you are coming from the golf course, you can stop at the Golf Club and Ryder Cup Grille for lunch or dinner, one of the few places men can leave their ties in their room when they dine. Try the pasta dishes, veal chops, or seafood specialties, and don't miss Sunday brunch, when a jazz band entertains.

There is also the Old White Club for cocktails and dancing and the Rhododendron Cocktail Lounge. In other words, there are plenty of places to eat, suitable for whatever mood you're in.

Much of the vegetables and fruits come from the local markets, and there are local specialties such as fresh trout. The Tavern serves its own ice cream, made daily. Especially popular at breakfast are the warm, homemade muffins and buckwheat cakes. And if you're into watching what you eat, The Greenbrier has introduced its Greenbrier Light Cuisine, with one third the calories and low fat.

You won't have to go very far if you want to shop. There is a major shopping arcade right in the main building, with stores like Orvis and The Sam Snead Memorabilia Shop. There is also another group of craft shops on the grounds, selling some really good handicraft items.

Address/Phone: White Sulphur Springs, WV 24986; (304) 536–1110; fax: (304) 536–7834

Reservations: (800) 624–6070

Owner/Manager: Ted Kleisner, president and managing director; Gil Patrick, general manager

Arrival/Departure: Amtrak offers train service to The Greenbrier from New York and Chicago, with intermediate stops in Philadelphia, Wilmington, Baltimore, Washington D.C., Indianapolis, and Cincinnati

Distance from Greenbrier Valley Airport, in Lewisburg: 6 miles (15 minutes)

Distance from Washington D.C.: 250 miles southwest

Accommodations: 566 rooms, 33 suites, 73 guest houses

Best Rooms/Suites: Guest houses (Paradise Row or Spring Row) or Garden Suites

Amenities: Air-conditioning, hair dryer, clock/radio, minibar, toiletries, bathrobes, wet bars or kitchens in some suites, TV, fireplaces in guest houses; nightly turndown service, 24-hour room service

Electricity: 110 volts

Sports and Facilities: 3 golf courses; 22 tennis courts (5 indoor Dynaturf, 15 Har-Tru, and 2 heated platform courts); indoor and outdoor swimming pools; mountain biking; falconry academy; horseback riding; carriage rides; croquet; shooting preserve; white-water rafting trips; hiking, jogging, and parcourse fitness trails; fishing; bowling; sleigh rides; ice skating and cross-country skiing. There is also a 29,000-square-foot spa with all sorts of mineral baths, massage, and exercise facilities.

Dress Code: Casual by day; jacket and tie for dinner, except in golf club restaurant

Weddings: Can be arranged

Rates/Packages: $138–$248 per person, including breakfast and dinner. Honeymoon packages are $478 per couple per night, including breakfast, dinner, champagne and a photo. However, if you're into golf or tennis, you'd do better to take the golf or tennis packages, which are priced from $484 and $462, respectively and give you breakfast, dinner, unlimited golf or plenty of tennis plus a clinic and some balls.

Payment/Credit Cards: Most major

Deposit: $175–$400, depending on time of reservations. Late arrival or early departure causes forfeiture of deposit unless cancellation or changes are made 7 to 15 days in advance, depending on reservation dates.

Government Taxes: 6 percent

Service Charges: $17 per person, per day

Canada

Quebec

La Pinsonnière, Quebec

La Pinsonnière

Location: On the banks of the St. Lawrence River, in the picturesque Charlevoix region north of Quebec City.
Romantic Features: Private fireplaces; terraces above the river; whirlpool baths for two.

This small inn, which lies between the Laurentian Mountains and the tidal flats of the St. Lawrence River, is a real find for those honeymooning in Canada. La Pinsonnière, which means "house of the finches," sits about 200 feet up a bluff overlooking the river, which at this point, is wider than one of the Finger Lakes is long. This sprawling white manor house, with its pointed towers and garden setting ringed by tall trees, would seem equally at home on the Loire River in France's château country.

The personal involvement of owners Jean and Janine Authier, who purchased the mansion eighteen years ago and converted it into an inn, is just one reason this property is so special. The Authiers, along with their daughter, Valérie, who serves as La Pinsonnière's innkeeper, are committed to providing their guests with an exceptional place to stay and dine. Their restaurant, with its French-trained chef, has already received a number of awards and has gained a reputation for serving some of the finest cuisine in Canada.

In addition to the hotel business, the Authiers have an avid interest in the arts. Contemporary paintings by Quebec artists, many for sale, hang in the dining room and in other places throughout the inn.

Each of the rooms has a personality all its own. For example, one has a king-size brass bed, fireplace, private sauna, and large whirlpool tub. Another is a vision of romantic Victoriana, with white wicker and rattan furniture, a white marble bath, lace duvet cover, and puffy white cushions.

Some rooms are decorated in muted traditional colors and feature Queen Anne–style furniture, brass lamps, and wing chairs; others are light and airy, decorated in soft sea colors with rattan and pine furniture and patio doors leading to terraces overlooking the river.

Large marble baths with designer soaps, fluffy down duvets, classical music, and chairs you can really sink into and fall asleep in, add up to accommodations that are comfortable but not obtrusive.

La Pinsonnière is located in the Charlevoix region, an area known for its rugged cliffs, rolling hills, coves, and exceptional river views. A late afternoon pleasure for the inn's guests is to sit on the terrace of the hotel's lovely large patio and watch the sun set over the tops of the tall cedar, spruce, and birch trees. You can also follow the path that leads down through a cedar forest to the inn's private, rugged beach, a great place for a picnic. Going down the 226 steps is easy. Going up you'll find rustic benches where you can stop and rest or just sit for a while.

The inn may be small, but it still offers a lot of choices for active couples. There is a tennis court, indoor pool, and a massage therapist who can pamper you with a variety of soothing treatments.

In the warmer months, you can hike on the trails in the surrounding hills, tour the gardens of Aux Quatre Vents, take a whale-watching cruise, and play golf at nearby Murray Bay. Cruise up the Saguenay Fjord, the world's southernmost fjord, and marvel at the spectacular scenery of sheer rocky cliffs plunging dramatically down to the river. Or visit the artists' town of Baie Saint Paul, a pleasant drive from the inn, where you can browse through about twenty galleries featuring Charlevoix and Quebec painters. There are also many summer theater productions and concerts held nearby.

If you come in the winter, you can cross-country and downhill ski at Mont Grand Fonds, go snowmobiling and ice skating, and at the end of the day curl up in front of a crackling fire in your room or in the lounge. Want an adventure? Climb into a red isothermic suit and head off by boat for the world of the belugas and blue whales that inhabit the Saguenay Marine Arctic Park.

Vistas from La Pinsonnière's restaurant as well as from most of the rooms, are expansive. Large windows afford marvelous views of the rivers, hills, and trees. Dining by candlelight at a beautifully appointed table is a special pleasure. Cuisine centered on continental fare with an emphasis on French cooking includes dishes such as rabbit mousse, rack of lamb encrusted with almonds, fresh salmon prepared a number of ways, and wild mushrooms served in a delicate sauce. The Authiers' 10,000 bottle wine cellar is impressive and you are invited to participate in frequent wine tastings.

An exquisite romantic hideaway, the inn is a member of the prestigious Relais & Chateaux group.

Address/Phone: Cap-à-l'Aigle, Charlevoix, Quebec G0T IB0 Canada; (418) 665–4431; fax: (418) 665–7156
Reservations: (800) 387–4431; fax: (800) 665–7154; Relais & Chateaux, (800) RELAIS 8
Owner/Manager: Jean and Janine Authier, owners; Jean Authier and Valérie Andrée Authier, innkeepers
Arrival/Departure: There is a very small airport, St.-Irenée, about 3 miles from the inn; free pickup can be arranged.
Distance from Quebec International Airport: 95 miles
Distance from Quebec City: 90 miles
Accommodations: 27 rooms, including 1 suite
Best Rooms/Suites: Room 315, which has king-size brass bed, whirlpool bath for two, fireplace, and patio; Room 211, a creamy white confection with king-size bed, white lace duvet cover, double whirlpool, fireplace, marble bath, and deck.
Amenities: Hair dryer, toiletries, fireplace (some rooms), TV, telephones, robes, balconies (some rooms)
Electricity: 110 volts
Sports and Facilities: Indoor pool, hiking, beach, kayaking, skiing, skating, sauna, whale watching, massage therapy
Dress Code: Smart casual; no jackets required for dinner
Weddings: Can be arranged
Rates/Packages: $200–$330 (Canadian dollars) per couple, per night including breakfast, dinner, and service (low season); $220–$350 (high season—warmer months and holidays); honeymoon package:

$1,090–$1,740 (low season, three nights); $1,190–$,1840 (high season, five nights); ski packages also available

Payment/Credit Cards: Most major

Deposit: 50 percent of total cost of stay required; balance due on arrival. Refundable if cancelled 15 days or more prior to date of arrival.

Government Taxes: 7 percent federal; 6.5 percent provincial; those staying two nights or more only pay federal taxes.

Service Charges: Included

Entry Requirements for U.S. Citizens: Proof of citizenship

Closed: November–mid-December

The Caribbean
and Bermuda

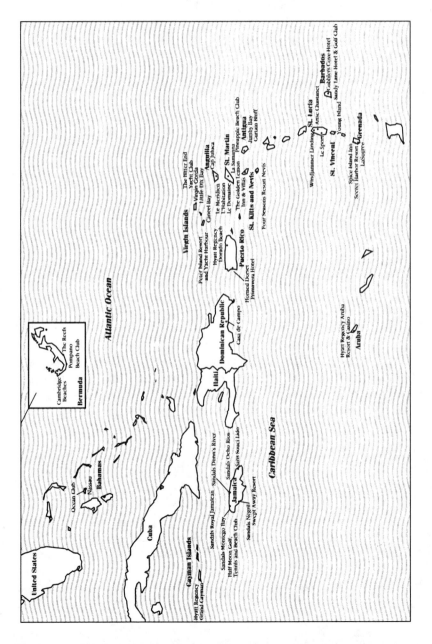

Anguilla

Cap Juluca

Location: On the western end of Maunday's Bay, on the southern coast of Anguilla, the northernmost island of the Caribbean's Lesser Antilles.
Romantic Features: Sugar-white crescent beach; palatial bathrooms, some with private solarium; intimate "garden rooms" for sunning and relaxing near pool.

Cap Juluca's dazzling white towers, turrets, and arches, set against the dense greens of the foliage and clear turquoise of the Caribbean waters, create a fairytale village straight out of the pages of *Arabian Nights*. Nothing but brightly hued blossoms of bougainvillea and waving palm fronds comes between you and your view of the sea from your terrace. Set on 170 acres, all of the resort's rooms and villas are just steps away from the white, sugary, sand crescent beach; no building is higher than the palm trees.

The exteriors of the buildings, with their parapets and domes, are dramatic enough, but wait until you get inside. Rooms are really large—at least 16 feet by 16 feet—and one-bedroom suites go up to 2,200 square feet. Villas, with up to five bedrooms, have private pools set in an enclosed, red-tiled garden courtyard. You can rent bedrooms and suites in the villas and share the pool with other guests or you can rent the entire villa yourself for complete privacy. Bathrooms are outrageously opulent, with tons of marble, double sinks, showers, and bidets. Some have double-size bathtubs with leather headrests; some open onto a private, walled solarium furnished with chaises and a table. Louvered windows let the sea breezes slip through, yet preserve your privacy. You can lie back and catch the sun wearing as little as you want or nothing at all.

Rattan furniture with thick cushions, king-size beds, fine linens, potted palms in clay pots, dark Brazilian walnut doors and trim, white walls, and ceramic tile floors in various muted colors provide a sumptuous setting for romance. Unique accessories, such as wooden bowls and sculpture, leather and clay as well as beautiful area rugs, inlaid mirrors and artwork, many imported from northern Africa, are found in some rooms; others lean toward a more European feeling, with traditional period furnishings and accessories.

There are three tennis courts, and the pro schedules round-robin tournaments every week. There is also a fitness center with state-of-the-art equipment and a croquet court set up British style. Complimentary water sports include waterskiing, sailing, and windsurfing. You can also go scuba diving (this is extra), or if you want to set off on your own "True Love" cruise, you can charter a yacht. You can also get a soothing massage.

No one will intrude on your privacy, even while you're on the beach, unless, of course, you plant a red flag in the sand. This means you want someone to come over and see what you want, whether it be a clean towel or another Sea Breeze. Intimate "garden rooms," partitioned with hedges, are located around the pool. If you want service, just ring a bell.

Cap Juluca's beaches are long and very walkable. The main beach stretches along Maunday's Bay for about a mile. Go around the eastern end of the headland, and there is another 2-mile beach running along Cove Bay. In the center of Maunday's Bay beach is an Olympic-size pool, which is surrounded by white market-style umbrellas and tables along with many lounge chairs—a popular gathering place.

Many guests, especially those who have terraces with great sea views, prefer to have breakfast brought to their room. Fresh fruits and juices, muffins and banana bread and steaming coffee or tea are beautifully set up on your patio table complete with linen and china. You also get a summary of the latest news from the *New York Times* faxed that morning from the States (just in case you've missed it).

One night you may wish to order a West Indian dinner served on your patio. Linger over a bottle of wine from the resort's extensive wine cellar, and see if you can spot the lights of St. Martin or tiny Saba twinkling across the water.

Cap Juluca has three restaurants: the casually elegant Pimms (named after the popular British brew) and the more informal Chattertons. Both restaurants are tucked into the corner of the protected eastern end of the cove and sit just 6 feet from the water's edge. There is also the striking, tented Beach Pavilion and pool terrace located in the middle of the beach, where you can get breakfast, light lunches, and drinks.

Pimms is known as one of the best restaurants on the island and is the place to come for fresh Caribbean and Mediterranean–inspired dishes such as Chinois fish with soy sauce, ginger, and green onions. Pimms invites chefs from other resorts to come and cook their specialties.

A special pleasure is to sit at your candlelit table, while you watch the sun set, its rich, radiant golds and reds framed by the arches and columns of the terraced restaurant.

After dinner, kick off your shoes and walk hand in hand back to your room along the moonlit beach and be lulled to sleep by the sound of waves rolling up on the shores. Or linger at your table at Chattertons for some dancing under the stars.

When you come to Anguilla, don't expect a roaring nightlife. After all, an island where the 30-mile-an-hour speed limit is reinforced by a series of speed bumps and the airport only allows prop jets to land is not a swinging place. Come here if you like to picnic on an uninhabited island or drift away in a hammock in a garden perfumed with the scents of frangipani, jasmine, and orchids.

Address/Phone: P.O. Box 240, Maunday's Bay, Anguilla, Leeward Islands, British West Indies; (809) 497–6666; fax: (809) 497–6617

U.S. Reservations: (800) 323–0139; (212) 425–4684; fax: (212) 363–8044

Owner/Manager: Leeward Isles Resorts, Ltd., owner; Brian Young, general manager

Arrival/Departure: Anguilla is reached via scheduled air service from San Juan (50 minutes) or St. Martin (5 minutes) or via ferry from Marigot in French St. Martin (25 minutes). Guests are met on arrival.

Distance from Wallblake Airport: 5 miles (15 minutes)

Distance from Marigot, St. Martin: 6 miles (25 minutes by ferry); 5 miles from the Valley

Accommodations: 71 units: 58 luxury rooms, 7 one-bedroom suites, 6 pool villas

Best Rooms/Suites: For privacy, try the end units: Pool Villa 19 and a room or suite in Villa Building 12

Amenities: Air-conditioning; ceiling fans; private, walled terraces; toiletries; refrigerator with ice maker, stocked minibar; hair dryer; oversize tub (some); solarium (some); bathrobes; kitchen in villas; twice-daily maid service

Electricity: 110/220 volts

Sports and Facilities: 3 Omni surface tennis courts (2 lighted), croquet; windsurfing, waterskiing, snorkeling, scuba diving; Hobie cats, Sunfishes; Olympic-size pool; 6 villa pools; 3 miles of beach. Extra charge for use of 32-foot motor cruiser; massages

Dress Code: Casually elegant and sophisticated; no jacket or tie required

Weddings: Can be arranged

Rates/Packages: $255–$390 per couple per night for rooms and junior suites (summer); $320–$475 (fall); $435–$700 (winter); $345–$515 (spring); 1-bedroom suites: $490–$1,125. Multibedroom villas with private pools also available. Meal plans available at $85 per person per day for three meals or $65 for breakfast plus lunch or dinner. Romantic Rendezvous package, $2,975–$4,775, includes 7 nights in beachfront accommodations, welcome bottle of champagne, 4 dinners, daily breakfast, sunset champagne cruise, snorkeling trip, 1-day car rental, complimentary tennis and water sports, and taxi transfers from Anguilla's Wallblake Airport. Four-night package and Aqua Adventures packages also available.

Payment/Credit Cards: Most major

Deposit: 3-night deposit within 14 days. Refunds made only when written notice is received by the hotel no later than 21 days prior to scheduled arrival. Other conditions may apply during peak periods.

Government Taxes: 8 percent (except for package where tax is included)

Service Charges: 10 percent (except for package where service charge is included)

Entry Requirements for U.S. citizens: Return ticket and proof of citizenship required; passport best

Antigua

Curtain Bluff

Location: Situated on Antigua's south shore, on a private peninsula jutting out into the water between two lovely beaches, one on the Atlantic, the other on the Caribbean.

Romantic Features: Terraces overlooking sea; dancing under the stars; hammocks for two on your own private patio; private dinner in the garden gazebo.

If there is a pot of gold at the end of one of Antigua's most winding, bumpy roads, it has to be Curtain Bluff. It's worth every torturous mile it takes to get you to this superb little resort, which seduces you from the moment you arrive. Consistently rated as one of the best resorts in the Caribbean for more than thirty years, Curtain Bluff rises from a narrow peninsula between two beaches, marking the place where the Caribbean and Atlantic meet, and giving you nonstop ocean views from every room. Bougainvillea, hibiscus, oleander, royal palms, and every other tropical flower you can think of line walkways, hug buildings, and fall in great clouds of blossoms from trellises and walls. And wherever you go, you never lose sight of the sea.

Some of the two-story buildings are spread out along the beach—just take a couple of steps from your patio and you can sink your toes into the sand. The villa suites climb gently up the slope of the peninsula. At the top of the bluff sits the home of the owner, Howard Hulford. It's the crown to Curtain Bluff's string of pink and white buildings and the site of many weddings as well as cocktail receptions honoring Curtain Bluff's guests.

There was nothing much on the land when Howard Hulford bought the property, but he brought seeds and cuttings from plants he liked from everywhere, started his own nursery, and soon the grounds were flourishing with palms, flowering shrubs, and other tropical plants. Today Hulford says he enjoys spending at least an hour a day tending to his fledging seedlings and newly grafted shrubs. This attention to detail by a man who once flew planes for a living is just part of the story, and helps explain the beauty and seductive influence Hulford and his beautiful wife, Chelle, have created at Curtain Bluff.

All the rooms and suites are decorated with impeccably good taste by Chelle in soft pastels and natural textures—clay pots, baskets filled with flowers, red tile, and an abundance of plants and real art. Rooms are airy and large with spacious patios, rattan furniture, puffy pillows, and natural fiber rugs on the Italian tile floors. Large sliding doors, which glide like butter, open onto a spacious well-furnished seaside patio. Ceiling fans (even in the bathrooms) along with louvered side windows let the sea breezes slip in and keep the rooms fresh and pleasantly cool. There is no air-conditioning, nor is it needed.

White walls and high, vaulted cedar ceilings distinguish the multilevel suites. In addition to the seaside patio, there is another, flower-filled, open-air patio on the inland side of your suite with walls just high enough to give you total privacy while letting the breezes in. A roomy hammock big enough for two is slung across a corner. A dining area, bedroom, bath, and another patio are located on the top level.

All of the bathrooms are large and luxurious, with lots of tile and marble. They boast twin vanities; endless shelf space; a bidet; a walk-in, no-curtain shower; large shower/tub; and mirrors ringed with small light bulbs. You also enjoy lots of hot water for those long showers and plenty of electricity.

Each year, the Curtain Bluff closes down for a couple of months in order to refurbish and refresh. Perhaps this is one reason nothing here ever looks tired or worn.

Dining is on an open terrace, where a band plays every evening. Dance under a spreading tamarind tree and a canopy of stars. Chef Ruedi Portmann, a classic Swiss chef who has been at Curtain Bluff since the mid-sixties and was named Caribbean Chef of the Year in 1991, is adept at preparing delicious American and European cuisine. Ingredients are the freshest you can find in the Caribbean: Fish is delivered every day and is filleted right on the property.

Curtain Bluff has an impressive 25,000-bottle wine cellar. Dust off a bottle of 1983 Louis Roederer Cristal and toast your bride or try a bottle of '83 Dom Perignon or an '81 Taittinger Brut Reserve.

On Wednesdays, you can warm up to reggae at the beach party, which is held at the beach bar and restaurant. You can also have lunch at the beachfront restaurant, where a lavish buffet tempts you with salads, fish, pasta, and meat dishes.

If you want to eat in the privacy of your room or on your patio, where you can watch the sun go down, just order room service. It's all included in the price.

Straddling the peninsula, the two beaches offer something for everyone. The waters off the ¾-mile beach on the Caribbean side are calm, gentle, and great for swimming. On the other side, the Atlantic stirs up more surf and the winds beckon to sailors and those looking for a little more excitement. You can windsurf, snorkel, sail, or just laze away the hours on the beach.

Tennis is big here. With four superbly maintained Laykold courts and a pro who once headed the Davis Cup team, lessons, clinics, round-robins, tournaments, or just friendly play keep the action rolling. There's a good-sized stadium for spectators to watch their favorite players as well as a squash court and a croquet field.

The fitness center is well equipped with Trotter treadmills, steppers, and the latest in health and fitness equipment. Aerobics classes are held each morning on an adjacent deck.

There are no TVs in the rooms, but there is Television House, perched high on stilts near the tennis courts and fitness center. Guests gather here to watch events like the Super Bowl and the Kentucky Derby.

The ages and interests of guests range from the older, well-heeled traditionalists to active, younger couples. You'll see a lot of Brits here, especially during January and February. If the idea of coat and tie is off-putting, come in the fall and spring, when this requirement is dropped. However, there's no doubt that the guests here like the idea of "dressing up" for dinner and appreciate the traditions that have evolved over the years since 1961, when Curtain Bluff first opened its doors.

At first glance, Curtain Bluff may seem a bit pricey at $3,500 to $4,000 for a week's honeymoon (in the deluxe rooms). But everything is included, even the scuba diving and the deep-sea fishing. Curtain Bluff is for those who love a beautiful, warm place by the sea where they can get away and totally unwind while a superb, dedicated group of people see to it that nothing interferes with this vision of what paradise should be.

Owner/Managers: Howard W. Hulford, owner and chairman, board of directors; Robert S. Sherman, managing director; Calvert A. Roberts, general manager

Address/Phone: P.O. Box 288, St. John's, Antigua, West Indies; (809) 462-8400; fax: (809) 462-8409

U.S. Reservations: (800) 67–BLUFF, (800) 672–5833 or (212) 289–8888 (brochures)

Arrival/Departure: Taxi to and from airport. Local regulations prevent hotel from sending drivers.

Distance from V.C. Bird International Airport in St. John's: 15 miles (35 minutes)

Distance from St. John's: 9 miles

Accommodations: 63 rooms and suites, all with terraces and all overlooking the sea: 51 deluxe with king-size bed or 2 double beds; the Terrace Room with four-poster king-size bed (popular with honeymooners); 5 two-bedroom suites with king-size bed and 2 double beds, and a one-bedroom suite.

Best Rooms/Suites: The Terrace Room, with its huge terrace, and the one-bedroom suites

Amenities: Hair dryer, wall safe, ceiling fans, bathrobes, telephones (3 to 4 per unit), fresh flowers daily, real hangers, suites have minibars, full room service at no extra charge

Electricity: 110 volts

Sports and Facilities: 4 tennis courts, squash court, putting green, fitness center; waterskiing, windsurfing, scuba diving, snorkeling, sailing, croquet, deep-sea fishing, swimming, hiking, aerobics

Dress Code: Casual during the day; jacket and tie required for men every evening except Wednesday and Sunday during high season (winter). No jacket or tie required during the rest of the year

Weddings: Can be arranged. Good locations are the garden gazebo and the terrace of the owner's house.

Rates/Packages: All-inclusive rates include accommodations, three meals daily, all bar drinks, afternoon tea, hors d'oeuvres, tennis, weekly beach party, entertainment, mail service, and water sports including scuba diving. $595–$1,550 per couple per night (mid-December to mid-April); $495–$1,350 per couple per night (mid-October to mid-December and mid-April to mid-May).

Payment/Credit Cards: American Express, personal check, traveler's check

Deposit: 3-night deposit; cancellation 30 days in advance for full refund, except for December 16 to January 1, when cancellation must be received before November 1.

Government Taxes: 7 percent

Service Charges: 10 percent

Entry Requirements for U.S. Citizens: Return ticket and proof of identity; passport best.

Closed: June 1 to October 14

Jumby Bay, Antigua

Jumby Bay

Location: A private island 2 miles north of Antigua.
Romantic Features: Idyllic private island; some villas have private pools; secluded beaches reached by bicycle; hammocks for two; picnics on the beach; garden showers; Jacuzzi tubs; his and her monogrammed bathrobes sent to newlyweds' home on their return.

From the lookout tower on Jumby Bay, you get a great view of the white sandy beaches that ring the 300-acre island. Look southeast and you'll notice the red tiled roofs of the harbor villas; east you'll see a handful of beautiful multimillion dollar estates (Robin Leach is rumored to have built a home here, but no one's telling if and where); glance in a southerly direction, and you'll find the tennis courts, the original sugar mill, the old Estate House, beach pavilion, dock and sports area—the heart of this tranquil resort. And tieing it all together are sandy colored, interlocking brick-paved "roads" reserved for bikes, walkers, and golf carts. The only real vehicle you'll find is a shuttle, which runs back and forth to pick up people for dinner and transport those who don't want to use the bikes. (From the time you arrive, your mode of transportation is a sturdy white bike with a good-sized wire basket.)

From your vantage point, you'll have a hard time of it trying to pick out any moving objects—like people. At Jumby Bay privacy is fiercely protected, and very little is allowed to penetrate the serenity and romance, which are at the heart of this very posh place. Even the lights illuminating the brick paths are unobtrusive, natural-looking objects that look more like pieces of garden sculpture.

Telephones also have their place. No one from the outside world will intrude on your privacy while you're in your room. Telephones are located elsewhere, in cozy booths and mini–telephone lounges placed strategically throughout the property. If you have a call coming in, they'll find you and direct you to the nearest phone.

Mediterranean-style, two-story white buildings with red roofs are arranged in clusters along the beach and around pools. The two-suite villas are set alongside Pond Bay House, an old Spanish-style house overlooking a long beach; other villas are located along paths leading from the main beach to the Estate House, where you'll find the restaurant and library. Junior suites are located in Pond Bay House, and there are a handful of luxurious private houses that are available for rent.

Brilliant flowers, looking like ads for Miracle-Gro, are everywhere. Huge ceramic and clay pots filled with flowering plants, orchids, and palms sit in romantic courtyards. Inside, the ceilings are high, with fans slowly moving the air gently around the room. Walls are decorated with original artwork, and tile murals and fresh cut flower arrangements sit on counters and in the bathrooms. Baskets in all shapes and sizes are artfully arranged. French doors frame the gardens just outside while louvered doors, made of Brazilian walnut, let in the breezes.

Some of the bedrooms have bamboo four-poster king-size beds adorned with filmy white net-covered canopies. Furniture and pillows are covered in designer fabrics in muted tones of blues, corals, greens, and yellows, echoing the colors of the flowers in the courtyards and patios. Skylights help make the rooms bright and sunny.

Bathrooms are worth a photo session. In the villas, one entire wall is devoted to the shower. It has no sides—just a beautifully decorated wall of colored ceramic tile. You stand somewhere under the shower head, which comes out of the tiled wall, and whatever water doesn't hit the large tiled basin you're standing on splashes into the lushly planted gardens located on either side. Look up and you can see the stars through the skylight. Other rooms also have unique showers with louvered doors opening onto private garden areas.

At Jumby Bay, no one locks doors. There's no need to, there are safes for those who might have an anxiety attack about leaving their valuables lying about.

Dinner is served in the Estate House. Dating back to the 1700s, this

lovely old building was once an English sugar plantation house. Its courtyard, with its tiles, flowers, arches, and columns, resembles an Italian
palazzo. Upstairs there is a comfortable bar and a library, where guests can
borrow books, games, and puzzles. A balcony overlooks the croquet field
set up for play in the British manner.

Jumby Bay has its own nursery, where fresh flowers and plants sit
under a shade canopy. This is also the area where Jumby Bay grows the
vegetables and herbs used in the preparation of some of the excellent
dishes served in the restaurants. A balanced choice of American and European dishes are featured on the menu, which changes daily. The wine cellar is also first-rate. As night falls on the island, the candles are lit at the
tables on the Estate House terrace, which overlooks the gardens and the
sea beyond. A band provides soft music for listening and dancing.

Breakfast can be delivered to your room, or you can head to the beach
pavilion near the main beach and the boat dock. You can also enjoy lunch
and afternoon tea at the pavilion on the open-air terrace, which woos you
with flowers, waving palms, and sea views. At dusk you can see the lights
of Antigua sparkling in the distance on the mainland.

During the day, there are plenty of things to do. Pack a picnic and head
to Pasture Beach, a smaller and more private beach than the main one. Explore the island on your bike or on foot; plant yourself under a thatched
umbrella with a cool drink; hang out in the hammock with a good book;
play tennis; go waterskiing or windsurfing; or try out one of the sea kayaks.

Jumby Bay appeals to those who want to honeymoon on an idyllic
tropical island and don't mind paying the price for this low-key elegance.

Address/Phone: P.O. Box 243, St. John's, Antigua, West Indies; (809)
462–6000; fax: (809) 462–6020

U.S. Reservations: (800) 421–9016; Relais & Châteaux, (800) RELAIS 8

Owner/Manager: William Andersen, general manager

Arrival/Departure: Met by Jumby Bay representative at airport and taken
to private pier for 6-minute boat ride to island

Distance from V.C. Bird International Airport (in St. John's): 2 miles
(5 minutes)

Distance from St. John's: 5 miles

Accommodations: 38 deluxe rooms

Best Rooms/Suites: Luxury villas by beach (numbers 32 to 36) with king-
size beds and garden shower. Also house rentals; Blue Pelican has its
own pool and is near Pasture Beach.

Amenities: Hair dryer, wall safe, ceiling fans, bathrobes, fresh flowers
daily, 24-hour security; villas have spacious, full kitchens; there is no
charge for room service.

Electricity: 110 volts

Sports and Facilities: 4½ miles hiking trails; biking trails; 3 tennis courts, 2 floodlit; several pools (private and shared); Sunfish, floats, waterskiing, sea-cycling, windsurfing, snorkeling; the yacht, *Moonshine,* is available for half- and full-day charters at $350 and $500 per couple with a captain.

Dress Code: Casual during the day; casual cocktail attire evenings; no jacket or ties for men required

Weddings: Can be arranged. Good locations are the old sugar mill, which is on a crest in the center of the island, and the Great House, which overlooks the water and Pasture Bay Beach. A tower that overlooks the entire island is also worth considering.

Rates/Packages: Rates include accommodations, three meals daily, all bar drinks, welcome champagne, departure bottle of rum, airport taxi service and boat transportation to and from island, hors d'oeuvres, tennis, croquet, weekly beach party, weekly sunset cruise, use of bicycles, entertainment, mail service, watersports. Villas $1,445–$1,775 per couple per night; luxury villas $1,195–$1,525; guest cottages $945–$1,275; resort rooms $645–$975; Honeymoon packages (per couple): 5 days/4 nights $2,580–$3,900; 8 days/7 nights $4,515–$6,825

Payment/Credit Cards: Most major

Deposit: 3-night deposit; cancellation 30 to 45 days in advance, depending on time of year.

Government Taxes: 7 percent

Service Charges: 10 percent (no tipping)

Entry Requirements for U.S. Citizens: Return ticket and proof of identity; passport best

Pineapple Beach Club

Location: Set on Long Bay, on the northeast coast of the island.

Romantic Features: All-inclusive, secluded beachfront resort; cottages only steps from sand; hillside gazebo overlooking sea; dancing under the stars every night.

Pineapple Beach is a small, very casual resort located right on a lovely piece of beach. Less elegant and less pretentious than some of its more upscale cousins on the island, Pineapple Beach is a good choice for those seeking a reasonably priced honeymoon. Its all-inclusive program means that you get a lot for your money, such as water sports instruction and brand-name bar drinks. Pineapple is a place where you can stroll along the beach under the starry skies while the music of the live band drifts over the moonlit sea. You can also wake up early, wander down to the coffee bar, and take a cup of hot brew and pastries to a chair on the beach to watch the sun come up.

The resort has a great white sand beach, one of the best on Antigua (an island known to have a beach for every day of the year). Sheltered by two sets of reefs, the water is perfect for water sports and swimming.

One of the reasons the resort works so well is due in large part to its tenacious owner, Rob Barrett, who virtually patrols the place and sees that everything is as it should be. This attention to detail has paid off since Barrett took over the property in 1986 and turned a somewhat down-at-the-heels resort of 30 rooms into a thumbs-up operation with 105 more rooms. The fact that Pineapple enjoys an almost constant 90 percent occupancy rate with a large number of guests returning each year attests to the fact that people who come here to vacation really like it.

The plantation-style pale peach buildings, which are pepped up with splashes of white and red tile roofs, are no higher than the coconut trees. Most fan out along the beach, and there are also some villas located about 50 feet above, on the hill that leads down to the sea. These suites give guests great privacy and superb views of the water. All rooms have balconies or patios and are decorated simply and in good taste. Red tile floors, rattan headboards, generous-sized closets, and pretty floral fabrics create a cheery, airy mood in the rooms, which are kept meticulously clean. The Standard rooms are small but comfortable, have limited views of the sea (but are only 350 feet away from the beach), and have a queen-size bed and patio area. Garden-view rooms have lovely garden vistas, and most have limited ocean views. These are furnished either with one queen-size or two double beds and have a balcony or patio. Baths come with showers, some also have tubs.

If you stay in the waterside rooms, where the beach is just a 60-second stroll from your door, you can leave your doors to the patio open and hear the sound of the waves gently rolling in on the shore and watch pelicans soar overhead, suddenly plunging smack into the water to scoop up their dinners.

You won't find any televisions, radios, or even phones in the rooms, but if you really need them, you can find all of these and a fax machine in the main reception building.

The resort is located on twenty-five acres in a rather secluded part of Antigua and is thus not on the main beat of the island's vendors. Since all the beaches in Antigua are public, vendors can often be a nuisance in areas where there are a number of easily accessible resorts strung along the beach. Guests of Pineapple are encouraged to buy from approved vendors who have set up some small shops on the edge of the property and sell a number of interesting items, including local crafts, jewelry, and T-shirts.

The grounds of the resort are lushly planted with a variety of flowers, plants, and trees that are cultivated in Pineapple's own nursery. Many of the fruits and vegetables served at meals are grown right on the property, too.

There are two restaurants at Pineapple: the intimate Pelican Grill, where you can enjoy a cozy, candlelit dinner and listen to Calypso Joe sing Caribbean melodies, and the large open-air restaurant near the beach. Snacks and drinks are available at the Outhouse, a hilltop retreat; tea is served every afternoon. As evening approaches, guests drift into the lounge/bar area for drinks and hors d'oeuvres before heading to dinner, where they eat at private tables, selecting from a menu that changes daily.

There is live musical entertainment in the evening for dancing under the stars. It may be a steel band, island pop, or contemporary band music. But if you're in the mood for some late nightlife, you'll have to head into town; Pineapple's beat folds up around midnight.

The resort has four new tennis courts. It also has numerous nonmotorized water sports activities, such as windsurfing, kayaking, sailing, snorkeling, and reef fishing as well as an open-air fitness center. Fishing excursions and a trip to some of the surrounding islands, including a romantic cruise to Bird Island, a sanctuary for exquisite, long-tailed birds, are all part of the scheduled activities here. You can also walk to Devil's Bridge, a natural bridge formation carved into the rocks by the sea; it is located in a national park adjacent to the resort.

At Pineapple there is absolutely no pressure to join in the various activities. However, the options are always there if you want to play volleyball or participate in a tennis round-robin. There is also the Pirate's Den, an electronic casino with about thirty-five slot machines, a video poker machine, and a satellite TV.

Honeymooners get a free bottle of champagne and are eligible to receive a 20 percent discount at Pineapple if they return for their first anniversary.

Address/Phone: P.O. Box 54, St. John's, Antigua, West Indies; (809) 463–2006 or (407) 994–5640; fax: (407) 994–6344

U.S. Reservations: (800) 966–4737

Owners/Managers: Robert Barret, owner; Bill Furlonge, general manager; Britton Forman, resident manager

Arrival/Departure: Taxi from airport costs $20 per couple; departure transfer included in all-inclusive price

Distance from V.C. Bird International Airport: 12 miles (30 minutes)

Distance from St. John's: 14 miles (30 minutes)

Accommodations: 135 rooms in Standard, Gardenview, Waterside, and Beachfront categories

Best Rooms/Suites: The Beachfront and Waterside rooms are very popular. The Waterside rooms are especially appealing as they are perched directly on the Caribbean Sea—just 15 feet from the water's edge, and thus very private. Each room has a private balcony that overlooks a 180-degree view of the water. The two favorite Beachfront rooms are called Bougainvillea and Hibiscus and are newer and larger than the Waterside rooms. Although not located smack on the beach, the sand is only about 25 steps away.

Amenities: All rooms are air-conditioned, but you'll need to bring your own hair dryer, shampoo, and lotions.

Electricity: 110 volts

Sports and Facilities: Four Laykold tennis courts, freshwater pool, snorkeling, windsurfing, sailing, shuffleboard, nature trails, kayaking, volleyball, and basketball

Dress Code: Casual; men requested to wear long pants at night; no tank tops at night

Weddings: Weddings free for couple staying 13 nights or more (not applicable to Standard category room bookings); otherwise, cost is $600. The basic wedding package consists of normal government fees, registrar costs, and ceremony charges; decorated site for the wedding and reception; bouquet of local garden flowers for the bride and boutonniere for the groom; wedding cake and one bottle of champagne; and all taxes, service charges, and gratuities for the above services.

Rates/Packages: Per couple per night summer rates are $320–$390; winter rates are $390–$460. Rates are all-inclusive and include accommodations, all meals, bar drinks, water sports and instruction, fitness center, tennis, evening entertainment, departure transfer, gratuities, service charges, government taxes.

Payment/Credit Cards: Most major

Deposit: 3-night deposit on booking reservation, refundable if cancelled 14 days or more prior to arrival date.

Government Taxes: Included

Service Charges: Included

Entry Requirements for U.S. Citizens: Proof of citizenship; passport best

Aruba

Hyatt Regency Aruba Resort & Casino

Location: On Aruba's historic Palm Beach, known for its white, sandy beaches and turquoise waters, on the southwestern coast of Aruba, 14 miles off the coast of Venezuela.

Romantic Features: Terraces overlooking the Caribbean; walking along the white sand beach under the moonlight.

When you get to Aruba, don't bother trying to find a weather report in any local newspaper or on the TV. You won't find one because the weather never changes. All they need to do is to put up a permanent sign reading, "about eighty-two to eighty-three degrees. Clear blue Caribbean skies with an occasional puffy white cloud shaped like popcorn floating by, winds about 16 miles per hour; and no rain. If anything's gonna change, we'll call you." This is just one reason Aruba is one of the more popular island destinations.

There are a lot of hotels here, most of them lined up along the broad, white Palm Beach, which stretches along the southwestern coast for several miles. An all-around good choice for romantics is the Hyatt Regency Aruba Resort & Casino. It's got a lot going for it.

As you check in and feel Aruba's famous trade winds blowing through the expansive, open-air lobby, you'll feel you've wandered back to a classic time of luxury and elegance. There are magnificent chandeliers, wooden beams, oriental rugs, and frescoes on the walls and ceilings. A sense of Aruban history pervades this relatively new resort: The architecture of the Hyatt borrows from the 1899 Gold Smelting Works of Balashi and Bushiribana on the North Coast of Aruba. The grounds, more lush than the rest of this desert island, do not disappoint.

Just off the lobby, walkways curve down toward the beach along waterfalls and the hotel's cascading, three-tiered pool—check out the two-story water slide. There's also a 5,000-square-foot pool stocked with tropical fish, and there are large aviaries of exotic birds. Here in this lush landscape, you'll find plenty of secluded areas in which to bask in the sun as well as larger patios if you wish to mingle.

The Hyatt's pools end where Aruba's white, sandy Palm Beach begins. The trade winds keep the temperature at a comfortable level, allowing you to loll in the sun with a tropical drink from one of the Hyatt's outdoor bars or to enjoy the shade at one of the resort's thatch umbrella tables. If you want to be more active, you can join in on a game of beach volleyball, go parasailing, scuba diving, windsurfing—something Aruba is known for—or simply float on a raft in the 80-degree Caribbean sea.

In addition to offering the usual water sports, the hotel's Red Sail Sports Center also features Balia catamaran cruises, canoe rentals, scuba diving, and sunset cruises.

While the turquoise water welcomes visitors with its gently rolling waves on this side of the island, you should pay a visit to the northeastern coast, where rough waves crash in carving out craggy cliffs. Here the remains of the island's original inhabitants, such as tools and hieroglyphics left in chalk caves, together with twisting rock formations, lend a historical, desert-island feel to Aruba. The windswept, native divi divi trees lean over in 45-degree angles like giant bonsai trees; iguanas perched on rocks, and cacti complete the picture. Land tours of the island are readily available and can be arranged through the Hyatt.

A sporting way to explore the desert landscape is to play a round of golf on Aruba's newly built Tierra del Sol, a championship golf course designed by Robert Trent Jones Jr. and managed by Golf Hyatt. Located at the base of the island's California Lighthouse, the course is distinctly Aruban in its landscape. All but three holes offer a panoramic view of the Caribbean as you play this challenging course. Built to complement the terrain, the roughs can be nasty. Errant balls find trouble in the form of cacti, divi divi and native desert grasses; hit it straight and you'll land in wonderfully lush, watered fairways. The Hyatt offers reserved tee times for guests and clubs can be rented at a reasonable fee.

Dining at the Hyatt gives you a number of options for a variety of tastes. There's Ole, a Spanish and tapas restaurant; Cafe Piccolo, an Italian cafe specializing in regional cuisine; Ruinas del Mar, featuring continental cuisine; and Palms, a casual restaurant serving Caribbean cuisine. Especially appealing is to dine at one of the cozy tables located out among the fountains and weeping walls of the Spanish-influenced hotel building—perfect for special romantic evenings.

Nightly entertainment is not forgotten. The resort's lively Casino Copacabana beckons to those who want to try their hand at blackjack, roulette, craps, or the slots. Bands play for dancing, and entertainment is regularly featured.

With 360 rooms, this is not your small intimate hotel. It is, however, a superb choice if you're looking for lovely accommodations in a tropical sun and sand destination. It's one of Hyatt's winners.

Author's note: With a reputation for being squeaky clean and safe, Aruba is popular among honeymooners. Only those bent on finding an island with a colorful, native culture with lots going on locally (i.e., politics, industry, working farms, sugar and banana plantations, etc.) may be disappointed. Aruba's main business is tourism; its hotels and casinos are where you'll find most of the action.

Address/Phone: L.G. Smith Boulevard, Number 85, Palm Beach, Aruba; 2978–61234; fax: 2978–61682

U.S. Reservations: (800) 233–1234

Owner/Manager: Hendrick Santos, general manager

Arrival/Departure: Taxis and car rentals available at airport

Distance from Queen Beatrix Airport: 7 miles

Distance from Oranjestad: 2 miles

Accommodations: 360 rooms, including 17 suites, 1 Regency Club floor, and 1 Governor's Suite

Best Rooms/Suites: Suites overlooking the Caribbean

Amenities: Air-conditioning, ceiling fans, minibar, cable TV, direct-dial phone with voice-activated dialing, in-room safe, coffeemaker, radio, hair dryer, toiletries; room service

Electricity: 110 volts

Sports and Facilities: Sailing, snorkeling, windsurfing, deep-sea fishing, 2 lighted tennis courts, volleyball, golf, beach, pools, health and fitness club

Dress Code: Casual

Weddings: Can be arranged

Rates/Packages: $340–$455 per room (winter); $210–$305 (spring and fall); $165–$260 (summer); suites $370–$770; Honeymoon Romance package (per couple): 4 days, $915–$1,545; 8 days, $1,655–$3,125; including accommodations, champagne, breakfast for two on first morning, sunset cruise, massage for two, jeep rental for 1 day, snorkel/sail with lunch, gratuities included for food and beverage items, service charges, taxes, and clothing discount at Red Sail Sports. Golf and scuba diving packages also available.

Payment/Credit Cards: Most major

Deposit: Reservations must be secured with deposit within 14 days of verbal confirmation; refundable if cancellation received in writing no later than October 1 for arrivals during Christmas season, 14 days in advance for all other periods.

Government Taxes: 5.5 percent, included in honeymoon plan

Service Charges: Included for items on honeymoon plan

Entry Requirements for U.S. Citizens: Proof of citizenship; passport best

Bahamas

Ocean Club

Location: On Paradise Island, off the northern edge of Nassau's New Providence Island.

Romantic Features: Intimate courtyard dining; hammocks for two; fountains and gardens.

From the moment you are greeted with a bubbling glass of fine champagne by warm, hospitable people, you know your honeymoon at this small, intimate resort on Paradise Island will live up to its reputation.

Recently the new owners of the Ocean Club, Sun International, closed the place and spent $7.5 million on renovating and restoring this little jewel. Once part of billionaire Huntington Hartford's holdings, the Ocean Club's new look is fresh and elegant. The resort's reputation for providing guests with superb service and luxurious accommodations is further enhanced with the addition of modern conveniences like minibars and central air-conditioning. With the Atlantic waters only about 20 yards from the guest rooms and a balcony or patio that takes full advantage of the marvelous sea views, the Ocean Club appeals to those seeking European ambience in a tropical setting.

Whether you are staying in a premier suite, an attractive tennis villa, or any of the other rooms in between, you are sure to be pampered by the kinds of services and amenities Croesus would have desired. Regal, king-size beds, softly colored pastel linens and fabrics, sink-in-your-toes carpeting, noiseless central air-conditioning, designer ceiling fans, stocked minibars, and 27-inch TVs are just the beginning. Bathrooms have state-of-the-art appointments, with imported marble, tile vanities, bidets, scales, and many other features you'd expect to find in fine European hotels, right down to the customized toiletries and bottled water. And something you probably wouldn't find across the "pond"—irons and ironing boards!

But that's not the total picture. Add twenty-four-hour room service, a maid who cleans your rooms three times a day, complimentary shoe shines, free shuttle transportation on Paradise Island, use of the bicycles, and a wonderful fruit basket in your room, and you have a pretty good idea of what's yet to come.

For such a small resort, the Ocean Club has a remarkable lineup of sports facilities. For the tennis player, there are nine Har-Tru clay courts, lit for night play and free to guests. There are also a teaching pro and a well-equipped pro shop. For golfers there is an award-winning eighteen-hole course less than a mile that is always open to guests of the Ocean Club. Greens fees and a cart are $86.

For pool loungers, there is an Olympic-size pool adjacent to both the tennis courts and a delightful open-air restaurant serving lunch and cocktails. The beach is one of the prettiest in the Bahamas. It's set in a protected cove and lined with palms and tropical plants, and the sand is white, soft, and deep. Lunch and drinks are served in a terrace restaurant overlooking the water, where you can watch parasailers flying in the brilliant, blue sky and luxury liners anchored offshore.

Hammocks-for-two dot the lush lawn just above the staircase to the beach. And in true Cecil B. DeMille fashion, would you believe, doves glide overhead, cooing their blessings.

Beautiful old trees, tropical flowers, and shrubs provide a rich setting for the terraced Versailles Gardens and plush lawns, which are tiered like a wedding cake up a gentle hillside. At the top is a thirteenth-century French cloister, which was imported from Europe and rebuilt stone by stone by Hartford. With its marble columns, arches, and statues, it is a lovely place to relax and enjoy the beauty of the gardens and the sea. (It's also a great place to have a wedding ceremony.)

You couldn't ask for a more seductive place to dine than the Courtyard Terrace restaurant, an intimate, outdoor courtyard where tables are arranged around fountains and gardens. With such a setting, you'd almost be willing to accept the most mundane of meals, but it will not be necessary. This restaurant is known for serving some of the finest cuisine in the islands. The a la carte menu features items such as Beluga caviar, homemade soups, lobster medallions with a warm sauce surrounded by local vegetables, chateaubriand for two, and a superb chocolate mousse. Dinner for two costs around $86.

Because Sun International owns about 75 percent of Paradise Island, you can use the facilities of their other property, the megasize Atlantis, which is located less than a mile down the road. At the Atlantis, there are twelve different restaurants and a 30,000-square-foot casino, complete with Las Vegas–style shows. The casino is open twenty-four hours a day for the slot machines and from 10:00 A.M. to 4:00 P.M. for the gaming tables. If you crave some action, this is the place to come, courtesy of the Ocean Club, which runs a free shuttle every half hour until midnight.

The Ocean Club may be close to the action, but it is worlds away from the glitter and glitz of its sibling down the road.

Address/Phone: P.O. Box N4–777, Nassau, the Bahamas; (809) 363–3000; fax: (809) 363–3703

U.S. Reservations: Sun International, (800) 321–3000

Owner/Manager: Sun International Bahamas, Ltd., owner; Jean Luc Naret, general manager

Arrival/Departure: Paradise Island Airlines leaves from Miami, Fort Lauderdale, and West Palm Beach twice a day and lands only five minutes from the Ocean Club. Delta, Kiwi, American, and United also fly into Nassau. Transfers can be arranged.

Distance from Paradise Island Airport: 1 mile (5 minutes); Nassau International Airport, 15 minutes

Distance from Nassau: 3 miles (10 to 15 minutes)

Accommodations: 71 newly refurbished rooms, including 4 suites and 5 two-bedroom villas (each with private whirlpool)

Best Rooms/Suites: Suites overlooking ocean

Amenities: Hair dryer, toiletries, central air-conditioning, ceiling fans, iron and ironing board, 27-inch TVs, bathrobes, scales, in-room safe, bidet, minibar; 24-hour room service, laundry and valet service

Electricity: 110 volts

Sports and Facilities: 9 Har-Tru lighted tennis courts; sailing, swimming, snorkeling, Aquacat sailing, kayaking; golf, cycling, croquet

Dress Code: Casual for daytime; jackets required for dinner at Courtyard Terrace

Weddings: Can be arranged

Rates/Packages: $279–$975 per couple per night. Ask about honeymoon packages.

Payment/Credit Cards: Most major

Deposit: 2-night deposit, refundable at no charge if cancelled 15 days or more prior to arrival.

Government Taxes: 10 percent room tax; $15 departure tax at airport

Service Charges: $3 housekeeping gratuity

Entry Requirements for U.S. citizens: Proof of citizenship; passport best

Barbados

Cobblers Cove Hotel

Location: On west coast of the island.

Romantic Features: Friendly, laid-back ambience; lovely beach.

Not as toney or as elegant as some of its more pricey neighbors on Barbados's western coast, Cobblers Cove is a jewel of a place: small and casual, yet lovely enough to be wildly romantic. It's the kind of place couples look for when they want to get away and simply enjoy each other for a serene few days. Cobbler's is very British in feeling; not slick, not elaborate, just an easy, laid-back kind of place. It offers water sports as well as tennis, but although you'll find Cobblers to be very friendly, no one tries to organize your time or urge you to play volleyball.

The hotel is located on only three acres, and you don't have to go very far to find anything. Sailboats? A quick snack or the resort's famous bar drink, the Cobbler's Cooler? Everything's very handy.

Each of the two-story, pink and white cottages has four suites with sitting rooms and louvered window/walls that open onto terraces or patios. The cottages and the main reception building and restaurant sit amid tropical gardens near the sea. Each suite, decorated in cheery colors, comes with a kitchenette, bamboo and contemporary white furniture, and good-sized closets. Although many of the suites are not right on the water, it's still hard to find a "bad" room here. For the most privacy, ask for the rooms to the left of the clubhouse (as you're facing the water). Those on the other side mostly overlook the gardens and lawns, where some people like to sit and sunbathe. The upper suites have peaked ceilings and better views.

If you really want to splurge, book the Camelot Suite, which is aptly named. This bilevel little spot of heaven appropriately decorated in blues and whites has a massive, white, four-poster, king-size canopied bed; spacious sitting room; huge bathroom with whirlpool tub; twin sinks; white marble floors; dhurrie carpets; and a luxurious, upholstered chaise and chairs. Climb the spiral stairway to your private pool on the furnished deck above, where you'll also find a wet bar and nonstop views.

The resort's kidney-shaped pool is not large, so if you find it a little too populated for your taste, all you have to do is walk about eight steps to one of the loveliest and quietest beaches in Barbados. For the more active there are complimentary tennis, waterskiing, windsurfing, and snorkeling right off the beach. The hotel will also make arrangements for you if you want to go deep-sea fishing, play golf, or take an island excursion.

The Terrace Restaurant is right by the sea. Here you can enjoy some of the best cuisine on the island, if not in the Caribbean. You'll have meals to write home about—guaranteed. French-trained chefs offer new choices every day. The emphasis is on Caribbean specialties with lots of fresh fish, fruits, and vegetables. You can sit on the open-air terrace right by the water and watch the sun set. Music and other entertainment is provided on various nights during the week.

Address/Phone: Road View, St. Peter, Barbados; (809) 422–2991; fax: (809) 422–1460

U.S. Reservations: Relais & Chateaux (800) RELAIS 8 or (212) 856–0115; fax: (212) 856–0193, Robert Reid Associates, (800) 223–6510; fax: (402) 398–5484

Owner/Manager: Hamish Watson, general manager

Arrival/Departure: Arrangements can be made for transfer from the airport for a fee; it's included in package rates.

Distance from Barbados International Airport: 18 miles (45 minutes)

Distance from Bridgetown: 12 miles (25 minutes); free shuttle weekdays

Accommodations: 40 suites, including 2 multilevel luxury suites with pools

Best Rooms/Suites: The new Colleton Suite and the Camelot Suite are to die for; otherwise go for the Sea View, second story suites.

Amenities: Air-conditioning, ceiling fans, direct-dial telephones, stocked minibar, hair dryer, bathrobes, drying racks, toiletries, ice service; in-room safes; radios and TV (can be arranged on request); room service from 8:00 A.M. to 9:00 P.M.

Electricity: 110/220 volts

Sports: Tennis; windsurfing, waterskiing; snorkeling; swimming at pool or beach; Sunfishes. Extra charge for deep-sea fishing and scuba diving

Dress Code: Casually elegant; jeans, shorts, and swimwear not allowed in bar after 7:00 P.M.

Weddings: In the staff's own words, "We help arrange it all, the ceremony, the champagne, and the cheers."

Rates/Packages: $590–$1,400 per room (high season); $180–$550 (low season). Honeymoon package, $758.50 per person, includes 6 nights in a Garden View suite, welcome drink, flower, fruit and wine basket, breakfasts, lobster dinner with champagne, tennis, water sports, and transfers

Payment/Credit Cards: Most major

Deposit: 3-night deposit required in winter and spring, 1-night deposit, summer and fall.

Government Taxes: 5 percent

Service Charges: 10 percent

Entry requirements for U.S. citizens: Return ticket and proof of citizenship required; passport best

Editor's Note: *At this book's press time, Cobblers Cove was completing a million-dollar upgrade of its suites and grounds.*

Sandy Lane Hotel & Golf Club

Location: On west coast of the island.
Romantic Features: Posh, estatelike surroundings; magical beach setting, especially at night.

Sandy Lane's pink-tinged, coral-stone hotel, with its graceful pillars and stately Palladian architecture, has long been the destination for the world's rich and famous, including Queen Elizabeth, the late Jacqueline Kennedy Onassis, and Kevin Costner. A traditional favorite with honeymooners for years, Sandy Lane has a lot going for it in addition to its location on one of the nicest islands in the Caribbean. Very British and perhaps a bit staid for some, the resort has a really nice buff-colored sand beach, unusually lush gardens shaded by the green canopies of trees that have been here a very long time, an ever-attentive staff, and very good sports facilities, including, until just recently, the only resort golf course on the island. Its special services, such as champagne transfers from the airport in a Rolls-Royce and breakfast in bed, are features honeymooners particularly enjoy. The views, they take for granted.

In 1991 Sandy Lane completed a $10 million renovation and restoration project, under which eighty-six of the bedrooms and bathrooms were enlarged and redesigned. Particularly classy are the eighteen beachfront, luxury, ocean-view rooms, which are now doubled in size. And just as important was the installation of new plumbing, ceilings, and walls. The public areas were also spiffed up with fresh new decor.

Guest rooms are light and airy, decorated in pastels, with predominantly white furniture. Large glass sliding patio doors open onto terraces spacious enough for tables, chairs, and lounges. And all around, the brilliantly colored ginger lilies, orchids, and hibiscus seduce you with their ambrosial perfumes.

Sandy Lane guests play free on the resort's eighteen-hole golf course, which is a very good thing if you're into golf. The two-story Plantation Clubhouse, where you can get a refreshing drink and light snacks and sandwiches, is unpretentious. You can rent clubs in the pro shop as well as purchase logo clothing, balls, and other golf-related items. Even if you're not a golfer, see if you can "steal" a golf cart and ride up to the back nine just as the sun is setting. This is the time when a whole community of Barbadian monkeys come swinging out of the trees that line a gully. Some are bold enough to come right up and sit on the tees. It's great fun to watch them play and romp over the fairways before they head back to the protection of the trees. And while you're at it, catch the view from the tee of the seventh hole, which sits high above the course, with the sea beyond. A neat photo opportunity!

The tennis center is located adjacent to the pool area. Use of the courts and racquets is complimentary, and there is a well-stocked pro shop that sells supplies and logo clothing.

You can start out your day with breakfast in your room or in the Sandy Bay Restaurant, overlooking the sea. Lunch can be buffet style or something light from the menu at the Seashell Restaurant. Dinners can be casual or more formal with gourmet cuisine prepared by European-trained chefs.

Tea is served every afternoon on the terrace. At night after dinner, walk down the winding staircase to the beach and look back at the white lights and candles glowing from the terraces of the sprawling white "great house," which is tucked under the towering mahogany trees—it's really quite beautiful.

There is live music for dancing and listening every evening, and on some nights you are entertained by a roving guitarist. A Barbadian floor show, steel band, and piano rounds out Sandy Lane's regular entertainment.

Address/Phone: St. James, Barbados, West Indies; (809) 432–1311; fax: (809) 432–2954

U.S. Reservations: The Leading Hotels of the World, (800) 223–6800

Owner/Manager: Richard Williams, general manager

Arrival/Departure: Arrangements can be made for a Concierge Welcome at the airport and complimentary luxury car transportation to and from the resort.

Distance from Barbados International Airport: 20 miles (30 minutes)

Distance from Bridgetown: 9 miles (15 minutes)

Accommodations: 80 rooms and 30 suites, each with a private terrace or balcony

Best Rooms/Suites: The luxury suites overlooking the beach on the north end

Amenities: Air-conditioning, ceiling fans, stocked minibar, hair dryer, telephones, clock/radios, toaster, bathrobes, in-room safes; 24-hour room service, toiletries, TV in suites; nightly turndown service

Electricity: 110/220 volts

Sports and Facilities: 18-hole golf course, driving area, putting and chipping greens; 5 Laykold floodlit tennis courts; windsurfing, waterskiing, snorkeling; Hobie cats; Sunfish; pool; beach. Extra charge for deep-sea fishing and scuba diving

Dress Code: Casually elegant. During the Christmas, winter, and spring seasons, jacket and tie are required twice weekly for gentlemen in the main dining room. Casual dining available in the seaside Italian restaurant.

Weddings: Sandy Lane can arrange any style wedding, from a simple, private ceremony to an elaborate gala affair. A waiting Rolls-Royce, private cruise, candlelight dinners, and romantic picnics are just a few of the resort's distinctive touches.

Rates/Packages: $720–$895 (January 1–April 10); $545–$695 (April 11–December 31); higher during holidays. Rates include breakfast and dinner.

Payment/Credit Cards: Most major

Deposit: 3-night deposit required in winter and spring and a 1-night deposit required in summer and fall. Refundable if cancelled 14 days before arrival.

Government Taxes: 5 percent

Service Charges: 10 percent

Entry requirements for U.S. citizens: Return ticket and proof of citizenship required; passport best

Bermuda

Cambridge Beaches

Location: On a twenty-five-acre peninsula on Bermuda's western coast, near Somerset Village.

Romantic Features: Dancing under the stars on the Mangrove Bay Terrace; boat ride to a private island for a picnic; five pink beaches to sink your toes into.

It's just about as far out on the island as you can get, but who cares? At Cambridge Beaches, you have five Bermuda-pink pristine beaches and numerous little coves to discover that are tucked into the rocky ledges of the peninsula, which meanders into the sea like a miniature Cape Cod. With water on three sides, the resort's pink-and-white limestone cottages nestle into the nooks and crannies of the well-manicured tropical gardens above and along the shoreline. White roofs and louvers, mellow stone walls and steps that turn golden in the late afternoon sun, and lush, flowering oleanders and hibiscus that have had many years to mature, transform Cambridge Beaches into a magical world where dreams are made and fulfilled.

It's truly one of the world's premier hideaway resorts and one of Bermuda's most exclusive properties. There are a variety of rooms and suites; some with king-size bed, vaulted beamed ceiling, and sitting areas; others with fireplaces and French doors leading to a large terrace and spec-

Cambridge Beaches, Bermuda

tacular views of the lovely harbor below, dotted with sleek yachts at anchor.

All rooms are individually decorated with cheerful English chintz in warm pinks, sunny golds, and blues, traditional Queen Anne furniture, and marble baths. Some of the larger suites feature charming antique pieces and extended grassy terraces. Attractive scenes of Bermuda decorate the walls. You have your own terrace, where you can enjoy a cozy, private breakfast or dinner, and it's only a short walk to the beaches.

The 275-year-old Great House, overlooking Mangrove Bay harbor, shelters a gracious lobby furnished with Bermudan and English antiques—it has that comfortable "been-here-a-long-while" feel. Downstairs you'll find the elegant Tamarisk Restaurant, where the food is a work of art. Your plate may be decorated with fans of fresh fruit, delicate lacy butterflies of chocolate, or swirls of raspberry sauce in a pool of vanilla custard. The panelled Port O'Call Bar, with its cozy fireplace, is a perfect spot to hide out when the weather is cool. Pastries, breads, and ice cream are made in Cambridge's own Pastry Shop.

For lunch and more casual dining, the Mangrove Bay Terrace invites you to dine and dance under trees and night sky. White wrought iron chairs and tables are set on the stone terrace, where you can see the harbor from just about anywhere you sit. For a change of pace, you can take advantage of the resort's exchange dining program, which invites you to eat at six other properties at no extra charge.

The water sports activities and the marina are down at the end of the beach. Rent a boat and explore the private islands just off the coast or head to nearby Turtle Cove beach, pick up the phone at the bottom of the steps, and order "room service." The resort has a number of boats you can use, including canoes, sailboats, and motorboats. Cruise on the 40-foot yacht, *Junkaroo,* and watch the sun set while sipping a Sea Breeze.

Want to be pampered? Then treat yourself to a massage or facial at the new European-American Spa or take in all the interesting sight-seeing activities in and around Hamilton. A free Cambridge Beaches ferry shuttles you to Hamilton three times a week. You can also explore the dockyard, located at this end of the island, or take a romantic horse and buggy ride in the nearby town of Somerset. Rent a moped or bicycle and ride off to discover the beauty of Bermuda. The speed limit on the island is about 25 miles per hour, so you can really enjoy an easy, carefree spin.

At Cambridge Beaches, entertainment is not forgotten. There is a Friday night barbecue, music for listening and dancing most evenings, and special evening cruises.

Address/Phone: 30 Kings Point Road, Somerset, MA 02, Bermuda; (809) 234–0331; fax: (809) 234–3352

U.S. Reservations: (800) 468–7300

Owner/Manager: Michael J. Winfield, managing director

Arrival/Departure: A 45-minute taxi ride from the airport costs approximately $35

Distance from Bermuda International Airport: 14 miles

Distance from Somerset: 3 miles

Accommodations: 82 rooms and suites in cottages, all refurbished within the past five years.

Best Rooms/Suites: Cambridge Suite, which has a bedroom and separate living room with panoramic water views; suites with water views also good.

Amenities: Air-conditioning, ceiling fans, toiletries, telephones, bathrobes, hair dryer; whirlpools in some baths; room service, free shuttle to Hamilton

Electricity: 110 volts

Sports and Facilities: 3 tennis courts (one lit for night play), croquet, swimming at heated saltwater pool or beach, snorkeling, scuba diving, sailing, canoeing, windsurfing, kayaking, fishing, motorboating; spa, Universal gym, sauna, whirlpool, aerobics; 40-foot yacht for special cruises; putting green, golf can be played at nearby Robert Trent Jones Port Royal and Mid Ocean Club courses; moped and bicycle rentals

Dress Code: Jacket and tie for formal evenings; smart casual for informal evenings

Weddings: Can be arranged
Rates/Packages: Rates are per couple per night, including breakfast, dinner, tea, use of tennis courts, putting green, and ferry service to Hamilton. $325–$525 (April 10–November 15); $230–$370 (March 1–April 9).
Payment/Credit Cards: Cash, personal checks; no credit cards
Deposit: 2-night deposit at time of booking to cover first and last night's accommodations; cancel 28 days or more prior to arrival for refund.
Government Taxes: 6 percent room tax
Service Charges: $12.50 per person per night
Entry requirements for U.S. citizens: Proof of citizenship; passport best

Pompano Beach Club

Location: On the southwestern coast of Bermuda.
Romantic Factors: Hillside Jacuzzis overlooking the sea; dramatic ocean views from every cottage; secluded and intimate family-run hotel.

Perched on a hill overlooking the turquoise sea, the Pompano Beach Club is a good choice for Bermuda-bound honeymooners seeking a quiet, relaxed, intimate resort at rates that won't bottom-out your pocketbook.

In 1955 this choice location on the picturesque southwest corner of the island was an ideal place for a group of avid fishermen to set up headquarters for a fishing club. In 1956 Thomas Lamb, an American from Boston, Massachusetts, purchased the club and went about, turning it into a first-class resort. The clubhouse was enlarged and designed with large windows looking out toward the sea, and several cottage accommodations were added.

Today Lamb's sons, Tom and Larry, are responsible for Pompano's operations. Their on-site management and personal enthusiasm for making sure their guests are happy, are part of the reason the resort is so popular.

The pretty pink cottages with white trim and roofs are terraced up the hill amid gardens and well-manicured lawns. Each room has a sitting area, balcony or patio, and great views of the turquoise sea below. Furnishings are a mix of traditional reproductions, rattan furniture, and soft pink, orange, and green fabric, and watercolor prints of Bermuda. As you stroll from your cottage along the walkways to the beach and dining room, you are always in sight of the sea.

Whether you're dining in the Cedar Room or sipping a cocktail in the lounge while the sun sets over the water, the mood is set for romance. The sea is so close, it's almost like being on a cruise ship. After dinner there is

music for listening and dancing, or you can head out for a moonlit stroll.
The beach, like many in Bermuda, is rather small and shallow. But the calm waters provide the perfect place to float on a raft, and when the tide is out, you can walk out on the wide sand bar for a long way without the water going over your head. The reefs that protect this cove provide wonderful snorkeling—some say it's the best in Bermuda.

If you love to sun and swim, Pompano's lovely mosaic pool overlooking the sea is a perfect place to settle with a frosty rum swizzle from the poolside bar. You can also sink into one of the bubbling, warm Jacuzzis, where day or night, you'll enjoy nonstop water views.

Want some action? Then head to the tennis courts or check out the water sports center at the beach. Here you'll find windsurfers, snorkeling equipment, sailboats, paddleboats, and other fun things to try out. Or you can take the ferry to Hamilton and indulge in some serious shopping. Bermuda has some great stores.

It also has one of the island's best golf courses right next door, the Port Royal Golf Course. Pompano can help you with tee times.

Tom and Larry will be able to tell you about all the places you can explore on the island. You can go by moped, bus, or taxi, or you can pick up a box lunch from the hotel's restaurant, rent a Boston Whaler, and go to one of the deserted islands around Hamilton Harbour for a picnic.

Although Bermuda is considered a year-round destination, and indeed is quite lovely in the fall, winter, and spring months, you should be aware that the water sports center is only open from May through early September. Winter months can be quite cool, although the trade winds moderate the weather, and the temperatures can be in the sixties and seventies even in February. Bermuda is not considered a tropical destination. So if hot hot weather is what you want, and you're getting married in the winter, you should probably head farther south.

For those who love fresh air, lovely scenery, walking, tennis, golf, and a comfortable, intimate place to stay, Pompano may be it.

Address/Phone: 36 Pompano Beach Road, Southampton SB 03, Bermuda; (809) 234–0222; fax: (809) 234–1694
U.S. Reservations: Bermuda Hotel Representatives, (800) 343–4155
Owner/Managers: Tom and Larry Lamb
Arrival/Departure: A 30-minute taxi ride from the airport costs approximately $30
Distance from Bermuda International Airport: Approximately 13 miles
Distance from Somerset: 3 miles
Accommodations: 54 rooms and suites in clusters of two-story cottages set into the hillside

Best Rooms/Suites: The deluxe suites in Flying Fish (numbers 1 and 2) and in Dolphin House (numbers 8 to 18)

Amenities: Hair dryer; iron and ironing board, umbrella, toiletries, air-conditioning, refrigerator, clock/radio, telephone; bottle of champagne on arrival

Electricity: 110 volts

Sports and Facilities: Fitness center; swim in heated pool or at beach, 2 outdoor Jacuzzis, windsurfing; Sunfish; paddleboats; snorkeling; 5 tennis courts (1 clay, 4 all-weather, 2 lit for night play)

Dress Code: Jacket and tie required for men on Tuesday, Thursday, and Saturday; other nights dress is smart casual

Weddings: Can be arranged

Rates/Packages: $270–$360 per couple per night, including breakfast and dinner. Fun in Sun is best package at $2,540 per couple, including 6 nights/7 days accommodations in deluxe ocean-view room with king-size bed and private balcony, breakfast and dinner daily, dine-around program with four other Bermuda Collection resorts, tax and service charges, round-trip airport transfers, welcome cocktail, round-trip ferry ride to Hamilton, tennis, and 1 day's use of snorkeling equipment.

Payment/Credit Cards: Cash, travelers checks, or personal checks if credit is established at hotel upon arrival. No credit cards.

Deposit: First and last night's room rate required. Full deposit is refunded if cancellation is received 21 days prior to arrival.

Government Taxes: 6 percent

Service Charges: 10 percent

Entry Requirement for U.S. Citizens: Return ticket and proof of citizenship; passport is best

The Reefs

Location: In Southampton, on the south shore of Bermuda.

Romantic Features: Hillside rooms overlooking the sea; room service breakfast on your private balcony; private pink beach with hidden coves to explore.

The Reefs is one of Bermuda's most romantic honeymoon resorts and has been consistently rated as one of the best on the island for a number of years. Sitting high above the beautiful pink beach and coral reefs below, the salmon-hued, low-rise lanai cottages ramble over the landscaped, terraced grounds. All have great views of the sea from the balconies.

Rooms are attractively furnished with rattan chairs, sofas, tables and bed, bright tropical prints, area rugs on red tiled floors, and cheery prints of Bermuda scenes. The upper level Premier Lanai Suites have a king-size bed, sitting area, and a private terrace where you can enjoy breakfast served on your table overlooking the sea.

The reception building houses an attractive lobby, comfortable lounge-bar, the dining room, and tropical conservatory, where you dine under a glass roof. In the warmer months, you can enjoy a candlelit dinner outside on the terrace under the stars, and there is often music for dining and dancing. The Reefs' delicious international cuisine is included in your room rate.

If you want to dine outside while the surf rolls in nearby, try eating at the casual, thatched-roof Coconuts, the beach level restaurant (warmer months only). You'll find the staff friendly and efficient.

The Reefs has a heated pool that overlooks the water and two all-weather tennis courts. There's a wonderful pink beach and more to discover if you walk around the big black boulders that lie at the ends of the beach. Here you'll come upon more delightful small beaches tucked into coves, which continue along the shoreline. And yes, the sand is really tinged pink from the bits of pulverized coral that have been mixed in over the years.

The Reefs is located within walking distance of the Sonesta Beach Hotel, so if you are in the mood for an evening show or some lively entertainment, simply walk next door. You can also rent a moped or go by bus or taxi to nearby Hamilton for some serious shopping.

The Reefs' traditions, such as serving tea each afternoon, are grounded in the British way of doing things, but the hotel is more informal than many Bermuda hotels. It appeals to the well-heeled, and guests tend to come back year after year. It's that kind of place.

Address/Phone: 56 South Road, Southampton SN 02, Bermuda; (809) 238–0222; fax: (809) 238–8372

U.S. Reservations: Islands Resorts Reservations Ltd., (800) 742–2008

Owner/Manager: David Dodwell, general manager

Arrival/Departure: A 25-minute taxi ride from the airport costs approximately $26 weekdays, $28 weekends

Distance from Bermuda International Airport: 11 miles

Distance from Hamilton: 7 miles

Accommodations: 56 guest cottages and lanais: 6 Poolside, 11 Superior, 23 Deluxe; 16 Premier

Best Rooms/Suites: Deluxe or premier lanais

Amenities: King-size bed, refrigerator, bathrobes, hair dryer, in-room safe, umbrella, toiletries, air-conditioning; daily newspaper, rum swizzle on arrival, in-room beverages

Electricity: 110 volts

Sports and Facilities: 2 tennis courts, pool, beach, fitness center, shuffle-board, croquet, cycle rentals, snorkeling, scuba diving; helmet diving and glass bottom boats nearby, golf at nearby courses, fishing and sailing can be arranged.

Dress Code: Casual during day; men required to wear coat and tie in restaurant except for Mondays and Thursdays, which are casual; beach restaurant and bar also casual.

Weddings: Can be arranged

Rates/Packages: Rates are per couple per night and include breakfast and dinner, local phone calls, in-room beverages on arrival, and use of sports facilities. $149–$180 for lanai rooms, $330 for one-bedroom cottage (high season spring and summer). Honeymoon package, $2,730–$3,250, includes 7 nights accommodations (lanai rooms), all the above inclusions plus a glass-bottom boat cruise, champagne, special gift, gratuities, and taxes. Rates are 20–35 percent less during the colder months.

Payment/Credit Cards: Cash, travelers checks, or personal check; no credit cards

Deposit: 2-night deposit at time of booking to cover first and last night's accommodations; fully refundable if cancelled 21 days prior to arrival.

Government Taxes: 6 percent of nightly rate; included in Honeymoon Package

Service Charges: 10 percent; included in Honeymoon Package

Entry requirements for U.S. citizens: Proof of citizenship; passport best

British Virgin Islands

Virgin Gorda

The Bitter End Yacht Club

Location: Covers 25 acres, stretching for a mile along the North Sound of Virgin Gorda.

Romantic Features: Magnificent sailing; thatched-roof bungalows on the beach; opportunity to combine a yacht cruise with an island stay; sunset sail; hammocks for two on your porch or balcony.

The Bitter End Yacht Club, Virgin Gorda

Don't let the name turn you off. This "Bitter End" could be your "Sweet Beginning." Artfully tucked into a cove on the northernmost tip of Virgin Gorda, one of the most picturesque of the British Virgin Islands, The Bitter End Yacht Club (BEYC) is a perfect place for newlyweds who love to sail. You can combine your passion for a romantic setting with a few days' cruise aboard a bare boat or crewed yacht, exploring the neighboring islands. Or you can spend all your nights at the resort, and venture out onto the gentle seas during the day.

World-class yachtsmen have known about this place for many years, and people like Jean-Michel Cousteau and Mel Fisher have rendezvoused often at this unique tropical haven, which has seventy deep-water moorings, two restaurants, and a host of water sports activities—all first class from beginning to end.

Protected by coral reefs and beach-fringed cays, this secluded, idyllic spot can most easily be reached by boat. The white sand beach, fringed by gnarled sea grape shrubs and palms, frames a lagoon, which seems more like a large, clear, turquoise lake dashed with flashes of the bright-colored sails of windsurfers.

From the time of your arrival at Virgin Gorda's tiny airport—hardly large enough to hold your luggage—everything is handled by the Bitter End staff with great style. After you've gathered your luggage, you're whisked up and over the steep hills to a landing area about twenty minutes away. Then it's a five-minute boat ride across a brilliant Caribbean-blue lagoon, where you are met by a smiling staff member at the dock. (Those landing at Tortola come to the BEYC via high-speed water taxi.)

Native stone lines the walkways and roads, and flowers and tropical plants, including fragrant frangipani, bougainvillea, hibiscus, oleander and sea grape, wind along the paths and up the hillside. Colorful nautical flags fly from the rafters of the bar, from poles along the walkways, and just about everywhere. Buildings are decorated with whimsical gingerbread trim and iron grillwork and are connected by a series of garden courtyards. Blue and white–painted wrought iron tables and chairs sit on brick-paved patios accented by tiered fountains and flowering plants. All very Mediterranean.

As the sun sets, you'll soon become aware that the lighting throughout the resort is seductively low. (Can this be due to the Caribbean-style electrical power or is it planned for romantics like you?) As you walk along the seaside paths to the dining room, you'll find the tiny flashlight you got at check-in extremely useful.

Because BEYC is actually the marriage of two different resorts, the styles of accommodations are quite different. There are rustic beachfront bungalows that blend into the hills, with their thatched roofs and weathered wood exteriors, and there are more contemporary hillside chalets. The bungalows are much closer to the water than the chalets—some are right on the beach—and are very Caribbean in feeling. You won't have a room key, because there are no locks. Nor are they needed. Open wraparound, palm-thatched verandas, ceiling fans, large walk-in showers, bamboo furniture, a tiled dressing area, and native art and quaint knickknacks lend a homey island feeling to the bungalows. Since most come with twin beds, request ahead to have them put together.

The deluxe 600-square-foot chalets, perched high over the water, are more spacious and luxurious, with vaulted ceilings, balconies, air-conditioning, two queen-size beds, and a very large marble inside/outside garden shower room. Connected by wooden walkways much like jungle catwalks, the chalets have wood peaked ceilings and glass doors leading out to balconies, and they are attractively decorated in rich fabrics, native art, and grass-cloth walls.

The chalets and bungalows come equipped with a refrigerator and coffeemaker, and each has telephone service to the front desk and a comfortable sitting area. The choice is yours: Lie in luxury overlooking the harbor or pick a casual, native-style beachfront villa.

When it comes to water sports, you're in sailing heaven. There are enough Mistral sailboards, Sunfish, Lasers, Laser IIs, Rhodes 19s, J-24s, and outboard-powered skiffs to get the whole guest population of the resort out on the water at the same time.

A semisubmersible is available for touring the underwater world, and there are daily escorted snorkeling trips, scuba lessons, dive trips, and lots of regattas. There is also the Nick Trotter Sailing School, a great way for new sailors to learn how to tell a *jib* from a *ready-about*. If you want to explore nearby shores, you can take one of the skiffs and chug over to other parts of the island for a picnic or a visit. For landlubbers a lovely pool and patio area is located on the eastern end of the resort, near the chalets.

Well worth seeing are Agadeda and Shipwreck Island as well as The Baths, giant granitelike boulders on the southwest coast. Take your bathing suit and swim in the pools located in, under, and around the huge rocks, some as high as 40 feet.

If you want the best of both worlds, you can live aboard one of the resort's Cal-27s, fully outfitted, luxurious yachts that you can sail into the sunset for a few days or a few hours, returning to your home base for the evening. All meals are included, whether you eat onboard or ashore.

The BEYC has two restaurants. The Clubhouse, on the shore, serves breakfast, lunch, and dinner. You can eat inside, on the tree-shaded terrace, or on the veranda. The terrace bar, poised on the edge of the water, is a popular gathering place for guests to enjoy morning coffee or a late afternoon cocktail.

Nearer the chalets is the Pavilion Dining Room of the English Carvery, which is open four nights a week for intimate candlelight dinners and dancing. You can also grab a quick snack or a light lunch at the English Pub at the Emporium, which serves pizza.

The BEYC attracts some big-name entertainers, and there is also entertainment in the piano bar, jazz club, and lounge. Bitter End's steel band plays several nights a week, and there are beach barbecues and sunset and moonlight cruises.

With close to 200 staff for just 90 rooms, the Bitter End gives you all the attention you want and need, but one of the best things of all, is that it's done in a totally unobtrusive manner. You can wash your hair, take a walk on the beach, and when you return, find a fresh towel in your room. Beds are turned down every night, and the beaches are raked every morning.

Although you will be surrounded by tempting things to do, you can find your own quiet spot on one of the secluded beaches and just sit back under a palm tree and watch a yellow finch eat sugar from your outstretched hand.

Address/Phone: North Sound, Virgin Gorda, B.V.I.; (809) 494–2746; fax: (809) 494–4756

U.S. Reservations: (800) USA–BEYC, (800) 872–2392 or (312) 944–5855; fax: (312) 944–2860

Owner/Manager: Bruce Hearn, COO and general manager

Arrival/Departure: Transfers from Beef Island Airport, Tortola, or Virgin Gorda Airport included in 7-day package; otherwise $20 per couple charge for transfer

Distance from Virgin Island Airport: 30-minute drive or bus ride plus 10-minute boat ride.

Distance from Spanish Town: 30 minutes

Accommodations: 83 rooms and suites with porches or balconies: 43 rustic bungalows and 38 chalets; 10 live-aboard yachts

Best Rooms/Suites: Beachfront bungalows for beach lovers; hillside chalets for those who prefer luxury and a birds-eye view of the water

Amenities: Air-conditioning (chalets only), ceiling fans, garden showers, hair dryer, coffeemaker, refrigerator, VCRs (in suites); turndown service; shops and convenience store

Electricity 110 volts

Sports and Facilities: Water sports galore; Mistral sailboards, Sunfish, Lasers, Laser IIs, Rhodes 19s, J-24s, and outboard-powered skiffs; snorkeling; scuba diving; swimming pool, 3 beaches, fitness trail; marina

Dress Code: Very casual. Leave your cocktail dresses and sports jackets at home.

Weddings: Can be arranged

Rates/Packages: From $320 per couple per night (spring–fall); $595 (winter); includes 3 meals and use of water sports equipment. For honeymooning sailors, there is the Admiral's Package; an 8-day/7-night plan, priced from $2,240 per couple (spring–fall) and from $4,165 (winter); includes accommodations, all meals, excursions, water sports and unlimited use of the Bitter End's fleet of boats. A package combining 5 nights on a yacht and 4 nights in the resort is priced from $2,730 per couple.

Payment/Credit Cards: Most major

Deposit: 3 nights; cancel 30 days prior to arrival date for refund, and by October 1 for Christmas season.

Government Taxes: 7 percent

Service Charges: $12 per person per day

Entry Requirements for U.S. Citizens: Proof of citizenship; passport best

Little Dix Bay

Location: Northwest corner of Virgin Gorda, just off the Sir Francis Drake Channel.

Romantic Features: Beautiful beachfront setting; garden shower rooms; romantic dining and dancing under the stars; hammocks for two; picnics on secluded beaches.

One of the most consistently appealing Caribbean resorts, Little Dix Bay was established over thirty years ago by Laurance S. Rockefeller, who visualized an ecological preserve and wilderness resort where privacy and solitude were paramount. Today Little Dix remains extremely romantic and seductive. It sits on 500 acres and has a lovely ½-mile crescent-shaped beach. The rooms and public areas are designed to blend into the surrounding gardens of flowering shrubs, sea grapes, and palms. Cottages containing two to eight rooms all face the sea. Some are on stilts and have cone-shaped roofs; others are more conventional. All have louvered window walls designed to catch the cooling trade winds.

Coral reefs and a cove create a calm, safe "harbor" for swimming and water sports. In 1993, Rosewood Hotels & Resorts took over the operation of the resort, giving the property a major face-lift, with new furniture and custom-designed fabrics, new lighting, telephones, redesigned bathrooms, and the addition of air-conditioning to about half the rooms. To lend a Polynesian ambience, bamboo beds and other interesting furniture pieces were imported from Asia, and unique touches were added, such as wicker baskets and artwork. Throughout the renovation, great care and sensitivity were taken to preserve the harmonious pact Little Dix has had with nature.

Cottages are constructed of native wood and stone with peaked wooden ceilings, circulating fans, and tile floors. Bamboo king-size beds; rattan furniture, including chaises roomy enough to hold two; and natural fiber area rugs are low-key yet elegant enough to satisfy the most discerning of guests. Rooms are located in clusters of cottages, some on ground level.

With more than 300 on staff, the hotel provides excellent, yet not overpowering, service. They pay attention to the little things like replenishing your ice bucket daily and providing an abundant supply of fresh towels.

Little Dix has three restaurants. The open-air Pavilion, which has four dramatic Polynesian-style pyramid roofs and a stone terrace, offers international and Caribbean specialties, lunch buffets, afternoon teas, and candlelight dinners. Rack of lamb, fresh salmon, red snapper, and grouper are served grilled or with wonderful light sauces. Guests often gather on the terrace early in the evening for cocktails as the sun sets. After dinner a band plays music for dancing under the open skies. This is your chance to get dressed up for a really lovely evening of good food, wine, and romance—the kind of night you always dreamed about.

The more casual seaside Sugar Mill, its roof and terraces splashed by the reds and oranges of bougainvillea, is a good place to enjoy Mediterranean-inspired cuisine. Pastas, pizzas, salads, and sandwiches are served at lunchtime, while dinner may include fresh grilled fish, lobster, and steaks. Freshly sliced turkey breast, grilled eggplant, and grilled fish are always popular choices.

The Beach Grill serves breakfast, light lunches, and dinner; at night you eat at candlelit tables overlooking the beach, alive with the glow of blazing torches.

At Little Dix, the beach is right in your "front yard." Float the afternoon away on a rubber raft, or sit under an umbrella of pond fronds. Take a box lunch and umbrella and climb aboard the resort's water taxi, which will shuttle you to a secluded beach. Snorkel in Devils Bay and explore Mosquito Island. Ask the boatman to drop you near the famous Baths, and spend a few hours climbing above, under, and around the huge boulders that create this unique natural phenomenon. Swim in the grotto pools and climb the path that leads from the beach to a hilltop restaurant/bar.

Guided snorkel tours are offered four times a week, and you can take Sunfish lessons, aerobic exercise, and even a tour of the gardens with the resident horticulturist. The tennis center offers complimentary clinics and round-robins twice a week, and movies are shown every evening in the large, open-air lounge.

Your honeymoon package includes a sunset cocktail cruise and a ride on a Boston Whaler to Spring Bay for a picnic. Full-day sails to nearby areas as well as scuba diving, fishing charters, and beauty treatments are also available as optional choices.

Well-heeled guests have been coming here for years, appreciating the easy ambience and the excellent service—they treat it rather like their personal island club. During the winter months, the guests tend to be on the more mature side. But in the spring—honeymoon season—the resort is popular with newly married young couples, many of whom have learned about the resort from their parents. Spring, summer, and fall are great times to come to Little Dix. Prices are lower, and the weather is great.

Address/Phone: P.O. Box 70, Virgin Gorda, B.V.I.; (809) 495–5555; fax: (809) 495–5661

U.S. Reservations: (800) 928–3000; fax: (214) 871–5444

Owner/Managers: Managed by Rosewood Hotels & Resorts

Arrival/Departure: Virgin Gorda can be reached via San Juan, Puerto Rico, and St. Thomas, U.S. Virgin Islands. Scheduled shuttles are also available to and from St. Thomas and Caneel Bay. Those arriving at Tortola International Airport are met by a Little Dix Bay representative and taken by private boat launch on a 20-minute ride to the resort .

Distance from Virgin Gorda Airport: 1 mile

Distance from Spanish Town: 2 miles

Accommodations: 98 rooms and 4 one-bedroom suites all facing the sea. Some rooms are set on stilts, and all have patios or balconies. Rooms on east side overlook gardens and sea beyond; rooms on west side are closer to beach.

Best Rooms/Suites: Newly created beachfront suites with oversize soaking tubs and showers and separate bedroom and living room, or the elevated hexagonal rooms on the west side, near the beach.

Amenities: Air-conditioning (about half), king-size bed, ceiling fans, hair dryer, generous kits of lotions and shampoo, telephones (can be removed at guest's request), clock/radios, TVs, minibars, and in-room safes.

Electricity: 110 volts

Sports and Facilities: Tennis day or night, scuba diving, snorkeling, windsurfing, sailing, Sunfish, kayaking, water skiing, aerobics

Dress Code: Informal during day; although jacket and tie are not required, most guests usually wear elegant attire when dining at Pavilion.

Weddings: Can be arranged

Rates/Packages: 7-night honeymoon package (per couple): $3,000-$4,000 (summer); $3,600-$6,000 (spring and fall); $4,500-$8,000 (winter); includes accommodations, meals, unlimited day sails, sunset cocktail cruises, Spring Bay afternoon picnic, champagne and fruit on arrival, transfers to and from Tortola, tennis, water sports, afternoon tea, water taxis to nearby beaches, guided snorkeling tour, Sunfish lessons, tennis clinic, aerobic exercise, and massage for two.

Payment/Credit Cards: Most major

Deposit: $1,000 for some packages, due 14 days from date reservations made. If booking 30 days prior to arrival, credit card deposit required within 24 hours of booking. A full deposit will be refunded if notice of cancellation is received at least 28 days in advance of arrival. For those travelling from April 1 to December 19, the full deposit will be refunded if reservation cancelled at least 7 days prior to arrival date.

Government Taxes/Service Charges: Daily rates and weekly package rates are subject to a 13 percent surcharge, which covers all room tax, service charges, and meal plan gratuities.

Entry Requirements for U.S. Citizens: A valid passport, authenticated birth certificate, or voter's registration card with a photo ID accepted as proof of citizenship

Peter Island

Peter Island Resort and Yacht Harbour

Location: A private, 1,800-acre island in the British Virgin Islands.
Romantic Features: Private honeymoon beach; garden showers; deserted beaches to explore on your own; hammocks under the palms; dining and dancing under the stars.

Peter Island is an easy, 20-minute boat ride from the Beef Island Airport, just long enough for you to stretch travel-weary limbs and bask in the warm sun and fresh salt air. As you pull up to the resort's pier, you'll see deserted white sandy beaches, coconut groves, and low hills covered with cactus and bougainvillea.

There aren't a lot of buildings here, and what structures do exist are so unobtrusive, you have to look hard to find them. There are only fifty rooms and three villas along with two restaurants, a lounge, library, reception area, fitness center, and dive shop on the entire 1,800-acre island. The two entrepreneurs who own most of Peter Island are passionately dedicated to preserving the low-key ambience of the resort. You'll find no Club Med sorts of "playmakers," no casino, no disco. What you will find is the oppor-

Peter Island

tunity to do pretty much what you want when you want to do it. If you like beaches, sun, and water sports, this island can be your nirvana. Like to sail? You can choose from a 42-foot yacht, a 48-foot Catamaran, Hobie Cats, 19-foot Squibs and Zumas along with kayaks and windsurfers. There are also power boats that can be chartered for deep-sea fishing.

If you feel a little green about climbing into a Sunfish by yourself, don't worry. The sail instructor keeps an eye on everyone. "I've never lost anyone yet," he'll tell you with a smile as he helps you push your boat into the water.

Peter Island is an excellent place for snorkeling and scuba diving as well as sailing. Snorkeling gear is free to guests and just offshore the main swimming beach is a reef where you can see a wonderful assortment of colorful fish, shellfish, corals, and aquatic plants. All you have to do is to wade out, don your mask and fins, and paddle off.

DIVE BVI offers scuba lessons and dives for all levels. One of the most popular dive sites is the Wreck of the Rhone, a nineteenth-century British mail ship and the site of the filming of Peter Benchley's *The Deep.*

If you like to go exploring, you can climb the rocks at the end of the main beach, follow the fitness trail and see who is the most flexible and the strongest, and walk to the really isolated long beach around the corner, where you can find lots of shells, coral, and bits of sea glass. Take along a blanket and a picnic lunch and enjoy a few hours on your own.

Peter Island has four Tru-flex tennis courts along with a small tennis center. A pro is available to give you lessons or arrange partners if you're looking for a set of doubles. Also located at the tennis center is a paperback book exchange library.

One of my criteria for a great beach resort is a place where you can go from your room to the beach in twenty paces and walk on that beach (and others) for miles. Peter Island passes the sand test. But there's more: king-size beds, attractive decor in the island mode, plenty of thirsty towels, lights bright enough for night reading, and a great view of the sea. You also have a minibar, sitting area, shower that looks into a small private garden, double sink, real hangers, a hair dryer that works well, a large walk-in closet, and lots of louvers that you can open to let in the breezes and the sounds of waves. Patios or balconies are furnished with Brown Jordan-type lounge chairs. If you want to watch TV, you'll have to head to the lounge in the main reception building, near the dock.

For entertainment there is music by local bands for dancing or listening almost nightly on the open-air patio. Excursions to neighboring islands such as St. Thomas, Jost Van Dyke, and Tortola are also offered.

Peter Island gets its fish daily from local fishermen, and the chef knows how to cook it! Especially good is the grilled tuna served with a homemade pineapple chutney. The resort also makes its own desserts and pastries. Fresh muffins in the mornings, great cookies with white chocolate chunks and macadamia nuts, and key lime pie made the traditional way are all delicious.

I would strongly advise that you take the meal plan when you come here. Peter Island's two restaurants are the only game in town. One glance at the menu will tell you that the high prices (no entree seems to be under $20) are designed to discourage all but the who-cares-what-it-costs types who arrive by boat, anchor offshore, and come in to eat.

Peter Island is for those who love beautiful beaches and water sports and don't need a lot of high-level activity. You're on your own here, with all the toys at your disposal.

Address/Phone: P.O. Box 211, Road Town, Tortola, B.V.I.; or P.O. Box 9409, St. Thomas, U.S.V.I. 00801; (809) 494–2561; fax: (809) 494–2313

U.S. Reservations: (800) 346–4451; fax: (616) 776–6496; Preferred Hotels and Resorts, (800) 323–7500

Owner/Manager: James Holmes, general manager

Arrival/Departure: Those arriving at the Beef Island Airport are met by a Peter Island representative, escorted to a pier right next to the airport, and taken by private launch to Peter Island, about a 12-minute ride. The resort also operates free round-trip ferry service several times a day to its dock at Baughers Bay, in Tortola. Helicopter transfers can be arranged from St. Thomas, San Juan, or several other islands. Peter Island has its own lighted helipad.

Distance from Beef Island Airport: About 4 miles by sea
Distance from Tortola: 4 miles
Accommodations: 54 rooms and suites: 30 with ocean or harbor view, 20 junior suites on beach
Best Rooms/Suites: Go for the beachfront suites.
Amenities: Air-conditioning, ceiling fans, minibar, Amway toiletries, coffeemaker, double sinks, hair dryer, bathrobes, umbrellas, and bug spray
Electricity: 110 volts
Sports and Facilities: Sunfish, windsurfers, kayaks, floaters, snorkeling gear, dive center (DIVE BVI), and fleet of Bertrams for fishing charters; 4 Tru-flex tennis courts (2 lighted) and tennis equipment; fitness trail with several "shape-up" stops and hiking trails; pool
Dress Code: Casual by day; casually elegant by night. No tie required at dinner, but men requested to wear sport jacket.
Weddings: Can be arranged. Good locations include the Crow's Nest, a spectacular villa on the highest part of the island; a lookout gazebo at the top of a hill; Honeymoon Beach, and the dining terrace.
Rates/Packages: $245–$525 per person per night. The meal plan is $65 extra per person per day for breakfast and dinner and $85 for all three meals, plus 15 percent gratuity. Two-bedroom/two-bath villas are priced from $475 per day. If you want to do a lot of diving, consider the Aqua Adventures package, priced from $3,150 per couple, for 7 nights, including room, meals, dives, and resort course. Perhaps your best bet is the Island Romance package, priced from $2,725 per couple for room, meals, day sail to Virgin Gorda, champagne, and photo album. For the truly rich and indulgent, there is the Crow's Nest, a luxurious hilltop villa that leases for $3,900 per day in high season (mid-December through mid-April). If you want to combine your stay on Peter Island with 1 or 2 overnights at sea on the resort's yacht with guide, cook, and crew, 4- and 7-night packages are available from $1,885 and $3,425, respectively.
Payment/Credit Cards: Most major
Deposit: 3 nights, due 10 days after reservations are made. Packages require full amount due 20 days after reservations; cancel 30 days prior to arrival date for refund.
Government Taxes: Included
Service Charges: Included
Entry Requirements for U.S. Citizens: Proof of citizenship necessary. Passport best, but an authenticated birth certificate, a citizenship certificate, or a voter's registration card with photo ID is acceptable.

Cayman Islands

Grand Cayman

Hyatt Regency Grand Cayman

Location: Directly across from Seven Mile Beach.
Romantic Features: Seven Mile Beach at sunset; tropical walkways laced through the property; sunset sail on the 65-foot *Spirit of Ppalu* catamaran.

Basking in the sun, playing golf on a unique championship course, and a side order of super scuba and snorkeling are all part of the honeymoon experience at the Hyatt Regency Grand Cayman. Entering the resort's palm-lined driveway you quickly leave the hubbub of life back home far behind. The Hyatt's British-inspired, low-rise colonial buildings are surrounded by lush green foliage and a rainbow of tropical flowers. The Caribbean is just across the way.

The pastel colors of the six buildings, all offset by the brilliant blue sky, set the mood. After checking in, couples who have requested the Honeymoon package are escorted out of the reception area past a stunning reflecting pool and tropical garden—the centerpiece of the Hyatt's courtyard—to a luxurious guest room, where a chilled bottle of champagne awaits. Rooms are typically Hyatt with a light tropical twist, but every amenity you could wish for is there, including for some, a garden Jacuzzi. Regency Club rooms located in a separate building are extra special and offer more amenities, private concierge, and complimentary continental breakfast and evening cocktails.

As you walk through the courtyard and gardens, all beautifully manicured, at every turn along the path you'll find romantic little enclaves. Whether it's a bench set in an alcove by a pond or a bridge over a stream running through the property, the setting seems designed for couples in love. The ⅓-acre free-form pool has a great swim-up bar, which serves some fabulous frozen drinks.

The Britannia Beach Club will be high on your exploration list. Located across the street, on Hyatt's pearl-white sand strip of Seven Mile Beach, it is here where you may encounter your toughest dilemma. What to do? Lie back and relax at the edge of the crystal-clear Caribbean with a dark rum and orange juice from the Britannia Beach Club's bar, or choose from the almost overwhelming number of activities available through Red Sail Sports—windsurfing, parasailing, Waverunners, and more.

After unwinding for a few days, if you crave some adventure, try scuba diving. Not certified? No problem. A resort course is available for beginners. You'll learn to dive in one day, and at the end of it all, you'll understand why the Grand Cayman is called the underwater capital of the Caribbean.

For a unique experience, don't miss the 20-foot dive to Stingray City, where you'll feed the stingrays and perhaps catch a glimpse of Psycho, the dive master's "friendly" pet eel! Even if you don't dive, take the trip with your snorkeling gear and watch the scene from on top of the water. But don't think you'll avoid an encounter with the stingrays, as the dive master usually coaxes the rays to the top for a closer look at guess who? You.

A dive along the famous North Wall is a fascinating Cayman exclusive—one sure to provide scuba enthusiasts with new thrills. For those nondivers who don't want to miss the sights, Atlantis Submarines offers several unique services. Choose from a personal submarine trip for two (with a captain) or a voyage aboard one of its larger subs. Both submerge to depths of over 100 feet. Through the Cayman's crystal-clear waters (there's a minimum $500,000 fine for dumping anything into the water), you'll see every type of tropical fish you've ever seen in an aquarium and then some. The corals and underwater "road" systems may even give you that needed push to try the one-day resort scuba course to get a closer look at this magnificent underwater world. Look carefully and you may spot some sea turtles!

After the excitement of Stingray City, all you may be up for is finding a lounge chair and watching the sun sink in the horizon while Calypso music plays in the background.

By this time you've probably worked up quite an appetite. The award-winning Hemingway's, located at the Britannia Beach Club directly on Seven Mile Beach, provides a wonderful setting for a romantic dinner for two. With some of the best cuisine on the Island, Hemingway's specialty is, of course, Caribbean cuisine, including fresh fish and seafood. The swordfish and crab cakes are a must-try!

If you have any time left for other activities, try golf. The Hyatt offers a unique Jack Nicklaus–designed layout. Says Victor Lopez, divisional vice president for Hyatt Hotels & Resorts, "The course configuration varies depending upon where the tees are located, so the forty-acre course can be played three ways: regulation golf, executive course golf, or Cayman ball." It's a challenge any way you play it.

For pure luxury in a tropical setting, with appealing activities and dining options, the Hyatt Grand Cayman delivers.

Address/Phone: Hyatt Regency Grand Cayman, Seven Mile Beach, Grand Cayman, B.W.I.; (809) 949–1234; fax: (809) 949–8528

U.S. Reservations: Hyatt Resorts, (800)233–1234

Owner/Manager: Ellesmere Britannia of Canada, owner; Hyatt Hotels & Resorts, operator; Doug Sears, general manager.

Arrival/Departure: Taxis available at airport; transfers can be arranged (are not included in the Honeymoon package).

Distance from Owens Roberts Airport: 5 miles (8 minutes)

Distance from Georgetown: 2 miles

Accommodations: 235 rooms and suites in 6 buildings; 44 Regency Club rooms, 2 Bilevel suites, and 35 villas offering one to four bedrooms with kitchen and laundry facilities. Villas overlook the Hyatt's private waterway to the Caribbean or the golf course.

Best Rooms/Suites: Bilevel Governor's and Georgetown Suites.

Amenities: Air-conditioning, minibar, satellite TV, direct-dial telephone, in-room safe, hair dryer, 24-hour room service, lotions, shampoos, and bath gels

Electricity: 110 volts

Sports and Facilities: Red Sail Sports has two locations on the Hyatt property and offers every water sport imaginable. Special activities include scuba/snorkeling trips to Stingray City and parasailing over Seven Mile Beach. The resort's golf course is designed by Jack Nicklaus.

Dress Code: Beach attire during the day; casual attire for evenings

Weddings: Arranged easily with the newly relaxed government regulations. A popular spot on the Hyatt property is the reflecting pool in the center courtyard. Weddings can also be arranged aboard the *Spirit of Ppalu* catamaran or for the adventurous couple—underwater. Advance notice is needed for all weddings.

Rates/Packages: $295–$415 per couple per night for a double room; $500 for a Regency Club room (winter); double $225–$345, Regency Club $415 (spring and fall); double $180–$300, Regency Club $370 (summer). Rates do not include 6 percent room tax or 10 percent service charge. For full breakfast and dinner daily add $62 per person per day. Honeymoon package includes accommodations, champagne, special Britannia honeymoon breakfast for two delivered to your room on the first morning (when meal plan is purchased), jeep rental for 1 day (minimum age, 25), sunset sail on the *Spirit of Ppalu*, massage for two, and a complimentary round of golf. Rates per couple: 4 days/3 nights $1,309, 8 days/7 nights $2,705 (winter); 4 days/3 nights $935, 8 days/7 nights $1,835 (spring and fall); 4 days/3 nights $829, 8 days/7 nights $1,585 (summer). Room upgrades for Honeymoon package available.

Payment/Credit Cards: Most major

Deposit: One to two nights' room rate required 14 days after verbal confirmation; refundable on advance cancellation received in writing no later than October 1 for arrivals during the Christmas season, or 14 days in advance for all other periods.

Government Taxes: 10 percent

Service Charges: 10 percent

Entry Requirements for U.S. Citizens: Proof of citizenship is required for U.S. and Canadian citizens. Birth certificate, voter's registration, and passport accepted.

Dominican Republic

Casa de Campo

Location: The resort sits on 7,000 acres, on the southeastern coast of the island.

Romantic Features: Moonlit horseback rides on the beach; vast tropical areas to explore.

Casa de Campo! It's big. Very big. It offers a mind-boggling list of things to do and it's got all the ingredients those looking for sun, sand, and sea require: pools galore, private beach, and lots of water toys, plus 13 tennis courts, an equestrian center, a fitness center, plenty of places to eat and drink, thousands of acres, a world-class shooting facility, splendid accommodations, and room service. What more could a body ask?

Want privacy? You've got it. There are 300 rooms and 150 villas, which may sound like a lot, but when they're spread out over 7,000 acres, planted with all sorts of tropical things, you can be assured of finding your own very special private places.

There are shuttle buses running regularly throughout the property, but you may want to pay $27 to $35 a day and rent your own golf cart. It's a great way to get around.

Casa de Campo, which is Spanish for "house in the country," has a variety of rooms and suites. Within the mix of accommodations are casitas and hacienda-like villas. The casitas, actually super-spacious hotel rooms, are located in one- and two-story clusters overlooking the golf links, which wind through the property. Designed and decorated by Oscar de la Renta, a Dominican, the stone and adobe casitas come with balconies, tile floors, louvered shutters, and designer furnishings. Two-, three-, and four-bedroom villas each have a living room, dining room, kitchen, terrace, gardens,

Casa de Campo, Dominican Republic

and maid service. They also come with private pools or Jacuzzis. All are exquisitely furnished.

Golfers will think they died and went to heaven, given the fifty-four magnificent holes to tee off on. This includes the world-class Teeth of the Dog course, which has been consistently ranked by *Golf Digest* in the "Top 100 in the World." Designed by Pete Dye, the course has eight holes that hug the rugged coastline, offering smashing views and teeth-rattling shots. Wait until you get those sand bunkers in your sights: Overshoot the bunkers, and you're likely to hit either the rocks or more sand—the beach.

And speaking of beaches, "lounge lizards" will be blissfully happy. There are three beaches, including the lovely, private Minitas Beach. Coconut palms and thatched umbrellas provide shade on the wide, white stretch of sand. Water sports include just about anything you can think of, from windsurfing to scuba diving. Package rates include some sports, but you may have to pay extra for things like scuba and deep-sea fishing.

Each of the nineteen pools is unique in design and patio landscaping; all are so inviting you'll want to plant yourself in a different one each day.

Play tennis, and you won't wear yourself out chasing an errant ball. Casa de Campo's tennis staff includes a number of ball boys who will run and fetch for the players. The pro will give you private lessons, or you can participate in the clinics and round-robins that are routinely scheduled.

Also located on the grounds is a shooting center, the finest of its kind outside England. It has a 110-foot tower and a variety of sport-shooting options.

There is an extensive equestrian center where you can learn to ride or practice skills you already have. Trails take you through sugar cane country and along the beaches. There are also an active polo operation, dude ranch, and rodeo arena.

Sitting atop some cliffs above the winding Chavon River is a must see—the Altos de Chavon. This replica of a sixteenth-century Italian village, designed by the Italian filmmaker, Roberto Copa, was constructed entirely by hand by local craftsmen. Cobblestone paths, stone carvings, arches, plant-shaded walks, and weathered stone buildings with red tiled roofs look very Old World, indeed. Although you might think it all a bit contrived, somehow it works.

Here you'll find a church, museum of archaeology, art gallery, art school, craft shops, boutiques, and four restaurants. There is a large outdoor Roman amphitheater, which has been the venue for a number of name-brand concerts and performances, drawing stars like Frank Sinatra and Julio Iglesias.

When you stay at Casa de Campo, you'll have a choice of eleven restaurants, running the gamut from gourmet candlelight dinners to barefoot-casual. Fresh fish like grouper, tuna, and red snapper along with quality meats and locally produced vegetables and fruits are artfully prepared. Try the banana milkshakes in the open-air, thatched Lago Grill. Enjoy the peerless views from the cliff-hugging Casa del Rio restaurant. Or have dinner prepared for you in the privacy of your villa. So many options.

Your best bet is to choose the Romance package providing you with casita accommodations, sports, food, and beverages. Villas are very pricey, and who needs to pay for an extra bedroom!

Address/Phone: P.O. Box 140, La Romana, Dominican Republic; (809) 523-3333; fax: (809) 523-8548

U.S. Reservations: (800) 877-3643 or (305) 856-7083; fax: (305) 858-4677

Owner/Manager: Claudio Silvestri, managing director

Arrival/Departure: Transfers can be arranged; Excel Club (a premium accommodations category) guests receive complimentary transportation from airport to resort.

Distance from Santo Domingo Airport: 1½ hours; La Romana Airport 5 minutes

Distance from Santo Domingo: 1½ hours

Accommodations: 300 casita rooms, 150 two-, three-, and four-bedroom villas

Best Rooms/Suites: Go for a casita nearest the location of your interests, such as a golf course, or the beach.

Amenities: Air-conditioning, ceiling fans, minibars, coffeemaker, TV, clock/radio, in-room safe, hair dryer. Excel Club guests also get private maid service, a scale, and bathrobes.

Electricity: 110 volts

Sports and Facilities: 3 championship 18-hole golf courses, Tennis Park with 13 red clay courts (10 lighted), racquetball court; aerobics in fitness center, gym, shooting center, 19 pools, equestrian center, polo, marina, hiking, full range of water sports, fishing in river

Dress Code: Casual smart

Weddings: Can be arranged

Rates/Packages: $125–$240 per couple per night (summer and fall); $180–$445 (winter); $235–$650 (Christmas). Romance package, $1,320–$1,648 per couple, includes 3 nights casita accommodations with king-size bed, airport greeting and transfer; champagne, breakfast, lunch, and dinner with no restrictions, unlimited drinks; unlimited horseback riding; tennis; water sports; use of the gym and fitness center; taxes and gratuities. Extra nights are $437–$546. Ask about special incentives and air–inclusive packages.

Payment/Credit Cards: Most major

Deposit: Secure with credit card.

Government Taxes: Rooms, 13 percent; food, 8 percent

Service Charges: 10 percent

Entry Requirements for U.S. Citizens: Proof of citizenship; passport best

Grenada

LaSource

Location: On forty acres on Pink Gin Beach.

Romantic Features: Lovely beachfront location; massages for two; especially romantic Great House restaurant, serving some of the best food in the Caribbean.

The only all-inclusive resort on Grenada, LaSource, like its sister property in St. Lucia, is themed around the ultimate "body holiday." In addition to a magnificent, long, gold-sand beach and large pool, LaSource has a wide array of pampering treatments in its Oasis Center, such as massage, aromatherapy, seaweed wrap, and salt and oil loofah rubs. It also offers yoga and meditation sessions.

The resort also has a highly energetic group of "body guards," who make sure everyone is having a good time. They'll join in the beachfront volleyball, lead you on sunset walks, and chat with you about Grenada's customs and history, if you're interested. One thing they won't do is infringe on your privacy. The bodyguards are adept in knowing who wants to be left alone and who needs some help in getting into the Caribbean swing of things.

LaSource's pink and buff–colored buildings with red roofs and dark wood trim are set into the hillside overlooking the sea. Connected by walkways and bridges, the resort is oriented toward a central courtyard, where you will find the reception building, gift shop, Oasis Center, and Great House Restaurant. Also here is the open-air Terrace restaurant and bar, topped by a soaring pyramid-shaped roof. Grounds are well landscaped, but because LaSource is located on the more arid side of the island, if you come at the end of the dry season (April and May), you will find the vegetation on the hillside less than lush. The resort has been struggling valiantly since it opened three years ago to establish lawns, flowering plants, shrubs, and palms, and it's looking better all the time.

The buff-colored beach is punctuated by the wind-twisted sea grapes and graceful palms, which, along with some palm-thatched umbrellas, give sunbathers as much protection as they need. The beach is long enough for a good brisk walk or a morning jog.

Rooms are a bit dark but well appointed, with mahogany four-poster beds, English-style fabrics and prints, and small sitting area. Suites, which are located at the ends of the buildings, have larger sitting areas with bow windows and are furnished with tapestry chairs and couches. The upholstery fabrics tend to be rather dreary, but the rooms are pepped up considerably by sparkling white bedspreads and large white eyelet pillows.

Windows open up, as do the doors leading to the terrace, but you will probably need your air-conditioning turned on, because the rooms back up against a hill and do not encourage cross-ventilation. On cooler nights, however, you can crank up your fan, open the door and windows, and fall asleep listening to the sound of the waves and rustling palms.

The terraces are small, with just enough room for two chairs and a tiny table, but the views are superb. Most of the rooms have ocean views, but from the standard rooms on the ground floor of the back building, you will see more roof than ocean.

The marble bath is bigger than average, and there is a small refrigerator in the room. (You'll have to stock it yourself, however, as this is not a mini-bar.)

The word is out in Grenada that if you want a great meal, come to La-Source's Great House. The resort's Australian chef is gaining a well-deserved reputation for creating some wonderful food. Whether it's a hearty fish soup, vegetable lasagne, or curried lambie (conch), here you really look forward to dinner. And wait until you try the chef's apple tart with a side order of homemade nutmeg ice cream.

The Great House is located one story above the courtyard level, and from its open terrace, you get a splendid view of the pool, ocean, and the lights of St. George's, just across the bay. White wrought iron chairs, pink lattice decoration, and banks of louvered doors make this a very pretty and romantic place to dine.

In addition to the Great House, there is the Terrace restaurant on the beach level where the weekly Caribbean buffet and barbecue nights are held. The restaurant and bar are in an open-air pavilion conveniently located right off the pool deck, so it's easy to drift from beach to pool to bar and restaurant. LaSource definitely gets high marks, not only for its food and body treatments, but also for the layout, which makes it easy to get from one place to another.

During the evening, there is usually live music for dancing. One of the regular bands is actually a group of moonlighting policemen who do a fabulous job of getting everyone on the dance floor. The music is just too toe-tapping good to sit out.

LaSource offers a long list of sports activities that are included in the price: waterskiing, sailing, windsurfing, tennis on two flood-lit courts; Ping-Pong, badminton, and scuba diving. Those who are certified get unlimited dives; beginners get a resort course and dive. If you want to take the full certification course, there is an extra charge of $375.

There is also a nine-hole golf course, but don't expect Doral. This one is strictly for fun and games, a kind of cross between a miniature golf course and a pitch-and-putt layout. But clubs and greens fees are included in the package, so try it out. Hitting the postage stamp–sized greens is a true test of accuracy and patience; putting tests your stamina.

La Source's location near the quaint capital of St. George's and its proximity to Grenada's lush green hills give you a lot of options for some interesting excursions. Check out the market on Fridays and Saturdays; hike from Concord Falls to another falls above, where you can take a dip in the clear, refreshing pool of water. Surrounded by lush green curtains of giant ferns and other plants of the rain forest as well as viney tendrils that cascade down the dark, moss-covered rocks, you'll feel rewarded for all that climbing. Or take a private "Jacuzzi" in one of the smaller rock pools along the way.

You can also charter a yacht and take a short plane hop or day sail to some of the neighboring islands, such as Carriacou, for snorkeling, swimming, and exploring.

Because of its location on Grenada's western shores, one of your special pleasures at LaSource is to snuggle back in a comfortable lounge under a palm tree and sip a rum punch as the sun sets all around you in brilliant reds, yellows, and oranges.

Address/Phone: Pink Gin Beach, P.O. Box 852, St. George's, Grenada, W.I.; (809) 444–2556; fax: (809) 444–2561

U.S. Reservations: (800) 544–2883

Owner/Manager: Gary Stephens, general manager

Arrival/Departure: A 5-minute taxi ride from the airport; complimentary transfers

Distance from Point Salines International Airport: ½ mile (five minutes)

Distance from St. Georges: 15 minutes

Accommodations: 100 rooms and suites in three- and four-story Mediterranean-style buildings; all rooms are alike except for the suites, which have an extended sitting area with bay windows. Each room has a balcony, and the top-floor rooms have vaulted ceilings. Rooms are priced according to location: 4 Standard rooms; 24 Ocean View Luxury rooms; 63 Oceanfront Luxury rooms; 2 Ocean View Luxury suites; 7 Oceanfront Luxury suites

Best Rooms/Suites: Suite 1519, third floor end unit near end of beach; Rooms 1423 and 1424, two Oceanfront Luxury rooms located on the ground floor in the end building, on a grassy terraced level with a private walk to the beach

Amenities: Hair dryer, air-conditioning, robes, ceiling fan, shampoo and conditioner, full-length mirror, refrigerator, telephone, AM/FM clock/radio

Electricity: 110 volts or 220 volts (110 volts outlet is behind bureau)

Sports and Facilities: 2 tennis courts lit for night play, Oasis Health and Body Center, snorkeling, scuba dive center, sailing, swimming, pool, whirlpool, waterskiing, windsurfing, Sunfish sailing, fencing, archery, volleyball, badminton, table tennis, aerobics, 9-hole golf course, gym

Dress Code: Casual elegance

Weddings: Wedding coordinator on premises; wedding package $375

Rates/Packages: All-inclusive rates include accommodations, meals, beverages (including bar drinks), snacks, tea, entertainment, transfers, sports, body and beauty treatments (except for manicures, pedicures, haircare services), gratuities and taxes. $240–$295 (winter); $200–$255 (early January); $210–$265 (spring through mid-December). Honeymooners are upgraded and also get a sunset cruise as well as champagne.

Payment/Credit Cards: Most major
Deposit: $300 refundable if reservation cancelled 21 days before arrival.
Government Taxes: Included; $14 departure tax at airport
Service Charges: Included
Entry Requirements for U.S. Citizens: Proof of citizenship; passport best

Secret Harbor Resort

Location: The deep, well-protected harbor of Mt. Hartman Bay, on Grenada's southeastern coast.
Romantic Features: Private en suite Jacuzzi with view of beautiful harbor through round window; spectacular views from every room.

There are those who yearn for what they consider the best of both worlds: a honeymoon at a lovely resort on the water, and a few days on a spiffy yacht sailing from island to island. Secret Harbor Resort, a Club Mariner property (the resort division of The Moorings) and one of the bases for the yacht chartering company, offers both in one great package. You get four nights at their intimate, twenty-room resort on Mt. Hartman Bay and three nights on a crewed yacht, complete with captain and cook.

Secret Harbor has more of a beachhead than a beach—the beach is pretty small. But if this isn't important to you, what you lose in sand, you gain in fabulous views of the harbor, which is cut into the steep hills, dotted with a few buildings here and there. Beyond the entrance to the harbor is the sea. From your perch on the terrace, all day long you can watch yachts sailing in and out, bound for the Tobago Cays, Isle de Ronde, or just a day's fun on the sea. The Grenadines, a string of islands stretching up to St. Vincent, are considered to be one of the best cruising areas in the Caribbean.

If you too want to hit the seas, you can climb aboard one of Secret Harbor's private yachts and cruise to some great little islands with deserted, white-sand beaches and excellent reefs for snorkeling. You can also sail to Carriacou, go ashore, and wander through the small fishing village, where they still make wooden boats the old-fashioned way—by hand.

The Moorings, considered the Cadillac of yacht leasing operations in the Caribbean, has several marina bases throughout the world. Secret Harbor is just one of them, and if you're a landlubber, it stands on its own as a fine resort, even if the closest you want to get to a boat is from your vantage point in the hillside swimming pool.

From the time you get up in the morning to a brilliant sunrise to when you call it a day, you can enjoy the ever-shifting world below. Several yachts are moored at the fifty-slip marina; others ride at anchor. By day you'll see sails being raised and yachts easing out into the winds; at night the lights from the cabins twinkle in the darkness.

You also get great views from the courtyard restaurant, lounge, and swimming pool, which is carved into the hillside just below the reception building.

The suites, though a bit on the dark side, are attractive and quite different from the usual Caribbean-style rooms. Each has two massive, elaborately carved mahogany four-poster beds imported from Italy; other furniture is similar. Beds are set on a platform facing the stunning sea views, framed by two large antique brick arches that divide the sleeping area from the lounge area and the stone terrace beyond. French doors open onto the terrace, which is furnished with lounges, chairs, and tables and is quite spacious.

Stained-glass side windows let in light but protect your privacy. Walls are built of stone and high, vaulted ceilings are of dark wood. Terra-cotta pots filled with flowers and plants along with decorative tiles here and there add to the ambience. Let your imagination wander, and you could be in a centuries-old cliffside Italian villa overlooking the Mediterranean.

The bath is decorative Italian tile, with a tub for two placed beneath a large, round, wagon-wheel window with another sea view. You also have a separate dressing area.

The restaurant, lounge, and bar areas are decoratively tiled and furnished with rattan chairs, mahogany tables, local art, and white wrought iron. All public areas are oriented to the harbor and take advantage of pleasant sea breezes, which waft their way through the flowering bougainvillea cascading over the stone walls and arches.

If you can tear yourself away from the views, you can enjoy Chicken La Grenada, stuffed with ham and bananas, breaded, fried, and served with a mango-ginger sauce that has been skillfully prepared by Morris the chef. Or you can try Chow-Chow Barbecued Filet of Fish, with paw-paw salsa and saffron toast.

Secret Harbor is a little gem of a resort, and when it's combined with a yachting experience, it gives you an exceptional value.

Address/Phone: P.O. Box 11, St. George's, Grenada, W.I.; (809) 444–4548; fax: (809) 444–4819
U.S. Reservations: (800) 437–7880; fax: (813) 538–8760
Owner/Manager: Evelyn Cvetic, hotel manager
Arrival/Departure: A 15-minute taxi ride from the airport; package rates include complimentary transfers.

Distance from Point Salines International Airport: 3½ miles (10 minutes)

Distance from St. George's: 5½ miles (15 minutes)

Accommodations: 20 bi-level hillside cottages, all with two double beds, large bath with Jacuzzi, lovely oval stone terrace, and separate sitting area

Best Rooms/Suites: It's a toss-up. Depends whether you want to be near the water or higher up with better views. Highest units are nearest the pool and restaurant.

Amenities: Hair dryer, air-conditioning, ceiling fan, shampoo and conditioner, refrigerator, telephone, coffee bar, tubs-for-two, AM/FM clock/radio

Electricity: 220 volts (English plug)

Sports and Facilities: Pool; tennis court; Jacuzzi; sailing on Sunfish, Catalina 14.8s, Impulse 21s; snorkeling; yacht charters

Dress Code: Tropically casual

Weddings: Can be arranged on land or sea; couple must be a resident in Grenada for three working days before the ceremony. The application process takes nine days of processing—papers can be sent down in advance.

Rates/Packages: Per couple per night, including complimentary water sports and tennis and one complimentary sail aboard a 43-foot yacht per 7-day stay, $225 (winter); $125 (spring, summer, fall). Breakfast and dinner per person, per day, $20. Special Fly/Sail fares available to Moorings guests; Honeymoon package $975–$1,549 per person, includes 4 nights at Secret Harbor and 3 nights on a crewed yacht plus welcome cocktail, fruit basket, all meals on the yacht, all soft drinks, beer and wine with dinner, immigration/departure taxes and customs fees when applicable. Hotel-only packages also available.

Payment/Credit Cards: Most major

Deposit: 50 percent of total; fully refundable if reservation cancelled 14 days before arrival (spring through fall), 8 days (winter)

Government Taxes: 8 percent; $14 departure tax at airport

Service Charges: 10 percent

Entry requirements for U.S. citizens: Proof of citizenship; passport best

Spice Island Inn

Location: On Grand Anse Beach.
Romantic Features: Private garden patios with pools; Jacuzzis for two;
patio a step away from the sand.

Sure it's on the quiet side, and it doesn't have marble baths and robes. It
also doesn't have TV in the rooms or activity leaders. But if being smack on
a great beach, having your own private pool in a walled garden courtyard,
and a large Jacuzzi tub for two interests you, then you should definitely
check out the Spice Island Inn. Here the white towels are thick and fluffy,
the king-size bed is dressed in high-thread-count linens, and the beach
chairs under the wind-sculpted sea grape trees are just too inviting to pass
by.

Spice is a well-seasoned beach resort that has been honed and per-
fected by its Grenadian owners, headed by Royston Hopkin and his brother
Arnold. The Hopkin family has been in the hotel business for many years
and really knows how to do it right. The resort has a high repeat guest
business, and heaven help the Hopkins if they decide to make any major
changes: They'll really hear it from their guests, who are happy with things
just as they are. And who can complain?

Set on 1,600 feet of wide, white beachfront are two meandering rows
of one- and two-story cottages huddled under palms and sea grapes. The
one-story beachfront cottages, where you literally step from your patio right
into the sand, have large Jacuzzis illuminated by a skylight, a sitting area, a
bath with super-size shower, and two twin or double beds. There is also a
terrace where you get unobstructed views of the water and the picturesque
capital of St. George's in the distance. If being on the beach is a top priority, these rooms should do it. But you will have to put up with guests walking back and forth right in your "front yard," as they go to, from, and along
the beach.

The pool suites are much more private, especially the older ones on
the northern end of the property, which have larger pools (about 16 feet by
20 feet) and raised garden terraces that give you excellent views of the sea
through wide breaks in the row of beachfront cottages. The pool, terrace,
and a large garden are all enclosed by an 8-foot wall that ensures your privacy. Your terrace comes with two lounges, an umbrella, round table, and
two chairs. Walls are draped with passion flowers, bougainvillea, hibiscus,
and other flowering plants.

The pool suites on the other side of the reception area are newer and
perhaps even a bit more private. They are also smaller, and when you sit

on your terrace, although the beach is only 20 steps away, you really can't see it. You can also choose one of the garden-view suites. These are located on the second story over the newer pool suites and have vaulted ceilings and wide, tiled terraces. Water views and sea breezes are superb from here.

All rooms have whirlpool bath; some have full-size hot tubs with all the bells and whistles. Most baths have bidets, and rooms are furnished with rattan furniture, original paintings by Grenadian artists, and tropical print fabrics. Floors are ceramic tile, and there are lots of louvers to open for cross ventilation, unless you want to crank up the mother of all air-conditioners; it's a big one. Lighting in the rooms is also more than adequate.

The property is well landscaped with a variety of tropical flowers and palms. Trellises, walls, and wood-slat roofs support lush vines, many covered with flowers like the showy, yellow buttercups.

The open-air bar and restaurant are adjacent to the beach, and there is entertainment three or more times a week; you can enjoy dancing to steel band music or a piano. Cuisine includes fresh local specialties and international dishes.

At the water sports center, you can arrange for complimentary snorkeling, windsurfing, and other water-based activities, and there is a tennis court that provides racquets if you need them. Lessons are extra. A boutique is also located on the property.

Spice is located near St. George's and is thus close to "the action," but Grenada is not a place you come to for a lively nightlife. There are a couple of local clubs, such as Fantasia 2001 and Le Sucrier, nearby, and a weekly Rhum Runner Cruise, where it is party time big time, but in general, you will have to be content with dancing to Spice's band, walking in the moonlight on the beach, sitting on your patio as the sun sets, and taking midnight swims in the sea or your own pool.

Grenada has a lot to offer in the way of hiking, scuba diving, and just sheer beauty. Its people couldn't be friendlier; its waters more inviting. Still relatively undiscovered by Americans, Grenada gives you a lot for your money. For those who love the beach and privacy, Spice is a real winner.

Address/Phone: P.O. Box 6, Grand Anse Beach, Grenada, W.I.; (809) 444–4423; fax: (809) 444–4807

U.S. Reservations: (800) 223–9815

Owner/Manager: Royston Hopkin, chairman and managing director; Arnold Hopkin, deputy chairman and deputy managing director; Augustus Cruickshank, general manager

Arrival/Departure: The resort is a 10-minute taxi ride from the airport (about $15).

Distance from Point Salines International Airport: 3 miles
Distance from St. George's: 6 miles (10 minutes)
Accommodations: 17 private pool suites and 39 whirlpool suites (beachfront and garden-view)
Best Rooms/Suites: Numbers 36, 37, 39, 41, 42, and 43 are large, private pool suites with the best views of the sea.
Amenities: Whirlpool tub for two or hot tub, bidet, hair dryer, air-conditioning, ceiling fan, shampoo and conditioner, telephone, AM/FM clock/radio, coffee and tea bar, minibar, room service, in-room safe; nightly turndown service
Electricity: 220 volts
Sports and Facilities: Swimming at beach, snorkeling, sailing a Sunfish, windsurfing; tennis court (lit for night play); gym; scuba diving nearby
Dress Code: Casual elegance (no shorts at dinner)
Weddings: Wedding coordinator on premises; wedding package available.
Rates/Packages: $320–$475 per couple per night and $430–$585 all-inclusive (winter); $250–$345 and $360–$455 all-inclusive (spring–fall). Honeymoon package, from $3,385, includes 7 nights in pool suite accommodation with king-size bed and whirlpool tub, all meals and drinks (except wine and champagne), water sports, bicycles, tennis, use of fitness center, bottle of champagne, taxes, service charges, and sunset cruise.
Payment/Credit Cards: Most major
Deposit: 1-night deposit during summer months; 3-night deposit in winter. Cancel 14 days or more (summer), and within 30 days (winter), before arrival date for full refund.
Government Taxes: 8 percent; included in Honeymoon package; $15 departure tax at airport
Service Charges: 10 percent; included in honeymoon and all-inclusive packages
Entry Requirements for U.S. Citizens: Proof of citizenship; passport best

Jamaica

Half Moon Golf, Tennis and Beach Club

Location: Set on 400 beachfront acres in Montego Bay.
Romantic Features: Clusters of villas and suites, some with private pools;

a wonderful beach; beautiful sunrises; candlelight dining and dancing
under the stars

Half Moon Golf, Tennis and Beach Club enjoys one of the most romantic
settings in the Caribbean. Put this together with one of the best managers in
the Caribbean, Heinz Simonitsch, part owner and managing director of Half
Moon since 1963, and it's no wonder that this resort attracts a sophisticated,
international clientele, including Sean Connery, the Beatles, Prince Charles,
and George Bush. Set on 400 acres of manicured gardens bordering a mile-
long, white crescent beach, most of Half Moon's stark-white, two-story,
plantation villas and beach houses are quietly arranged along the edge of a
lovely, palm-fringed beach. Gardens are interspersed among the buildings,
which serve as a brilliant backdrop for the red and orange bougainvillea
that climbs up the walls and hugs the arches. Some of the rooms open onto
wrought iron balconies; first-floor rooms have arched Palladian windows
with French doors that open onto a seaside terrace. The villas are really superb, with private pools and gardens.

Golfing couples will enjoy the excellent par 72 championship golf
course designed by Robert Trent Jones, and racquet players can challenge
their partners on the squash or tennis courts and meet other couples at the
tennis pavilion. There is a full-service health center with Nautilus and life
fitness equipment as well as aerobics classes, and there are biking, horseback riding, and paths for walking. Swimmers and sunbathers have a
choice of several freshwater pools, located throughout the grounds, or they
can head to the beach. You don't even have to get up when you want a
drink poolside or on the beach. Waiters will scurry to bring drinks and refreshments right to your chair. Snorkeling, scuba diving, sailing, windsurfing, and deep-sea fishing are readily available, and if you want to totally
relax, you can try a sauna, massage, or even an herbal wrap.

Your choice of accommodations includes deluxe rooms, suites, and villas, most strung along the beach and some set in the gardens. Rooms are
airy and spacious, and most have sitting areas. They are furnished with
white wicker and Queen Anne–inspired pieces made out of Jamaican mahogany. Black-and-white-tiled floors, sisal throw rugs and oriental carpets,
English flowered chintz, and authentic Jamaican art create an elegant yet
exuberant mood, somewhat different from the usual Caribbean style. Worth
considering are the Royal Beachfront Suites, which are enclosed in their
own garden courtyard with two pools and a central lounge reserved exclusively for Royal Suite guests, where continental breakfast and evening cocktails are served each day.

Half Moon has three outstanding restaurants, the open-air Seagrape
Terrace, the Sugarmill Restaurant and the newest addition to the family, the

El Giardino satisfies those who crave Italian and Mediterranean cuisine. Guests can select over one hundred different kinds of wines from several countries at any of the restaurants. The Seagrape specializes in Caribbean cuisine, and diners can sit on the tree-shaded seaside patio and enjoy dining by candlelight under the starry skies. If you're in the mood for chicken marinated in lime and fresh herbs, *duckanoo* (sweet potato dessert), or breadfruit vichyssoise, this is the place to come. During and after dinner, there is a resident band for dancing well into the evening and a discothèque for late-night fun.

Under the direction of the Swiss chef, Hans Schenk, the Victorian-style Sugarmill Restaurant is located on the grounds of—surprise—a sugar plantation, where you'll find the remains of a 200-year-old water-powered mill. Here diners are treated to dishes such as freshly made pastas, prime rib, flambéed entrees, and shrimp stuffed with ripe bananas and cooked in coconut batter. You can dine on the open-air terrace or inside while enjoying live music for listening and dancing.

For a change of pace, you can order room service and indulge in a lazy morning with breakfast in bed. Try the coconut waffles, fresh fruits, and Blue Mountain coffee. A Night Owl menu is available from 10:00 P.M. to 1:00 A.M. There are also beach parties, floor shows with native entertainers, and steel drum bands scheduled on various days. As if there weren't enough places to hang out, there is also the breezy, beachside bar.

Since the choices and quality of food at Half Moon are among the best in Jamaica, if not the Caribbean, take one of the plans that includes food as well as the various sports activities.The Royal Plan is the most comprehensive, followed by the Platinum Plan. There are also programs that allow you to dine around and/or stay overnight at sister properties (Tryall, Round Hill, and Trident).

Address/Phone: P.O. Box 80, Montego Bay, Jamaica, W.I.; (809) 953–2211; fax: (809) 953–2731
U.S. Reservations: Charms, (800) 742–4276; Robert Reid, (800) 223–6510; Elegant Resorts of Jamaica, (800) 237–3237
Owner/Manager: Heinz W. Simonitsch, managing director
Arrival/Departure: Transfer complimentary with Royal and Platinum Plans
Distance from Donald Sangster International Airport, Montego Bay: 6 miles
Distance from Montego Bay: 6 miles
Accommodations: 222 rooms and suites: 98 rooms, 78 suites, 46 villas; many with private pools.
Best Rooms/Suites: Royal Suites or beachfront cottages
Amenities: Air-conditioning, ceiling fans, hair dryer, minibar, kitchen (in

some units), toiletries, cable TV, radio, double sinks (villas and Royal Suites), in-room safe deposit box; shopping arcade with small grocery store

Electricity 110 volts

Sports and Facilities: 18-hole championship golf course, putting green; 13 Laykold tennis courts (7 lit for night play), 4 squash courts; scuba diving, snorkeling, windsurfing, sailing; paddleboats, glass-bottom boat; deep-sea fishing; horseback riding, bicycles; saunas; aerobics classes; 2 large pools and 19 smaller ones

Dress Code: Smartly casual

Weddings: A special wedding package, priced at $600, includes marriage officer, witnesses, flowers, champagne, video, cake, and photos. Allow one month to set it up. The fairytale gazebo, which sits at the end of a sliver of land that juts into the water, is a popular place to hold the ceremony.

Rates/Packages: The Platinum Plan, $280–$580 per person per night (winter), $225–$380 (summer); includes airport transfers, champagne on arrival, all meals, afternoon tea, bar drinks, minibar drinks, room service bar, dine and lunch around program, tennis, golf, sailing, windsurfing, glass-bottom boat ride, scuba diving, snorkeling, sauna, use of gym, bicycles, beach chairs and towels, squash, horseback riding, government tax, and 10 percent service charge. The Royal/Imperial Plan, $350–$650 (winter); $295–$400 (summer); includes everything in the Platinum Plan plus private car transfers, sight-seeing tours, room service, bottles of wine and champagne, golf cart, caddy fees, golf gift, club and shoe storage, club rental, golf clinic, spa service and health programs, massage, aerobics and fitness classes. EP (no meals, few sports) packages are also available as well as spa and golf packages. (Don't try to figure out what you are going to have to pay from their rate card; Half Moon wins the prize for having the most confusing published rate information. Call your travel agent or ask one of the reservation representatives.)

Payment/Credit Cards: Most major

Deposit: 3 nights required for confirmation; cancel within 14 days (summer); 30 days (winter); 45 days (Christmas) to avoid late charge of 1 night's room rate.

Government Taxes: Included

Service Charges: Included

Entry Requirements for U.S. Citizens: Valid passport, or birth certificate with raised seal along with two recent photo IDs.

Sandals Resorts

Sandals Dunn's River, Sandals Montego Bay, Sandals Negril, Sandals Ocho Rios, Sandals Royal Jamaican

Location: Montego Bay, Negril, Ocho Rios.

Romantic Features: Couples only; nonstop activities and quiet hideaway places; romantic restaurants; Stay at One, Enjoy All program—use all the Sandals resorts at no extra charge.

Sandals Resorts packages romance with a capital "R." Starting in Montego Bay, Jamaica, with the first property, Sandals now has more than a dozen (and growing) spread out over several other islands including St. Lucia, Antigua, Barbados, and the Bahamas. The resort company's all-inclusive, couples-only concept continues to score a "ten" with honeymooners for a number of reasons.

For starters, their Ultra-Inclusive plan, whereby you pay one price up front for virtually everything, is a real winner. Accommodations, meals, snacks, bar beverages including name-brand liquors, water sports, tennis, golf, tips, and just about anything else you can think of are all rolled into the package. Since many young couples have just a set amount to spend, knowing there will be no surprises when they check out provides a high level of emotional comfort. It also eliminates the "Do we have enough cash to eat here tonight?" kind of discussion. But no matter how good an idea, this wouldn't work unless the resorts themselves were really romantic and special. They are.

Guided all along the way by its dynamic founder and chairman, Butch Stewart, Sandals has attained a well-deserved reputation for consistently delivering what it promises: a "no problem," romantic holiday with all the bells and whistles. Standard with Sandals are king-size beds, beautiful decor, a whole range of sports and fitness facilities, every water sport you can think of, including scuba diving, and a staff that radiates as much good cheer as kids on their first day of summer vacation.

The fact that you can walk up to any of the bars and order a drink or food at will without having to sign a chit or pull out your wallet is a big plus. This also goes for the restaurants. You can eat at the same one every night or eat around. You can order anything on the menu—wine, beer, mixed drinks—whatever you're in the mood for, and it's all part of the package.

There is a huge list of activities available to guests, all complimentary. On hand to keep the mood upbeat and arrange special activities and parties are the energetic Playmakers. If you like to be on the go from dawn to dusk waterskiing, hiking, playing tennis or golf, you can pig out on the vast array of activities on tap at any of the Sandals properties. And if you tire of the scenery where you're staying, you can hop on a shuttle and spend the day and evening at one of the other Sandals resorts as part of their Play at One, Enjoy All concept.

You'll find many other young newlyweds to exchange wedding stories with on your honeymoon at a Sandals, and since the resorts operate exclusively for couples, you won't have to share your pool space with any kids. Many couples marry here and go on to make friendships with other guests that may last a lifetime.

Each of the Sandals properties offers the same quality of services and amenities. Where you choose to stay, however, will depend on what is really important to you. Each place has its own unique allure.

Sandals Montego Bay, the oldest of the properties and one of the most intimate, enjoys a wonderful beach. Its 243 rooms and suites are located in two-story buildings and two-unit cottages that are literally a stone's throw from the sand. The lobby is not as elegant as those of the other properties, and the resort's location close to the airport can be a distraction. However, the staff and guests cheerfully make light of the occasional jets that zoom in and out by waving to them—a Montego Bay tradition. And being so close to the airport means you can land, clear customs, and be on the beach inside about a half hour. The beachfront suite with separate sitting room, marble bath, four-poster bed, and patio with a private pool is wonderful. And especially good here are the restaurants.

The 190-room Sandals Royal Jamaican is also close to the airport and is set on seventeen acres fringed by a series of six white, sandy beaches. The rooms, which are located in two- and three-story pink and white buildings, are designed in the spirit of a traditional Georgian great house and are elegantly furnished with four-poster beds, English flowered chintz drapes and bedspreads, and classic mahogany furniture. The buildings, arranged around three nice little pools, are named after homes owned by British royalty and look to the sea.

If you love white sandy beaches and don't mind being a bit out of the way, try the 219-room Sandals Negril. Ask for the loft suites, which are set into the palms and gardens along a 7-mile, powdery, white sand beach. It's about a two-hour ride from the airport and has a more laid-back ambience than the other Sandals resorts.

Set in a virtual Garden of Eden, Sandals Ocho Rios is like a botanical wonderland of flowers, trees, and shrubs. Hammocks are hidden in little glades, small streams bubble through the ferns and grasses, and bridges span the waterways. Two pools are action centers for high-energy sports like water volleyball and swimming races. There is also a smaller pool, hidden in the dense "jungle," where you can escape and simply loll around. If you're looking for a long stretch of white sand beach, you may be disappointed; the beach here is small. The views from your oceanside room are great, though, and the satisfaction level of the property's guests is high.

Sandals Dunn's River, one of Sandal's newest resorts in Jamaica, resembles a posh establishment on the Italian Riviera. Rooms are located in two large, red-roofed, six-story buildings facing the sea. Here the grounds have been sculpted, molded, and planted to the nines, creating a playground of pleasure. The largest pool in Jamaica, with its own waterfall and swim-up bar, along with seaside gazebos, Jacuzzis, bridges, and a piano bar are spread out over a large area. Rooms are elegantly furnished, and the beach is good.

You might assume, since the food is already included and paid for, that a place like Sandals could get away with providing rather average restaurants. Not so. At Sandals, the restaurant side of the resort operation is first-rate. Dinners feature a la carte menus, and couples can dine alone or with other couples. Breakfast and lunch are buffets, but a nice Sandals touch is the "white glove" service—a waiter carries your tray to your table. Each resort averages four restaurants, and all offer a distinctly different dining experience, ranging from informal to elegantly casual. Most of the restaurants are oriented to the sea, and the Bali Hai restaurant at Royal Jamaican is actually on its own little island.

If you like Italian food, you can head to Cuccina Romana, the new restaurant at Sandals Montego Bay, where you can dine on a freshly made pasta of your choice while enjoying the sunset view from your table on the open-air deck. Next door, at Sandals Royal Jamaican, the Courtyard Grille treats its diners to Spanish cuisine. If the flair and flourish of a teppanyaki Japanese restaurant is tempting, you can try Kimonos at Sandals Negril. Here you'll dine on exotic oriental entrees prepared right in front of you.

Sandals went all the way to Holland to find an authentic Indonesian chef for Bali Hai. Since the restaurant is located just offshore from Sandals Royal Jamaican, getting there via the resort's private boat launch is part of the fun. Once you arrive at the entrance of the ornate, carved-wood building, a hostess wraps a colorful silk scarf around you, your "costume" for the evening. Diners sit at long tables where hot and spicy as well as mild dishes (for more timid palates) are placed in the center for everyone to sample.

In the elegant category, Sandals Montego Bay's Oleander Room, brainchild of Horace Peterkin, the resort's enterprising general manager, has stenciling on the ceiling, and a warm coral decor accented with brass lamps, chandeliers, and Palladian windows overlooking the sea. Most romantic.

Get hungry between meals? Each Sandals resort has an "anytime grill," open well into the night, offering snacks as well as made-to-order meals. A new Sandals restaurant is located on the newly redesigned golf course at Ocho Rios. The only resemblance Upton House on the Green bears to the typical golf course restaurant is its location on a knoll above the first tee. The former clubhouse has been turned into an exquisite replica of an elegant Jamaican great house, richly furnished with antiques, English chintz draperies, ruby cut glass hurricane lamps, and brass chandeliers. The cuisine—gourmet French with a Jamaican twist—includes items such as shrimp Bavarois; fresh fish and vegetables baked in a paper bag; duck with glazed turnips, green beans, and a balsamic vinegar sauce; and chilled terrine of white chocolate and lime with a tangy ginger sauce. Chef Cadiou creates dishes that look as good as they taste. If you have any room left after the last course, you can top it all off with chocolate truffles, cookies, and a special house concoction of mulled rum and fruit.

Dollar for dollar, the Sandals resorts offer a lot of value and a lot more unexpected pleasures.

Author's note: Too late for a review, the new Sandals Royal Bahamian just opened in the Bahamas on Nassau's Cable Beach. Formerly known as the Le Meridien Royal Bahamian and in the fifties and sixties as the Balmoral Club, this lovely old Bahamian-style property is set on a superb white sand beach. I have every confidence that this Sandals will be one of the best bets for honeymooners in the Bahamas if not the Caribbean. It has 145 rooms and 27 secluded honeymoon suites with private pools and all the romantic extras Sandals offers. There is even an offshore island, the Balmoral, designed for theme parties and special events.

Address/Phone: In Jamaica, W.I.: Sandals Dunn's River, P.O. Box 51, Ocho Rios, St. Ann; (809) 972–1610; fax: (809) 972–1611; Sandals Montego Bay, P.O. Box 100, Kent Avenue, Montego Bay, St. James; (809) 952–5510 or 952–5515; fax: (809) 952–0816; Sandals Negril, P.O. Box 12, Negril; (809) 957–4216 or 957–4217; fax: (809) 957–4338; Sandals Ocho Rios, P.O. Box 771, Ocho Rios, St. Ann; (809) 974–5691; fax: (809) 974–5700; Sandal's Royal Jamaican, Mahoe Bay, Box 167, Montego Bay, St. James; (809) 953–2231 or 953–2232; fax: (809) 953–2788

U.S. Reservations: (800) SANDALS

Owner/Manager: Butch Stewart, chairman of the board; Louis Grant, general manager, Sandals Dunn's River; Horace Peterkin, general manager, Sandals Montego Bay; Baldwin Powell, general manager, Sandals Negril; Brian Roper, general manager, Sandals Ocho Rios; Earl Foster, general manager, Sandals Royal Jamaican

Arrival/Departure: Sandals guests are met at the airport and escorted to their resort.

Distance from Donald Sangster International Airport, Montego Bay: Driving time: Montego Bay 5 minutes; Ocho Rios 1¾ hours; Negril 1½ hours

Accommodations: Rooms, suites, bungalows: Sandals Dunn's River, 256 rooms and suites in six categories; Sandals Montego Bay, 243 rooms and suites in nine categories; Sandals Ocho Rios, 237 rooms in five categories; Sandals Negril, 219 rooms in six categories, including loft suites; Sandals Royal Jamaican, 190 rooms

Best Rooms/Suites: At Sandals Dunn's River, ask for the Penthouse Honeymoon Suite or the one-bedroom Ocean Suite; Sandals Montego Bay, the Presidential or Prime Minister Suites or the beachfront suite with the private pool (shared only with adjacent suite); Sandals Negril, Beachfront Honeymoon Suite or Beachfront Loft Suites; Sandals Ocho Rios, Grande Luxe Oceanfront Suite; Sandals Royal Jamaican, Grand Luxe Honeymoon Beachfront or Beachfront Royal Suites. These accommodations will run you approximately $500 more (for 7 nights) than the most inexpensive room but are worth it if you care to splurge a bit.

Amenities: Air-conditioning, king-size beds, ceiling fans, hair dryer, generous kits of lotions and shampoo, telephones, clock/radios, TV, minibar, and safe deposit box

Electricity: 110 volts

Sports and Facilities: Tennis day or night, scuba diving, snorkeling, windsurfing, sailing; Hobie cats, paddleboats, canoes, kayaks; racquetball, golf, pitch-and-putt golf, volleyball, basketball; pool tables, shuffleboard, horseshoes, croquet, Ping-Pong, aquatriking, squash, and waterskiing (except Ocho Rios). Also "Fit-Shape" program, exercise rooms, aerobics classes

Dress Code: Casual

Weddings: Over 500 weddings are performed annually at the various Sandals properties. On-site wedding coordinators arrange all the details including taking care of the paperwork, leading the couple through the process of getting the marriage license, flowers, music, and reception. "WeddingMoons"—Sandals's term—can be as intimate as a couple getting married at the beach or under a gazebo with a best man and attendant "borrowed" from the Sandals staff. Or it can be a more elaborate affair held at one of the Sandals villas with a reception for the couple's family and friends.

The base price of a Sandals wedding in Jamaica is $50. The package includes a prewedding massage for the groom and a manicure and pedicure for the bride, services of a justice of the peace or clergyman, tropical flowers, wedding cake, champagne, personalized candlelight dinner, and wedding video. Options include special treats such as sunset cruise, reception, gift baskets, and upgraded villa accommodations. There are many places a couple can choose to be married. Most popular are places like the gazebo at Sandals Montego Bay and the beach or the gardens in Sandals Ocho Rios. Brides can bring their own dresses or use one provided by Sandals. One bride who got married in Sandals Dunn's River wore a white, two-piece swimsuit with her veil, gloves, and garter. The groom wore a pair of white shorts, a bow tie, cummerbund, and a boutonniere attached to one of his shirt garters. Taking a quick dip in the Caribbean after the ceremony was "no problem."

Rates/Packages: All-inclusive, per person rates for 7 nights: Sandals Dunn's River, from $1,570; Sandals Montego Bay, from $1,310; Sandals Negril, from $1,515; Sandals Ocho Rios, from $1,385; and Sandals Royal Jamaican, from $1,355.

Payment/Credit Cards: Most major

Deposit: Guarantee with credit card

Government Taxes: Included

Service Charges: Included

Entry Requirements for U.S. Citizens: Proof of citizenship; passport best

Sans Souci Lido

Location: Near Ocho Rios, on Jamaica's north shore.

Romantic Features: Adults-only resort; private Jacuzzi; dancing under the stars alongside the beach.

According to legend, the natural mineral springs located on the grounds of Sans Souci Lido will fill the hearts of couples who take a dip with the power of the forbidden, passionate love secretly shared by an old English admiral and a Spanish maiden. All this aside, you won't need much inducement to feel the romance at this seaside property, which combines the elegance of a bygone era with the comforts you look for today.

After going through several ownership and management changes over the years, Sans Souci is now part of the all-inclusive SuperClubs family. At this upscale and quietly elegant resort, you can now enjoy the benefits of package pricing. Everything—even name-brand liquors, meals, golf fees, and scuba instruction—is all rolled into one price, paid before you come. Even weddings are complimentary.

Wedding Gazebo at Sans Souci Lido, Jamaica

Sans Souci enjoys a wonderful beachfront setting; part of it is tucked into the cliff at one end of the property, which drops to a white-sand beach where the newest suites are located. The resort's pinky beige, three-story buildings are cheerfully accented with white gingerbread trim and terraces. One of the oldest resorts in Jamaica, it has been drawing people since the 1700s to partake in the curative powers of the natural mineral springs, which still flow down the rocks to the sea.

In the 1960s Sans Souci established itself as a holiday residential community for wealthy Brits who purchased apartments on the grounds. In the 1980s, new owners renovated the entire place, turning the apartments into guest quarters. Recently an entire new group of buildings were constructed on the 400-foot beach at the west end of the property.

Over the years the gardens, one of the most charming aspects of Sans Souci, have had plenty of time to grow and mature. Follow the winding walks, which eventually lead to the spa, pool, and beach, and take in the beauty of the hibiscus, bougainvillea, red tulip trees, palms, and exotic flowering shrubs planted all along the way.

Rooms and suites that overlook the ocean are spacious; most have separate sitting areas and large balconies. The newer suites on the beach are decorated in soft, light colors and have French doors that separate the bedroom from the living room area. Baths are natural-colored tile and marble with double sinks, and many have Jacuzzis.

You have a choice of four restaurants, including the casual Ristorante Palazzina, an indoor/outdoor eatery serving breakfast and lunch; Casanova, which features gourmet cuisine and is the most formal of the restaurants; and for romantic dining under the stars, there is La Terrazza. Snacks and local specialties are served at the Beach Grill.

If you want to be active, there are plenty of water sports as well as tennis, golf, croquet—you name it. You can also relax at Charlie's Spa: get a massage, facial or manicure. At night there is music for dancing under the stars, and local entertainers often perform on the Terrace.

In French, Sans Souci means "carefree." Once you spend a few days here, you'll understand why the name is so apt.

Address: P.O. Box 103, Ocho Rios, Jamaica, W.I.; (809) 974–2353; fax: (809) 974–2544
U.S. Reservations: (800) 859–SUPER 7873
Owner/Manager: John J. Issa, chairman; Patrick Drake, general manager
Arrival/Departure: Transfers included in rate
Distance from Donald Sangster International Airport, Montego Bay: 70 miles (1¾ hours)
Distance from Ocho Rios: 2 miles (5 minutes)

Accommodations: 111 rooms and suites: 97 suites, 8 deluxe rooms, 6 penthouse suites

Best Rooms/Suites: Beachfront suite with Jacuzzi

Amenities: Air-conditioning, hair dryer, double vanities, whirlpool tubs (most), direct-dial telephones, TV, AM/FM clock/radio, minirefrigerator, in-room coffee and tea; 24-hour room service; laundry, valet, and dry cleaning services

Electricity: 110 volts

Sports and Facilities: 2 tennis courts (lit for night play), 2 pools; windsurfing, Sunfish sailing, waterskiing, snorkeling, kayaking, glass bottom boat rides, scuba diving with resort certification; Hobie cats, watertrikes; mineral whirlpool tub, natural mineral spring pool, beach; Ping-Pong, table tennis, basketball, volleyball, shuffleboard, bocci ball, darts, croquet; bicycling, morning walks, golf, aerobics, aquacize, fitness center

Dress Code: Tropically casual; jackets for men requested for dinner at Casanova

Weddings: "Super-Inclusive" weddings are complimentary and include marriage license, minister, witnesses, flowers, music, champagne, and cake. The ceremony can take place in the seaside gazebo, on the beach, or in the gardens.

Rates/Packages: 3-night package priced $1,035–$1,640 per couple; 7 nights $2,100–$3,325 (summer); $880–$1,380 for 3 nights and $1,785–$2,800 for 7 nights (spring–fall). Minimum of 7 nights and a surcharge may apply during holiday seasons.

Payment/Credit Cards: Most major

Deposit: Guarantee with credit card

Government Taxes: Included

Service Charges: Included

Entry Requirements for U.S. Citizens: Proof of citizenship; passport best

Swept Away Resort

Location: Located on twenty acres on Long Bay in Negril, at the western tip of Jamaica.

Romantic Features: Superb sports and fitness complex; a great white-sand beach; couples only.

Swept Away's romantic beachfront setting, gardens, and spacious villa suites along with its exceptional health and fitness complex have been wooing honeymooners ever since the resort opened just a few years ago. The spacious veranda suites, which sit amid tropical gardens overlooking

Swept Away Resort, Jamaica

the turquoise sea, are as tastefully decorated as they are comfortable. Jamaican in style and character, the decor is designed to complement the natural colors of the outdoors with the use of local woods, rattan chaises and chairs with puffy off-white cushions, king-size beds made up with creamy linens, red tile floors, and soft neutral beige fabrics. Your bedroom opens onto a very large veranda where you can enjoy the views of the gardens and sea. Rooms are air-conditioned, but you will probably find that the louvered window walls along with a gently turning ceiling fan will keep you cool.

You might be tempted just to chill out on your veranda, but you'll find it hard to resist the wide array of tempting things to do. Tennis buffs won't have to line up at the tennis courts to wait to play, as there are ten courts, five of them clay, unusual in the Caribbean, where courts are most often of the hard-surface variety. There are an Olympic-size pool, complete with lap lanes, racquetball and squash courts, an easy-on-your-feet aerobics floor, a parcourse fitness circuit, and even a basketball court. And if you want to work out, you can head to the gym, which has all the latest equipment. A free round of golf at the new Negril Hills Golf Club, five minutes away, is included in your package.

Sitting on a twenty-acre piece of pristine beachfront on the western end of Jamaica, Swept Away has a boatload of water sports, such as sailing, kayaking, windsurfing, and waterskiing. Certified scuba divers get two free dives daily, and you can join others for a game of beach volleyball—always a good way to meet other couples.

Swept Away earns a lot of kudos for its cuisine, which tastes as good as it looks. Since the resort stresses a healthy lifestyle, you'll find a lot of choices on the menu that are low in fat, yet very tasty. There is a fruit and veggie bar on the grounds and a beachside grill where you can get things like fresh fruit and vegetable juice concoctions, pita sandwiches, and fish sandwiches. When it come to serious eating, you can dine in either the open-air, beachside restaurant or Feathers Restaurant, which offers gourmet cuisine. Be sure to try the pumpkin soup and fresh red snapper.

When night falls, you can dance under the stars to the music of a resident band or you can sit back and relax in the piano lounge.

Newlyweds are invited to a special party just for honeymooners, where they can win a one-week return stay at the resort, a dinner for two at a nearby restaurant, catamaran cruise, horseback rides, or a 30 percent discount at the boutique.

You can be as active—or as lazy—as you want to be. No one coaxes you to do anything. One of the most difficult choices you may have to make is just what you want to do first. Do you want to dawdle in bed in the early morning and have room service bring you breakfast? Do you want to settle into a comfy chaise on the beach or by the smaller seaside pool, or do you feel up to the early morning beachfront power walk?

Swept Away packs a lot of value in its all-inclusive package, even a special massage class, where you can learn techniques to reduce and relieve stress in your mate. Just about the only thing you'll have to pay extra for are the services provided by the new full-service spa facility, where you can get massages and beauty treatments.

Address/Phone: Long Bay, Negril, Jamaica, W.I.; (809) 957–4061; fax: (809) 957–4060; U.S. address: 4944 LeJeune Road South, Coral Gables, FL 33146

U.S. Reservations: (800) 545–7937

Owner/Manager: Lee Issa, managing director; Jeremy Jones, general manager

Arrival/Departure: A representative from the resort will meet you at the airport for transfer to the resort.

Distance from Donald Sangster International Airport, Montego Bay: 60 miles (1½ hours by car); 2 miles (5 minutes) from Negril Airport

Distance from Negril Center: 5 minutes

Accommodations: 134 Caribbean-style veranda suites housed in 26 two-story villas

Best Rooms/Suites: Beachfront suites

Amenities: Hair dryer, telephone, in-room safe, ceiling fan, toiletries, air-conditioning; room service for breakfast

Electricity: 110 volts

Sports and Facilities: 10 lighted tennis courts (5 hard, 5 clay), pool tables, 2 pools, bicycles, jogging track, golf course, basketball court; sailing, kayaking, waterskiing, windsurfing, snorkeling, scuba diving; fully equipped gym; aerobics; racquetball, squash, volleyball; saunas, Jacuzzis

Dress Code: For daytime dining, women are requested to wear coverups and men, shirts; evenings are casually elegant.

Weddings: Swept Away averages six weddings a week. Complimentary with any package, it includes minister's fee, marriage license, flowers, wedding cake, two half-hour massages, and champagne. Popular places to wed include a thatched-roof gazebo and seaside at sunset.

Rates/Packages: All-inclusive packages are priced per couple and include accommodations, transfers, all meals, unlimited drinks, wine with lunch and dinner, late-night snacks, water sports and use of fitness facilities, afternoon tea, nightly entertainment, classes and clinics, two daily dives for certified divers, one round of golf, and glass-bottom boat rides. 7 nights from $2,765; 6 nights from $2,370; 5 nights from $2,100; 4 nights from $1,760; and 3 nights from $1,320.

Payment/Credit Cards: Most major

Deposit: 1-night deposit for 3- to 7-night stay, 3-night deposit for stays over 7 nights; deposit due within 1 week of booking; balance due 30 days prior to arrival. Cancel 8 to 21 days prior to arrival date for full refund; 3-night charge if you cancel 7 days or less prior to arrival date.

Government Taxes: Included

Service Charges: Included

Entry Requirements for U.S Citizens: Proof of citizenship required; passport best

Puerto Rico

Horned Dorset Primavera Hotel

Location: On four acres, tucked away on the west coast of Puerto Rico.

Romantic Features: Small, intimate inn by the sea; cocktails on seaside veranda as the sun sets.

The elegant Horned Dorset Primavera Hotel, which is hidden away on Puerto Rico's western shores, focuses more on relaxation than recreation and offers only a few facilities. The resort attracts solitude-seeking guests who want a small hotel with plush European standards. Located 2½ hours from San Juan, the Horned Dorset isn't the easiest of places to find. But once you do, you may never want to leave. And that is just part of its mystique.

Its name sounds like a weird kind of English pasta, but the hotel, directly on the pounding surf, is named after a breed of sheep raised on the grounds of the owner's upstate New York inn. No sheep are in sight, but still the setting is bucolic.

The grounds are lavishly landscaped with exotic plants. A recently built Spanish colonial hacienda with a curving split staircase brings you to the stunning, tiled-floor breezeway/lobby and an open porch cantilevered over to catch the sea spray. Below is a courtyard with a gigantic fountain, and beyond that is a large swimming pool with a wide lounging deck set up with Japanese umbrellas.

Off the lobby is a smaller, open dining terrace for breakfasts of warm banana bread, local fresh-ground coffee, finger bananas, papaya, and pineapple from local fields. Light lunches might feature fresh, grilled fish and a yummy salad. Drinks are served in the charming, wicker-furnished library, home to Pompideau, a pampered macaw in a huge cage.

The walk up the hacienda's stairway to dinner, with the tree frogs chirping a chorus, brings you to the second-floor dining room, where you are served a six-course prix-fixe dinner by candlelight. A member of the elite Relais & Chateaux group, the resort serves fine, French-inspired cuisine. A typical dinner might include Carrot Soup, Lobster and Grilled Vegetable Salad, Passion Fruit Granité, Roasted Sierra with Red Wine Sauce, Radicchio and Celery Salad, Assorted Cheeses, and Papaya Soufflé with Lemon Sauce.

As you dine, romantic ballads are softly played in the background by a classical guitarist. You can sit by French doors that open onto a balcony overlooking the ocean and the tiny beach.

The tropical grounds are extremely quiet. No pets, no TVs, no radios, and no children are allowed on the property. What to do? How about lazing by the pool or reading a novel from the library? Fishing, whale watching, and golf are only thirty minutes away and can be easily arranged. Or walk along an almost deserted beach for a couple of miles past a small fishing settlement.

Temptation in this languorous, lush bit of paradise lurks behind the mahogany-shuttered windows of well-appointed suites that match the plush public rooms in quality. There are Persian rugs over tile floors, jalousied and mullioned windows, roomy armoires, and large, lavish European baths with quirky features, like big, old-fashioned tubs and brass antique shower fixtures.

Woodwork is from island artisans, and four-poster beds, claw-footed tubs, and some of the only bidets on the island are unexpected amenities. All units have individual air-conditioning, queen-size sofa beds in sitting areas, and furnished balconies looking out on the water and beach.

A new ultraluxurious unit housing eight suites with plunge pools was finished in 1995, and these are the most superb accommodations.

The Horned Dorset is located in a part of Puerto Rico you may not even have a clue exists: quiet, quiet, and yes, quiet. No casinos, no discos, no glitz. Just the Straits of Mona separating you from another island far across the water.

Address/Phone: Rincon, Puerto Rico 00677; (809) 823–4030; fax: (809) 823-5580

U.S. Reservations: Relais & Chateaux, (800) RELAIS 8

Owners: Harold Davies and Kingsley Wratten

Arrival/Departure: Transfers can be arranged from the San Juan or Mayaguez Airports.

Distance from San Juan International Airport: 120 miles (2½ hours); Mayaguez Airport, 6 miles (10 minutes)

Distance from Rincon: 5 miles

Accommodations: 22 suites in five adjoining villas

Best Rooms/Suites: New suites with plunge pools

Amenities: Air-conditioning, hair dryer, marble bath, toiletries, ceiling fans; ice service, room service (breakfast)

Electricity: 110 volts

Sports and Facilities: Pool, water sports, golf nearby, scuba and deep-sea fishing can be arranged.

Dress Code: Semiformal, evenings

Weddings: Can be arranged

Rates/Packages: $162.50–$220 per person per night (winter); $112–$162 (summer); $63.25 per person includes breakfast, dinner, and gratuity; Romance package, $1,998–$2,998 per couple, includes 7 nights' accommodations, dinner, transfers, and champagne.

Payment/Credit Cards: All major

Deposit: Credit-card deposit for 4 nights (winter); 1 night (summer); for refund cancel within 45 days of arrival date (winter); 15 days (summer).

Government Taxes: 7 percent

Service Charges: 15 percent on food and beverages; 3 percent for general service

Hyatt Regency Dorado Beach

Location: Twenty-two miles west of San Juan on the north shore of Puerto Rico.

Romantic Features: Beachside casitas; long walks amid lushly planted gardens.

Formerly a grapefruit and coconut plantation, the classic Hyatt Regency Dorado Beach, which sits, along with its sister hotel, the Cerromar Beach, on 1,000 beautifully landscaped acres by the sea, gives you lots of room to spread out. This sprawling, former private playground of the Rockefellers was designed and built to respect the ecosystem surrounding it long before it became a cliché to do so. Lushly planted, the hotel supplies maps to guests interested in knowing more about the tropical trees and exotic plants; many are clearly labeled for identification. Long walks here can be educational as well as romantic.

To blend in with its environs, the Dorado's clean, modern lines are partially hidden in a cloak of palms, the resort overlooks two championship golf courses and the pounding surf. The main building, a modernized plantation house, looks to the Atlantic. It features a trilevel terrace restaurant aptly named the Surf Room, where Caribbean and continental cookery is accompanied by the sound of crashing waves. Service is excellent, and the nightly menu changes to reflect international themes. Big windows and a breezy walkway outside give this Hyatt restaurant added panache.

Another charming restaurant, housed in an original 1905 hacienda, combines Caribbean and Mediterranean menus, while a more prosaic clubhouse restaurant sells snacks to golfers. Food prices are high, and if you have to ask, you should probably choose another resort.

Drinks are poured at various bars and lounges, some offering live entertainment and dancing. Two pools will keep you cool, one Olympic-size with wide patios. Other diversions, all shared with the neighboring Hyatt Regency Cerromar Beach, include a casino, seven tennis courts, two championship, Robert Trent Jones eighteen-hole golf courses, and a complete water sports program—including a certified windsurfing course. The surging surf here is tamed by a breakwater, but the steep, curving beach is more suitable for sunning or windsurfing than for swimming.

If you like water play as well as swimming, a shuttle runs continuously to the Cerromar, 1 mile away, where one of the world's longest "river" swimming pools offers splashy fun. Rent a bike and pedal along trails laced through the grounds, which are planted with citrus, wild orchids, and over 600 varieties of native plants.

If you want to explore the area around the Dorado, you can head into Old San Juan and enjoy the pleasures of this old Spanish colonial city. It has some great shops with real bargains in jewelry and handcrafted items. You can also take a horse and buggy ride along the cobbled streets.

Completely refurbished accommodations in the fourteen, two-story buildings that flank the central section are designed to take advantage of views and ventilation. The spacious, air-conditioned units have earth-toned and pastel furnishings, terra-cotta tile floors, safes, minibars, telephones, TVs, jalousies, and terraces or balconies. Separate dressing areas and marble combination baths add a deluxe spin. Ground-floor units have double beds; upper rooms have four-poster kings. The three-story, pool-view wing, which overlooks the beach and is linked to the lobby by elevator, houses balconied superior rooms.

For privacy, there are better choices. Two- and three-story golf-view buildings have private verandas facing the fairways and are set in a cool coconut grove near the lobby and dining area. Most special are the casitas on the beach. With tile floors, ceiling fans, baths with skylighted showers, and terraces on the lawn sweeping down to the beach, these are the most romantic accommodations of the resort—a perfect place to hang out a DO NOT DISTURB sign, order room service, and watch the sun set.

Address/Phone: Road 693, Dorado, Puerto Rico 00646; (809) 796–1234; fax: (809) 796–2022

U.S. Reservations: Hyatt Hotels, (800) 233–1234

Owner/Operator: Hyatt Hotels & Resorts

Arrival/Departure: You might want to fly in to the private air strip, or, as most mortals do, drive in from the San Juan Airport. Taxis available at airport. Transfers arranged for a fee.

Distance from San Juan International Airport: 31 miles; Dorado Airport, 1 mile

Distance from San Juan: 22 miles west

Accommodations: 298 rooms, including 17 casitas and 1 two-bedroom suite

Best Rooms/Suites: Upper oceanfront rooms, which have four-poster king-size beds; or casitas, which have showers with skylights and king-size beds and are located between the beach and the pool.

Amenities: Air-conditioning, climate control, ceiling fans, hair dryer, bathrobes, minibar, coffeemaker, in-room safe, iron and ironing board, TV, clock/radio, telephone, toiletries; nightly turndown service, 24-hour room service

Electricity: 110 volts

Sports and Facilities: 7 tennis courts, pool, 2 golf courses; water sports,

jogging and biking trails, windsurfing school, health spa, computerized
exercise room, aerobics, in-line skating, Ping-Pong, casino
Dress Code: Casually elegant; jackets required for men for dining in winter
Weddings: Can be arranged
Rates/Packages: $160–$350 per couple per night (summer); $230–$425
(spring and fall); $345–$610 (winter); Honeymoon package, including
accommodations, champagne, a honeymoon breakfast, a candlelight
dinner with wine, and transfers, from $839 for 4 days; $1,515 for 8 days.
Payment/Credit Cards: All major
Deposit: 3 nights; cancellation 14 days prior to arrival date for refund
Government Taxes: 9 percent
Service Charges: 15 percent on food and beverages suggested
Entry Requirements for U.S. Citizens: U.S. Commonwealth; none re-
quired for U.S. citizens

St. Kitts and Nevis

Four Seasons Resort Nevis

Location: Set on 2,000 feet of beachfront on Nevis's leeward coast.
Romantic Features: Catamaran cruise to private beach; candlelight dinners
on your veranda; a pristine setting amid palms, sand, and sea.

Two plane flights, a short hop in a taxi, and a leisurely boat ride may
sound like a lot of travelling, but once you hear the rustle of the swaying
palms, feel the gentle breezes crossing the beach, and see the flourishing
tropical rain forest from your private veranda, you will no doubt believe
that getting to this secluded island retreat was a piece of cake.

Four Seasons Resort Nevis, which is part of the Four Seasons group of
prestigious, upscale resorts located in exotic locations around the world,
lives up to its reputation for providing a bundle of services and luxurious
appointments, such as the large marble baths and the Evian water sprayed
gently on your face by attendants to cool you while you lounge on the
beach or by the pool. This resort also delivers high prices and can make a
serious dent in your budget.

One of the best things Four Seasons has going for it is its location—
really spectacular, with a long, golden sand beach lined by what seem to
be hundreds of tall, graceful palm trees that blend into the hillside beyond.

It also has an impressive 6,725-yard, eighteen-hole Robert Trent Jones II golf course that climbs from sea level up the volcanic slopes of Mount Nevis to the fifteenth hole, where, from your perch at about 1,000 feet above sea level, you will see some incredible views of the sea and craggy hills. The course takes you up and down the mountainside, over deep ravines and along the ocean. What more could a golfer want!

Tennis players have a fancy complex of ten courts, a pro shop, and organized lessons and clinics. And if this isn't enough, there is a fully equipped health club, a complete water sports center, two pools, Ping-Pong, croquet, hiking paths, and myriad other activities that may pull you away from your lounge on one of the most beautiful beaches in the Caribbean.

Occasionally even those with a passion for *plein air* find it necessary to come inside. Because the restaurants and lounges have been designed to ensure maximum exposure to the outdoor environment, even when you are technically indoors at the resort, you can still enjoy a magnificent view, trade-wind breezes, and the sound of lapping waves.

Most of the public rooms are located in the sumptuous Great House, the heart of the resort. Many public rooms are open-air, with patios and terraces leading to gardens of tropical Nevisian flowers. The Library Bar is enclosed, cozy, and could have come straight from England—it even has a fireplace and paintings of tall ships. On the rare occasions when the sun is not shining, this is a wonderful place for cocktails before and after dinner.

The two-story bungalow buildings that stretch along the beach have rather uninspired architectural designs, but the interiors of the rooms and suites are spacious and decorated to the nines. Deep chestnut brown armoires, carved headboards, brass lamps, and botanical prints contribute to the British ambience. The use of rattan chairs, tropical-colored fabrics and prints, and tile floors keep the rooms from looking too heavy. Fresh flowers and potted palms also help lighten it all up.

The bathrooms will really knock your socks off. They're simply superb, with lots of marble, double vanities, attractive lighting, and plenty of fluffy towels. The Four Seasons toiletries are especially fine.

There are two gourmet restaurants that serve Caribbean-inspired meat, fish, and seafood dishes, and fresh fruits and vegetables: the more formal Dining Room, with its French doors, high ceiling and chandeliers; and the casual, open-air Grill Room. The casual Ocean Terrace overlooks the pool and the beach, and there is the Tap Room, with a game area and entertainment lounge, a pool cabana, and a sports pavilion.

Evenings you will be able to enjoy dancing and listening to local bands, including a steel drum group.

So if you don't mind blowing a lot of cash, be prepared to revel in one of the most ultraluxurious mega-resorts in the islands.

Address/Phone: P.O. Box 565, Pinney's Beach, Charlestown, Nevis, W.I.;
(809) 469–1111; fax: (809) 469–1112

U.S. Reservations: (800) 332–3442

Owner/Manager: Mark Hellrung, general manager

Arrival/Departure: Most fly to Antigua, San Juan, or St. Martin for quick
flight to St. Kitts, where guests are met by a hotel representative and
whisked to the private dock in Basseterre to board a boat for the 30-
minute ride to the resort. While on board, you complete check-in formalities and enjoy some refreshments.

Distance from St. Kitts Airport: 30 minutes by boat; 6 miles by land

Distance from Charlestown: 1½ miles

Accommodations: 196 rooms and suites, each with a large veranda ranging from 120 to 160 square feet, overlooking the ocean, Nevis Peak, or
the golf course

Best Rooms/Suites: The oceanfront Nelson or Hamilton Suites

Amenities: Air-conditioning, ceiling fan, toiletries, telephone, TV, VCR,
clock/radio, ice maker, minibar, hair dryer, twin vanities, separate
shower and tub, magnifying mirror, bathrobes, bath scale; 24-hour
room service

Electricity: 110 volts

Sports and Facilities: 10 tennis courts (3 lighted), eighteen-hole championship golf course, health club with saunas, whirlpool baths, gym with
Nautilus equipment; fitness program, aerobics, massage therapies;
beach, pool, snorkeling equipment, sailboards, kayaks, sailboats, sea
cycles, catamarans; waterskiing, fishing, scuba diving, croquet, volleyball, shuffleboard, and hiking

Dress Code: Casual elegance

Weddings: Wedding coordinator on premises can arrange all the legalities
as well as the ceremony, reception, wedding cake, music, photogra-
phy, and flowers.

Rates/Packages: $500–$1,050 per couple per night (winter); $200–$500
(spring–fall); Romance in Paradise package, $3,600–$6,200 per couple,
includes 7 nights in deluxe oceanfront accommodations, flowers,
champagne, and truffles, candlelight dinners, unlimited golf and tennis,
and half-day catamaran cruise to private beach.

Payment/Credit Cards: Most major

Deposit: 3-night deposit applied toward first and last night's stay (if staying
for a week); refundable if cancelled 3 weeks or more prior to arrival.

Government Taxes: 7 percent

Service Charges: 10 percent

Entry Requirements for U.S. Citizens: Proof of citizenship; passport best

The Golden Lemon Inn & Villas

Location: On Dieppe Bay, on the northeast coast of St. Kitts.
Romantic Features: Private sunning areas; intimate inn; a moonlight dip in your own villa pool.

This special, small resort got its name when owner Arthur Leaman's friends told him he had bought a "lemon" when he purchased the seventeenth-century stone and wood former Huguenot warehouse on Dieppe Bay. Leaman, a former editor at *House Beautiful*, decided to make this lemon into more than lemonade. He created the glorious, Golden Lemon, bathed by light that filters through the graceful coconut palms surrounding it.

Staying at this stylish, one-of-a-kind country inn in St. Kitts is like being a guest at a private home. The main building has been renovated to look like a plantation house, but with sophisticated pizzazz only a designer like Leaman could pull off: vivid, lemon-hued walls trimmed with white, painted floors, whimsical and offbeat mixes of old and new, mainland and local bibelots. All highly creative.

Breakfast can be taken on the second-floor balcony of the great house, lunch is served outdoors on a stone terrace, and afternoon tea is presented on the garden patio, ringed with lush, tropical foliage. Guests gather at 7:00 P.M. at the Brimstone Bar for a convivial cocktail hour with the scent of night-blooming flowers all around.

Dinner is the main event, presented at two long tables in the great house, much like a formal dinner party. Antiques glow under candlelight and chandeliers, and Leaman sits at the head of one table. Talk flows as smoothly as the fine wine from the resort's wine cellar. Seating is rotated over the minimum four-day stay, so you get to meet the other lucky guests who have spent the day luxuriating here or around this pretty island, with its fort and beaches. If all this togetherness unhinges you, you can ask to have your dinner served in your suite or at a private table—the staff enjoys catering to honeymooners. The fixed dinner menu is graciously served, and usually includes a soup, fresh fish or continental dish, local produce, and a grand dessert and coffee.

Exceptional guest rooms in the great house are filled with fun, style, and fantasy, and have names such as Parrot, Victoria, and Paisley. All are unique. The two-story villa accommodations of the Lemon Court and Lemon Grove are spacious and eclectically furnished with a combination of antiques, oriental rugs, four-poster beds, wicker, wrought iron, island artifacts, and objets d'art. Many have walled gardens and private pools right off the living areas. There are no TVs, radios, or air-conditioning here, and they aren't missed.

The Golden Lemon sits on a rather plain black-sand beach behind a lava stone wall. Industrious fishermen mend nets nearby, for the everyday life of the islanders goes on just outside the resort's boundaries. A reef located just offshore is great for snorkeling, and a tennis court offers a chance for further exercise. But this is not a resort for the hyperactive. Lazing around the main pool, reading a book, getting a massage, or sipping an island drink are popular activities. Or as Leaman will tell you, the Golden Lemon is for those who are good at doing nothing in grand style.

Address/Phone: Dieppe Bay, St. Kitts, W.I.; (809) 465–7260; fax: (809) 465–4019

U.S. Reservations: Caribbean Inns, Ltd., (800) 633–7411

Owner/Manager: Arthur Leaman, owner; Ann Spencer and Malcolm Nesbett, managers

Arrival/Departure: Guests are met on arrival at Golden Rock Airport and transported to the hotel; taxis are available at the airport.

Distance from Golden Rock Airport: 14 miles (30 minutes)

Distance from Basseterre: 14 miles (30 minutes)

Accommodations: 32 rooms and suites: 8 in main building, 6 in Golden Lemon Court, with pools; 10 in villa cottages, with pools and terraces

Best Rooms/Suites: Lemon Grove villas, cottages, with walled gardens and private pools

Amenities: Ceiling fans, telephones, hair dryer, toiletries; room service

Electricity: 110 volts

Sports: Pool, tennis court, snorkeling; scuba diving and hiking can be arranged

Dress Code: Casual

Weddings: $600 wedding package includes ceremony, flowers, cake, witnesses, and dinner.

Rates/Packages: From $260 per couple per night; Honeymoon package from $2,335 (summer) and from $2,825 (winter); one-bedroom villas with pool $3,175 (summer); $3,840 (winter); including 7 nights' accommodations, breakfasts, dinners, tea, champagne, sight-seeing tour, use of tennis court, 1-day car rental, massage for two.

Payment/Credit Cards: Most major

Deposit: 3 nights; cancel 21 days prior to arrival date for refund (winter); 14 days (summer).

Government Taxes: 7 percent

Service Charges: 10 percent

Entry Requirements for U.S. Citizens: Proof of citizenship; passport best

St. Lucia

Anse Chastanet

Location: Sits on 500 hillside acres on the southwestern coast of the island.

Romantic Features: Dramatic open rooms with spectacular views of the Pitons on the edge of the sea; huge open showers (one with a tree growing right through it); candlelight dining and dancing in the Treetops Restaurant.

There are no televisions, no room phones, nothing really to break the spell of tropical moonlight, refreshing sea breezes, and the scent of frangipani in this dense, green, jungly paradise that is the idyllic setting for Anse Chastanet. Your room may be wide open to lofty views of the blue-green pyramidlike peaks of the Pitons and the variegated blue sea. And this is exactly what Nick Troubetzkoy had in mind when he created Anse Chastanet.

Nick, an architect, and his wife, Karolin, have carved into the thick tropical forests on this remote hillside one of the most unique and romantic resorts you'll find anywhere in the world. This is the way you imagine a resort in the Caribbean should be—and better. Cooled by the sea breezes, not by air-conditioners; open louvers, and in the premium rooms, no walls at all, so that you can hear the birds, the waves, and the rustling of palms; and a view from your balcony that looks through the tops of the trees out to the mountains and sea beyond. Waking up to see the cones of the two Pitons framed by the arches of your octagonal "treehouse" can blow you away. It's that good.

There are only 48 cottages, partially camouflaged by the lush, tropical foliage that rises like a thick green carpet from a lovely, coconut palm–fringed beach. Thirty six of the cottages are staggered up the hillside, and twelve are located at the beach level; most have views of the two Pitons—Gros and Petit—that distinguish St. Lucia. As you walk up the hillside to your cottage, you may wonder if the climb is worth it. It is. The higher you are, the better the view and the privacy.

Each room is fun and dramatically different not only in decor but in shape. Standard hillside rooms are rectangular and slightly smaller than the superior rooms, which are octagonal or rectangular in shape and feature two twins or one king-size bed. Beachside rooms are quite spacious, with either two double or one king-size bed, a bath with two sinks, shower, and large balcony or patio. Although these are just steps from the beach and probably the best choice for those who can't or don't want to climb the hill, they have garden, not ocean, views.

It is the premium rooms located high up the hill that are so spectacular. Many guests have grumbled on their first climb up to their suite and asked to be transferred to a beachfront room. But after one night, would they move? No way. These rooms are just too special.

Even the showers are worth writing home about; many are as large as a garage. Ginger (number 14B) has a gommier tree growing right through it. Some open onto gardens, others to the sea. Most have no curtains or doors. "There is a fan club for every room," exclaims Karolin. "Even the original octagonal rooms have a loyal following."

It's not just that the rooms are super spacious—7B is roughly 30 feet by 30 feet—it's the way they blend into the surroundings. Mahoe (number 14A), for example, is totally open on two sides. The only creatures that will share your private moments are the birds (which you'd expect would fly in and out, but they don't). You have mosquito netting to drape around your bed, but unless you want it for the romantic effect, you really don't need it.

The Troubetzkoys have carried their good taste and creativity into the decor of the resort as well. Furniture, designed by Nick and constructed from local woods, has been made locally. Thick, puffy cushions covered in a cheerful plaid madras sit on the chair frames and beds. The madras theme is also carried throughout the property: tablecloths, staff uniforms, napkins, and bedspreads are made out of this traditional island fabric by local seamstresses.

Red tile or wood floors, original art by Reina Nieland, a Dutch-Canadian artist who works in burlap and mixed media to create superb abstract collage, and woodcarvings by Lawrence Deligny, a St. Lucian artist, are located throughout the rooms and public areas. Simple but effective basket lamp shades with yellow insect repellent bulbs hang around the perimeters of the rooms, balconies, and restaurants.

If you can tear yourself away from your room, you'll find there's plenty to do here if you like water sports, hiking, or relaxing with a soothing massage. Deborah Adams, the resident massage therapist, is available to give a variety of treatments, including reflexology, Swedish massage, aromatherapy, and deep tissue therapy. Charges range from $15 to $80, the latter for a 50-minute massage for two.

There is a palm tree or palm-roofed umbrella for every guest who wants some shade on the picturesque, volcanic sand beach, which seems to sparkle with diamond dust in the sun. At one end of the beach, you'll find the casual Trou-au-Diable restaurant and bar, two boutiques, and the scuba center.

Two more restaurants, a bar, and reception area are located midway up the hill. Dining up here in the Tree House Restaurant is literally dining in the treetops. You look through leafy green foliage and the feathery branches of the Flamboyant trees down to the beach and the turquoise waters, which slowly roll onto the shore. Breakfast is served at the Piton Restaurant, on the same level as the Tree House.

Food is excellent, especially the fresh grilled catch of the day, which might be red snapper or grouper. Fresh fruits and vegetables such as breadfruit and christophine (tastes and looks a bit like a potato) as well as curries are very tasty. Soups are a meal in themselves. And be sure to try the banana pancakes, a house specialty.

There is live entertainment six nights a week, a manager's rum punch party on Mondays, and an underwater slide show on Wednesdays. One of the Troubetzkoys' major commitments is to the crafts of St. Lucia. Already a woodcarver has his own workshop area at the northern end of the beach, and a pottery shop has been established on the grounds. Many of the articles these craftspeople make, such as the carved wood fish, can be purchased at the boutiques.

For scuba enthusiasts, Anse Chastanet is a dream come true. The waters off the beach are brilliantly clean and clear. A reef on the southern end of the beach, which is known for its excellent underwater plant and fish life, was recently declared a marine preserve.

Michael and Karen Allard, managers of the Scuba St. Lucia Dive Center, maintain a staff of seven fully qualified dive instructors and offer a complete range of courses and facilities for beginners up to experts. Dive trips operate daily to sites around the island. If you ever wanted to learn to scuba, this is the place to do it. After some basic instruction, you can actually take your first dive right off the beach, where the reef falls from 20 to 140 feet.

Whether you're diving or snorkeling, you'll find the reef alive with corals, sponges, black spiny sea urchins, chromis, sea cucumbers, and schools of fish in wonderful bright colors. A resort course perfect for beginners is priced at $75; the open-water certification course is $350.

A must-do while you're here is an excursion with Murray, Anse's resident horticultural guide. With a mother who was a midwife and a grandfather who was a witch doctor, Murray knows a lot about the flora and fauna of the island. One of the most interesting tours is a trip with Murray to the ruins of an eighteenth-century French sugar plantation located off the resort's Anse Mamin Beach.

A complimentary water taxi, *Peace on Earth* takes you to Anse
Mamin and Soufrière, just around the corner, the first capital of St.
Lucia and now a sleepy fishing village. In Soufrière you'll find some well-
weathered houses, shops, and a crafts market.

If you want to explore the many beautiful coves and small islands
that ring St. Lucia, you can charter the resort's 37-foot yacht for a half or
full day's sail and snorkeling tour. The trip costs between $200 and
$300.

Anse Chastanet is not for everyone. There are more than one hundred steps leading from the beach to the hillside rooms. So if steps are
out for you, you probably should go elsewhere. Anse Chastanet is also
not for those who need ready access to phones, TVs, and faxes. The
only public phones are found in the reception area midway up the hill.
There's a fax machine in the office, and that's it.

But if living well in spacious accommodations amid the stunning
sights, sounds, and sweet fragrances of nature appeals to you, then
think Anse Chastanet. There's no better place to be.

Address/Phone: P.O.Box 7000, Soufrière, St. Lucia, W.I.; (809)
459–7000 or (809) 459–7554; fax: (809) 459–7700

U.S. Reservations: Ralph Locke Islands, (800) 223–1108 or (310)
440–4225; fax: (310) 440–4220

Owner/Manager: Nick Troubetzkoy, owner and managing director;
Karolin Guler Troubetzkoy, director of marketing and operations;
Richard Barnett, resident manager

Arrival/Departure: Pickup can be arranged at the airport; the fare is
approximately $45 per car (four people) from Hewanorra Airport;
$47 per car from Virgie Airport.

Distance from Hewanorra International Airport: 18 miles (one
hour); Virgie Airport, 30 miles (1¾ hours)

Distance from Soufriere: 1½ miles

Accommodations: 48 rooms: 4 spacious, open-style, Premium rooms
on hillside, with dramatic Piton views; 12 large, open Deluxe hillside rooms with Piton or ocean views; 12 deluxe beachfront rooms;
16 Superior hillside rooms with wraparound balconies; 4 Standard
hillside rooms (smaller with queen- or king-size bed)

Best Rooms/Suites: Room 7F, huge and totally open on two sides;
14B, another wide-open room with a tree growing through the
shower; 14A, with a giant, four-poster bed and wide-open vistas

Amenities: Hair dryer (a really good one), refrigerator; tea and coffee
bar, ceiling fans; super-size baths (most), bidets (some), louvered
walls, toiletries; boutique

Electricity: 220 volts

Sports and Facilities: Scuba diving with Scuba St. Lucia; snorkeling, windsurfing; Sunfish sailing, hiking, swimming at beach; massage therapist; yoga and meditation instructor; tennis, table tennis; half- and full-day yacht charters aboard a 37-foot O-Day craft; plantation tour

Dress Code: Men requested to wear long slacks or long-cut Bermuda shorts at Tree House Restaurant

Weddings: Can be arranged; popular sites are the Tree House Restaurant or the beach; each wedding is treated as a unique affair. Wedding package priced at $390, with a number of options, such as private boat charter, live entertainment, and video available.

Rates/Packages: Double room, including breakfast and dinner, $360–$595 (winter); the breakfast and dinner plan is optional in the shoulder and summer seasons and is available at $50 per person, per day; double room $190–$390, meals not included (spring and fall); $156–$350 (summer); drinks packages to stock refrigerator can be prebooked or booked on arrival. Escape package includes 7 nights' accommodations, transfers, volcano tour, champagne, fruit, and resort scuba course; plus breakfasts and dinners, winter season only; $2,958–$4,078 (winter); $1,798–$2,708 (spring and fall); $1,498–$2,408 (summer). Scuba packages also available.

Payment/Credit Cards: Most major

Deposit: 3 nights in winter; 2 nights in summer and shoulder seasons; all weekly packages must be prebooked and prepaid in full. Cancellations subject to 3 nights' fee (winter) or 2 nights' (summer and shoulder) if notification is not received 21 days prior to arrival date, (winter); 28 days (Christmas) or 14 days (summer and shoulder).

Government Taxes: 8 percent

Service Charges: 10 percent

Entry Requirements for U.S. Citizens: Proof of citizenship; passport best

Le Sport

Location: On the northernmost tip of the island.

Romantic Features: Sunsets from your seaside terrace; body massages for two; hilltop Oasis spa.

Looking for a tropical sun destination that offers sports and activities geared to help you shape up your body and feed your spirit? Then try Le Sport. Tucked into a secluded cove between a high outcropping of rocks, Le

Le Sport, St. Lucia

Sport lets you really unwind and be pampered with soothing treatments like Swedish massages, seaweed wraps, facials, and salt loofah rubs.

Want more action? There's tennis, aerobics, jogging, golf, water sports, scuba diving, snorkeling, Ping-Pong, wake-up walks, and a whole bulletin board of activities. You can do it all or do nothing at all.

Since the resort is all-inclusive, you don't have to reach for your wallet every time you want to have a drink or meal, indulge in a massage, or try the windsurfer. Instruction, ranging from scuba and golf lessons to fencing and archery, is also included. Couples can even take part in a one-hour honeymoon massage class to learn massage techniques with their partners.

The stunning $3.5 million temple of pleasure, called the Oasis, sits at the top of the hill, overlooking the sea and the hotel, and was modeled after the Alhambra in Granada, Spain. It's a bit of a long walk up the hill to the Oasis, but what a view. Resembling an old cloister, the Oasis is built around an open courtyard. In the middle is a beautiful, serene, dark-water pool bordered by a grassy apron and several lounges set under low palm trees. Guests come up here for total peace and quiet. Even the pool aerobics, which takes place here once a day, doesn't upset the mood; music is not part of the program. Just about the only sounds you hear are the bubbling fountains that flow into pools. And from just about anywhere you sit, you can see the turquoise sea framed through the stark white arches and columns of the building.

There are more than thirty small treatment rooms housed in the Oasis, designed for such earthly indulgences as reflexology, hydro massage and tai chi. Many guests bring a book, suntan lotion, and towels and come up here to spend the day, leaving their lounge only long enough to keep their appointments.

Upon arrival, after filling out a health questionnaire, you meet with the medical staff and decide what treatments you want to schedule and when. Then you'll get a printout of your appointments. From here it's on to days of pampering and playing.

Down at the beach, you can waterski, snorkel, or swim. Sit under one of the thatched umbrellas and no one will intrude on your privacy unless, of course, you want a cool drink. Then all you have to do is to plant your orange flag in the sand, and an attendant will come to take your order.

There are plenty of activities for those who want to keep busy, starting with the power walk at 7:00 A.M. You can play tennis day or night, play Ping-Pong, take the resort scuba course, or go on an excursion to see St. Lucia's volcano and working cocoa and coconut plantation.

There are three pools at Le Sport, including a water volleyball pool, the Oasis pool, which is a lap and exercise pool, and a full-size swimming pool. Golf greens fees, clubs, and transportation are all included in the daily rate, and there is a golf practice area with nets, putting green, and sand trap.

At night there is music at the open-air beachfront restaurant, where you have dinner. Dinner is served by candlelight, and you can choose from a regular gourmet menu or one featuring *cuisine légère,* a lighter and more nutritious style of cooking. Monday nights there is a Caribbean buffet featuring a wide variety of local dishes and Thursday is barbecue night.

Later the beat heats up at the disco in the Terrace Bar and Theater, where there is often entertainment, with various local performers and an exceptionally good staff show. It's hard to believe that Trevor the dancer is also Trevor your waiter. This guy really knows how to dance!

Afternoon tea is served from 4:00 to 5:30 P.M. and includes finger sandwiches, light cakes, and scones. The air-conditioned piano bar is a popular spot to meet friends or just stop for a cocktail. After dinner, Le Sport's resident pianist plays from 7:00 P.M. until the last guest retires.

Rooms and suites are located in three main buildings of two, three, and four stories. The most desirable are the luxury beachfront rooms and suites, which have balconies overlooking the water and come with four-poster canopy beds, white rattan furniture upholstered in soft pink, peach, and mint fabric, and marble floors. The bathrooms are white Italian and rose-salmon Portuguese marble.

For those who are active and fit enough to want every imaginable exercise and treatment facility available along with a wide variety of sports activities, yet also want a relaxing, romantic Caribbean vacation, Le Sport offers this unique combination. And with everything included, it's one of the best values around.

Address/Phone: Cariblue Beach, P.O. Box 437, Castries, St. Lucia, W.I.; (809) 450–8551; fax: (809) 450–0368

U.S. Reservations: SunSwept Resorts, (800) 544–2883

Owner/Manager: SunSwept Resorts, owner; Michael Matthews, general manager

Arrival/Departure: Transfers included with weekly package

Distance from Virgie Airport: 7 miles (20 minutes); Hewanorra International Airport, 28 miles (1½ to 2 hours)

Distance from Castries: 8 miles

Accommodations: 102 rooms in three buildings. All rooms feature ocean views and individual terraces or patios. There are 20 deluxe ocean-view rooms, 24 oceanfront rooms, 56 standard ocean-view rooms, and two oceanfront suites.

Best Rooms/Suites: Oceanfront luxury rooms or oceanfront luxury suites

Amenities: Hair dryer, bathrobe, Gilchrist & Soames herbal soaps, lotions, shampoos, TV, telephones, air-conditioning, ceiling fans, refrigerators (deluxe ocean-view and oceanfront rooms only); room service for continental breakfast and fresh fruit; beauty salon on premises (extra charge)

Electricity: 220/110 volts

Sports: Snorkeling, windsurfing, Sunfish sailing, tennis, hiking, swimming at beach or in pools, golf, croquet, bicycling, fencing, archery, volleyball, Ping-Pong, stretch classes and yoga classes, variety of body treatments, weight training, aerobics, sauna, Swiss needle showers, stress management, meditation, mixology classes, and dance classes

Dress Code: Casual

Weddings: Can be arranged with a week's notice

Rates/Packages: All-inclusive per person per night rates include accommodations, sports, treatments, meals, beverages, classes, tips, taxes, and service charges: $200–$450 (winter); $210–$420 (spring, summer, and fall)

Payment/Credit Cards: Most major

Deposit: $300 per person within 10 days of booking; cancel 21 days prior to arrival for refund.

Government Taxes: Included

Service Charges: Included

Entry Requirements for U.S. Citizens: Proof of citizenship; passport best

Windjammer Landing

Location: Set on a hillside on Labrelotte Bay, on the northwestern coast of St. Lucia.

Romantic Features: Private dinner on your garden terrace overlooking the sea; your own plunge pool.

You can reach Windjammer by land or sea. Either way, you'll be impressed with this little seaside "village" of white villas with red roofs and white adobe turrets and arches reminiscent of Mykonos in the Greek islands. Narrow, winding brick paths, which meander up the hillside to the villas, are lined with a profusion of flowering bougainvillea, hibiscus, and oleander. Since the villas are clustered together comfortably, there is room on this 55-acre resort to explore: to poke around the nooks and crannies defined by the villas, gardens, pools, restaurants, and beaches.

An open-air car with a fringed top shuttles you up and down the hill to and from your villa to the beach, pools, and restaurants. But you'll find it tempting to laze away the day at your own private plunge pool, which is set in a tiled courtyard surrounded by flowers. From here, the views of the sea and the hills in the distance are magnificent.

The one-bedroom villas, with 1,200 to 1,300 square feet of space, are a perfect choice for a romantic hideaway. The living rooms are large and airy, furnished with wicker furniture with pastel fabric cushions that contrast nicely with the red tile floors and thick, round arches and windows. Cocoa straw mats, hand-painted tiles, and original art along with fresh flower arrangements add splashes of color to the white plaster walls, and lofty ceilings are light, pickled pine. There is a lovely tiled terrace with a dining area as well as a good-sized kitchen.

Water sports on the grounds are complimentary, including an introductory scuba lesson. You can join in the aerobics, participate in the waterskiing contest, go on a snorkeling trip, or take part in a sailing regatta. There are fashion shows, games in the main pool, beach volleyball, water polo, and calypso lessons. Tennis courts are lighted for night play.

Windjammer has three restaurants and three cocktail lounges along with a minimart, boutique, and on-site car rental office. One of the most popular restaurants, Jammers, carries you into the world of the South Seas with its Polynesian decor. Its sprawling, open-air veranda, covered with a thatched roof, is a great place to enjoy breakfast, lunch, and dinner. Seafood, grilled fish, and fresh island vegetables are superbly prepared by the resident chef. Try a cocktail of mango shrimps dressed in honey and ginger vinaigrette.

Dine at Ernestines, and you'll be able to savor dishes that reflect the Caribbean culture. Here you are served by staff dressed in traditional costume. The Conch & Bandshell is made up of gazebos, pavilions, and terraces where you will have a variety of dining options from 11:00 A.M. until late evening.

A wood-fired oven set into the wall is a feature of Papa Don's, where you can get pizza, pasta, and other good things. (You can also order a pizza and have it delivered to your room.)

Want a very private dinner for just the two of you? Just ask the kitchen staff to prepare and serve a special meal on your terrace. Start with Chilled Breadfruit Vichyssoise and follow it up with a Mille-Feuille of Fresh Mahi Mahi with a Saffron Cream Sauce and a Panache of Vegetables. You'll find it looks as good as it tastes.

Address/Phone: P.O. Box 1504, Labrelotte, Castries, St. Lucia, W.I.; (809) 452–0913; fax: (809) 452–9454

U.S. Reservations: (800) 743–9609; L.R.I. (Loews Representation International), (800) 223–0888

Owner/Manager: Anthony Bowen, general manager

Arrival/Departure: Round-trip transfers included in Honeymoon package

Distance from Hewanorra International Airport: 32 miles (1¾ hours); 5 miles (20 minutes) from Virgie Airport

Distance from Castries: 5 miles

Accommodations: 227 rooms in 114 villas: 21 deluxe; 21 superior; 35 one-bedroom villas; 27 two-bedroom villas; 28 three-bedroom villas; 3 four-bedroom villas

Best Rooms/Suites: One-bedroom villas (two have private Jacuzzis overlooking the bay)

Amenities: Hair dryer, air-conditioning, sun terrace, cable TV, ceiling fans, toiletries, bathrobes, in-room safe, cassette players, golf umbrellas, VCRs on request; closets are roomy; villas have fully equipped kitchen, microwave, blender, and coffeemaker

Electricity: 110 volts

Sports and Facilities: 4 pools, beach, PADI scuba program, snorkeling, waterskiing, windsurfing, fitness center, aerobics, golf nearby; deep-sea fishing can be arranged, 42-foot cruiser available for charter

Dress Code: Casually elegant

Weddings: Windjammer's wedding package is priced at $700 per couple and includes the ceremony, marriage license, certificate, fees, cake, champagne, photographer, sunset cruise, candlelight dinner served in your villa, taxi to and from the lawyer's office, and upgrade to villa with private plunge pool (based on availability). Options include a video, live music, and special flowers.

Rates/Packages: $230–$560 per couple per night (Christmas); $200–$560 (winter); $140–$425 (spring, summer, and fall). Honeymoon Plan, $2,100–$3,300, includes 7 nights' accommodations, champagne, candlelight dinner in your suite, sunset cruise, kimonos, complimentary tennis, Sunfish sailing, waterskiing, and transfers. Golden Honeymoon Plan, $2,800–$4,000, includes all meals and beverages.

Payment/Credit Cards: Most major

Deposit: 3-night deposit at time of booking; for full refund, cancel 7 days or more prior to arrival date (winter); 3 days (spring, summer and fall); 45 days (Christmas)

Government Taxes: 8 percent

Service Charges: 10 percent

Entry Requirements for U.S. Citizens: Passport

St. Martin

Le Meridien L'Habitation Le Domaine

Location: On French St. Martin's northwestern shore, opposite the island of Anguilla, the resort is nestled on Marcel Cove, surrounded by a 150-acre nature preserve.

Romantic Features: A casual but elegant Caribbean resort with charming French accents. The private cove setting is made for lost-in-each-other walks along the white-sand beach. Perfect for a 'do-nothing' escape, the resort nevertheless has the added attractions of fine continental restaurants, casinos, and elegant duty-free shopping a short drive away.

As your taxi coasts down the last hill, you'll find yourself relaxing. Your first criteria have very obviously been met. You had wanted gorgeous sun and sand and an upmarket full-service resort as well as the aura of a foreign destination. So far, so good.

Surrounded by lush green mountains, basking in the clear blues and whites of the sea and beach spread out below, L'Habitation sits amid French-inspired gardens abundantly planted with latticed flowering vines, red and yellow bougainvillea, hibiscus, and oleander. The resort is on the sophisticated French side of this small, hilly island. The smallest island in the world to be shared by two sovereign powers, St. Maarten/St. Martin offers an enticing blend of two European cultures, Dutch and French, combined with the beauty of the tropics. The island is considered by many to be the culinary capital of the West Indies.

The Creole-influenced architecture, accented by gingerbread balconies in island colors, provides all the ingredients for a traditional beach-escape honeymoon. The interiors of the resort do not disappoint. The Winter Garden Lounge, inside the main building, is bright and eclectically decorated with the changing displays of local artists. A mezzanine overlooks the beautiful, marbled lobby.

While all the rooms at the resort are well done, especially recommended for honeymooners is the new luxury wing, Le Domaine. A resort within a resort, the complex is situated to the west of L'Habitation proper. With its own pool and bar, Le Domaine comprises five two- and three-story buildings that echo the Creole motif. Room decor could be considered "rustic Caribbean," with wood country-style furniture and cheerful accessories such as hand-painted lily pads. You have a choice of king-size or twin beds (so ask!).

Both the spacious living room and bedroom have sliding doors to an oversized balcony with white wicker furniture. A unique, romantic touch is an oversized round tub set at the far end of the bedroom, overlooking the windows (drapes surround the area for privacy when needed, and there is a separate vanity area and water closet for the toilet). White tile floors are accented with bright rugs that carry out the country theme. The whole package radiates airiness and freshness.

At L'Habitation, you can choose from four excellent resort restaurants: La Belle France specializes in French cuisine made with local products; Le Barbecue is a casual beachfront eatery; open-air La Veranda serves Italian-accented specialties; and Le Balaou offers an elaborate buffet breakfast daily. If you want a change of scenery, try one of the many acclaimed St. Martin restaurants in the charming town of Marigot, which also has a number of wonderful little French-inspired cafes, some so close to the water, you can see the fish below.

Enjoy the two freshwater swimming pools and Jacuzzis, or take advantage of the myriad water sports available at the 1,600-foot-long beach. Adjacent is the one hundred-slip Port Lonvilliers Marina, where excursions and day boat charters go to remote islands for barbecues and sight-seeing; or take in a day of deep-sea fishing. You can also hire a helicopter to tour nearby islands.

A state-of-the-art hillside health club (it is also open for local membership) offers an array of activities such as aerobics, tennis, racquetball, and squash as well as massages. And, while there are some lovely boutiques at the resort, there is regular shuttle service to Philipsburg and Marigot for some world-class shopping.

A variety of nightly entertainment programs are staged at the pool bar and in the restaurants. Music for dancing is a regular feature.

Address/Phone: Anse Marcel BP 581, 97056 Saint Martin Cedex, F.W.I.; 590–87–67–00; fax: 590–87–30–38

U.S. Reservations: (800) 543–4300

Owner/Manager: Philippe Seigle, general manager

Arrival/Departure: Taxis available from the airport; round-trip transfer fee is $20.

Distance from Queen Juliana International Airport: 12 miles (30 minutes)

Distance from Grand Case: 3 miles; 6 miles from Marigot, the French capital; 7 miles from Philipsburg, the Dutch capital

Accommodations: 396 rooms divided between L'Habitation and the new wing, Le Domaine: 314 deluxe rooms, 50 suites, and 32 deluxe suites

Best Rooms/Suites: Book one of the deluxe suites in the Le Domaine section. These suites are on the second and third floors overlooking the tropical gardens and Caribbean Sea.

Amenities: Air-conditioning, hair dryer, direct-dial telephone, toiletries, satellite TV, in-room safe, minibar

Electricity: 110/220 volts

Sports and Facilities: Tennis, squash, racquetball; mini golf, volleyball, shuffleboard, water aerobics, jogging, water polo, horseback riding; kayaking, waterskiing, jet skiing, scuba diving, canoeing; fitness center

Dress Code: Casual beachwear

Rates/Packages: Rates per couple per night range from $190 (spring–fall) to $720 (winter). A 4- or 7-night honeymoon package is available, ranging from $770 for 4 nights in a double room (low season), to $3,250 for 7 nights in a deluxe suite (winter). Package includes accommodations, 1 gourmet dinner for two with wine, bottle of French champagne, gift T-shirts, use of health club facilities, free daytime tennis, weekly manager's cocktail party, complimentary casino transfers, and complimentary nonmotorized water sports.

Weddings: St. Martin's wedding rules are strict. You have to be on the island for at least forty-five days before you can be married. Why not consider this popular option? The rules for nearby Anguilla are lenient: forty-eight hours on the island before you can tie the knot. So book an elegant Anguillan villa for two nights (or choose one of the very upscale Anguillan resorts). Relax, entertain any family or friends that you've invited down, and get married! Then, charter a romantic sunset cruise that will deposit you right at the L'Habitation dock to start your honeymoon. If you've invited guests down to share the wedding with you, this cruise can make a wonderful reception.

Payment/Credit Cards: Most major

Deposit: 1 night's deposit due 30 days before arrival; cancel 24 hours prior to arrival date for refund.

Government Taxes: $3:00 island tax per person per night

Service Charges: All service charges for dining and accommodations are included in room rate.

Entry Requirements for U.S. Citizens: Valid passport or original birth certificate (or certified copy), naturalization certificate or voter's registration card, return travel tickets, documents for next destination, and sufficient funds.

La Samanna

Location: Sits on fifty-five acres of beachfront property on the French side of the island.

Romantic Features: Spectacular ocean views; private terraces opening onto a white-sand, pristine beach.

After setting a standard for the ultimate in luxury resorts in the Caribbean since the mid-seventies, La Samanna went through a period of decline in the late eighties. Under the new management of Rosewood Hotels, however, the property has undergone a multimillion-dollar renovation, including new furnishings and decor throughout the public and guest rooms.

The decor is light, elegant, and airy with lots of wicker, bamboo, and wood. Furniture upholstery and cushions are covered in pretty fabrics in blues, greens, and coral. Custom-designed wood and natural hemp headboards, large hand-carved bedside chests, limestone-topped dining tables on bamboo bases, and majavey-wood director's chairs for dining on the terrace provide guests with a comfortable, attractive environment. Appointments include hand-blown glass candle cylinders and classic Caribbean artwork. Suites have oversized sofas, mahogany desks and chairs, and new tiled kitchen counters.

The stark, white buildings, softened by the brilliant colors of bougainvillea, hibiscus, and other tropical flowers and the cerulean blue doors, stand at one end of a pristine beach, which you can see from just about every spot on the property. Very Mediterranean in style, with white arched windows and doors and terra-cotta tile floors, your room's terrace or patio opens onto the beach. The twisted shapes of wind-sculpted sea grape trees frame patches of bright turquoise sea just outside your room.

While at La Samanna, you'll be pampered with a number of special services. For example, you will have been asked prior to your arrival which newspapers and magazines you like and which beverages you prefer. Duly noted by the attentive staff, these will be waiting for you when you check in. Cuisine is French-inspired, although you will also find some regional Caribbean dishes on the menu. You can dine in the main restaurant or alfresco on the terrace. The bar, with its multihued Indian wedding tent ceiling, is furnished with comfortable cushioned wicker chairs—a lovely place to sip a chilled glass of champagne while you enjoy the cooling sea breezes.

There is also a new rotisserie grill located at the poolside bar where you can order lunch and beverages. Want to take a picnic and have lunch at a secluded beach? All you have to do is ask and everything will be arranged.

The pool is a serene haven for those who simply want to lie back on their cushioned teak lounges and enjoy the sun.

Water sports available at La Samanna include sailing, windsurfing, snorkeling, waterskiing, and swimming. You can also play tennis, exercise in the Fitness Pavilion, or charter a yacht for some deep-sea fishing.

The library is a quiet place to relax, read, or play a game. Browse through the rows of books and find something for the beach. Or indulge in a little shopping spree in the picturesque seaside village of Marigot, just 10 minutes away. Here you'll find a number of upscale designer boutiques along with some trendy restaurants. On Saturdays, the waterfront area is alive with the busy, colorful market where residents come to buy fresh fruits, vegetables, meats, and fish.

Address/Phone: P.O. Box 4077, 97064 St. Martin CEDEX, F.W.I.; 590–87–51–22; fax: 590–87–87–86
U.S. Reservations: Rosewood Hotels, (800) 854–2252
Owner/Manager: Ulrich Krauer, managing director
Arrival/Departure: A La Samanna representative greets guests at the airport and has a prearranged taxi service waiting for a prompt transfer to the resort. Transfer is included with package; others pay $15 each way.
Distance from Juliana International Airport: ½ mile (five minutes)
Distance from Marigot: 5 minutes
Accommodations: 80 ocean-view accommodations include traditional guest rooms, one- and two-bedroom suites, and three-bedroom villas, all with living rooms, dining areas, and private patios or terraces.
Best Rooms/Suites: The Terrace Suite is located on the top floor of the resort's main building on the cliff, giving you dramatic views of the

beach and sunsets. The suite has a thatched-covered terrace as well as an open-air, octagonal terrace affording guests complete privacy.

Amenities: Hair dryer, air-conditioning, robes, ceiling fan, toiletries, telephone, AM/FM clock/radio, minibar, vanity mirrors; nightly turndown service, 24-hour room service; daily newspaper, welcome gift; VCR players and video library available, TV and movie room located in main building

Electricity: 220 volts

Sports and Facilities: 3 tennis courts, pool, snorkeling, windsurfing, waterskiing, fishing, and sailboat rental; fitness center; massages and beauty treatments

Dress Code: Casual elegance

Weddings: Can be arranged (see L'Habitation for legal guidelines)

Rates/Packages: $490–860 per couple per night (winter), including breakfasts, use of tennis courts, and some water sports; $410–$625 (spring and fall); $325–$625 (summer). Terrace Suite, $1,300 (winter), $1,100 (spring and fall); $900 (summer). Add $70 per person per night for breakfast and dinner. Escape Package includes 3 nights accommodations, picnic basket lunch, rental car for 1 day, transportation to and from the resort, breakfasts and all water sports, aerobics instruction, and tennis (available spring, summer, and fall only): $1,200–$2,070 (spring and fall); $945–$1,845 (summer); with accommodations in Terrace Suite, $3,270 (spring and fall) and $2,670 (summer). 7-night packages also available, including champagne, rental car for 2 days, candlelight dinner on your terrace, picnic lunch or massage for two, and all of the above, starting at $3,220 per couple.

Payment/Credit Cards: Most major

Deposit: Three-night deposit; balance due 30 days prior to arrival. Full refund if cancelled 21 days or more prior to arrival date; less than 21 days, forfeit 3-night deposit.

Government Taxes: $4.00 per person per day

Service Charges: Included

Entry Requirements for U.S. Citizens: Proof of citizenship; passport best

Editor's Note: *La Samanna sustained extensive damage as a result of hurricane activity in 1995 and was closed for several months. At press time no reopen date was available. We recommend that you call your travel agent or La Samanna for information on the resort's current operational status.*

St. Vincent and the Grenadines

Young Island

Location: A thirty-five-acre island 200 yards off the southern coast of St. Vincent.

Romantic Features: Private tropical island; lush gardens; hammocks for two; open-air garden showers; option to spend two or three nights on yacht cruise through the Grenadines.

It seems like only a coin's toss from the southern coast of St. Vincent to Young Island, a private island resort set in a lush wildlife reserve. The colorful Vincentian parrots along with several other species of birds cohabit these thirty-five acres with a few people who come here to unwind in this tropical garden paradise. Clouds of bougainvillea and hibiscus thrive in the sun, while white ginger, colorful crotons, and ferns grow profusely under the palms, giant almond, mango, Flamboyant, and breadfruit trees. Over 1,000 varieties of flowers, trees, and shrubs are planted here—a smashing Garden of Eden.

There are twenty-nine thatched cottages located along the beach, poolside, and in the low hills connected to the beach and public areas by winding stone paths. Many of the cottages are so hidden by the foliage, you have to look hard to spot them when you're arriving on your Amazonian boat. All have private patios and wonderful views of the sea. Some have combination bedroom-sitting areas; luxury cottages have a separate sitting room with terrace. Two of the cottages were recently expanded and now boast plunge pools and separate living rooms. If you like to be on top of the world and don't mind an aerobic climb, you might find the hillside cottages most desirable. Others might prefer the beachside bungalows, located just steps from the sand.

Rooms are decorated to blend with the gardens just outside. Lofty wood ceilings, stonework, and expansive sliding glass doors leading onto the private patio create a romantic bower where outside and inside spaces seem to meld into one. Soft, natural fabrics, rattan furniture, and wonderfully roomy garden showers set the mood. King-size bed, louvered walls that let in the sea breezes, ceiling fans, a refrigerator, and luxurious towels and linens help make your days here just about perfect.

Although the beach is a bit small, it's still a good place to head if you like to relax on a chaise, sip a cool drink, and swim in the fantastically clear waters of the Caribbean. One of the best places to sit, read, and snooze is on your own spacious patio. Ease back into the comfortable pillowy lounges, gaze out at the water, and watch the yachts sailing in and out of the small harbor. Sheer bliss.

Dinner is served at the two-level restaurant, a candlelit grotto carved out of the hillside. Fresh fish—the catch of the day—along with West Indian dishes and other more international choices are offered. Meals as well as the weekly barbecue can be enjoyed in one of the clusters of open, thatch-roofed *bohios* set in the gardens by the beach. You'll have to get wet to reach the unique, floating Coconut Bar located within easy swimming distance. Here you can get tasty brews served in—what else—fresh coconuts.

If you want to escape for a few hours by yourselves and explore the island, ask for a box lunch. Want to have breakfast in bed? No problem. Room service is available on request.

Every Friday, you are invited to a manager's cocktail party at the Rock Fort on Fort Duvernette, a tiny island just off the coast. Blazing torches light your way up the steep path to the top of the fort, where you are treated to complimentary drinks, live music, and hors d'oeuvres. Lights softly illuminate the ruins of an eighteenth-century fort perched on the rocks around you. Several nights a week, a band at the top of the island plays for listening and dancing.

The waters around the island are calm and protected, perfect for windsurfing or sailing. The resort has several watercraft available for the use of its guests, and lessons can be arranged for those who are new to sailing. A lovely, free-form pool meanders around the gardens and under the palms.

Tennis is complimentary during the day (a small fee is charged for night play), and clinics and private lessons are offered by the pro. If you want to explore St. Vincent and some of the neighboring islands, which make up the Grenadine chain, you can take the ferry to St. Vincent, which runs on demand, sail on one of the resort's crewed yachts to Bequia or Mustique for the day, or go by scheduled ferry to the various islands.

If sailing off to other islands for a few days on your honeymoon appeals, Young Island gives you the best of both worlds with its lovers Sail-away plan, included in the price of your Lovers package. Couples who take the seven-night package can choose to spend two nights of their stay aboard one of Young Island's four yachts. One 44-foot yacht accommodates one couple; others take two couples, and another 50-foot boat accommodates up to three couples. The yachts carry a crew that includes a cook, who prepares all the meals. Typically you'll sail to Mustique for the first night and Bequia for the second. The three-night option takes you through the uninhabited and beautiful Tobago Cays.

It is said that Chatoyer, a powerful Carib Chief, wanted a majestic black steed belonging to Sir William Young. Young wanted the chief's island, so a mutually agreeable trade was made, which is how the island got its name. It took a number of years and some shifts in ownership before the birth of Young Island as a resort took place in 1963. Some horse!

Address/Phone: P.O. Box 211, St. Vincent, W.I.; (809) 458–4826; fax: (809) 457–4567

U.S. Reservations: Ralph Locke Islands, (800) 223–1108; fax: (914) 763–5362

Owner/Manager: David Settle, general manager

Arrival/Departure: Fly to Barbados and connect there with a Liat or Mustique Airways (800–526–4789) charter flight to St. Vincent, just 35 minutes away. On arrival at Arnos Vale Airport, it's a 10-minute taxi ride to the Young Island dock, where the resort's launch will meet you for the five-minute ride across the water to the island.

Distance from St. Vincent Airport: 1½ miles (8 minutes)

Distance from Kingstown: 3 miles (10 minutes)

Accommodations: 29 cottages, all with ocean views

Best Rooms/Suites: Two luxury beachfront cottages have plunge pools and separate living rooms.

Amenities: Ceiling fans, hair dryer, garden shower, toiletries, bathrobes, ice machine, small refrigerator, in-room safe, hammocks; room service for breakfast

Electricity: 110/240 volts

Sports and Facilities: Tennis; saltwater pool, windsurfers, small sailboats, glass-bottom boat, snorkeling gear; waterskiing and scuba available nearby at local rates

Dress Code: Informal

Weddings: A special wedding program includes services of a wedding coordinator, who will make the arrangements for the wedding and personally take you to the registrar for your license; bride's bouquet, groom's boutonniere, and decorations; minister's fee; champagne; hors d'oeuvres; wedding cake; photographer and photos. You also celebrate with a candlelight dinner that evening and a champagne breakfast the next morning. Cost is $550. Waiting requirement on the island is 72 hours, excluding the day of arrival.

Rates/Packages: 7- and 10-night Lovers packages from $1,065 and $2,860, respectively, per couple (summer); from $3,300 and $4,615 (winter). Rates include accommodations in ocean-view cottage with king-size bed and private terrace, 3 meals daily, round-trip taxi from airport and ferry trip, use of Sunfish, snorkels, glass-bottom boat, windsurfers, tennis, and simple laundry services. The Sailaway option is also included if reserved before arrival.

Payment/Credit Cards: Most major
Deposit: $1,000 deposit for packages, refundable if cancelled up to 30 days
  prior to confirmed arrival date.
Government Taxes: Included
Service Charges: Included
Entry Requirements for U.S. Citizens: Proof of citizenship; passport best

U.S. Virgin Islands

St. John

Caneel Bay

Location: Situated on a private, 170-acre peninsula on St. John.
Romantic Features: A different beach for each day; natural splendor of
6,500 acres of national park surrounding the resort; candlelit dining amid
the flower-bedecked ruins of a sugar plantation.

With 5,000 acres of tropical jungle around you, there is plenty of room to
spread out on Caneel Bay, one of Laurance Rockefeller's most beautiful creations. He discovered this pristine, jungle-covered island in 1952 when he
was on a sailing trip. After purchasing a good portion of the island, he set
about to personally oversee the building of Caneel Bay, insisting that it be a
low-key, ideal vacation resort for those who wanted to escape to a peaceful, natural retreat.

Over the years, many couples have started their married lives here,
and their children have come after them on *their* honeymoons. It's traditionally been ranked as one of the best honeymoon resorts in the world,
the kind of place "old money" likes—elegance without the glitz or bells and
whistles.

For many years the resort was managed by the Rockresorts hotel group
until, in 1993, the upscale Rosewood Hotels & Resorts took on its management and undertook a multimillion-dollar renovation project, redecorating
just about everything except the scenery.

The cottages, which are constructed of natural stone and weathered
wood, are spread out along the fringes of the beaches and in the gardens
and manicured lawns. Designed to blend into the lush tropical plants and
trees that surround them, the cottages have louvered windows that let in
the cooling sea breezes and wonderful views of the beaches or gardens.

The new decor emphasizes a palette brought in from the outdoors including corals, blues, and greens. Accessories and furniture also echo nature's design—in clay, cane, bamboo, and local hardwood. There are six categories of rooms: courtside, tennis garden, ocean-view, beachfront, and premium as well as Cottage 7, a luxury villa popular with visiting bigwigs.

On the whole, the rooms are not super luxurious, nor are the baths mega-marble marvels. But with Caneel's setting and amazing natural assets, who can complain?

If you come here for a week's honeymoon, you will be able to plunk yourself on a different beach every day, but the alluring Honeymoon Beach may seem most appropriate. At Caneel, your day spreads out before you like a sybaritic feast of wonderful things to do and see. If you love nature, you'll have miles of trails to follow that wind through the 5,000-acre Virgin Islands National Park. At night, you can take walks along the pathways, which are softly lit with low mushroom lights to aid hikers, joggers, and strollers.

Feel adventurous? Then take a jeep or boat to other islands or to Caneel's sister property, Little Dix Bay on Virgin Gorda. Ask Caneel to pack a picnic lunch for you and spend a relaxing day on your own. You can also head to Cruz Bay for shopping and browsing. There are several excellent shops in this little town along with some good restaurants.

Tennis players will be in racquet heaven, with eleven courts surrounded by tropical gardens in the terraced Tennis Park. The resort offers complimentary clinics and private lessons, and there is an on-staff pro and a fully stocked shop.

Water sports abound. Stop at the Beach Hut and get a Sunfish or windsurfer and sail off into the calm waters in the bay. You can go snorkeling either by yourself or with a guide or charter a boat for deep-sea fishing. The best snorkeling is off the north end of Caneel Beach, where you can see bright green parrot fish, funny-looking needle fish, and sinister moray eels tucked into crevices of coral. The brilliant world underwater also comes to life through the eyes of Lucy Portlock, the staff marine biologist, who personally escorts guests on weekly snorkel tours through the island's undersea treasures.

More than 1,400 different kinds of plants and trees flourish on Caneel's property. The resort's horticulturist, Eleanor Gibney, will take you on a tour of the grounds.

Caneel's three restaurants and terrace lounge look out over the sea. Turtle Bay Estate House, a gourmet restaurant reminiscent of a grand plantation house, invites you to enjoy open-air dining while looking out over gardens to the deep turquoise sea beyond. At the Beach Terrace, a casual, open dining room along the beach, you can indulge in a sumptuous lunch buffet every day. From your table in The Sugar Mill, set in the ruins of an ancient sugar plantation, you can see the twinkling lights of St. Thomas across the water; the Breezeway and Terrace provide a casual, comfortable place to meet friends and relax with a cool rum punch.

Meals are included in the romance and other packages. Those on daily rates should budget for the meal plan: $65 per person per day for breakfast and dinner; $85 for all meals.

At night there is live music for dancing under the stars while the torches set in the lush foliage turn the resort into a tropical wonderland.

Address/Phone: P.O. Box 720, Cruz Bay, St. John, U.S.V.I. 00831–0720; or (809) 776–6111; fax: (809) 693–8280

U.S. Reservations: Rosewood Hotels & Resorts, (800) 928–8889

Owner/Manager: Rosewood Hotels & Resorts, management company; Martin P. Nicholson, general manager

Arrival/Departure: Caneel Bay can be reached via San Juan, Puerto Rico, and St. Thomas, U.S.V.I. St. John and St. Thomas are served by frequent flights from major U.S. gateways. Caneel Bay's regular ferry service operates between downtown St. Thomas and Caneel Bay several times each day. The resort also operates regular ferry service three times each week to its sister resort, Little Dix Bay, on Virgin Gorda, B.V.I. Look for the Caneel Bay desk at the Cyril E. King Airport, St. Thomas.

Distance from Cyril E. King Airport: 12 nautical miles (40 minutes)

Distance from Cruz Bay: 3 miles

Accommodations: 171 rooms and cottages. All have terraces; many have king-size beds.

Best Rooms/Suites: Secluded Cottage Point area

Amenities: Ceiling fans, direct-dial telephones, minibar, hair dryer, bathrobes, TV, toiletries, in-room safes; ice service; room service

Electricity: 110 volts

Sports and Facilities: 11 tennis courts (5 lighted), pool, boating, sailing, snorkeling, and swimming; scuba diving can be arranged.

Dress Code: Casual during the day; men required to wear slacks, collared shirts, and closed-in footwear in evening; jackets required during height of winter season for dinner in Turtle Bay restaurant.

Weddings: Can be arranged

Rates/Packages: Per couple per night rates include use of nonmotorized boats, snorkeling gear, shopping trip to St. Thomas, tennis and weekly clinics, introductory scuba clinic, feature movie presentations, rum tasting, and garden walk. $335–$695 (winter); $275–$525 (spring and fall); $225–$450 (summer). Pure Romance package includes all of above plus 7 nights' accommodations, fresh berries and champagne on arrival; all meals; unlimited half-day "ensign" sails; day trips to Little Dix Bay; sunset cocktail cruise; transfers to and from St. Thomas; massage for two. $3,600–$6,000 per couple (winter); $3,200–$4,900 (spring and fall); $2,800–$4,000 (summer). Tennis, Island Hopper, and other packages also available.

Payment/Credit Cards: Most major

Deposit: 3-night deposit; balance due 30 days prior to arrival. Full refund if cancelled 21 days or more prior to arrival date (winter); 7 days (summer); otherwise forfeit deposit. $1,000 deposit for packages, due 14 days from date of booking; remainder due at checkout.

Government Taxes: 8 percent on room rate only; packages are subject to a 15 percent surcharge, which covers all room tax, service charges, and meal plan gratuities.

Service Charges: 7.5 percent

Entry requirements for U.S. citizens: Proof of citizenship required when travelling between the United States and British Virgin Islands.

Latin America
and Mexico

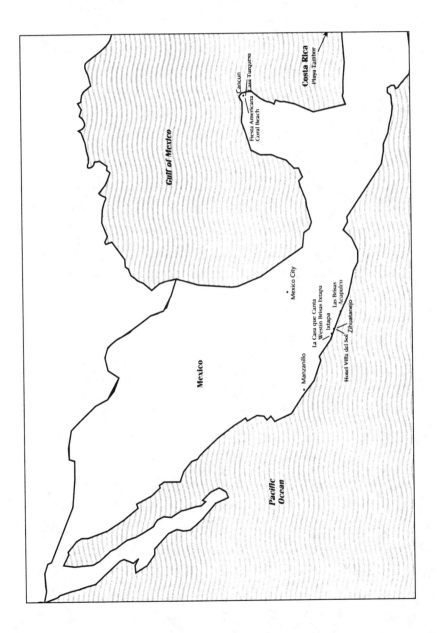

Costa Rica

Playa Tambor, Costa Rica

Playa Tambor

Location: Located on Tambor Beach in Ballena Bay on the west coast of Costa Rica, on the southern tip of the Nicoya Peninsula.
Romantic Features: Loving and lazing in the lap of luxury at an all-inclusive resort; primordial excursions to the nearby, world-famous rain forests and biological reserves of Costa Rica.

You are not planning to have an ordinary marriage, so why should you choose an ordinary honeymoon? Stay at the five-star Playa Tambor, and you can have all of the fun and amenities of an all-inclusive resort, and still indulge your interests in things natural and environmental—like the wonders of pristine rain forests. Uniquely located in one of the most beautiful areas of Costa Rica, with its long stretches of unspoiled Pacific Ocean beaches, Playa Tambor is set in the midst of one of the most important systems of national parks and biological reserves in the world. The resort itself has private, parklike grounds and is blessed with its own sandy cove, shady woods, streams, and a rich variety of exotic subtropical flora and fauna including toucans, parrots, and lizards.

On arrival, you are welcomed with a cool drink at the large open-air reception and lounge area, which is filled with tropical plants. In the distance you can see a huge, free-form pool, swim-up bar, poolside bar and grill, and, beyond that, the palm trees that, you will soon discover, fringe a private crescent of golden sand beach, where you can try out one of the sea kayaks or windsurfers.

Large, rolling lawns are interspersed with colorful bushes and flowerbeds, which are spread throughout the beautifully landscaped grounds, where the white-balconied, pastel-colored accommodations are located. Easygoing yet tropically elegant, this bright and cheerful resort was built on what was once a cattle ranch. None of the buildings is higher than two stories, and all rooms, which are decorated in a bright, tropical style, come with a balcony or terrace.

You never have to go beyond the Playa's boundaries if you don't want to. Days can be spent in the sun lying by the pool or at the beach, or wandering down the many paths of lush, natural forest greenery. Like all good all-inclusive resorts, Playa Tambor has many planned activities during the day—such as water polo, dancing lessons, and aerobics classes. Special nightly entertainment is always planned, the disco pulses with Latin rhythms, and your luck can be tested in the casino. You can choose to eat at the a la carte restaurant, the sumptuous buffet spread, or the beach grill.

But there is more. One of the reasons you may have come here is to explore Costa Rica. This amazing little country is home to more than 4 percent of the world's total flora and fauna, and about 25 percent of its national territory is protected. Whether you walk along the water's edge to the nearby fishing village (at low tide!) or sign up for an excursion farther afield to one of the country's volcanoes, biological reserves, or national parks, you will come away with a strong sense of how dependent we are on nature for enrichment, beauty, and balance in our lives. Not a bad honeymoon gift to take home!

The resort is very helpful in setting up these adventures. One nearby excursion takes you to Cabo Blanco National Rain Forest on the tip of the Nicoya Peninsula. You can wander with a guide in the marine bird sanctuary and catch glimpses of pelicans, brown boobies, and magnificent frigate birds, not to mention howler monkeys, kinkajous, anteaters, and collared peccaries. There are also more than 119 tree species.

Playa Tambor is for those with a keen sense of adventure and a desire for an exotic, tropical vacation. The fact that it's all-inclusive makes it even better.

Address/Phone: (Puntarenas, Costa Rica), c/o Edificio Palacio Hotel, San Jose, Costa Rica; (506) 661–1923; fax: (506) 661–2069

U.S. Reservations: (800) 858–0606

Owner/Manager: Vicente Raventos, manager

Arrival/Departure: Land transfers from San Jose airport via bus, ferry, and another bus take about 3½ hours ($72 round-trip); air transfers take about 25 minutes flying time ($132 round-trip). If you have to stay overnight in the capital city of San Jose because of international flight connections to transfers, arrangements will be made for accommodations at a sister hotel, the elegant, five-star San Jose Palacio (about 20 minutes by taxi from the airport). You are entitled to all-inclusive privileges during your stay there, with certain restrictions.

Distance from San Jose Airport: 3½ hours by buses and ferry, 25 minutes by charter airplane

Distance from Tambor: 10 minutes; the nearest large town is Puntarenas, about one hour by ferry .

Accommodations: 402 doubles. Each room has two European double beds (close to the familiar queen-sized bed), and en suite bathrooms with deep tubs.

Best Rooms/Suites: All rooms are in the same deluxe category and are priced as such. Requests for a sea or garden view can be made at time of booking.

Amenities: Air-conditioning, telephone, satellite TV, and in-room safe deposit box

Electricity: 110/220 volts, 60 Hz. Two-pin plugs are standard. (These are. U.S. equivalents.)

Sports and Facilities: 3 tennis courts, 2 multipurpose courts (football, basketball, volleyball); water polo, aerobics, fitness center; scuba diving, sailing, catamarans, windsurfing, kayaking, deep-sea fishing; horseback riding

Dress Code: Casual

Rates/Packages: $90 per person per night (April–December); $110 (December 15–April 15). Price includes all meals, local brand beverages, nonmotorized water sports, nightly entertainment, daily activities. Air/land packages are available. A 3-night package from Miami is $589. Call for most recent promotions.

Payment/Credit Cards: Most major

Deposit: $150 per person upon booking, and full payment 30 days prior to arrival. Cancel 46 (or more) days prior to arrival date for full refund less $25; 30–45 days for refund less 25 percent of the package value; 21–30 days for refund less 50 percent of the package value; 15–20 days for refund less 75 percent of the package value; 14 days or less, no refund.

Government Taxes: Departure tax, $6.00
Service Charges: Included in room rate
Entry Requirements for U.S. Citizens: Valid passport

Mexico

Casa Turquesa

Location: On Cancun's main hotel strip, near the end of the beach.
Romantic Features: Large suites with Jacuzzi on each terrace; small intimate property with its own semiprivate beach.

Most of Cancun's hotels along the main beach are large, many with huge pools. Casa Turquesa is not. Nor is it a high-rise. With only thirty-one suites, this small, intimate hotel is a real find for those who want to honeymoon in Cancun, but don't want to stay in a mega-resort. Located on the beach near the end of the hotel zone, on the narrow peninsula that lies between the Caribbean Sea and Nichupte Lagoon, Casa Turquesa is lovely, exclusive, and pricier than its neighbors.

The resort's buff, peachy exterior with its various levels, terraces, Palladian windows, and arches is architecturally quite beautiful—more like a palace than a hotel. Inside you'll find lots of white, pink, and gray marble on the floors and in the bathrooms. Beautiful Mexican artifacts and paintings along with soft pastel fabrics and glass tables help set a serene, elegant mood. Walls are painted in light colors, and there are plenty of fresh flowers and tropical plants in ceramic urns throughout the guest rooms and public areas.

Each suite has either one king- or two queen-size beds, a sitting area, desk, and large terrace with a Jacuzzi and daybed. Glass doors lead out to terraces, from where you'll have lovely views of the Caribbean Sea.

A large pool overlooks the water and is designed with a step just below the top of the deck and wide enough so you can put your chaise right in the water. The lounges are plushly cushioned, and there are enough for everyone—no need to rush out to save a chair!

Casa Turquesa has two restaurants: The Bellevue, serving continental cuisine, and Celebrity, featuring seafood, pasta, and Black Angus beef.

Although you might be tempted to stay put in your elegant hideaway, consider a day trip to one of the Mayan archaeological sites. Tulum is 80 miles south of Cancun on the sea. Chichen Itza, the more extensive site by far, is a full-day adventure. You can also go to Tikal or Uxmal/Merida. A special package includes airfare to Merida, a delightful colonial city.

If you are interested in the archaeological programs, Casa Turquesa offers special packages that include a choice of sites.

Address/Phone: Boulevard Kukulcan Km 13.5, Zona Hotelera, 77500 Cancun, Q.R., Mexico; 52–98–85–2924; fax: 98–85–2922

U.S. Reservations: Small Luxury Hotels of the World, (800) 525–4800

Owner/Manager: Gastón Alegre

Arrival/Departure: You are met by the resort's airline representatives and provided with complimentary transfers (minimum stay, 3 nights).

Distance from Cancun Airport: 20 minutes

Accommodations: 31 suites, 29 junior suites, 1 two-bedroom Presidential Suite, 1 three-bedroom Royal Suite

Best Rooms/Suites: Except for the Presidential and Royal Suites, all suites are identical. Honeymooners are upgraded to the top floor and guaranteed a king-size bed suite.

Amenities: Hair dryer, air-conditioning, bathrobes, makeup table mirror, toiletries, telephones, satellite TV, VCR, CD player, full bar; 24-hour butler and maid service, manicures and pedicures on request; fax/computer connections (if you dare bring work with you); video library

Electricity: 110 volts

Sports and Facilities: Lighted tennis courts; most water sports, including boating, waterskiing, and snorkeling; 2 golf courses nearby

Dress Code: Casually elegant

Weddings: Can be arranged

Rates/Packages: $300–$500 per couple per day (November 1–mid-April and July 1–August 31); $275–$500 (mid-April–June 30 and September 1–December 15); executive suites $1,500–$2,500. Honeymoon package includes accommodations, champagne, flowers, private transfers, candlelight dinner for two in the Gazebo, daily breakfast (the first served with champagne), all taxes and gratuities, 2-hour city or shopping tour, and gift: 3 nights, $1,777; 4 nights $2,487; and 5 nights $2,887. For the 4- and 5-night stays you get more champagne, a dinner show, and a dinner cruise.

Payment/Credit Cards: Most major

Deposit: Guarantee with credit card; cancel within 7 days of arrival date to avoid 1-night charge.

Government Taxes: 10 percent VAT (included in packages); $10 departure tax

Service Charges: Included in packages

Entry Requirements for U.S. Citizens: Passport or original birth certificate

Fiesta Americana Coral Beach

Location: In the Yucatan on the northern end of the Cancun peninsula, across from Plaza Caracol Mall.
Romantic Features: A luxurious mega-resort with all the bells and whistles.

This is one of Cancun's biggies. Two U-shaped multistory pink and white buildings sit side by side facing the Caribbean. The Fiesta Americana Coral Beach cannot be called an intimate hideaway resort, but it can be called one of the best of the many hotels on Cancun's busy hotel strip.

About twenty years ago, no one had ever heard of Cancun as a resort destination. It simply didn't exist, until the Mexican government selected this coastal area on the easternmost coast of the Yucatan for development because of its many virtues: Crystalline waters of the Caribbean rolled in on the pristine white sand beaches, weather was hot and balmy year-round, interesting Mayan archaeological sites were located nearby, and air access would be good.

Once this area was earmarked to become Mexico's newest tourist destination, developers came in like gangbusters, and new hotels were built one next to the other along the skinny peninsula, which boasts a lagoon on one side and the open sea on the other.

Today the beach is lined by resorts, many with huge, lakelike pools. Although it might be easy to overlook the fact that you are indeed in Mexico, the margaritas are real, the ruins at Tulum and Chichen Itza are awesomely authentic, and Cancun's tourism machine runs full tilt to attract vacationers, offering highly competitive prices and nonstop nightlife and activities. If you're looking for action, Cancun delivers. Jet skiing, parasailing, discos—the whole banana.

Considered the flagship hotel of the popular Fiesta Americana chain, the Coral Beach has more than 600 rooms, all with balconies overlooking the sea, 1,000 feet of beachfront, eleven places you can eat and drink, three indoor tennis courts, and a health center and spa.

The 660-foot-long pool, the size of two football fields, winds around a huge tiled patio punctuated by two swim-up bars, fountains, waterfalls and "oasis" areas planted with grass, trees, and flowers. When you stand at one end of the pool, it would not be a far-fetched idea to wish you had a boat to get you to the other side. Lap swimmers will love it!

All rooms have marble floors, a step-down sitting room leading out to a terrace through sliding glass doors, and tasteful decor. Junior suites are more than 500 square feet in size; master suites are more than 800 square feet and have terraces. Off-white wood furniture is upholstered in tropical prints and clear blues, corals, lavenders, and whites.

Tall palm trees grow in the elegant atrium lobby, where light filters through the stained-glass conservatory roof. Here light marble floors, columns, Palladian windows, and lots of tropical plants create an open, airy feeling.

You can eat indoors or outside under the stars on a terraced garden patio. The Isla Contoy, a thatched-roof restaurant-bar nestled between the pool and the beaches, serves great seafood and light meals and is especially fun.

The Coral Reef, a gourmet seafood restaurant, is decorated in shrimp pink; chair backs are in the shape of shells. La Joya, decorated in a Mexican theme, is another gourmet restaurant, where you can enjoy that elegant dinner and then dance to music by a local band. And you can always order room service for complete privacy.

You won't have to get taxis to explore Cancun, for right across the street from the Coral Beach are two big shopping malls where you can shop at designer outlets and take in the nightlife at spots like the Hard Rock Cafe.

There are all kinds of water sports available on the beach. It will cost you extra to do things like parasail, Jet Ski or scuba dive, but you'll find the prices from the operators are competitive.

Address/Phone: Boulevard Kukulkan Lote 6, Zona Hotelera, Cancun, Quintana Roo, Mexico 77500; 52–988–32900; fax: 52–988–33076
U.S. Reservations: (800) FIESTA 1
Owner/Manager: Gustavo Arce, general manager
Arrival/Departure: Frequent daily flights to Cancun from most major U.S. gateways; taxi from airport; hotel shuttle $7.00 per person
Distance from Cancun International Airport: 20 minutes
Distance from Cancun center: 10 minutes
Accommodations: 602 oceanfront rooms with balconies: 178 junior suites with king-size beds; 334 junior suites with two double beds; 8 special junior suites; 68 master suites with king-size beds, dressing room, Jacuzzi, large terraces, and double vanities; 10 Caribbean suites with king-size bed and two doubles; and 10 multiuse suites
Best Rooms/Suites: Master suites or junior suites with king-size beds
Amenities: Climate control, toiletries, hair dryer, direct-dial telephones, in-room safe, minibar, satellite TV, in-room movies, AM-FM clock/radio, purified drinking water
Electricity: 110 volts
Sports and Facilities: Health club and spa; 3 indoor tennis courts; 660-foot

outdoor pool; beach, water sports, including beach volleyball, parasailing, Jet Skiing, windsurfing, deep-sea fishing, scuba diving, snorkeling.
Dress Code: Casual
Weddings: Can be arranged
Rates/Packages: From $240 per couple per night (high season); from $230 (low season). Honeymoon package, from $209 per couple, includes deluxe room accommodations, champagne, breakfast in bed, and candlelight dinner with wine.
Payment/Credit Cards: Most major
Deposit: 1-night credit card deposit; cancel 3 days before arrival date for refund.
Government Taxes: 10 percent
Service Charges: 15 percent suggested
Entry Requirements for U.S. Citizens: Proof of citizenship; passport best

Hotel Villa del Sol

Location: On palm-lined La Ropa Beach in the quaint village of Zihuatanejo. 150 miles northwest of Acapulco on the Pacific coast.
Romantic Features: Lovely white, crescent-shaped private beach.

It's only 6 miles from Ixtapa, but this small gem is quite different, indeed, from the large chain of hotels in nearby Ixtapa. It has a beauty of a beach sheltered by a dense canopy of palms and framed by a carpet of tropical foliage that begins at the edge of the beach, rising up into the hills behind. Nestled in this greenery are thirty-six suites in adobelike bungalow cottages. Winding stone walkways lead from the cottages to the two palapa-roofed bar/restaurants and the beach. Water runs in a meandering channel from the main fountain, along the paths, and into the pool.

Once you've had time to let the magic of Villa del Sol sink in, you'll be hooked. From the time you step up into the rather unpretentious yet charming tiled reception area and pass through to the gardens just beyond, you've entered the Mexican version of the Garden of Eden, and in this garden, everything works: from the high-tech faucets that glide open like butter to the attractive lights that line the walkways. Created by Helmut Leins, who came to Mexico several years ago from Germany, Villa del Sol combines the casual and colorful ambience of Mexico with the superb service-oriented traditions of Europe.

Passionate about details, Leins says he makes sure he sleeps in every room at least once a year. This way he knows if everything is as it should be. It's only when you stay here that you notice how well thought out it all is—subtle things like soap dishes, towel bars, and shelves are all perfectly placed.

Leins's charming French wife, Muriel, oversees the room decor and goes to great lengths to get just the right accessories and furnishings. Each of the thirty-six split-level suites are unique and appointed with authentic Mexican artifacts such as wooden masks, terra-cotta pots, and ceramic birds. Suites have king- or queen-size beds, separate sitting areas, terraces or balconies, and luxurious baths with large walk-in showers. Rooms are decorated in rich, Mexican-loomed fabrics and enhanced by colorful hand-made Mexican tiles. Terra-cotta and white ceramic tile floors are accented by area rugs; beds are draped in filmy, white gauze and a hammock is strung in a corner of each patio, providing a pleasant retreat for an afternoon siesta.

Villa del Sol's beachfront suite is about as romantic as it gets. The problem is, once you've seen it, you'll not want to leave. This two-story, two-bath casita is pure Mexican magic at its best. It has a large patio smack on the beach with a hammock for two as well as a table and chairs; you can wake up slowly there to fresh coffee and croissants each morning. The first floor has a sitting area with a built-in lounge about the size of a double bed. A spiral stairway brings you up to the second floor and yet another patio overhanging the beach, with an outdoor Jacuzzi. The king-size bed is swathed in white netting and a long vanity counter topped by handmade blue and bright yellow tiles runs along one side of the room, separating a shower on one side from an enclosed bath on the other. Red tile floors, fresh flowers, shelves, and roomy closets all add to the wonderful ambience.

If one wants to nitpick (and that's all it is): Some of the bungalows are a bit on the dark side, especially those that front on the gardens. The heavy, tropical vegetation overhanging the roofs tends to keep sunlight at bay. But this is a minor thing and will soon be forgotten once you settle in. The newer casitas, some with private plunge pools, are more open but don't have quite the charm of the older ones.

A large, round, palapa-thatched roof, which looks much like a giant sombrero, houses an open-air bar and restaurant. Orlando's Bar, named after the affable master of the bar, whose wit and diplomacy are legendary, is also housed under its own thatched roof. Repeat guests always look forward to swapping stories with Orlando, who will serve you exotic drinks such as coco loco.

The white-sand beach, shaded by palms and palm-frond umbrellas, is set up with comfortable lounges with thick cushions, where you can crash and snooze. Want a frosty margarita and some freshly made guacamole and tortilla chips? Just signal the beach attendant, and it will be brought to you in speedy fashion. Generally the waters off La Ropa, unlike the rougher beach areas in neighboring Ixtapa, are very swimmable. When the surf kicks up, however, you can cool off in one of the resort's two pools. There are two tennis courts, which like everything else on the property, are well maintained. If you're looking for a game of tennis and your spouse isn't up to it, ask Leins if he'd like a set or two. In addition to running the resort, he likes to keep fit by running around the tennis court.

Dining at the Villa del Sol under the palapa roof is just about everything you could want: excellent, well-prepared food, candlelit tables by the sea, and warm smiles from those who serve you. Just outside the resort entrance lies the picturesque village of Zihuatanejo. Still very much a sleepy fishing village in spite of the recent tourism influx at nearby Ixtapa, here you can still watch the fishermen bring in their daily catch, and you can stroll down decorative brick-paved streets past small shops and cozy little restaurants. If you crave a bit of lively nightlife, you can head to one of the large hotels on Ixtapa's Palmar Beach. But then, who really wants to leave the Villa del Sol for very long!

Address/Phone: P.O. Box 84, Zihuatanejo, Gro., Mexico 40880; 52–753–42239 or 52–753–43239; fax: 52–753–42758 or 52–753–44066

U.S. Reservations: (800) 223–6510; Small Luxury Hotels, (800) 525–4800

Owner/Managers: Helmut and Muriel Leins

Arrival/Departure: Taxis are available at the airport (about $7.00 each way per carload).

Distance from Ixtapa-Zihuatanejo International Airport: 15 minutes

Distance from Zihuatanejo: 5 minutes; from Ixtapa, 10 minutes

Accommodations: 22 minisuites; 8 deluxe suites; 6 master suites

Best Rooms/Suites: Master beachfront suite

Amenities: Air-conditioning, ceiling fans, king- or queen-size beds, toiletries, in-room safes, TV in master and minisuites, refrigerator and telephone in master suites, some have whirlpools or minipools; laundry and valet service

Electricity: 110 volts

Sports and Facilities: Hobie Cats, waterskiing, snorkeling, 2 freshwater pools, golf on a Robert Trent Jones course nearby, 2 tennis courts

Dress Code: Casual

Weddings: Can be arranged

Rates/Packages: $130–$330 per couple per night (summer); $180–$460 (winter). During the winter season, the meal plan, for breakfast and dinner, is mandatory ($40 in summer). No children under 14 during winter months.

Payment/Credit Cards: Most major
Deposit: 2 nights deposit; cancel 7 days before arrival for full refund
Government Taxes: 15 percent
Service Charges: 10 percent suggested
Entry Requirements for U.S. Citizens: Proof of citizenship; passport best

La Casa que Canta

Location: On a cliff above the sea adjacent to La Ropa Beach, near the center of Zihuatanejo.
Romantic Features: Views, view, views; intimate private suites; wonderful small terraced places where you can drink or dine.

La Casa que Canta, "the house that sings," is one of those rare finds in Mexico, a small, intimate, five-star inn perched on the top of a cliff overlooking the Pacific. The clusters of pink-hued adobelike casitas with balconies and thatched roofs that look like giant mops atop little blockhouses are staggered down the hillside so that you get a great view of the sea from each room.

Eclectically and creatively furnished with authentic Mexican artifacts and furniture, the casitas have chairs with arms that are brightly painted to resemble birds and legs carved like feathers. A large, colorful striped animal (could it be a pig or a tapir?) sits on the floor balancing a carved bird on its back. A large terra-cotta bird with real, brightly colored feathers sits on a table, one of the many cleverly designed lamps scattered here and there in the public areas and casitas. Furniture painted by well-known Mexican artists such as Frida Kahlo and Diego Rivera, mermaids, and ceramic angels along with tons of plants and Mexican tapestries and paintings add beauty and a sense of fun to La Casa que Canta.

Your casita, with its bedroom, sitting room, and separate patio, is home to a number of valuable and whimsical art pieces: hand-painted desks, folk art from Erongaricuaro and *equapal* chairs. All these wonderful things are set against a background of creamy white walls and bed linens and red tile floors edged with shiny, polished pebbles. Wood louvered doors open out to the terraces, which are partially thatched and have two extra-long lounge chairs, colorfully painted wrought iron tables and chairs and hammocks. In the harbor below, you'll see a scattering of beautiful yachts—picture postcard stuff. Don't look for a TV: There isn't one—but who needs it, with such views! (If you really need a quick catch-up on the world outside, there's a TV in the lounge.) Your bath has a granite counter with double

La Casa que Canta, Mexico

vanity, a pink marble walk-in shower, and oversize bath towels.

Other resorts might be able to duplicate the decor (although I doubt it, unless the designers are prepared to spend years searching for interesting Mexican art and furniture pieces), but a better setting would be hard to find. Your patio, the pool, the dining room, the various terraced rooms tucked into the descending hillside—everything—sits over the sea, which continually crashes into the wet, dark, jagged rocks at the base of the cliff. There are a saltwater pool and Jacuzzi cut into the rocks near the bottom of the cliff and a second saltwater "Jacuzzi" is being carved into another rock basin nearby. The freshwater pool, near the top of the cliff, is constructed so that the water seems to simply slip over the side of the pool down to the sea. You can quite happily while away the entire day sitting on the patio here, enjoying the scenery and sun.

In the evening when you come into your room, you'll find a floral surprise waiting for you: an elaborate pattern of flower petals on your bed, perhaps shaped into a heart. You also might find flowers tucked into washcloths, in soap trays, and on your bedside table.

Casa que Canta has its own private beach club on nearby La Ropa, where you can get chaises and refreshments. It's about a five-minute walk from the resort. You can also arrange to participate in a variety of water sports here, ranging from windsurfing to waterskiing.

Meals are served in a palapa palm frond–thatched structure, where you'll also find a reception area, lounge, and bar. Dining hours are relaxed. You can eat anytime after 8:00 A.M., and Mexican specialties, salads, and grilled items are offered at both pool terraces. Like tequila? The resort features twelve different brands. Try a frosty and yummy papaya cocktail or go for a cold Corona, the local beer.

Enjoying cocktails and dinner on the terrace at night is about as romantic as it gets: The soft, yellow lights play on the lofty, palm-thatched ceilings and endless views of the sea are punctuated by the winking lights of Zihuatanejo in the distance. Light peeks through the holes of large round terra-cotta pots and gently glows from hanging wicker shades; there are enough private cozy sitting areas tucked here and there for every couple who wants their own space.

Just five minutes away is Zihuatanejo, a charming fishing village nestled into the curve of a bay cut sharply into the hills. Small white houses with red tile roofs, a variety of fishing vessels anchored in the bay or pulled up on the shore, and a small population of happy, easygoing people make this a fun place to visit. If you crave some modern-day action, the new beach development, Ixtapa, is just a 10-minute drive around the corner.

This all may seem familiar if you saw the movie *When a Man Loves a Woman,* starring Meg Ryan and Andy Garcia, which was filmed here. A glance at the guest book says it all: A honeymoon couple writes, "La Casa que Canta was the best place to start the first day of the rest of our lives." Another says simply, "Wow! Pure magic."

Address/Phone: Camiono Escenico a la Playa La Ropa, 40880 Zihuatanejo, Gro., Mexico; 52–753–47030; toll free: 91–800–093–45; fax: 52–753–47040

U.S. Reservations: Small Luxury Hotels, (800) 525–4800; Robert Reid, (800) 223–6510

Owner/Manager: Jacques Baldassari, owner; Cecelia Gonzalez, general manager

Arrival/Departure: Transfers from Ixtapa/Zihuatanejo Airport provided with prior arrangement

Distance from Ixtapa-Zihuatanejo International Airport: 12 miles (20 minutes; 35-minute flight from Mexico City)

Distance from Zihuatanejo center: 5 minutes

Accommodations: 18 suites, each with its own living room and terrace; suites range in size from 540 to 1,500 square feet.

Best Rooms/Suites: Private pool suites are great, but all suites have great views and balconies.

Amenities: Air-conditioning, fans, bidet, large walk-in shower, magnifying mirror, toiletries, hair dryer, telephones, in-room safe, minibar, bathrobes; room service, massages available

Electricity: 110 volts
Sports and Facilities: 2 pools (1 freshwater, 1 saltwater), saltwater Jacuzzi, private beach club offering most water sports, horseback riding; golf and tennis nearby
Dress Code: Casually elegant
Weddings: Can be arranged
Rates/Packages: $215–$235 per couple per night for a grand suite, $280–$340 for a pool suite (low season); $275 for a grand suite, $370–$390 for a pool suite (high season).
Payment/Credit Cards: Most major
Deposit: 2-night deposit; refund if cancelled 15 days prior to arrival date (45 days for Christmas and Easter).
Government Taxes: 15 percent
Service Charges: 10 percent suggested
Entry Requirements for U.S. Citizens: Proof of identity; passport best

Las Brisas

Location: Terraced up a hillside overlooking Acapulco Bay.
Romantic Features: Casitas with private pools dotted with floating fresh flowers; spectacular views of the sunset from your terrace; midnight swim in private pool.

Imagine this: Just the two of you are alone on your private garden terrace. The sun is setting over the water and the islands in the bay as the lights of Acapulco turn on. You linger as the red-golden glow becomes blue-black. It's not long before thousands of twinkling lights come alive. You take a dip in your pool and linger in the warm water, enjoying the soft, night air. You are at Las Brisas, known as one of the world's most romantic resorts. Its grounds, which are covered with over 110 acres of pink fuchsia blossoms, hibiscus, wavy palms, and cascading bougainvillea bushes, are terraced up the hillside like a giant amphitheater, so that those who stay here get first-row seats for the spectacular sunsets and views of the city.

When Las Brisas first opened more than forty years ago, Acapulco was considered the most exotic place to go in Mexico. Unique at the time of its conception, Las Brisas features 300 charming white casitas, 250 of them with private or semiprivate pools, tucked into the hillsides overlooking Acapulco Bay. Rooms are tastefully, though not opulently, decorated and have king-size beds and sliding glass doors opening onto wonderful stone garden terraces banked by tropical plants and flowers. Baths are marble, and there are separate vanities, wet bars, and minibars.

The multilevel suites are much roomier than the single-room casitas. Each has a separate dining area, large wet bar, sitting room, one and a half baths, a patio, pool, and on another level, a bedroom opening onto another terrace with a Jacuzzi. Baths are large with sunken marble tubs and double vanities. Furniture is hand-painted in gay designs.

Because the casitas are terraced one atop another, ask for one where your patio and pool are shielded from those around and above you; otherwise you won't have as much privacy as you might expect. The top villas are the best. You also have to decide whether you want a bay view or ocean view—or both. Placido Domingo stayed in number 328 when he came here recently and enjoyed bay and sea views.

To enjoy your stay, you've got to like the idea of Acapulco and a resort that overlooks the water but is not itself directly on a beach. However, jitneys will shuttle you to a swim club on the coast, La Concha, where you'll find a lovely freshwater pool, saltwater lagoon with a raft anchored in the middle, and an open-air restaurant. There are also tented cabanas, water sports, a fitness center and spa, and a refreshment area. The public beach is nearby. In the not too distant past, vendors on Acapulco's beaches have been pretty aggressive. Thanks to a strong stand by the government, this situation is much better now, and vendors now have their own market areas.

Each morning a basket of fresh fruit, pastries, and coffee is placed in the "magic box," a special two-way cupboard in your wall, so you can wake up to another morning of breakfast on your patio. Later in the day, when it comes time to eat, there are three choices: the Bellavista, which features continental cuisine and provides nightly music for dancing out on the starlit terrace; El Mexicano, overlooking Acapulco Bay and specializing in—you guessed it—regional fare; and La Concha, the restaurant and bar at the swim club.

A fleet of pink and white jeeps is stationed at the reception area at the base of the hill, just off the main road. These are available around the clock to transport you up to your casita. Shuttle service also runs regularly to downtown Acapulco, five minutes away.

You can rent these jeeps for $35 (plus 10 percent tax) per day. Just beyond the entrance of your luxurious sanctuary, the sights and sound of one of Mexico's most colorful cities beckons. The highly charged nightlife of this aged city still dazzles. Discos, nightclubs, and bars galore are open until the wee hours. You'll find most of the action along the Costera Miguel Aleman, the city's main street, which stretches along most of the beach areas and through the center of town.

At the top of Las Brisas, catch the sunset at the new Sunset Bar, which is open just 1½ hours every day. A spectacular close to another day in paradise. And before you leave Acapulco, be sure to visit the La Quebrada divers, a fearless group of young athletes who four times daily climb a steep rock cliff, kiss a statue of the Virgin of Guadalupe, and hurl themselves 130 feet into the ocean.

Address/Phone: P.O. Box 281, 39868 Acapulco, Gro., Mexico 39868; 52-74-84-1580; fax: 52-74-84-6071

U.S. Reservations: Leading Hotels of the World, (800) 223-6800; Westin Hotels & Resorts, (800) 228-3000

Owner/Manager: Francisco José Garcia, general manager

Arrival/Departure: Guests staying in a suite are met at the airport on request; taxis available.

Distance from Acapulco International Airport: 20 minutes

Distance from Acapulco: 1 mile

Accommodations: 300 rooms and suites in casitas, some with private pools, others with shared pool. (250 pools in all): 96 casitas with semiprivate pools, 104 casitas with private pools, 38 Royal Beach Casitas, 22 junior suites or villas, 5 one-bedroom suites, and 3 two-bedroom suites.

Best Rooms/Suites: The higher the better, as the lower casitas are closer to the traffic noise and have less privacy; also the views are better on the top. Ask for a Royal Beach Club room or a junior suite on the fifth level. Number 328, a junior suite, has both bay and ocean views and is a favorite with repeat guests; in number 402 you can lie in your bed and gaze out at Acapulco and the bay.

Amenities: Hair dryer, air-conditioning, ceiling fans, toiletries, telephone, minibar, wet bar, bathroom scale, separate vanity, Jacuzzis in suites, cotton robes, in-room safe; "magic box" for room service, jeep shuttle, welcome drink, shopping arcade, private gas station, deli shop, laundry service

Electricity: 110 volts

Sports and Facilities: 5 lighted tennis courts (3 with artificial lawn); private swim club with large freshwater pool, and 2 saltwater lagoons, and most water sports; jeep safaris and rentals

Dress Code: Casual elegance; jackets optional for dinner

Weddings: The Chapel of Peace, at the top of the hill, has been the site of hundreds of weddings over the years.

Rates/Packages: $150–$365, per room for a double, including continental breakfast; $352–$1,192 for a suite. Honeymoon package "Romantically Las Brisas"

Payment/Credit Cards: Most major

Deposit: 1 to 2 nights' room rate, guaranteed with credit card prior to arrival. Cancel 3 days prior to arrival for refund.

Government Taxes: 15 percent
Service Charges: $16 daily
Entry Requirements for U.S. Citizens: Proof of citizenship; passport best

Las Hadas

Location: Sits on 650 acres on Santiago Peninsula about three hours south of Puerto Vallarta on Mexico's Pacific coast.
Romantic Features: Private tented cabanas; Moorish fantasy suites overlooking the Pacific; suites with private pools.

The beach isn't the most spectacular in the world—actually rather small as beaches go—but that didn't stop Bo Derek and Dudley Moore from having a romantic fling there in the classic movie *10.* They ate in the El Terral restaurant, with the Pacific surf and night skies as a backdrop, and indulged in a friendly frolic in their posh suite. The setting was Las Hadas, on Mexico's picturesque Pacific coast.

When architect Jose Luis Ezquerra applied his audacious, creative powers to designing Las Hadas (which means "the fairies" in Spanish), he conjured up a Moorish fantasyland composed of dazzling white towers, domes, minarets, arches, and spires. The resort is terraced up the green foliage–carpeted hillside, looking much like an elaborate, tiered wedding cake. Bright clouds of bougainvillea cascade over walls and into courtyards, brilliant blossoms of hibiscus and mimosa, palms, and many varieties of cactus paint beautiful patterns against the white adobe walls.

Moorish tented white cabanas on the beach provide private retreats from the hot sun, and another tented outdoor "room" shelters a poolside bar. All these fanciful structures are linked by a network of cobblestone walkways, edged by marble and lined by tropical plants.

In addition to the beach, Las Hadas has two pools; one is quiet and secluded; the other is more like a sprawling lagoon with waterfalls, flower-covered little islands, and a rope bridge. You don't have to look very hard to spot a lazy iguana catching some sun on one of the islands. Pick a red hibiscus blossom, and he (or she) will eat it right from your fingers.

There are several kinds of rooms and suites, ranging from standard right up to the Presidential Suite, which is very private, with a living room, large walk-in closet, private pool and Jacuzzi, an upstairs dining terrace, and a private entrance. The Las Hadas Suite is another luxurious accommodation (please see "Best Room," which follows). All rooms have marble floors, air-conditioning, balcony or terrace, and a number of amenities.

Las Hadas, Mexico

The Camino Club rooms give you more privacy as well as the use of a private pool. Fantasia suites are larger, with king-size beds. Some have living rooms, more than one balcony, two bathrooms, a wet bar, and spacious terraces. The decor is in keeping with the Moorish theme, and colorful artwork and fresh flowers are used to pep up the white walls.

Las Hadas has several restaurants, including the elegant Legazpi, which serves classic international cuisine; El Terral, a more informal, open-air restaurant, where you can try some excellent Mexican dishes along with grilled meats; Los Delfines, a thatched-roof, seaside eatery serving lunch and beverages; and El Palmar, an informal restaurant overlooking the main pool where you can have breakfast, lunch, and dinner.

There are also a popular swim-up pool bar, a piano lounge, a tented beach bar, and a disco.

You'll find plenty to do if you like water sports and when the day cools down, you can head to the tennis courts. If you want to see what lies outside the gates of Las Hadas, hop aboard the resort's trimaran, which runs daily excursions to Manzanillo, and take a romantic Sunset Bay cruise.

As sensual as Las Hadas is during the day, it really turns up the steam when night falls: Golden lights dance in and around the pointed spiral roof towers, scalloped tiers of open balconies, and arched windows, creating a magical wonderland designed for romance.

Address/Phone: Rincor de las Hadas, P.O. Box 158, 28200 Manzanillo, Colima, Mexico; 52–333–4–00–00; fax: 52–333–4–19–50

U.S. Reservations: (800) 7 CAMINO or Leading Hotels of the World, (800) 223–6800

Owner/Manager: Richard Pfeifer, general manager

Arrival/Departure: Regular air service to Playa de Oro Airport; private transfers, at $50 per couple round-trip can be arranged; shuttle service and taxis available at $15 per person each way.

Distance from Playa de Oro Airport: 30 minutes

Distance from Manzanillo: 15 minutes

Accommodations: 220 rooms, including 41 suites grouped in multistory towers and terraced rows; some suites are set apart with their own pools

Best Rooms/Suites: If you want the one where Derek and Moore cavorted to Ravel's *Bolero,* ask for the Las Hadas Suite. It has two living rooms, two bathrooms, a private pool with terrace, wet bar, upstairs dining terrace, and great views of the sea. For more modest budgets, a room in the Camino Real Club or a Fantasia suite are recommended. The higher up, the more privacy and the better the view.

Amenities: Air-conditioning, satellite TV, minibar, toiletries, marble baths,

telephone; room service
Electricity: 110 volts
Sports and Facilities: 10 tennis courts lit for night play, 2 of them clay, ($9–$15 per court, per hour); La Mantarraya 18-hole golf course ($66 greens fees with caddy, $90 with cart), club rentals ($25); marina, beach, 2 pools; water sports, including snorkeling, sailing, swimming, waterskiing, windsurfing, Sunfish sailing, speedboat rides, and deep-sea fishing
Dress Code: Tropical elegance
Weddings: Can be arranged
Rates/Packages: $155–$185 per couple per night for a room; $310–$900 for suites; breakfast and dinner, $45 per person. Book a package at $230 per couple per night for 4 nights and the last night is free, plus you get accommodations in a Camino Real Club room, welcome cocktail, breakfasts, and free tennis.
Payment/Credit Cards: Most major
Deposit: 1-night deposit due 15 days before arrival; cancel 3 days or more before arrival date for full refund.
Government Taxes: 15 percent
Service Charges: 15 percent
Entry Requirements for U.S. Citizens: Proof of citizenship; passport best

Westin Brisas Ixtapa

Location: 120 miles northwest of Acapulco, on Mexico's western coast.
Romantic Features: The only large hotel in Ixtapa on its own beach; magnificent suites; lobby bar is *the* place to be for sunset.

It creeps up on you. At first this monolithic structure of high ceilings, ochre-colored, concrete walls pierced by patterns of square and rectangular openings, which let in light and air, seems strangely stark. Plain. Even ugly, to some. The reception area is softened only by a few pieces of simple, sturdy, varnished wood tables and a long bench reminding one of the sitting area in a railroad station. Look up and see geometric splashes of bright canary yellow and magenta. Clay pots, looking much like relics from an archaeological dig, sit in clusters on the pitted quarry tile floor. Giant stone marbles of various sizes sit in a corner of the lobby. Strange place this.

   Then just about the time you're pulling out your credit card, you start to feel the breezes. No matter how hot it is just outside in the glaring Mexican sun, you are cooled and soothed. The architect, Ricardo Legorreta, who designed the hotel, built it without actual windows—just open spaces to take full advantage of the building's cliffside location on the edge of the sea. Unless you actually get out on the water, you can't really see the entire structure, which is constructed in the shape of a pyramid, its balconies climbing up the receding sides. All rooms have spectacular views and capture the refreshing breezes coming in from the Pacific.

At the base of the resort is a lovely cove beach that belongs exclusively to the Westin Ixtapa for, unlike the other resorts just around the bend, which are lined up side by side along the 2-mile stretch of Palmar Beach, guests at the Westin need not share their sand with anyone else. You get down to the beach by shuttle or elevator, or you can take an eco-walk along paths lined with rain-forest-like tropical foliage.

When he created this hotel, Legorreta, one of Mexico's most renowned architects, produced an excellent example of the minimalist style of Mexican architecture. Corridors are lit by open squares cut into the ceiling; large-scale contemporary art hangs on walls in both the public areas and guest rooms. Nothing is frivolous here.

The most romantic accommodations are the junior suites, located on the top (twenty-second) floor. You have a sitting room, bedroom, roomy bath with granite-topped vanities, and two patios, one with a Jacuzzi. You can sit in the Jacuzzi under the stars and gaze out at the sea. These patios, though terraced up the face of the pyramid, are really very private. A hammock is slung in a corner of a patio and the whole shebang is furnished with lounges, chairs, and tables with plushy cushions you can really sink into.

Furnishings are understated and very classy: cobalt blue glass–based lamps, three-dimensional wall murals, Mexican red tile floors, blue tiled headboards, flowers in wonderful pots and vases, and lots of space. Beds are covered with brightly colored cotton spreads and pillows.

These are not suites you want to leave. Sofas have double-thick cushions covered in brilliant Mexican woven fabrics in magentas, yellows, and turquoises. Closets, in keeping with the natural look, have nets instead of doors.

There are four pools, one just for adults; all sit on a hill overlooking the sea. The adjacent solarium serves light meals, including fresh seafood, and Les Fuentes is the place to go for drinks.

Westin's restaurants include El Mexicano, a romantic hacienda-like eatery with an inner garden courtyard; the Portofino, serving Italian cuisine, and Bellavista, where you eat outdoors on a covered terrace looking out over the Pacific.

At dusk, the Westin Ixtapa glows warmly as the golden rays of the sinking sun turn the hotel into a temple of gold.

Address/Phone: Playa Vista Hermosa 40880, Ixtapa Zihuatanejo, Gro., Mexico; 52–753–321–21; fax: 52–753–307–51

U.S. Reservations: (800) 228–3000

Owner/Manager: Rafael Millan, general manager

Arrival/Departure: The Ixtapa-Zihuatanejo Airport is 20 minutes away by taxi (45 pesos, about $7); transfers by van can be arranged.

Distance from Ixtapa-Zihuatanejo International Airport: 20 minutes

Distance from Ixtapa center : 3 minutes

Accommodations: 428 rooms and suites, each with patio

Best Rooms/Suites: Go for the junior suites on the top floor, or the master suites, which have private pools.

Amenities: Air-conditioning, ceiling fans, king- or queen-size beds, toiletries, TV, radio, cotton bathrobes, real hangers, hammocks; hair dryer in suites; refrigerator and telephones in master suites, some have whirlpools or minipools; laundry and valet service, 24-hour room service

Electricity: 110 volts

Sports and Facilities: 4 lighted tennis courts, gym, 4 pools, beach, Jacuzzis, most water sports; golf 5 minutes away

Dress Code: Casual

Weddings: Can be arranged

Rates/Packages: $130–$300 per couple per night; 4 days/3 nights package: $201 per couple (spring through fall); $300 (winter); including ocean-view room, breakfast, 1 hour of tennis daily, 15 percent discount on car rental, 20 percent discount on greens fees. Honeymoon package: $405 per couple for 2 nights; $673, 4 nights; $1,075, 7 nights; including accommodations, breakfasts, welcome cocktail, 1 hour of tennis court time daily, 15 percent car rental discount, 20 percent golf discount, 1 dinner for two, and champagne.

Payment/Credit Cards: Most major

Deposit: 2-night deposit; cancel 7 to 14 days prior to arrival date (depending on season) for refund.

Government Taxes: 15 percent

Service Charges: 15 percent suggested

Entry Requirements for U.S. Citizens: Proof of citizenship; passport best

Europe

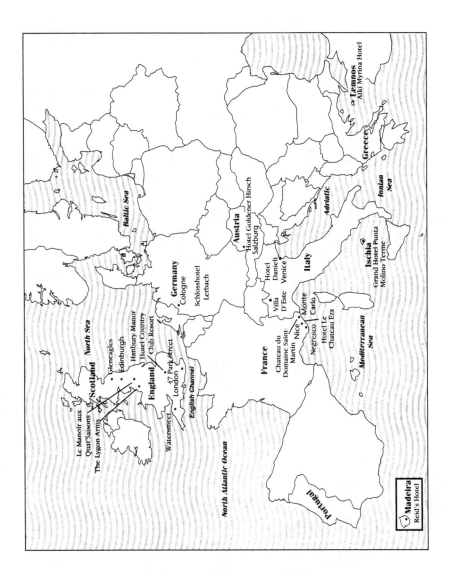

Lennos
Alki Myrina Hotel

Greece

Ionian
Sea

Adriatic

Baltic Sea

Austria
Hotel Goldener Hirsch
Salzburg

Ischia
Grand Hotel Punta
Molino Terme

Germany
Cologne

Schlosshotel
Lerbach

Italy

Hotel
Danieli
Venice

Villa
D'Este

Monte
Carlo

Mediterranean
Sea

North Sea

Gleneagles

Edinburgh

Hanbury Manor
Hotel Country
Club Resort

Scotland

47 Park Street
London

England

Chateau du
Domaine Saint-
Martin Nice

Negresco

Hotel Le
Chateau Eza

France

Le Manoir aux
Quat'Saisons
The Lygon Arms

Watersmeet

English Channel

North Atlantic Ocean

Portugal

Madeira
Reid's Hotel

Austria

Hotel Goldener Hirsch, Austria

Hotel Goldener Hirsch

Location: In the heart of Salzburg, on elegant Getreidegasse.
Romantic Features: Antique beds; Old World charm in fifteenth-century inn, the magic of Salzburg just outside your door.

The Hotel Goldener Hirsch is pure Austrian, from the puffy duvets to the quaint, wrought-iron folk art lamps which decorate the rooms. If you are coming to Austria for your honeymoon and want an historic inn in the heart of Salzburg, try this one. You'll know you're there when you spot among the many beautifully wrought hanging signs along the narrow street the one with a gold deer atop an ornate golden circle—Goldener Hirsch stands for "gold deer." From the time you check in at the elaborately carved front reception desk and follow the bellman to your room on a rather circuitous route, you'll begin to realize that this is indeed a unique place.
   The Goldener Hirsch is not just one building, but a combination of in-

terconnected buildings that stand smack on one of the most elegant streets in the baroque, historic heart of Salzburg. The Getreidegasse is lined with trendy boutiques and antiques shops, and just down the street is Mozart's birthplace; close by is the Festspielhaus (Theater).

Each of the seventy-three rooms and suites is individually furnished with cozy sitting areas, a conglomeration of antiques and masterpieces of rural art. On the beds are those wonderful creations of European refinement—goose down duvets and fine, soft linens. Headboards, desks, tables, and bureaus are likely to be mellowed orange pine. The baths are modern, and rooms come with comfortable amenities such as telephones, a TV, radio, and a minibar.

There is no way you can spend a night here and not be touched in some way by the rich heritage of this fine old inn. Its character and place in the world are due in part, to the work of a very special lady, Countess Walderdorff. She is the one who rescued the centuries-old structure from its sad state of disrepair and began its reconstruction during the difficult years following World War II. During the renovations, the countess supervised every detail of the hotel's rebirth, from the hand-wrought iron light fixtures to the specially made china.

Almost from the first day it opened its doors, the Goldener Hirsch became known as the "in" place for notables to stay and be seen when they came to Salzburg. Heads of state and the elite of the world have come to overnight and sup at this famous hostelry, among them the Duke and Duchess of Windsor, Herbert von Karajan, and Leonard Bernstein.

Today it's the lady's son, Count Johannes Walderdorff, who heartily welcomes guests from near and far places. Enjoy a quiet cocktail at the bar before sitting down to dinner. You can try local specialties and delicious draught beer in the rustic Herzl-Taverne, with its attractive inner courtyard. Indulge in all kinds of good things at the hotel's Goldener Hirsch restaurant, one of the best in Austria. Ask Count Walderdorff to recommend his favorite dishes, and he may suggest that you try the goose liver and *tafelspitz* (a boiled beef dish). Top it all off with a delectable caramel soufflé and caramel and walnut pancakes. "I tried twenty-eight versions of this recipe until I got it right," said the Count.

The Goldener Hirsch is not a particularly elegant place, nor is it one that offers much in the way of entertainment or activities. It doesn't need to. It's friendly, charming, and imagine: The whole wonderful city of Salzburg is right outside your door, with just about everything within easy walking distance. There are museums to explore, concert performances to attend, romantic little restaurants to try out, shops to browse through and endless, interesting streets to discover.

Address/Phone: Getreidegasse 37, A–5020, Salzburg, Austria; 43–662–848–511; fax: 43–662–843–349

U.S. Reservations: Ciga Hotels, (800) 221–2340

Owner/Manager: Johannes Walderdorff, director

Arrival/Departure: Taxi from airport or train station

Distance from Munich International Airport: Approximately 84 miles (2 hours); 3 miles (20 minutes) from Salzburg Airport

Distance from Salzburg: Located in heart of town

Accommodations: 70 rooms, 3 suites

Best Rooms/Suites: Room 23 with its antique, painted bed is charming; suites are roomier

Amenities: Hair dryer, telephone, radio, toiletries, air-conditioning, mini-bar, TV; room service, valet service

Electricity: 110 volts

Sports and Facilities: Guest privileges at Gut Altentann Golf & Country Club with payment of greens fees; other sports nearby include tennis, swimming, skiing, squash, and horseback riding.

Dress Code: Informal by day; jacket and tie for men appreciated for dinner

Weddings: Can be arranged

Rates/Packages: From ATS 3,300 per couple per night; Ciga Hotels offers a Welcome to Europe package: $299 per couple per night that requires a minimum of 7 nights and includes accommodations, breakfast, lunch or dinner, taxes, and service charges.

Payment/Credit Cards: Most major

Deposit: Guarantee with credit card

Government Taxes: Included

Service Charges: Included

Entry Requirements for U.S. Citizens: Passport

England

47 Park Street

Location: In London's fashionable Mayfair area near Grosvenor Square, Hyde Park, and trendy shops.

Romantic Features: Private, luxurious, apartmentlike accommodations in the heart of London; 24-hour room service menu provided by La Gavroche, a top-rated British restaurant.

When you walk into 47 Park Street, you are entering one of London's top hotels, although it is not as well known as others in its class. It has but 52 suites, and its brick Georgian facade looks more like the private townhouse of a wealthy British magnate or a titled lord than the elegant hotel that it is. It's discreet; it's classy; and it's divinely comfortable. The guests are rich or famous or both. Their temporary address at 47 Park Street affords them all the privacy they could ever want.

For honeymooners who want the ultimate in comfort and a quiet, gracious retreat after a busy, exciting day in London, this is really the cat's meow. The property was built in 1927 as the luxury pad for country gentry visiting the city, and in the 1960s the neighboring structures (numbers 45 and 49) were added to it. In 1982 the apartments were totally refurbished, and Albert Roux, one of Britain's most highly respected chefs, moved his famous restaurant, La Gavroche, to the premises and became the managing director of the hotel. Roux's wife, Monique, an accomplished interior designer, contributed her expertise to create 47 Park's sumptuous and stylish decor, blending English style with French chic.

The "apartments" on the first three floors have the highest ceilings; walls are panelled—some painted in soft pastels or ivory, others left natural to bring out the warm wood tones. Rich tapestries along with cheerful designer chintz are generously used throughout, and the suites are appointed with crystal chandeliers, brass and porcelain lamps, antique plates, and fine paintings and prints. Leatherbound books, fine old clocks, brass fireplace fenders, oriental area rugs, and mahogany writing boxes add warmth and character to the rooms. Bows are tied around sweeping draperies, and round tables and dressing vanities are covered with fabrics that reach the floor. King-size beds have padded headboards; some have canopies and "crowns" of flowing chintz. Each suite has a writing desk and a highly polished dining room table with six chairs, where you can enjoy breakfast, private dinners, and midnight repasts.

Curl up on one of the comfortable upholstered couches or chairs and sip a fine wine or champagne; when the weather is crisp and cool, savor the warmth of a fire in the fireplace.

The hotel is unique in that it technically has no restaurant if its own, although guests can enter Roux's La Gavroche through a private entrance off the lobby and get priority reservations. The restaurant is only open Monday through Friday for lunch and dinner, but not to worry: 47 Park has twenty-four-hour room service. You can have your meals or snacks delivered right to your door and the selection of food and wines is guaranteed to please the most discerning of palates. They come from the kitchens of La Gavroche, and the menu is extensive and totally tempting.

If you want to cook a meal for yourself, it's easy as your suite comes with a fully equipped kitchen. You can even have someone else to do your grocery shopping for you.

The rates are not for the timid, but the hotel is priced in the same ballpark as other top places in London, and for privacy and luxury, it ranks at the top of the list. The danger here is that you may find your "apartment" at 47 Park Street just too comfortable to leave, and with London's many treasures just outside your door, you'll want to venture out sometime.

Address/Phone: 47 Park Street, Mayfair, London W1Y 4EB; 44–171–491–7282; fax: 44–171–491–7281

U.S. Reservations: Relais & Chateaux, (800) RELAIS 8; Sterling International Reservation Service, (800) 637–7200; Utell International, (800) 44 UTELL

Owner/Manager: Compagnie Internationale Phénix Hotels, owner; Albert Roux, managing director; Ian Merrick, general manager

Arrival/Departure: Pickup at London's airports can be arranged from Heathrow via private limousine (approximately $140), hotel Jaguar ($110), or hotel sedan ($95); transportation from Gatwick slightly higher.

Distance from Heathrow International Airport: 15 miles

Distance from London Center: In heart of Mayfair

Accommodations: 52 private suites: 41 one-bedroom; 4 studios; 7 two-bedroom. All have separate living rooms; most have foyers and fully equipped kitchens.

Best Rooms/Suites: The deluxe one-bedroom suites on the first three floors have fireplaces, king-size beds, and two baths.

Amenities: Air-conditioning, TV, telephone, radio, terry robes, slippers, hair dryer, sewing kit, clothes brush, Moulton Brown toiletries, magnifying mirror, full-length mirror, padded hangers, in-room safe; daily newspaper, minibars, mineral water, fresh flowers, VCRs on request; most have fireplaces; fully equipped kitchens have refrigerator, coffeemaker, toaster, stove, and wet bar; twice-daily maid service, 24-hour room service, shopping service

Electricity: 220/240 volts

Sports and Facilities: For a nominal charge, guests have memberships at a health club 2 minutes away, at Grosvenor House, where there is a pool, sauna, sun beds, spa and treatment services; short walk to Hyde Park and jogging trails.

Dress Code: Casual smart during day; men must wear a jacket and tie for lunch and dinner at La Gavroche.

Weddings: A private dining room can be used for receptions or dinners for up to twenty guests.

Rates/Packages: From £235 per couple per night for a studio; £255–£380 for a one-bedroom suite
Payment/Credit Cards: Most major
Deposit: Guarantee with credit card; cancel 24 hours prior to arrival date to avoid 1-night room and tax charge.
Government Taxes: Included
Service Charges: Included
Entry Requirements for U.S. Citizens: Passport

Hanbury Manor Hotel Country Club Resort

Location: Near Ware, 25 miles north of London.
Romantic Features: Secret garden; suites with fireplaces; four-poster canopied beds; stepping through the moongate to the walled garden.

Driving north on the A10 about 25 miles out of London, you catch a glimpse of a stately Jacobean-style brick mansion on your left as you round a bend. You have just about arrived at Hanbury Manor, an impressive estate sitting comfortably on 200 acres of Hertfordshire countryside. With its luxurious accommodations, European health spa, gourmet restaurant, squash courts, tennis courts, walled gardens, arboretum, croquet lawn, snooker room, and eighteen-hole golf course, this bastion of British tradition appeals to just about anyone.

Once the sporting retreat of Edmund and Amy Hanbury, the mansion boasts a library with richly carved mahogany and rosewood panels, and its ornate great hall is home to some magnificent eighteenth-century tapestries. For a period of time, the estate served as an all-girls convent and boarding school before being transformed into a ninety-six-bedroom country house resort. Today Hanbury Manor greets guests from all over the world.

Golfing couples will find this a particularly good place to stay. About 170 of the property's picturesque, rolling acres have been carved into a new golf course designed by Jack Nicklaus II. During the construction of the course, an older layout was discovered, later determined to have been designed by the golf great Harry Vardon. The new course retains some of the features of the original course built in the early 1900s. A memorial to Vardon can be found on the seventeenth hole in the form of a unique bunker.

The new course is designed to test the skills of the more advanced players as well as provide a good day of golf for average mortals. Significant elevation changes and some magnificent stands of trees, as well as lakes and brooks, lend both beauty and interest to the layout. The course is open to members only and guests of the hotel who pay a nominal fee or book a golf package. Peter Blaze, the course's golf professional who served as the pro at Moor Allerton in Leeds for sixteen years, is on hand to give private golf lessons.

The ninety-six rooms and suites are located throughout the manor and adjacent garden court. Leaded glass windows overlook the meadows, golf course, and croquet field, and rooms are elegantly furnished with period pieces, English chintz, and marble baths. Some have canopied beds, fireplaces, and sitting areas. Fresh flowers are brought in each day, and in the large, luxurious bathrooms you'll find wonderfully thick towels, bathrobes, and Taylor's of London toiletries.

The rooms have twin or double beds, so be sure to ask for what you want at the time you make your reservations. Many of the king and junior suites have four-poster beds, separate sitting areas, and fireplaces.

Hanbury Manor has three restaurants: the classic and elegant Zodiac; the brasserie-style Vardon's, where you can sit inside or on the terrace overlooking the golf course; and the Conservatory, which features lighter fare for breakfast and lunch. Rory Kennedy, the executive chef, goes out of his way to find fresh local produce and offers dishes such as pressed Foie Gras with Braised Goose or Assiette of white and dark chocolate. The hotel has an extensive wine list with selections from France, Australia, the Americas, and England.

Hanbury Manor is a vast playground for active couples. In addition to golf, you can take a swim in the spectacular indoor pool, ringed with white columns and inlaid tile, or challenge your mate to a game of tennis, croquet, squash, or snooker (the closest thing to our game of pool). The gym provides the opportunity for a good workout; you can also arrange for clay pigeon shooting, archery, fishing, horseback riding, hunting, or hot air ballooning. After all, this is the land of kings and queens, where all these sybaritic pleasures are commonplace.

For a more leisurely afternoon, stroll through the gardens, which were established in the late 1850s. Discover the romantic "secret garden" set in a sunken glade with paths, lily ponds filled with goldfish, grottos, and intimate bowers. Explore the walled garden where two domed greenhouses are filled with exotic plants and trees. Step through the round archway carved in the hedge—the moongate.

Or take a picnic to the orchard, set in a meadow with large drifts of wildflowers. A woodland walk takes you from the back pond to the main arboretum, giving you a chance to enjoy the beauty of tall redwood, pine, and oak trees.

Feel like being pampered? Then sign up for a soothing massage or indulge in a number of special spa treatments such as aromatherapy, herbal baths, or facials. The spa is a particularly good place to go to help you unwind after all your wedding activities and the long plane ride. Should you want to leave your elegant "country house" for a few hours, you will find Hanbury Manor is ideally situated for exploring some of England's most interesting and historic places. Cambridge, Ascot, Newmarket, Hatfield House, and Wimpole Hall are within easy driving distance.

Address/Phone: Thundridge, Nr. Ware, Hertfordshire, SG12 0SD England; 44–192–048–7722; fax: 44–192–048–7692

U.S. Reservations: Small Luxury Hotels of the World, (800) 525–4800

Owner/Manager: Poles Limited, owners; Richard McKevitt, executive director

Arrival/Departure: Trains run frequently from London to Hertford North and East and to Ware. Taxis and chauffeur-driven cars can be arranged to Hanbury Manor from London's airports and local stations. By car, London is less than 1 hour away. The hotel also has a helipad.

Distance from London Heathrow Airport: 48 miles; 16 miles from London Stansted

Distance from London: 25 miles north

Accommodations: 96 rooms and suites

Best Rooms/Suites: King or junior corner suites overlooking golf course

Amenities: Hair dryer, in-house video, direct-dial telephone, TV, trouser press, toiletries, personal bars; 24-hour room service; laundry, dry cleaning, pressing, and shoe shine are also available.

Electricity: 240 volts

Sports and Facilities: 18-hole championship golf course, fitness center, indoor pool, 2 squash courts, steam bath, sauna, spa, gym, snooker room, 3 outdoor tennis courts; clay pigeon shooting, archery, croquet, horseback riding, fishing, and hot-air ballooning available nearby

Dress Code: Casual by day; dressier for dinner in the Zodiac restaurant. Vardon's is casual for all meals.

Weddings: In addition to many lovely garden settings throughout the property, there are 6 private rooms in the manor house and three in the garden court as well as Poles Hall, a deconsecrated chapel.

Rates/Packages: From about $300 per couple per night, including breakfast and VAT (March 1–Mid-July and mid-September–November 30); from about $245 (mid-July–mid-September and December 1–February 28). A Champagne Package giving couples accommodations, breakfast, dinner, and champagne is priced from about $273.

Payment/Credit Cards: Most major

Deposit: 1-night deposit, which may be cancelled 48 hours prior to arrival

for full refund; 50 percent refund if cancelled 24 hours prior to arrival
date
Government Taxes: Included
Service Charges: Not included
Entry Requirements for U.S. Citizens: Valid passport required

Le Manoir aux Quat' Saisons

Location: In a small country village between the Chilterns and the Cotswolds.
Romantic Features: Cocktails on the terrace overlooking the meadows
and gardens; a stroll through the tranquil Japanese gardens; sleeping in a
round, stone, medieval dovecote.

Those who dream of honeymooning in a centuries-old stone manor house
and have the wherewithal to pay the bill should head to Le Manoir aux
Quat' Saisons. England has a lot of wonderful castles and estate hotels, but
you'd have to look far and wide to find a place with as much going for it as
this one: romantic rooms, idyllic setting, superb service, convenient location
near the Cotswolds and London, plus one of the best restaurants in all the
kingdom.

Once a favorite country retreat of Lord Coventry, trusted servant of
James I, and a refuge for public officials in high standing, this magnificent
estate became a hotel in 1984 when Raymond Blanc opened Le Manoir.
During the past few years, the property has been totally refurbished, and a
garden wing and two glass conservatory dining rooms have been added.

One of the most unique accommodations, the Michael Priest Suite, is
located in the fifteenth-century dovecote, a round, stone tower with a coni-
cal pointed roof. The bathroom has a huge antique tub on feet that has
been painted with fanciful pink and white doves and flowers. A great
shower gives you the option of steam super jets coming at you from all
sides. A wide, soft, pink carpeted staircase winds up to the second level,
where a queen-size bed is topped by "garlands" of white and pink fabric
swags held aloft by white doves suspended from the ceiling by invisible
wires. The thick walls of the tower are painted in a warm yellow and decorated with pretty pictures hanging from wide pink ribbons. There is also a
skirted dressing table, cabana-like pink and white striped tented "closet,"
and a small leaded window opening onto the gardens. The only downside
of this blissful romantic bower is its size—it's a bit tight; other suites are
roomier. But for sheer romance, this is a honeymoon favorite.

Hollyhocks is in the main building and was the bedroom of one of the

Le Manoir aux Quat' Saisons, England

former owners of the estate. It is extremely spacious, furnished with a couch, chairs, dressing table, desk, coffee table, and large, canopied bed. A number of leaded windows open onto the courtyard. Also popular are the two-story garden suites, which have a sitting room on the lower level along with a furnished patio; the bedroom is upstairs. All are exquisitely decorated with a combination of traditional English furniture, antiques, artwork, chintz, and French accents.

Flowers are lavishly spread through the public areas and guest rooms. An in-house florist has her own cutting garden and flower house tucked into the corner of the property. A recent addition to the hotel, a Japanese garden, may seem a bit out of sync with the English gardens, but somehow it fits. A delicate mist of water falls from hidden places between the trees that overhang the pond, and a teahouse welcomes those who want to stop and be soothed.

Throughout the grounds, you'll find a number of original sculptures. A bronze work of birds rising through the reeds is particularly appealing. Many are for sale, as the gardens serve as an excellent showcase for artists such as Judith Holmes Drewry and Lloyd Le Blanc. Prices range from about $300 up to over $50,000.

Walk through the three acres of vegetable gardens and you'll begin to understand why the food here is so good. The thirty or so chefs who prepare the meals each day use only the freshest of ingredients. Baby zucchini picked just minutes before serving, with blossoms still attached (to stuff with crabmeat and truffles); beetroot, runner beans, artichokes, leek, spinach, tomatoes—more than one hundred varieties of vegetables, herbs, and fruits planted here supply the hotel with most of its produce. Meat comes from a local butcher just down the road. Take a peek in the kitchen, and on the shelves you'll see huge glass jars filled with plums, cherries, raspberries, and other fruits.

But having the right ingredients is just the beginning of the road leading to a Michelin two-star rating. It takes a great chef like Raymond Blanc to complete the picture: Blanc's list of credits fill a page and more. Each of his creations not only looks like a work of art, it titillates taste sensations you never knew you had. Your meal may also seem to be priced like an art object (hors d'oeuvres such as pressed duck confit and foie gras in a truffle gelée costs about $36; entrees such as pan-fried wild salmon fillet on a sorrel sabayon will set you back about $47; homemade sorbets on a waffle "painter's palette" cost around $23), but look at it this way. Sure it costs a lot, but here you're not just paying for dinner, you're investing in a delectable memory guaranteed to last a lifetime. If you come to the hotel and can't afford to try the restaurant, you might as well go somewhere else.

Meals are served in three different dining rooms: the original one and two new conservatory rooms, which are pleasant and pretty year-round. (The new rooms are air-conditioned.)

Lest you be tempted to simply loll on the grounds and take in the never-ending vistas of pure English countryside, there is a tennis court, croquet court, and lovely pool set in its own garden courtyard, enclosed by hedges. You can go biking, walking, fishing, or arrange with the concierge to play golf or go horseback riding. And Le Manoir is in a great location for exploring the Cotswolds, Oxford, and other historic and interesting places such as Blenheim Palace, the Royal Shakespeare Theatre and Windsor Castle.

Le Manoir Quat' Saisons combines the country charm of merry old England, the cuisine of France, and the technical expertise of today's engineering: a real winner! Now if the price of a room here in 1474—about 95 cents for a week—could be matched today, you'd really be in heaven.

Address/Phone: Church Road, Great Milton, Oxford OX44 7PD; 44–1184–427–881; fax: 44–0184–427–8847

U.S. Reservations: Relais & Chateaux, (800) RELAIS 8

Owner/Manager: Raymond Blanc, chef-patron; Simon Rhatigan, general manager

Arrival/Departure: Pickup at London's airports can be arranged; from Heathrow via private limousine (about $135 per car); from Gatwick

Airport (about $235); helipad on grounds

Distance from Heathrow International Airport: 40 miles (under 1 hour); Gatwick, 55 miles (1½ hours)

Distance from Oxford: 8 miles south

Accommodations: 19: 10 in main house; 9 in dovecote and garden wing; 4 rooms with four-poster beds

Best Rooms/Suites: The two-story Michael Priest Suite, built in a fifteenth-century dovecote; Hollyhocks, a spacious room with a four-poster bed in the main building; and the two-story suites in the new garden wing.

Amenities: Hair dryer, TV, telephone, radio, terry robes, sewing kit, heated towel bar, bidet, double sinks, toiletries, magnifying mirror, full-length mirror, padded hangers, trouser press; daily newspaper, fresh fruit, Madeira, mineral water, 24-hour room service, fresh flowers, VCRs on request

Electricity: 220/240 volts

Sports and Facilities: Latex tennis court, croquet, pool, bicycles, walking trails, fishing; riding and golf nearby

Dress Code: Country elegant

Weddings: Can be arranged; gardens and terraces make lovely setting.

Rates/Packages: £375 per couple per night for a suite, £325 for a junior suite, £275 for a superior room, £235 for a deluxe room, £175 for a standard room; includes early morning tea and coffee, taxes, and service charges, October to April midweek rates, £125 per couple per night; includes standard accommodations, breakfast, dinner, newspaper, morning tea and coffee, taxes, and service charges.

Payment/Credit Cards: Most major

Deposit: $150 per couple per night; cancel 2 weeks prior to arrival date for full refund.

Government Taxes: Included

Service Charges: Included

Entry Requirements for U.S. Citizens: Passport

The Lygon Arms

Location: In the center of the town of Broadway in the Cotswolds.

Romantic Features: Canopy beds and fireplaces; garden lunches.

You couldn't ask for a better base from which to explore the beautiful Cotswolds. Located right on the main street in the heart of Broadway (one of the Cotswolds' most charming towns), The Lygon Arms is steeped with old English charm and character, from its hand-hewn rafters to its massive stone fireplaces and antique four-poster canopy beds. A member of the Savoy Group of hotels, The Lygon Arms has a history of welcoming travelers for more than 470 years.

The sixteenth-century front doorway is believed to have been built in the year the *Mayflower* sailed for the New World, and in 1651 Oliver Cromwell was a guest at the inn the night before the Battle of Worcester (the final battle of the Civil War between Charles II and his Cavaliers and the Parliament's Roundheads). The room where he slept contains a handsome Elizabethan fireplace, original oil paintings, antique Jacobean-style furniture, and an ornate seventeenth-century plaster ceiling frieze. An ancient staircase used by King Charles II and original oak panelling can be found in the cozy first-floor sitting room.

The hotel's accommodations are divided between the old, original structure and a relatively new (1960s) east wing. Although I would choose the older rooms, with their uneven floors, plastered walls, exposed beams, and antique furniture, the newer rooms are also quite charming and are decorated in softer, lighter colors. They can also be quieter. Some of the rooms located at the front of the building have windows that open over the main street and can thus be noisy at times.

Because the Cotswolds is one of England's most popular tourism destinations, this area is often teeming with tourists during the warmer months. Nevertheless, when I visited in August, I found The Lygon Arms to be a wonderful haven from the browsers and shoppers just outside the entrance.

The hotel has a lovely inner courtyard where you can sit at an umbrella table and have a cup of tea or lunch, and in the lounge areas there are a lot of nooks and crannies where you can settle into a comfortable chair and read a paper, sip a cocktail, or just watch the world go by.

A new $3-million country club was added in 1991 and is connected to the hotel so that guests can walk from their rooms to the facilities without going outside. The club has a large, attractive, Roman-style indoor pool with a retractable glass roof that opens (weather permitting), a jogging track, spa bath, fully equipped fitness room, solaria, steam room, saunas, and a billiards room. A floodlit tennis court is also on the premises, and a croquet lawn is located in the gardens.

The truly adventurous can take off from the hotel in the early morning or evening for a balloon ride over the rolling countryside or get a bird's-eye view of the area from a helicopter—The Lygon Arms has its own helipad. Other activities, such as golf, fishing, riding, and sightseeing, can be arranged through the concierge.

Elegant dining takes place in the Great Hall, which boasts a seventeenth-century minstrel's gallery, stags' heads, heraldic friezes, and a barrel-vaulted ceiling. Complete gourmet meals are created by the hotel's award-winning chef, Roger Narbett, who turns out dishes such as salmon and barley pie and Cotswold partridge. He uses fresh, locally grown produce when in season. A three-course vegetarian menu is also offered. Goblets Wine Bar is popular with guests who want to eat in a more casual atmosphere, and light lunches are served in the cocktail bar.

There is lots to see in the area, including Blenheim Palace (Churchill's birthplace); Stratford, Sudeley, and Warwick castles; Cambridge; and Hidcote Garden. Quaint Cotswolds villages such as Chipping Campden, Burton-on-the-Water, and Upper and Lower Slaughter are also great fun to explore.

In one of the lounges you'll find inscribed on the wall, "The hay is so good, the dog so fat," an old saying meaning, "The beds are good, the food is delicious." So it was when it was written many years ago; so it is today at The Lygon Arms.

Address/Phone: Broadway, Worcester WR12 7DU; 44–138–685–2255; fax: 44–138–685–8611

U.S. Reservations: Leading Hotels of the World, (800) 223–6800

Owner/Manager: Kirk Ritchie, managing director and general manager; Barry Hancox, hotel manager

Arrival/Departure: Taxi and chauffeur-driven car transportation can be arranged to The Lygon Arms from London's airports and local stations. A complimentary meet-and-greet service at Heathrow will help you get on your way. A private car transfer costs £120 (about $185) per car from Heathrow. The hotel also has a helipad.

Distance from London Heathrow Airport: About 75 miles (2 hours)

Distance from London: 75 miles

Accommodations: 58 rooms and 5 suites, some with four-poster beds; most have queen-size beds; 6 rooms have patios

Best Rooms/Suites: Four-poster rooms, The Great Bedchamber has a vaulted Tudor beamed ceiling and a marvelous, heavy, mahogany four-poster bed; Room 35 in the old section is located directly across from the Cromwell Room. If the Cromwell Room is not being used for a private party, you can use it at no extra charge and enjoy a candlelight dinner for two in front of the fireplace.

Amenities: Hair dryer, radio, TV, telephone, in-room safe, toiletries

Electricity: 240 volts

Sports and Facilities: The country club has a fitness center, billiards room, beauty treatment facilities, table tennis, indoor pool, steam bath, sauna, and spa bath. There is also a tennis court (lit for night play) and a croquet lawn. Golf, horseback riding, squash, fishing, and hot air ballooning can be arranged.

Dress Code: Casual by day; dressier for dinner in the Great Hall restaurant

Weddings: Can be arranged

Rates/Packages: £140–£305 per couple per night, including accommodations, breakfast, early morning tea, and newspaper. A special midweek package priced at £205 per person includes two nights' accommodations, breakfast and tea each morning, newspaper, and dinner each evening. A Champagne Break package priced at £225 per person includes two nights' accommodations, champagne on arrival, fruit and flowers in your room, breakfast each morning, and dinner, plus a special gift (extra nights are £98 per person).

Payment/Credit Cards: Most major

Deposit: Guarantee with credit card

Government Taxes: 17.5 percent

Service Charges: Not included

Entry Requirements for U.S. Citizens: Valid passport

Watersmeet

Location: Perched on a cliff on Devon's dramatic coastline, on Woolacombe Bay

Romantic Features: Spectacular views of the sea from just about every window; unusually wide, moonscapelike beach; wonderful footpaths along the coastline.

Located on the north coast of Devon, the award-winning Watersmeet Hotel is the kind of place people return to year after year, asking for the same room and coming to meet with friends at the same week of the same month. It's got a superb beachfront location, the best food you'll find anywhere, and it's near two of the finest golf courses in England.

The Watersmeet doesn't have pink marble baths or multistory lobbies with fountains. What it does have are comfortable chairs and sofas arranged along the length of a long lounge overlooking the sea. It has a spectacular dining room with circular glass windows and views of the water and gardens and guest rooms you wouldn't mind hanging out in for a few hours. But most important of all, it has Pat and Brian Wheeldon, owners and innkeepers, who have renovated the old hotel from top to bottom and put a lot of love and hard work into maintaining it and keeping their guests happy.

Using her flair for design and color, Pat has decorated each of the

Watersmeet, England

twenty-five rooms with soft pastel colors and prints. The lovely draperies, canopies, bedspreads, and table covers in pinks, aquas, yellows, and greens reflect the colors of the sea and sunsets. All rooms are different. Room 22 is on a corner and has a great view of the coastline from a window at the end of the shower! Another room overlooking the sea has an antique four-poster bed and armoire as well as a sitting area. Some rooms have queen-size beds, others twins, and all rooms have TV, tiled modern baths, and sitting areas.

Brian, an excellent cook, can often be found in the kitchen creating some of his well-known dishes. His soups are outstanding; his liver pâté is smooth and rich. All fish, meat, and produce served at the Watersmeet is fresh. Brian told me, "Over the years I have found where to get the best. Our bacon, for instance, comes from Belgium." The Watersmeet has won a number of awards for its cuisine and fine wine cellar. The hotel's Devon cream tea, a specialty of the area, is served each afternoon.

Dining at the Watersmeet becomes a ritual. You come down to the lounge dressed for dinner (no jeans here), sit at one of the comfortable chairs, perhaps by the fireplace or in one of the nooks along the lounge, then order a drink or two. Pat or one of the waitresses brings you a small plate of impossible-to-resist hors d'oeuvres and gives you a menu. After you have ordered, you continue to enjoy your cocktails until you're told your table (always the same one) is ready. Your first course is in place when you get to the table. It's rather like a large, lovely house party.

If you're normally a toast-coffee-juice person, once you've tried Watersmeet's fresh sautéed mushrooms, wonderful English sausage, omelets, back bacon, and homemade muffins, you may temporarily convert to a fat-intensive-breakfast devotee. Rates include breakfast and dinner, and in this case, you wouldn't want to eat anywhere else. When you stay at the Watersmeet, whether you're on the golf course or exploring one of the quaint villages nearby, you find yourself looking at your watch to make sure to get back to the hotel by dinnertime. The food is that good.

Watersmeet is a great location for those who want to play golf at one of the superb courses nearby, which, by the way, eat balls on contact. Saunton Golf Club, just a few minutes away, has two seaside courses that were described in *Golfweek* as the best in England. Stay at Watersmeet, and Brian will help arrange your tee times.

Just outside the hotel are some good walking trails that lead you by rolling pastures dotted with grazing sheep. Amble up the narrow road to the top, where you'll find a fine pub and the small village of Ilfracombe. In these little villages in the countryside, roads are so narrow in places, only one car can pass at a time, squeezing by the hedgerows.

Watersmeet has a grass tennis court (which doubles as a croquet court, depending on the interests of the guests) and a large heated swimming pool. Below the hotel, a path heads to a huge, sprawling beach edged by jagged dark rocks near the base of the cliff. As the tide retreats, glistening rock pools are left behind. Serious swimmers should be aware that the water can test the endurance of the hardiest of souls. It can be very cold. But even in October, you'll see surfers in wet suits riding the rolling waves.

If you want to travel in England and enjoy the luxury of a lovely country home, Watersmeet provides an excellent base for exploring the Devon countryside. You'll find guests of all ages here, and you won't find many Americans—they haven't discovered it yet.

Address/Phone: Mortehoe, Woolacombe, Devon EX34 7EB, England; 44–2718–703–33; fax: 44–2718–708–90

U.S. Reservations: NA

Owners/Manager: Brian and Pat Wheeldon

Arrival/Departure: Rental cars available at airport

Distance from London Heathrow International Airport: 2½ to 3 hours

Distance from London: 3 hours

Accommodations: 25 rooms, all individually furnished

Best Rooms/Suites: Oceanfront room with antique canopy bed, armoire, and sitting area

Amenities: Tea and coffee bar, ceiling fans, toiletries, TV; hair dryer avail-

able; turndown service, room service (breakfast)
Electricity: 220/240 volts
Sports and Facilities: Tennis (grass court), beach, heated swimming pool
(warm months), undercover golf practice area, pool table, Ping-Pong,
bar billiards, croquet; golf nearby at Saunton Golf Club
Dress Code: Jacket and tie requested for evening dining
Weddings: Can be arranged
Rates/Packages: £68–£87 per person per night, including breakfast and
dinner. Weekly rate £476–£553; Special Breaks package, 2 night mini-
mum, £58–£76 per person per night; £406–£483 (weekly) (early and
late summer); £47–£63 per person per night (spring and fall)
Payment/Credit Cards: Most major
Deposit: £50 per person per week, £10 per day; one-third refund if can-
celled, unless room can be relet.
Government Taxes: Included
Service Charges: Included
Entry Requirements for U.S. Citizens: Passport
Closed: December and January

France

Château du Domaine Saint-Martin

Location: Centrally located in the center of the French Riviera on six hilltop
acres overlooking the Mediterranean.
Romantic Features: Villas with private terraces looking out to the sea;
serene setting steeped in history.

As you approach the unassuming entrance to the Château du Domaine
Saint-Martin after a rather heady ride through narrow, loopy roads, a break
in a lush, thick, clipped hedgerow takes you into the quaint complex of
charming old buildings with roots dating back to A.D. 350. Once the residence of the Knights Templar, this serene place is a haven for those who
love history and peace, graciousness and good food.
    There are several rooms in the château itself that are beautifully ap-
pointed with antique furniture, Persian and Flemish carpets, original art,
and fresh flowers that set a mood of timeless elegance. There are also several *bastides* and villas randomly placed on the wooded estate. Each of
these suites has its own sitting room, bedroom, and bath and a whole lot of

privacy. Enjoy the sunset while sipping a glass of fine French champagne from your private terrace and look out over the tops of the trees and old stone houses staggered down the hill to the sea beyond. In the vivid late afternoon light, this shimmering vision conjures up a page from a romantic novel.

Wander into the gracefully landscaped lawns and gardens, where you'll find chairs and tables for relaxing; head to the tennis court for a bit of exercise or to the swimming pool, where there are lounges, umbrella tables, and chairs. During the summer months, you'll also find a grill restaurant that serves beverages and light meals.

The restaurant, awarded one star by the Michelin guidebook, is known for its fresh fish, which in all likelihood has been purchased by the chef himself the same morning from local fishermen. The skillful use of herbs and preparation of vegetables and fruits harvested from the Domaine's own gardens are what has given this restaurant a reputation as one of the best in the region. Homemade pasta and soups, rack of lamb, and superb soufflés are hard to resist. The hotel's selection of regional wines is also excellent.

The Domaine is ideally situated to serve as a base for exploring the Riviera; the excitement of Cannes and Nice as well as Monaco is not far away. Also nearby are some extraordinary art galleries, such as the Maeght Foundation, where you'll find Miró, Calder, Chagall, Kandinsky, and Matisse paintings and sculptures. Several large sculptures are also located on the beautiful, sprawling grounds.

A short drive away is the medieval town of Vence, which has preserved its old ramparts and has some wonderful little shops and streets. Not far from Vence is Cagnes-sur-Mer, where you'll find Les Collettes, once the home and studio of Renoir. It's with a sense of reverence that you see the chair he sat in when he painted, the brushes he used, the lounge with its fragile silk covering where his models lay, and the old shed and twisted old olive trees that appear in many of Renoir's best known works.

Visit one of the loveliest fortified medieval towns in Europe, St. Paul de Vence, which sits high on a hilltop and is still partially ringed by ancient stone walls. Wander through the narrow, twisting, cobbled streets, watch the men play a game of *boules* in the village square, and browse through the many antiques shops. One of the prize souvenir items you'll find here are the miniature ceramic house "blocks" by Jean-Pierre Gault and other artists, which replicate the French houses in these medieval towns.

And after you've been out exploring the countryside and small villages, you can return to spend the rest of the day and evening amid the quiet elegance of Château du Domaine Saint-Martin. What more could you want!

Address/Phone: Route de Coursegoules, 06140 Vence, France; 33–93–58–

0202; fax: 33–93–24–0891
U.S. Reservations: Relais & Chateaux, (800) RELAIS 8
Owners/Manager: Andrée Brunet, director
Arrival/Departure: Rental cars available at Marseilles
Distance from Nice Côte d'Azur Airport: 12 miles (20 minutes)
Distance from Nice: 12 miles
Accommodations: 24 rooms and suites: 14 rooms in château; 10 suites in
the villas and *bastides* with double bed, sitting room, and terrace
Best Rooms/Suites: Private villas or *bastides*
Amenities: Hair dryer, toiletries, air-conditioning, bathrobes
Electricity: 220 volts
Sports and Facilities: Tennis court (clay), heated pool; golf nearby at Biot,
Valbonne, and Mougins
Dress Code: Jacket and tie required for dinner
Weddings: Can be arranged
Rates/Packages: ff 2,280–ff 3,200 per couple per night (March and Novem-
ber); ff 1,370–ff 2,630 (Easter to end of October); breakfast is ff 110.
Payment/Credit Cards: Most major, not accepted for payment of deposit
Deposit: 2 to 4 nights at time of booking; prepayment of balance due 1
month prior to arrival, credit card not accepted for payment of this part
of account; cancel 1 month in advance in high season; 2 weeks in low
season.
Government Taxes: Included
Service Charges: Included
Entry requirements for U.S. Citizens: Passport
Closed: December to February

Hotel Le Château Eza

Location: Situated on the Moyenne Corniche between Nice and Monaco,
on the Côte d'Azur.
Romantic Features: Dramatic setting on cliff overlooking the Mediterranean; elegant theme rooms, some with terraces.

Like the legendary Camelot, Le Château Eza stands in a medieval village
awash in romance and mystery. But while King Arthur's domain was an in-
vention of British folklore, this exquisite, intimate hotel tucked away in a
1,000-year-old fortress village is very real.

Modern-day Lancelots and Guineveres will love this castle of stone, the
former summer residence of the Swedish royal family. Set on a narrow cob-

Hotel Le Château Eza, France

blestone street, it clings to the side of the ancient rock wall of Eze, more than 1,300 feet above the Mediterranean.

Situated midway between Nice and Monte Carlo, it is conveniently located on the Moyenne Corniche (the middle road running between the two cities), allowing guests easy access to the many attractions of the famous Côte d'Azur—providing they can tear themselves away from the breathtaking views of Cap Ferrat and the sea.

Stone passages and walkways lead to ten guest accommodations, which have been newly decorated. All have modern conveniences such as air-conditioning and fine baths, and the rooms are enhanced by charming fireplaces, stone walls, beamed ceilings, balconies, and the pièces de résistance: the views.

Each room is thematically different: There is a quaint room perched on the cliff's edge overlooking the mountains, and there is an intimate, romantic room with a canopy bed, fireplace, and balcony as well as a very grand Louis XVI chamber with a separate dressing area fit for a queen. La Suite du Château, a three-room suite with a floral and ivy theme, has a bedroom with loft, sitting room, separate dressing room, private terrace with garden, and a spectacular sea view. Another suite is especially dramatic, with high ceilings, arches, columns, and an enormous iron bed. Take your pick! All the rooms are elaborately furnished with oriental rugs, antique furniture, upholstered chairs, and stunning accessories. Fresh flowers are replaced daily.

Although there are no sports facilities on the property, within the walled city of Eze there is the Jardin Exotique, filled with cacti as well as gift shops, art galleries, and restaurants.

Dinner at Le Château Eza is served in either the indoor glass dining room or outdoor terrace atop the cliffs. It is considered one of the most romantic dining spots in the world. Chef Andre Signoret, formerly of the Crillon and the Grand Véfour, has just received a Michelin star for his cuisine, which might include sautéed fresh foie gras on a bed of pasta au gratin with truffles; lobster with ratatouille; sautéed Mediterranean bass with wild baby fennel; or roasted rack of lamb with tiny stuffed vegetables.

Desserts include wild strawberry tarts; a bitter-black concoction that is coffee liqueur heart with a cacao bean crust; or petals of zucchini flowers with vanilla ice cream flavored with apricot marmalade. The wine list is extensive. Although dinner for two with wine could set you back $300, there is a special lunch menu for only $20 per person without wine that is a bargain.

The staff at the hotel is efficient, friendly, and helpful; restaurant service excellent.

You would need a time machine to travel back more than a thousand years to the medieval era, unless of course you chose to visit Château Eza. Here, on a spell-binding cliff overlooking the Mediterranean, all the romance and chivalry of King Arthur is yours, albeit for the modern-day equivalent of a king's ransom.

Address/Phone: 06360 Eze Village, Côte d'Azur, France; 93–41–1224; fax: 93–41–1664

U.S. Reservations: (800) 507–8250

Owner/Manager: Mr. and Mrs. Terry Giles, owners; Jesper Jerrik, general manager

Arrival/Departure: By taxi, available at airport

Distance from Côte d'Azur Airport: 10 miles

Distance from Nice: 10 miles, 15 minutes; 2 minutes from Eze

Accommodations: 4 suites; 6 guest rooms

Best Rooms/Suites: Le Suite du Château

Amenities: Air-conditioning, safe, TV, video, telephone, hair dryer, toiletries, bathrobes, flowers, champagne, candy

Electricity: 220 volts

Sports/Facilities: Beach 10 minutes away.

Dress Code: Men should wear a jacket at dinner.

Weddings: One of their specialties

Rates/Packages: $200–$400 per couple per night for a room (Dec. 1 to mid-April); suites $350–$500; $275–$630 for a room (July 1 to Aug. 31);

suites $450–$630; $300–$600 for a room (mid-April to June 30 and Sept. 1 to Oct. 31); suites $500–$700.
Payment/Credit Cards: Most major
Deposit: 1-night deposit; 15-day cancellation notice for full refund
Government Taxes: Included
Service Charges: Included
Entry Requirements for U.S. Citizens: Valid passport
Closed: November

Negresco

Location: Sits right on the famed French Riviera, or the Côte d'Azur, in Nice, which is cradled in a mountain range that plunges straight down to the sea.
Romantic Features: A veritable palace where guests are treated like the royalty who frequent the resort; four-poster beds, mink bedspreads, marble baths with gold sinks, and charming terraces facing the sea.

If you have ever dreamed of rubbing shoulders with royalty, Nice's Hotel Negresco may be as close as you will ever get to an invitation to Buckingham Palace.

The Negresco is a step back to La Belle Epoque, when crown princes and monarchs fled the harsh European winters and escaped southward to this jewel on the French Riviera.

Located in Nice on the legendary Côte d'Azur, the gilt-edged Negresco is the queen of the Riviera hotels. Staying here is an exercise in luxury and excess, and it is not surprising to find the hotel was inspired by the Palace of Versailles. Built in 1912 by Rumanian immigrant Henri Negresco, it was intended as a haven for the upper crust of Europe. It still is. Classified by the French government as a historic monument in 1974, the Negresco is frequented by movie stars, heads of state, and the world's beautiful people.

Unlike many of those venerable grandes dames that have fallen on hard times, the Negresco has not lost its luster. It has been polished and honed to a fare-thee-well. In fact when you walk through the various rooms—each one different from the other—you may be taken aback by the riot of bright colors, patterns, ornate accessories, and frivolities used in the decor. Only the Negresco can get away with bright blue flowered drapes, vivid red carpeting, gilt mirrors, and gold-flecked tubs. Walls are brocade, beds are huge (some are four-poster) with puffy down pillows and thick comforters, fur spreads, antique needlepoint chairs, and gold double sinks.

These rooms are beyond elaborate! (A sense of humor helps.)

The hall porters and doormen are dressed in traditional French costumes, copies of the uniforms worn by the staffs of aristocratic homes during the eighteenth and nineteenth centuries. The reception hall, with its fine gold molding, is decorated with Louis XVI period furnishings. To the left is the Salon Massena, which is adorned in the Empire style with gold thread tapestries that are exact replicas of the fabrics of the throne room at the Château of Fontainebleau. Straight ahead, under the world-famous glass dome made in the workshop of Gustave Eiffel, is the majestic Salon Royal. On the floor is the largest carpet ever made by the Savonnerie factory—so large that it took an oversize truck and a huge crane to handle it when it was sent out for cleaning.

The Baccarat chandelier, one of a pair ordered by the Tsar of Russia at the end of the nineteenth century, is a nice touch. Its mate hangs in the Kremlin. Works by Picasso, Leger, and Cocteau hang on the walls, and everywhere you'll see period pieces, tapestries, and antique furniture. If you ever wanted to stay overnight in a museum, this is it.

Amid all this splendor, there is something breezy and fun about the Negresco. Perhaps it is the impeccable staff, who are bent on providing each guest with every possible service and are never overbearing or stuffy.

There are two restaurants, the brasserie-style La Rotonde, with its cheerful merry-go-round decor, complete with painted wooden horses, and the well known Chantecler. La Rotonde serves outstanding pasta, hors d'oeuvres, fish, and meats along with exemplary pastries. Prices are surprisingly moderate.

The Regency-style Chantecler restaurant, with its sumptuous wood panelling, flower-patterned silk curtains, Aubusson tapestry, red velvet chairs, and fine portraiture, is the setting for a trip to gastronomic heaven. Ravioli with Artichokes, St. Peter's Fish with Ratatouille, Coquilles Saint-Jacques with Caviar, and Gateau of Chocolate Nougatine are just a few of the specialties turned out by the award-winning chef, Dominique Le Stanc. And wait 'til you try the crème brûlée. Chantecler received two Michelin stars in 1993.

At the Negresco, all you need is a crown and scepter for your royal honeymoon.

Address/Phone: 37 Promenade des Anglais, BP 379, 06007 Nice Cedex, France; 33–93–88–3951; fax: 33–93–88–3568
U.S. Reservations: Leading Hotels of the World, (800) 223–6800
Owner/Manager: Mr. and Mrs. Paul Augier; Michael Palmer, general manager; Guy Bellet, manager
Arrival/Departure: Taxis available at airport

Distance from Côte d'Azur Airport: 4 miles (10 minutes)
Distance from Nice: Is in the heart of Nice
Accommodations: 140 rooms, 18 suites
Best Rooms/Suites: Deluxe room on fifth floor
Amenities: Air-conditioning, bidet, radio, cable TV, minibar, direct-dial
  telephones, robes, toiletries, fresh flowers; stereo on request
Electricity: 220 volts
Sports and Facilities: Swimming at beach, waterskiing, massage; golf and
  tennis nearby
Dress Code: Elegantly casual; jacket required in Chantecler restaurant in
  the evening
Weddings: Can be arranged
Rates/Packages: $250–$750 per night per room, EP (October–April);
  $325–$800 (May–Sepember)
Payment/Credit Cards: Most major
Deposit: 1-night deposit; 15-day cancellation notice for refund
Government Taxes: $1 per person per day city tax (high season)
Service Charges: Included
Entry Requirements for U.S. Citizens: Valid passport

Germany

Schlosshotel Lerbach

Location: East of Cologne, in the wooded valleys of Bergischesland.
Romantic Features: Relaxing in quiet country setting; ballooning over the
countryside.

When you stay at the ivy-covered Schlosshotel Lerbach, once a private castle, you feel much like you are visiting privileged friends in the country.
The sprawling grounds, rooted in a setting of gently rolling green hills and
meandering streams, are bucolic. Situated in Germany's Bergischesland,
east of Cologne, the castle is surrounded by fine old trees, and double
stone stairs lead down to a nice garden area and a glimmering fish pond.
The Lerbach staff, who treat you as if you were privileged guests of an old
friend, make it easy to settle in here very quickly.
  Over the past 600 years, the hotel, once Burg Lerbach Castle, has gone
through a lot of changes. Built around 1384, the castle was converted to the
classic English manor house style in 1838. After serving as a private palace

and later as headquarters for a film company, this magnificent estate was transformed into a stylish hotel just a few years ago.

Each of the fifty-four rooms and suites is individually decorated and distinguished by little touches like books on the shelves and fresh flowers. Some have canopy beds, others brass beds. Many suites are multilevel with nice sitting areas with writing desks. Rooms are furnished with period furniture and artwork, tapestries, oriental carpets, and interesting accessories like puffy throw pillows, porcelain pieces, and leatherbound books. Bathrooms are large and have tubs and showers.

The castle sits in a park of more than seventy acres, which gives you plenty of room to find your own private place. For a special treat, arrange for a hot air balloon tour of the countryside. Your journey starts in the park and lifts you over the hills, valleys, vineyards, and lakes, which are so very beautiful here. Enjoy a delightful picnic later under the trees.

One of the most dreamy places to relax is on the pretty terrace, which is set up with wrought iron tables and perky yellow umbrellas. In good weather, you can have your breakfast, lunch, or tea here. For more active souls, there is a red-clay tennis court on the grounds as well as a well-equipped health club.

Or how about a hiking trip in the Siebengebirge? You start out with a gourmet breakfast in the hotel, then it's off on a guided hike in the mountains with a picnic lunch served in the countryside.

The hotel has two restaurants: the Restaurant Dieter Müller, featuring creative, modern French specialties such as Homard Rôti Parfumé aux Truffes Exotique Saint-Pierre, and Sorbet au Champagne. The Dieter Müller has earned a two-star Michelin rating as well as other honors. The more moderately priced but also excellent Restaurant Schlosschänke specializes in regionally influenced new German cuisine. There are also a bar and a terrace overlooking the park.

Schlosshotel Lerbach is an excellent base for exploring this exceptionally beautiful area of Germany. History buffs will want to visit nearby Cologne, where there is a lot to see besides the famous cathedral, such as an original Roman mosaic floor, museums, and art galleries. Have lunch in an old brewery. Take a day cruise on the lovely Rhine River.

Address/Phone: Lerbacher Weg, D–51469, Bergisch Gladbach, Germany; 49–2202–2040; fax: 49–2202–204940

U.S. Reservations: Relais & Chateaux, (800) RELAIS 8

Owner/Manager: Thomas H. Althoff, owner; Kurt Wagner, director

Arrival/Departure: Private transfers from airport can be arranged

Distance from airport (Cologne/Bonn): 15 miles

Distance from Cologne: 12 miles (20 minutes)

Accommodations: 47 rooms, 7 suites
Best Rooms/Suites: Each is different; ask for a room with a canopy bed.
Amenities: Hair dryer, minibar, TV, in-room safe, music system, telephones; portable fax machine on request
Electricity: 220 volts
Sports and Facilities: Archery, swimming pool, sauna, solarium, massages, fishing, hiking, jogging trails, tennis, horseback riding (in season), ballooning (arranged); golf nearby,
Dress Code: Casual by day; jacket requested in dining room for dinner
Weddings: Can be arranged
Rates/Packages: DM 380–DM 540 per couple per night for a room; junior suite, DM 580–DM 780; suite, DM 780–DM 1,280; including breakfast, parking, and use of swimming pool and sauna.
Payment/Credit Cards: Most major
Deposit: Credit card guarantee
Government Taxes: 15 percent VAT included
Service Charges: Included
Entry Requirements for U.S. Citizens: Passport

Greece

Lemnos

Akti Myrina Hotel

Location: On west coast of Lemnos, in the northern Aegean Sea.
Romantic Features: Stone cottages with private terraces overlooking sea and private beach; unspoiled Greek island with aura of mythology; resort ferries guests to beaches so remote, there is no access by land.

Nestled into forty-one rolling acres filled with flowers and fruit trees, the weathered stone bungalows and cottages of Akti Myrina Hotel visually meld into the rugged stone hills of the island of Lemnos, serving as a dramatic backdrop for this unique hideaway. Lemnos, an island of about 182 square miles and home to only about 18,000 people, is where the ancient Greeks first staged their Hephaestian Games, sports contests from which the Olympics evolved.

The resort has been here for more than thirty years, building up in that time a loyal group of repeat guests, including celebrities, famous industrialists, authors, artists, and politicians who come here seeking a relaxed vacation in a serene and beautiful environment. Akti Myrina is not a pretentious or particularly luxurious resort. That's not what it's all about. Rather it's valued for its traditions, its sheer natural beauty, its hospitality, and its sense of place on an island that has not yet been touched by mass tourism. It fulfills your dreams of what a Greek island is and should be. This is a place where you can have breakfast delivered to your garden terrace and linger over fresh breads and delicious coffee as you watch the sea roll in on the beach below.

The owner and on-site managing director, Helen G. Dalacouras, fell in love with the property many years ago when she came here with her husband, George, a Greek shipowner, and her family to vacation each summer. In 1988 the Delacourases bought the resort and since then, Mrs. Delacouras has put her heart and substantial financial resources into Akti to make sure her guests yearn to come back again. She sees to it that rooms and grounds are meticulously maintained, linens immaculate and fine, food fresh and beautifully presented, and the staff attentive and friendly.

It's like a wonderful little Greek village set on one of the prettiest sites you'll find anywhere. Bungalows and cottages climb gently up a small hill from the beach, connected by stone walls, walkways, and flower-filled courtyards. Terra-cotta pots filled with flowers sit on walls and along the paths and stone steps leading to the beach. The original cottages were built by a group of Greek business people as holiday homes for themselves and were designed to carefully harmonize with the surrounding land.

Unlike the majority of Greek beaches, which are public, the Akti's strip of sand is private, a designation acquired at great expense and effort by the Delacourases.

The rooms are spacious, with native stone walls and floors; wood ceilings and trim are offset by the bold colors and patterns of the bedspreads and pillows. The chairs are well-designed caned pieces, and the tables and other furniture are simply designed out of wood as well. Twin beds are placed side by side and can be converted to king-size beds. French doors lead out to the patios, which are very private—many have wonderful old trees creating a green, leafy canopy. Here a garden table and chairs invite guests to order room service for an intimate breakfast or dinner. At night, you can see the lights of the small village of Myrina twinkling in the distance, spreading their reflections over the water.

There are three restaurants on the grounds as well as a beach bar, pool bar, piano bar, and Hephaestos Disco. A colorful buffet lunch is set up at the simple, but pleasant restaurant by the beach. Tables covered with blue and white checkered tablecloths sit on the grassy area adjacent to the beach. At night you can dine at Taverna Castro, the Hephaistia, or Caviria restaurants, and you can choose to eat inside or on the open terrace overlooking the pool and sea. Enjoy fresh lobsters and fish such as gilthead bream and red mullet, which are caught locally, or try traditional Greek specialties such as *Dolmadakia Yalantzi* (stuffed grape leaves), *Moschari Stifado* (a sort of beef ragout), or *Taramossalata* (fish salad). Continental cuisine is also offered. A wide selection of Greek and French wines are featured, and locally produced honey, cheeses, figs, raisins, and almonds are always available.

After a long trip, you may decide simply to chill out under one of the blue and yellow umbrellas located along the beach or at one of the heated pools. If you're up for some exercise, challenge your partner to tennis or try out some of the water sports activities, such as waterskiing or windsurfing. There are also canoes and pedal-boats available. Or discover the romance of the island's secluded bays by sailing with Captain Yannis aboard the resort's *caique* (a typical Greek sailing vessel).

From the air, Lemnos looks like a giant butterfly resting on the water, its edges scalloped with deserted sandy beaches carved into rugged rocks. Though not a particularly lush island, a variety of flowers and plants have stubbornly survived and thrived, including the dense carpetlike Burnet shrub, rock roses, thyme, wild olive trees, and oleander. Of particular interest are the fossilized forests that were created centuries ago. In addition to walking, one interesting way to see the island is to join one of the guided horseback trips that takes you along the hilly trails.

The capital and main town, Myrina, is a picture postcard harbor village of one-, two- and occasionally three-story white buildings with red tile roofs hugging a small harbor, where little fishing boats fight for space along the piers. These graceful craft are mostly white-trimmed with touches of blues and reds and greens, their bows and sterns swooping gracefully up to points.

It's only a fifteen-minute walk into town from the Akti, and once you get there, you can browse in the shops, have a snack and a glass of retsina at a taverna, and take in the activity as the boats come and go. In the evening, walk along the Romeikos Yalos road when everything takes on a hazy purple hue in the fading light.

On Lemnos you can explore some interesting archaeological sites, including the remains of prehistoric Poliochni, a Minoan civilization, the ruins of Pelagian walls, which date back to 551 B.C., and the thirteenth-century Venetian fortress that once guarded the harbor. At night the ruins, which sprawl along the hill above the town, are floodlit and look much like a golden, lacy fringe sitting atop the black rocky cliffs below. It's all there to seduce you—the island, the people, the beaches, the mythology, and of course, Akti.

Address/Phone: Myrina, 814 00 Lemnos, Greece (summer); 107 VAS, Pavlou Kastella, 185 33 Piraeus, Greece (winter); 30–254–22310 (summer); 30–1–4138001 (winter); fax: 30–254–22352 (summer); 30–1–4137639 (winter)

U.S. Reservations: Prima Hotels, (800) 447–7462; (212) 223–2848

Owner/Manager: Helen G. Dalacouras, owner and managing director

Arrival/Departure: Guests can be met at Lemnos Airport with prior arrangement.

Distance from Lemnos Airport: 15 miles southeast; 1 mile west of marina

Distance from Myrina: 15-minute walk

Accommodations: 110 rooms in stone bungalows; 15 cottages

Best Rooms/Suites: Rooms 305 to 312 on end overlooking sea; also Cottages 214 and 215

Amenities: Air-conditioning, minibar, telephone, writing desk

Electricity: 220 volts

Sports and Facilities: Private beach, 2 heated pools, 3 floodlit tennis courts, fitness center, mini golf, table tennis, volleyball, fishing, swimming, water sports, billiards; private *caique* for trips to neighboring islands

Dress Code: Casual

Weddings: Can be arranged

Rates/Packages: About $280–$419 per couple per night including breakfast, dinner, taxes, and service charges

Payment/Credit Cards: All major

Closed: October–end of April

Deposit: 1-night deposit; cancel within 14 days for refund

Government Taxes: Included

Service Charges: Included

Entry Requirements for U.S. Citizens: Valid passport

Italy

Grand Hotel Punta Molino Terme

Location: On the northern coast of the island of Ischia, near Ischia Porto.

Romantic Features: Dancing under the moon, shining on the Bay of Naples.

If the term "romantic" suggests a private hideaway, then the Grand Hotel Punta Molino Terme, overlooking the Bay of Naples, is about as romantic as it gets. This contoured, white-as-snow hotel sits in a vast pine woods park opposite the Aragonese Castle, on the little fisherman's island of Ischia.

The boat to the island takes a couple of hours from Naples, and is slow, breezy, and dreamy. You pass the fabled Isle of Capri, and then Ischia appears in the distance guarded by the picturesque castle on the cliffs.

Ischia (pronounced Iskea) is still undiscovered by tourists, and certainly few Americans know about it. Mention the name even to an Italy-lover and he or she will probably say "God bless you." The island is just too peaceful and sleepy to be popular, but for some, this is exactly what makes it such a find.

After a short drive from the dock, you reach the hotel, which is set among lush landscaping, and fronts on a beach walkway that runs along the coastline. The public rooms are cool and classically elegant, decorated with custom-made Italian tiles, traditional furniture, white walls, tapestries, and original paintings. Fresh flowers are everywhere, and the understated decor features a mix of antiques and art pieces.

The dining room, with lavender tablecloths and tapestry chairs, has picture windows overlooking the dark blue pool and aqua water beyond. You can eat outside, on the terrace, or on the roof garden to catch the breeze and enjoy the fishing boats going out for the catch.

The cuisine is Italian or international, featuring local seafood, of course, and it is graciously served. A pianist plays for the cocktail hour, through dinner, and on into the night, when couples can dance under a moon shimmering on the bay.

The cool, stylish guest rooms have ceramic tile floors, beds with antique headboards, minibars, TVs, and balconies with panoramic views of the sea. The dominant color is blue, reflecting the sea and sky. Mirrored bathrooms have showers or baths and amenities such as hair dryers, robes, and plants.

What to do here on this quiet island? You can swim in the stunning pool and relax on the little private beach, where topless bathing is an option, and you can participate in a variety of water sports. If you like to walk, you can go to the nearby woods and follow the footpaths. You can also take a four-hour boat ride around the island.

The most popular activities center on the hotel's well equipped spa. Since ancient times, the thermal waters here have been enjoyed by travelers seeking soothing treatments and relaxation. Today the hotel's spa still offers thermal baths, mud packs, saunas, hydromassage, and facials.

After an invigorating massage, you can sunbathe and sip a Campari on the little jetty that juts into the lapping water. Watch the local children playing nearby on the rocky public beach, catch the distant sounds of family life coming from the fishermen's houses, or gaze at the beautiful castle just across a bridge. Or do all three. It's all part of soaking up the laid-back life in Ischia.

At twilight walk along the beach as the lights turn on in the small buildings in the distance. The peaceful serenity of this place can really creep up on you.

Address/Phone: Lungomare Cristoforo Colombo 23, Porto, Italy; 39–81–991–544; fax: 39–81–991–562

U.S. Reservations: Leading Hotels of the World, (800) 223-6800

Owner/Manager: Eugenio Ossani, owner and general manager

Arrival/Departure: By boat from Naples seaport of Mollo Beverello: 40 minutes by hydrofoil, 1½ hours by ferry; transfers can be arranged on request.

Distance from Naples Airport: 24 miles via ferry

Distance from Naples: 24 miles via ferry

Accommodations: 865 rooms; 10 suites

Best Rooms/Suites: Ocean-view suite

Amenities: Air-conditioning, minibar, telephone, radio, TV, bathrobe, toiletries, magnifying mirror

Electricity: 220 volts

Sports and Facilities: Pool, beach, spa, water sports, game room; tennis nearby

Dress Code: Casual

Weddings: Can be arranged

Rates/Packages: ITL 420,000–ITL 500,000 per night per couple, including breakfast and dinner

Payment/Credit Cards: Most major

Deposit: Guarantee with credit card

Government Taxes: Included

Service Charges: Included

Entry Requirements for U.S. Citizens: Passport

Hotel Danieli

Location: Prime location on Venice's famed lagoon next to the Doge's Palace and near the entrance to the Grand Canal. Situated right in the heart of the city, it is a two-minute walk to St. Mark's Square.

Romantic Features: Venice's opulence and history are combined in this authentically elegant grand hotel of the world, which once hosted visiting royalty and ambassadors (and continues to do so).

Hotel Danieli, Italy

To stay at the super deluxe Hotel Danieli is to embrace the romantic heart and soul of this unique city of gondolas and canals, flower boxes, and foot bridges, cathedrals, and ancient architecture. As with every corner of Venice, every nook and cranny of the Danieli begs to be photographed. The fourteenth-century palace of the Doge Dandolo is the central building of three attached wings that house 230 recently restored rooms and suites of varying vintage, decor, and views, but all definitely in the deluxe category.

Arriving by private water taxi right to the doorstep of the hotel, you walk into what is now a covered courtyard foyer with a gorgeous, golden stairway leading up to the rooms (elevators, of course, are always there for the travel weary). The lobby is sublime, darkly opulent, and unforgettable, with its marble arches, ornate ceilings, breathtaking Venetian glass chandelier, and huge fireplace. The ghosts of such eminent and historic guests as George Sand, Charles Dickens, and Richard Wagner can easily be conjured up as you sip a drink in the Bar Danieli.

And right outside the front door is Venice itself. If you haven't already prearranged a package of sight-seeing and excursions, the concierge will be happy to help you to arrange a gondola ride, a guided city sight-seeing tour, an excursion to the islands of the lagoon—Murano, Burano, and Torcello—to see the famed Venetian glass being made (with plenty of opportunity to shop), to visit the school of lace-making, and to tour the ancient cathedral of Torcello.

When you want to take a break from sight-seeing, you can spend the afternoon at the world-renowned Venice Lido (beach). A free water taxi takes you over to the Excelsior Lido Hotel to swim and sunbathe at the swimming pool or right on the beach, with its rows of cabanas. You can try your hand at the nearby casino or take in a round of golf.

On more than one morning, you may very well forgo a breakfast served in your room to eat at the hotel's open-air (in good weather) rooftop Terrace Restaurant to take in the early morning Venetian light and the breathtaking views of the lagoon.

Address/Phone: Riva degli Schiavoni, 4196, 30122 Venice, Italy; 41–522–6480, fax: 41–520–0208

U.S. Reservations: (800) 325–3535

Owner/Manager: Ugo Balaudo, general manager

Arrival/Departure: By air to the Marco Polo Airport, just outside of Venice, and then by private water taxi from the airport to the hotel. By train (Santa Lucia Station), then 20 minutes by boat.

Distance from Marco Polo Airport: 35 minutes by boat

Distance from Venice center: In the heart of the city

Accommodations: 230 deluxe rooms of varying vintage, decor, and views, including 9 suites and 177 double rooms

Best Rooms/Suites: 6 suites, 3 junior suites, and 50 double rooms are available with wonderful lagoon views.

Amenities: Air-conditioning, hair dryer, minibar, shaver outlets, TV with international programs via satellite, direct-dial telephone, toiletries; robes in suites; room service

Electricity: 110/220 Volts

Sports and Facilities: In season, there are many sporting options on Venice Lido. The concierge can arrange tennis, horseback riding, golf, waterskiing, windsurfing, and yachting. Free boat service to the Lido is available.

Dress Code: Smart casual for daytime, dressier in the evening

Weddings: Can be arranged

Rates/Packages: $340–$415 per couple per night for a room. No honeymoon package, but special arrangements can be made for amenities such as champagne, breakfast in bed, fruit, and flowers.

Payment/Credit Cards: Most major

Deposit: Guarantee with credit card; cancel up to 24 hours in advance

without penalty.
Government Taxes: 10 percent
Service Charges: Not included
Entry Requirements for U.S. Citizens: Valid U.S. passport

Villa D'Este

Location: Set on ten acres on the western shore of Lake Como.
Romantic Features: Spectacular lakeside setting; floating pool; dancing under age-old trees in the foothills of the Alps; watching the sun set over the lake and the mist waft down from the mountains.

The ultimate vacation resort on Lake Como, one of the loveliest lakes in the world, is Villa D'Este. Built by a cardinal as his personal home in the sixteenth century, this impressive neoclassic pleasure palace sits amid ten acres of gardens, manicured lawns, magnolias, and towering trees. Once you pass through the elegant entrance, you will have everything you need to enjoy a relaxed, yet fun-filled honeymoon. In addition to the heart-stopping lakeside setting framed by the high ridges of the mountains, the resort boasts a full range of sports and fitness facilities, several restaurants, a night club, and a cozy piano bar.

As you come into the palatial lobby, with its high, vaulted ceiling, graceful white columns, wide double marble staircase, and fine period furniture, you enter another world, where you will be pampered like royalty, but not so much so that it becomes overbearing. The staff here strikes just the right note between service and respect for your privacy.

Each of the 112 spacious rooms and 46 suites is different, and many, including those rooms located in the Queen's Pavilion, have balconies overlooking the lake. Rooms are elaborately decorated with rich, jewel-like fabrics and colors. Chandeliers, comfortable upholstered chairs and sofas, luxurious full drapes pulled back with golden cords and brocade ties, Renaissance-style artwork, and plush carpets give you accommodations fit for a king and queen.

Clark Gable, Paul McCartney, Ali McGraw, Woody Allen, Arnold Schwarzenegger, John Cleese, and Carly Simon have all stayed here along with other notables. It's a good place to unwind and fall in love all over again with the person you care most about.

In 1875 Franz Liszt remarked, "When you write of two happy lovers, let the story be set on the banks of Lake Como." No doubt he had in mind strolls along the shore in the moonlight and serene afternoons lying on the

Villa D'Este, Italy

banks when he wrote this. But today this is only part of what you can do here. For active couples, there are plenty of options. One of the resort's useful novelties is its large, freshwater pool, which actually floats in the water on its own island, just off the water's edge. (Early risers will have to wait until 10:00 A.M. when it opens.) There is also an indoor pool and a childen's pool as well.

There are eight tennis courts as well as a squash court, waterskiing, sailing, and even hang-gliding along with various sports lessons and clinics scheduled throughout the week. Take a canoe and spend a peaceful afternoon gliding along the waters. If staying fit is on your agenda, you'll find the gym well equipped with the latest exercise and weight-lifting equipment. Or relax in the Turkish baths or saunas and get a soothing massage. Golf enthusiasts can practice their putting on the special green located on the villa grounds and later get in a game at a course just down the road.

All the dining facilities are oriented toward the lake. In good weather meals are served outdoors either on the open-air Verandah, which is covered by bright yellow awnings, or the Grill Room, set up on a large open terrace set under a canopy of leafy, ancient plane trees; the walls are dense, green hedges and the views are of the shimmering lake. At breakfast you can order a specially prepared omelette from the trolley and watch it being cooked, or you can ponder your choices from the lavish breakfast buffet. Head to the terrace or sit poolside for lunch and enjoy a selection of fresh fruits, salads, fish, and pastas.

At night the Verandah lowers its glass walls to shelter diners from the night breezes and turns up the romance factor with candles, lots of fresh flowers, and soft lights. The presentation of food is a work of art: grilled salmon is served with red, green and yellow peppers in the shape of leaves, and a lemon tartlet in a pool of vanilla custard laced by a delicate pinwheel pattern of chocolate and strawberry sauce. You almost hate to stick your spoon into it and disturb the fragile beauty of that confection. But when you do, you'll scrape every last drop from your plate. It's just too good. After dinner, mellow out at the piano bar or dance the night away at the disco.

If you should wish to venture out, you can visit the nearby quaint medieval villages with red-roofed buildings and narrow, winding streets and explore ruins of centuries-old castles and fortresses. One of the best ways to see the area is to take a boat ride around the lake where you will see spectacular villas.

Address/Phone: Via Regina 40, 22012 Cernobbio, Lake Como, Italy; 39–31–3481; fax: 39–31–348844

U.S. Reservations: Leading Hotels of the World, (800) 223–6800 or (212) 838–3110; fax: (212) 758–7367

Owner/Manager: Jean-Marc Droulers, chairman and CEO; Marco Sorbellini, general manager

Arrival/Departure: You can arrange for pickup by the hotel at the airport, but check rates. The resort is easily accessible by car (car rental at airport); helipad at hotel.

Distance from Airport: 27 miles (45 minutes) from Malpensa and Linate, Milan's two airports

Distance from Como: 3 miles; Cernobbia is less than 1 mile; Milan, 35 miles

Accommodations: 112 rooms, 46 suites. Many have balconies overlooking the water; others face gardens.

Best Rooms/Suites: Rooms in the nineteenth-century Queen's Pavilion and suites in the main building overlooking lake

Amenities: Hair dryers, telephone, in-room safe, toiletries, air-conditioning, minibar, TV; room service; U.S. newspaper faxed daily

Electricity: 220 volts

Sports and Facilities: 8 tennis courts (6 clay, 2 manteco), squash court, gym, putting green, jogging route with 15 checkpoints, sauna, Turkish bath, 3 pools (2 outdoor, 1 indoor); waterskiing, sailing; canoeing;

windsurfing; golf 20 minutes away

Dress Code: Casual sports clothes during day; evening: jacket and ties required for men in the dining room.

Weddings: Can be arranged. Outside terrace popular.

Rates/Packages: ITL 500,000–ITL 563,000 per couple per night, including buffet breakfast. Honeymoon package: from ITL 824,000 per person, including welcome fruit baskets and wine; 2 nights' accommodations; 1 dinner in Verandah restaurant, including house wines; 1 dinner in Grill Room with house wines; entry card to casino; 20 percent discount on use of outboard boat plus use of most of the sports facilities. 5- and 7-day packages available

Payment/Credit Cards: Most major

Deposit: Depending on season

Government Taxes: Included

Service Charges: Included

Entry Requirements for U.S. Citizens: Valid passport

Closed: December–February

Portugal

Madeira

Reid's Hotel

Location: Perched on the Santa Catalina hill overlooking the Bay of Funchal.

Romantic Features: Wrought iron balconies overlooking sea; Old World elegance.

Madeira has been called a floating garden. Indeed, this 287-square-mile island plunked about 600 miles off the coast of Lisbon, Portugal, in the middle of the North Atlantic, is exuberantly lush with flowers and tropical vegetation. Its volcanic origins have created an island of contrasts: dramatic green mountains, coastal plantations of sugarcane, bananas, and other crops terraced up the hillsides; deepwater bays and clear mountain streams. It's not really a place you come for beaches: It has few. But because of its charm, its beauty, and its subtropical climate, Madeira has been attracting sun seekers from the damper climes in northern Europe for more than one hundred years.

The oldie but goodie grandee of Madeira's many resorts is Reid's Hotel. Sitting high on its own promontory on the southern coast near the center of Funchal, Madeira's principal city, Reid's enjoys a commanding view of the Atlantic and the bay. What it lacks in beaches it makes up for in views and service. After all, Reid's has had more than a century to get it right, and it has.

From the time you arrive, you don't have to sniff it out—you know it at once. Reid's is a place "old money" likes to come to. The British-style hotel's guest list amassed over the years reads like a *Who's Who:* Sir Winston Churchill, Prince Edward, George Bernard Shaw, Gregory Peck, Queen Ingrid of Denmark, and Roger Moore, to name a few.

With its clubby bars, polished antique furniture mellowed with lemon oil, crystal chandeliers, silk brocades, and cushioned wicker terrace furniture as well as contemporary amenities like air-conditioning and modern baths, Reid's continues to be *the* place to stay in Madeira.

There are 169 rooms and suites located in the main Victoria building and in the newer wings. Most have balconies facing the sea. Those on the upper floors of the main building are preferred for their views and their character, aged like fine wine over the years.

There's no beach, but there are plenty of sports and activities to keep you as busy as you want to be. There are two large heated saltwater pools with ample lounging space on the patio and lawn, a nifty jetty at the base of the cliff for private swimming and sunbathing, windsurfing, sailing, scuba diving, and game fishing, two all-weather courts for tennis, and lots of hiking trails. Boat trips around the island are available, and there is golf at nearby Santo da Serra.

The Health Center offers a variety of massages and treatments with specially priced spa packages; the saunas are free of charge to guests.

There is no skimping on service or food at the various restaurants. They're simply superb. The casual Garden Restaurant looks over the pools and sea—a great place to have breakfast and lunch; chandeliers, gleaming crystal, Palladian windows, and Old World elegance characterize the main dining room; regional cuisine and fresh fish are featured at the informal Villa Cliff Restaurant; gourmet fare is offered at Les Faunes, and a buffet lunch is served poolside.

A pianist plays every evening in the main dining room and Les Faunes and there is dancing to a live band nightly in the cocktail bar.

Currently some of the rooms in the hotel are being redecorated to lighten up the whole look. One only hopes the redo will incorporate the best of the characteristics of the original guest room decor, which made these rooms unique and special.

You'll want to take time to explore the island and perhaps walk along some of the many trails that wind through the hills. Squeaky clean like Bermuda, scenic like Hawaii, it's a beautiful place to be.

Address/Phone: P-9000 Funchal, Madeira, Portugal; 351–91–7630–01; fax: 351–9176–4499

U.S. Reservations: Leading Hotels of the World (800) 223–6800; fax: (212) 758–7367

Owner/Manager: Kurt E. Schmid, general manager

Arrival/Departure: Transfers to and from Funchal Airport included in honeymoon package; otherwise can be arranged for a fee ($50 for private transfer per car); approximately $25 per carload for taxi.

Distance from Funchal Airport: 40 minutes; 75 minutes by air from Lisbon

Distance from Funchal center: 10 minutes

Accommodations: 169 rooms and suites

Best Rooms/Suites: Deluxe rooms or suites on higher floors of main building.

Amenities: Air-conditioning, hair dryer, minibar (free soft drinks), toiletries, TV, radio, telephone; personal safes, 24-hour room service

Electricity: 220 volts

Sports and Facilities: 2 heated saltwater pools, seaside terrace/swimming area, 2 all-weather tennis courts, Ping-Pong, billiards, Health Center with sauna and massage, waterskiing, scuba diving; golf at Santo da Serra, hiking trails nearby

Dress Code: Casual during day; jacket and tie for men for dinner in more formal restaurants

Weddings: Can be arranged

Rates/Packages: $269–$345 per couple per night (summer) including breakfast, tax, and service charges. $345–$431 (winter); Honeymoon package $1,078–$1,401 per couple, includes 3 nights' accommodations; breakfasts; gourmet meal in Les Faunes, island tour; vineyard tour; gift; wine; flowers and fruit; transfers; free use of tennis court, pools, and sauna; taxes and service charges; special rate for fourth night. 7 nights, $2,228–$2,982, includes all of above features plus 2-day car rental with insurance and 2 sports lessons or massage for two. Golf packages and meal plans available.

Payment/Credit Cards: Major credit cards

Deposit: Credit card deposit; cancel 14 days or more before date of arrival for full refund.

Government Taxes: Included

Service Charges: Included

Entry Requirements for U.S. Citizens: Passport

Scotland

Gleneagles

Location: On 830 acres north of Edinburgh in Perthshire, the gateway to the Highlands.
Romantic Features: Walks into the heather-covered hills; fireside cocktails after a brisk horseback ride; four-poster beds.

When it first opened, people titled and/or ridiculously rich flocked to this venerable estate in the Scottish countryside. The golf courses quickly gained an international reputation as the finest in the realm. Today Gleneagles is a first-rate resort appealing particularly to those who love to be active, for there is a lot to do here on this sprawling property. Three golf courses plus the "wee" nine-hole course, a full-blown equestrian center, tennis courts, falconry school, health club and spa, even an off-road driving school, plus a number of other sports and activities assure that those with an itch to see and do are blissfully happy.

The setting in the wild and wonderful heather-clad Perthshire Hills is magnificent, a perfect venue for those who love to hike, ride, and enjoy the outdoors. Shimmering lochs and rivers invite anglers to fish in the fresh, cool waters; equestrians will find some of the most spectacular riding country in Europe at their doorstep. And with a complete riding school and forty-five horses, there is instruction for every level.

Ever wanted to learn the fine art of falconry, one of the world's most aristocratic sports? At Gleneagles you'll find the British School of Falconry right on the grounds; you can try your hand at handling and flying Harris hawks. Or what about popping a clay pigeon out of the sky? At Gleneagles's Jackie Stewart Shooting School, set smack on a grouse moor, you can learn how to master this unique sport.

Golfers can't help but love Gleneagles. Besides the original King's and Queen's Courses, there is the Monarch's Course, a new eighteen-hole layout designed by Jack Nicklaus, opened in 1993. And for those who want to brush up on their game or even learn how to play, there is a superb golf school. Tuition is included in some of the package plans.

Other activities are located in the resort's country club. Here you'll find a pool, Jacuzzi, hot tubs, sauna, Turkish baths, gym, squash courts, snooker tables, croquet, bowls, pitch and putt course, tennis courts, and bicycles. All these things are free to Gleneagles guests. Within the club, there is also Champneys—the spa where you can enjoy a wide number of therapies and

Gleneagles, Scotland

treatments, such as aromatherapy and massages. Except for those on a special package, these treatments cost extra.

Lest you think Gleneagles is all about fun and games, there is more. Guests have a choice of six places to eat and drink and can choose from a wide assortment of cuisines, ranging from Scottish specialties to continental. Try grouse, salmon, kippers, scones and cream, and venison.

Rooms and suites are furnished traditionally with chintz bedspreads and draperies; comfortable upholstered chairs and sofas are covered in rich greens, golds, blues, and reds. You'll find highly polished wood tables and desks, brass lamps, leather stools, silk-lined walls, and handwoven carpets, and some rooms have four-poster, canopy beds. In the summer, French doors can be opened to let the fresh breezes in. In the colder months, some suites have working fireplaces guaranteed to banish winter chills.

Gleneagles's grounds are beautifully landscaped with gardens, trees, and lawns. Take your camera and walk or cycle along the paths or venture farther over the moors and hills. Ask the kitchen to pack a picnic for you and discover a special glade by a lake where you can have lunch.

In the summer daylight hours are long and can last until 10:00 or 11:00 P.M. giving you plenty of time to explore the countryside, where you can see hundreds of castles. For some local flavor, attend the local Highland Games or sheepdog trials. And remember, if you can tear yourself away for a day or two, Glasgow and Edinburgh are only an hour away and well worth a visit.

Address/Phone: Auchterarder, Perthshire, Scotland, PH3 1NF; 44-1764-662231; fax: 44-1764-662022

Reservations: The Leading Hotels of the World, (800) 223-6800

Owner/Manager: Peter J. Lederer, managing director; Guinness plc, owner

Arrival/Departure: Arrangements can be made for private transfer to the hotel. The charge for a chauffeur-driven car is about $100. Gleneagles train station is 1 mile from the resort, and all trains are met by the hotel's minibus (no charge). Free transfer to Edinburgh Airport on Monday morning for those staying Sunday night.

Distance from Edinburgh or Glasgow Airport: 45 miles, 1 hour's drive; taxi about $80, limousine $110

Distance from Perth or Stirling: 20 miles

Accommodations: 216 rooms plus 18 suites

Best Rooms/Suites: Suites are ideal; the Royal Lochnagar is the best and costs a king's ransom.

Amenities: Hair dryer, TV, minibar, toiletries, telephones, terry bathrobes, trouser press

Electricity: 220/240 volts

Sports and Facilities: 5 tennis courts (4 all-weather, 1 grass), 3 championship 18-hole golf courses, 1 nine-hole course, 2 squash courts; riding, shooting, gym, spa, pool, falconry, fishing, mountain biking, snooker, jogging, hiking (it's a good idea to book sports activities such as golf at time you make your reservation)
Dress Code: Smart casual
Weddings: Can be arranged; garden weddings are particularly lovely; bagpipers serenade newlyweds
Rates/Packages: £195–£270 per couple per night for a room, £290–£1,100 for a suite (November to April); £230–£320 for a room and £350–£1,100 for a suite (May to October), including accommodations, full Scottish breakfast and VAT. Honeymoon package, £400–£480 per couple per night including VAT, includes suite accommodations, flowers, chocolates, champagne breakfast in your suite, carriage drive around the estate, chauffeur transfer to any airport in Scotland, and dinner for two on your first anniversary. Stay 6 nights and get 7th night free. Carte Blanche rates, at £280–£290 per person, cover accommodations, all meals, tea, and unlimited choice of all sports and leisure activities, such as golf, golf school, riding, spa treatments, beauty services—even a half day Discover Scotland Land Rover tour. Add £170 for suite accommodations. Ask about special-interest packages, such as golf, spa, and riding.
Payment/Credit Cards: Most major
Deposit: Guarantee with credit card
Government Taxes: Included
Service Charges: Not included
Entry Requirement for U.S. Citizens: Passport

Asia
and the Pacific

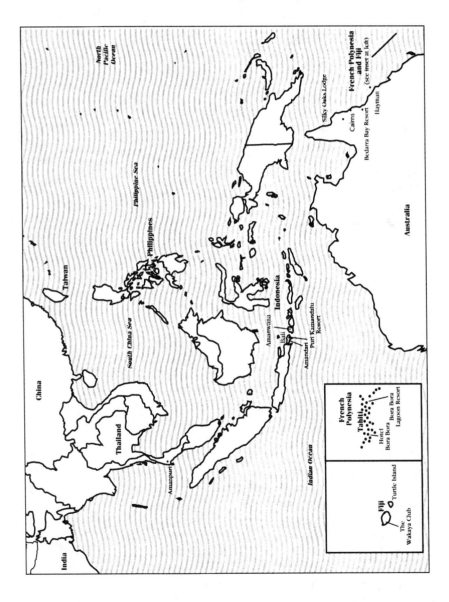

North Pacific Ocean

Philippine Sea

French Polynesia and Fiji (see inset at left)

Silky Oaks Lodge

Cairns

Bedarra Bay Resort

Hayman

Australia

Taiwan

Philippines

Indonesia

Amanwana

Bali

Amandari

Puri Kamandalu Resort

South China Sea

China

Thailand

Amanpuri

Indian Ocean

India

French Polynesia

Tahiti

Bora Bora

Bora Bora Lagoon Resort

Hotel Bora Bora

Fiji

The Wakaya Club

Turtle Island

Australia

Bedarra Bay Resort, Australia

Bedarra Bay Resort

Location: On Bedarra Island, 3 miles off the northern Queensland coast.
Romantic Features: Very, very quiet private island; lovely beaches.

When you hear an Australian say, "Going troppo, mate," he or she could be heading to Bedarra Island, a sunny tropical bit of paradise located just off the northern coast of Queensland—Great Barrier Reef territory. For this cheery saying means you're going to a place guaranteed to provide lots of hot sun, sand, and sea. Bedarra offers all this and more—or less, depending on how you look at it. It's secluded, it's quiet. Very quiet. Here there are no schedules to follow and very little in the way of nightlife.

A white, sandy oasis in the middle of a brilliant turquoise sea, Bedarra Bay Resort is a small, intimate resort. Staying here is much like staying at the home of a wealthy relative who just happens to be out of town: members of the staff are in attendance and have been told to do everything in their power to keep you happy. And they do!

At this sybaritic destination, besides being waited on, you're quite welcome to help yourself to anything you desire, at any time. If you want something special, all you have to do is ask. Caviar? They'll bring it. An omelette at three in the afternoon? They'll cook it. Want to go over to Dunk Island for some action? They'll get the boat fired up. You just name it.

Your multilevel villa is yours alone. Crafted from native timbers, it sits on stilts amid lush gardens. Ceilings are high, with exposed beams; floors are made of highly polished wood. The bright, airy decor reflects the colors from outside. Linens are smooth and lovely; pillows are puffy, soft down. (If you want something different, just ask.) Towels are thick and thirsty and are changed often.

Each villa has a balcony, a good place to enjoy "brekkie" (breakfast) while gazing out at the sea. Only a few steps from the beach, each villa comes with one queen-size bed and one single bed and a separate lounge area with desk and refrigerator. (Why the extra single bed in such a romantic place? No one could say.)

Since Bedarra is a very private island, you'll have no trouble finding innumerable places to be alone. Discover hidden coves; walk in the lush rain forest, which flourishes alongside the beaches, or float side by side on rubber rafts. Swing gently in one of the hammocks slung between palms on the beach, or ask for a picnic hamper filled with delicious food to take with you to a secluded spot.

Although Bedarra's chefs find new ways to tempt you daily, they also make a point of asking if you have any personal requests. The open bar, which is available to you twenty-four hours a day, is stocked with domestic and imported beers, champagnes, fine vintage reds and white wines, spirits, and liqueurs.

The restaurant, which is round and constructed of local woods, overlooks the gardens and turquoise lagoons, a perfect setting for that special romantic dinner. Enjoy the excellent cuisine and be sure to top it all off by indulging in a delectable Pavlova (a meringue dessert). There are only fifteen other couples, at most, so if you're looking for a lively nightlife with lots of socializing, this might not be the place for you to come. If, however, a serene, beautiful natural setting and lots of pampering by an extremely competent and caring staff appeals, then Bedarra is worth the trip.

Address/Phone: P.O. Box 1033, Bedarra Island via Townsville, Queensland, Australia 4810; 61–70–68–8233; fax: 61–70–68–8215
U.S. Reservations: Australian Resorts, (800) 227–4411
Owner/Manager: Quantas, owner; Michael Ruff, general manager
Arrival/Departure: Private resort launch to and from Dunk Island airstrip
Distance from Airport: 20-minute launch ride from Dunk airstrip

Distance from Cairns: About 150 miles
Accommodations: 16 private, two-level and split-level villas crafted from native timbers
Best Rooms/Suites: Villa number 1 is most secluded.
Amenities: Hair dryer, toiletries, air-conditioning, ceiling fans, ISD telephones, radio, ironing facilities, TV, VCR, and bathrobes
Electricity: 240 volts
Sports and Facilities: Tennis, sailing, swimming, snorkeling, fishing, sailboarding. Guests may use sporting facilities at nearby Dunk Island, just 20 minutes away, at no extra charge
Dress Code: Casual
Weddings: Can be arranged
Rates/Packages: All-inclusive rates, approximately $783 per couple per night, include accommodations, 3 meals daily, open bar, snacks, tennis, water sports, and laundry.
Payment/Credit Cards: Most major
Deposit: Credit card guarantee; no charge for cancellation made 30 days prior to arrival date; less than 30 days, a 1-night charge.
Govenment Taxes: Included
Service Charges: None
Entry Requirements for U.S. Citizens: Valid passport and visa

Hayman

Location: 20 miles from the Australian mainland, on 960 acres of one of the Whitsunday Islands, considered to be the most beautiful of all the Barrier Reef Islands.
Romantic Features: Private dinners for two on beach or in tropical gardens; themed penthouses filled with antiques; island picnics and snorkeling on Bali Hai and Langford Reef.

Hayman, a long, low, sprawling property with reflecting pools filled with swans, tropical gardens, waterfalls, and palm-lined beaches is designed for romance. The Great Barrier Reef is close by, but you may find it hard to tear yourself away from your Hayman Island paradise. Situated at the tip of the Whitsunday Islands, this luxurious, 214-room resort is the only place on this 960-acre island. And what a place!

It takes a bit of doing to get here, but it's worth it. First you have to get to Australia, then you can fly from Sydney or Brisbane to Hamilton Island, where you board a sleek yacht for the forty-five-minute cruise to Hayman.

While on board, you enjoy complimentary flutes of champagne and get all the registration formalities out of the way, so you can head right to your room on arrival.

The resort, which stretches along a cove on the southern part of Hayman Island, fronts two lovely beaches. Some say the waters around this island offer some of the finest sailing in the world. Hayman Island, 3 miles in length and a mile wide, is shaped like a crescent with mountains running along its spine, punctuated by a tall peak standing 820 feet above sea level. The island is covered with a dense blanket of native eucalyptus trees, and the Australian bushland goes right to the edge of the white beaches.

All rooms and suites have either private balconies or terraces with views of the pools, lagoons, and beaches or gardens. Rooms are low-key but elegant, decorated in soft pastels and florals that complement the tropical setting. Your room or suite comes with large glass patio doors, white sliding louvers, handwoven rugs and dhurries, original paintings and sculpture, comfortable upholstered chairs and sofas, and lavish marble baths. The one-, two-, and three-bedroom penthouses on the top floor of the East Wing are each decorated in a different style, accented with a stunning selection of furnishings and objets d'art. You can choose from a variety of themes including Greek, Japanese, Italian palazzo, Moroccan, South Seas, contemporary, North Queensland, California, Art Deco, and French provincial.

You don't have to be water-oriented to be enraptured by the dazzling freshwater pool floating in the midst of a huge saltwater lagoon—it's seven times larger than an Olympic pool. There are also two more intimate pools surrounded by palms, tropical gardens, and fish ponds. Here you'll have as much privacy as you want. Wander through exotic gardens and along the beaches and never see another soul.

In addition to a full range of water sports facilities and six tennis courts, Hayman has an excellent health club equipped with Hydragym computerized workout equipment such as rowing machines, aerobicycles, and treadmills along with spas, saunas, and steam rooms. Want to be pampered? Indulge in a Swedish or aromatherapy body massage.

There are many things that make Hayman an exceptional resort, but its proximity to the Great Barrier Reef really sets it apart. This incredible natural wonder is more than 1,200 miles long and is made up of 2,000 individual reefs and 71 coral-based islands. Snorkelers and scuba divers universally classify the reef as the ultimate underwater experience. The waters around Hayman churn with fish of all shapes and colors, and even for a rank novice, it is a thrill to glide above and through their world. If you prefer to stay dry, you can take a glass-bottom boat ride or a helicopter or seaplane excursion, which will take you directly over the reef.

Hayman has its own marina and offers chartered fishing excursions aboard the *Sun Aura*, a 40-foot game fishing boat. Since these waters offer some of the finest fishing in the world, you might get lucky and catch some dinner, which the Hayman chefs will be happy to prepare for you.

In all there are six restaurants, each one featuring its own unique fare. There is also an extensive wine cellar of more than 35,000 bottles. La Fontaine, the resort's signature restaurant, is the most formal, with Waterford chandeliers and Louis XVI furniture. Its "cuisine moderne" is outstanding and beautifully presented. There is also the Oriental Seafood Restaurant, where you can try Morton Bay "bugs," a cross between lobster and crab, served in an outstanding black bean sauce. The menu includes food selections from China, Malaysia, Thailand, and Japan. Fresh herbs from the resort's gardens are used in preparation of the meals. Hayman bakes its own breads and makes chocolates and ice creams. La Trattoria is a lively, informal, indoor/outdoor Italian bistro featuring pastas, salads, and antipastos at moderate prices. Planters is your ultimate Australian-style bar and grill, and you can also eat at the Coffee House, a casual beachfront restaurant serving buffet breakfasts, lunches, and pastries throughout the day. The Beach Pavilion offers daily blackboard specials, barbecues, snacks, and drinks. And there is always room service, available at any hour.

After dinner, you can enjoy nightly performances by resident and guest artists, and you can dance the night away in the island's nightspot, Hernando's.

Hayman's guests give the staff high marks for professionalism, friendliness, courtesy, and dedication. These, combined with an idyllic setting and superb facilities, add up to a top-notch honeymoon resort.

Address/Phone: Great Barrier Reef, North Queensland, Australia 4801; 61–79–46–9100; fax: 61–79–46–9410

U.S. Reservations: Leading Hotels of the World, (800) 223–6800; Ansett Airlines, (800) 366–1300

Owner/Manager: Ansett Airlines, owners; Tom Klein, general manager

Arrival/Departure: Fly Ansett Airlines or Eastward Airlines to Hamilton Island, where guests board one of Hayman's two luxury yachts for the 45-minute trip to the island. A minibus will pick you up at the wharf for the 10-minute ride to Hayman.

Distance from Hamilton Island Airport: 45 minutes by boat plus 10 minutes by van

Distance from Hamilton Island: 25 miles, approximately 1 hour

Accommodations: 203 rooms and 11 penthouse suites

Best Rooms/Suites: Beachfront rooms or suites, which allow you to walk from private terrace onto beach

Amenities: Air-conditioning, TV, telephones, ceiling fan, minibar, in-room safe, refrigerator, tea/coffeemaker; hair dryer, toiletries, robe and slippers

Electricity: 240 volts

Sports and Facilities: No charge for snorkeling, Hobie Cats, windsurfing, paddle skiing; use of 6 tennis courts, golf target range, putting green; playing billiards, table tennis, and badminton; hiking trails lace the island. Activities incurring charges include parasailing, water sleigh, yacht charter, reef trips, dinghy hire, snorkelling excursions, aerobics; tennis lessons, full diving services with instruction and equipment, diving trips

Dress code: Casual during the day; jacket required for dinner at La Fontaine; elegantly casual at other five restaurants

Weddings: Exquisite setting for garden weddings. Choice locations: gardens or in front of sparkling waterfall.

Rates/Packages: Rates per couple per night range from $227 for a garden-view room to $754 for an East Wing suite overlooking the Whitsunday Passage. The three-bedroom penthouse suite is $1,800 daily, including breakfast. Airline packages available through Ansett Airlines of Australia. Honeymoon package, priced at $2,070 per couple, includes 3 nights' accommodations, breakfast, use of all nonmotorized water sports, limousine transfers, flowers, champagne, sunset cruise, and candlelit dinner.

Payment/Credit Cards: Most major

Deposit: 1 night; cancellation 1 week prior to arrival for full refund.

Government Taxes: None

Service Charges: Included

Entry Requirements for U.S. Citizens: Valid passport and visa

Silky Oaks Lodge

Location: Adjoins the Daintree Rain Forest National Park, on the northern bank of the Mossman River Gorge, near Port Douglas and Cairns.

Romantic Features: Very private wilderness cabins.

This one is definitely for the adventurous couple. Located on the edge of the Daintree Rain Forest National Park, Silky Oaks gives you the wilderness experience without the bugs and the cold showers. If you were to look up into the treetops from the Mossman River as the night darkness arrives, you would see the twinkling lights and windows of cottages glowing through the leafy canopy of the forest. Silky Oaks chalets are built on stilts to sit high in the dense tropical foliage. Constructed of wood inside and outside, large sliding glass doors open onto a veranda, giving you a marvelous perch from which to view the world below. Tarzan and Jane would have loved it.

The suites are spacious, comfortable, and very private with sitting areas, queen-size beds, and lots of windows. When you arrive, you are warmly greeted by Moss and Theresa Hunt, who are justly proud of their award-winning hotel and restaurant. Although it's set in the Mossman River Gorge in a lush ancient rain forest, you'll find that your private "treetop" chalet has air-conditioning, an en suite bath, a hair dryer—even a minibar. From your veranda, look carefully and you may be able to catch a glimpse of a platypus or tortoise.

Winner of several tourism awards, the lodge features a superb open-air restaurant set high in the treetops overlooking the natural rock swimming pool and the river that flows below. The observation lounge and guest lounge, which is ringed with large windows, are furnished with rattan chairs with comfortable cushions and oriental carpets. The lodge, chalets, and rain forest are connected by a series of paths and boardwalks on stilts.

There is plenty to do at Silky Oaks. You can go kayaking, hiking, and swimming and even play tennis. The one thing you must absolutely do is visit the Kangaroo Nursery located on the property. This is where orphaned wallabies, wallaroos, and kangaroos are nurtured and raised. Perhaps you'll even get to feed one of the babies from a bottle. It's not unusual to arrive at the restaurant for cocktails and find a wee guest: a baby roo hanging in a specially made pouch from the back of a chair.

Silky Oaks is only fifteen minutes from Cairns, the jumping-off point for the Great Barrier Reef, which is really a must-see if you've come all this way. Stay four nights at the lodge and your excursion to the reef is on the house. You also get free guided rain forest walks and nighttime animal spotlight walks. On the shelves of the lodge's reference library is an impressive selection of books to help you understand the wilderness surrounding you.

Just outside your doorstep is a whole world of interesting flora and fauna to discover. After morning tea at the lodge's Tree House Restaurant, you can walk to the World Heritage–listed Daintree National Park, the oldest living rain forest in the world, where you will be surrounded by huge trees, primitive plants, and myriad collections of birds, butterflies, and little creatures such as lizards. Sling bridges take you over bubbling creeks, and marked paths show you the way to some spectacular sights—electric blue butterflies, bright yellow-and-green birds, and tiny frogs.

Take a refreshing dip in the crystal-clear billabong, a natural pool surrounded by big boulders and lush tropical foliage. Take a picnic lunch (provided by the hotel) for a fun day on your own. Or explore the rain forest on horseback, retracing the steps of the old teamsters. Back at the lodge's bar, you can make new friends from all over the world. The food is worth writing home about. This may look like a wilderness lodge, but there is nothing primitive about the cuisine served here. You may not be able to remember exactly what you ate, but you will remember that the food was some of the tastiest you've ever had—anywhere. Fresh tropical fruits and lots of great seafood from the nearby Barrier Reef along with Asian and continental dishes are prepared with great skill. As one recent guest put it, "Every day we really looked forward to returning to the lodge for dinner. It got to be a habit."

There are several safari companies, such as Tauck Tours and Swain Australia, that take you to Australia and combine a wilderness adventure with a stay at Silky Oaks. A typical program takes in the Daintree Rain Forest, Cape Tribulation, and the Bloomfield Track and includes a Daintree River cruise. Maybe you'll catch a peek at an Estuarine Crocodile sunning on the river banks.

Address/Phone: Finlayvale Road, via Syndicate Road, Mossman; P.O. Box 396, Mossman 4873, Australia; 61–70–981–666; fax: 61–70–981–983

U.S. Reservations: P&O Resort Holidays, (800) 225–9849

Owner/Manager: James Baillie, general manager

Arrival/Departure: From Cairns you can rent a car, take a limousine (seats up to 6), or go by bus (check at desk in airport, you'll go by coach to Mossman where Silky Oaks Lodge will pick you up). Pickup can also be arranged at various Cairns hotels.

Distance from Cairns Airport: 1¼ hours by limousine (AU$230 round-trip per car)

Distance from Cairns: 16 miles north (20 minutes) from Port Douglas; 51 miles (an hour and 15 minutes) from Cairns

Accommodations: 60 private "treehouse" chalets on stilts located near the lodge overlooking the lagoon or the treetop canopy or situated deeper in the rain forest itself. Recently 25 new chalets were completed, many with Jacuzzis.

Best Rooms/Suites: New chalets with Jacuzzis

Amenities: Air-conditioning, ceiling fan, minibar, tea/coffee facilities, hair dryer, toiletries, clock/radio (no TVs or telephones—public phone in lodge); massages available; nightly turndown service, laundry service

Electricity: 220 volts

Sports and Facilities: Hiking in the rain forest, tennis, swimming, canoeing, river kayaking, horseback riding, wilderness safaris, bicycling, trips to the Great Barrier Reef, golf at the Mirage Country Club (20 minutes

from Silky Oaks), fishing, night animal spotting
Dress Code: Casual
Rates/Packages: Per person per night from AU$175, including breakfast. Four-night package that includes accommodations, breakfasts, limo transfers from Cairns, and Great Barrier Reef tour via Quicksilver: AU$799 per person. Wilderness safaris available with stay at Silky Oaks.
Payment/Credit Cards: Most major
Deposit: Credit card guarantee
Government Taxes: None
Service Charges: None
Entry Requirements for U.S. Citizens: Passport and visa

Fiji

Turtle Island

Location: 500-acre privately owned island in the South Pacific.
Romantic Features: Thatched beachfront cottages; seventeen beaches; dining by candlelight on the beach or on a mountaintop.

Some call it the most romantic place on earth. Apparently Columbia Pictures thought so, as it picked this island as the site for its 1980 movie *Blue Lagoon* starring Brooke Shields. The original 1949 version with Jean Simmons was also shot here.

One recent bride said they had to carry her off the island because she didn't want to leave. This is a true fantasy island, where you live in your own thatch-roofed beachfront *bure* (cottage), spend lazy barefoot days on the beach, and get to know, at the most, thirteen other couples (the whole place only accommodates 14 couples).

When Turtle was simply a relatively unknown Fijian island located somewhere in the South Pacific, Richard Evanson, an American, came here to find a simpler life apart from the hectic world of television, where he had achieved success working on the West Coast. Evanson liked it so much, he stayed, eventually purchasing the island in 1972 and building a small resort with the help of Joe Naisali, a Fijian.

In constructing Turtle, Evanson was extremely careful not to upset the beauty and balance of the environment. He planted thousands of trees, including many Honduras mahoganies, carved a small road from the under-

Turtle Island, Fiji

brush to go around the island, and protected the natural development of Turtle with a 500-year-old trust. Small and intimate, Turtle is a jewel not only because of its unspoiled physical beauty, but because of the interaction of its guests with the warm, loving, Fijian people. Sitting under a banyan tree and singing with guests and staff in the late evening can be a spiritual experience.

Only English-speaking, heterosexual couples are welcomed, as Evanson feels it is important that his few guests be able to communicate and enjoy each other's company. When dinnertime rolls around, it's like one big house party. (Unless, of course, a couple wants to have a romantic dinner someplace on their own, such as on a lantern-lit beach or at the top of a mountain, all easily arranged.)

The minimum stay of six days gives you time to relax, unwind, and explore Turtle's many pleasures. Turtle's all-inclusive fee frees you to go with the flow. No bills to sign. No need to wonder about additional charges, since everything is included.

A seaplane brings you to Turtle from Nadi, Fiji's main airport. As you approach, you'll see the brilliant colors of the Blue Lagoon and miles of white, powdery sand ringing the island. From the time you step from the boat to the shore, you are warmly attended to by a very hospitable staff who call you by your first name (only first names are used here). Your picture is taken when you arrive so the staff will recognize you on sight. If you have any special requests or needs, they'll already know about them from the questionnaire you filled out before you came. Like a white omelette every morning? You'll get it. Don't eat meat? No problem. Get ready for some great vegetarian meals.

Here the sea is calm, with gently rolling waves, perfect for swimming and snorkeling. Perhaps you'd like to meet some Fijian tribal chiefs. All you have to do is to hop on the boat for a trip to one of the outer islands. You can also escape to one of the seventeen beaches around Turtle and be totally alone.

Thatched-roof two-room *bures* built of coral stone are roomy, comfortable, and private with separate sitting areas, wet bars, his and her baths, four-poster queen-size beds, rattan furniture, rush mats, and louvered walls. Vaulted ceilings are constructed in the traditional Fijian way, by hand shaping and lashing noko noko poles in a decorative pattern. And perhaps best of all, you have plenty of space around your *bure,* which is located directly on the Blue Lagoon.

Lali drums and guitar music announce that it's cocktail time. Food is fresh and delicious, with an emphasis on organically grown produce and fruits just picked from the trees. Turtle's three-acre garden provides plenty of food. Grilled lobster with lemongrass, all kinds of seafood, fresh fish caught earlier in the day by local fishermen, and wine from Turtle's extensive wine cellar are prepared with skill and flair. Try *Kokoda,* a Fijian dish of fish marinated in lime and oil or mud crabs dipped in vinaigrette sauce.

At Turtle you have so many choices: go horseback riding or have a champagne picnic on the beach; take a nap in a hammock strung between two coconut palms; hike into the jungle hillsides; or visit the market on a nearby island. And participate in weekly love feasts and Fijian sing-alongs, where you share *kava,* the Fijian ceremonial drink.

You will probably find the most difficult thing about Turtle is leaving. After a week here, among some of the friendliest people you'll find anywhere, life for you will be just like a beautiful song—"*Vovosa malva mai vei au.*"

Address: P.O. Box 9317, Nadi, Fiji Islands 72921
U.S. Reservations: (800) 826–3083
Owner: Richard Evanson
Arrival/Departure: Fly from Los Angeles or San Francisco to Fiji with a brief stop in Honolulu. Round-trip transfer via seaplane from Nadi, Fiji, to Turtle Island is $572 per couple (make arrangements when booking main flight).
Distance from Nadi International Airport: 30 minutes

Accommodations: 14 suites

Best Rooms/Suites: *Bure* number 1, with endless views of the water

Amenities: Ceiling fans, hair dryer, iron, ironing board, coffeemaker, toiletries, insect spray, beach bag, bathrobe, baseball cap, refrigerator, stocked bar

Electricity: 240/110 volts

Sports and Facilities: Water sports such as boating and snorkeling, deep-sea fishing, hiking on trails, horseback riding

Dress Code: Casual (you don't even need shoes); pack light as you are limited to 40 pounds of luggage for the seaplane flight. Extra luggage can be stored at Turtle's facility in Nadi.

Weddings: Can be married in traditional Fijian ceremony held at sunset on the Blue Lagoon. Your wedding attire is hand-painted *tapa* cloth (you may look like pears, but who cares?) and you wear garlands of fresh flowers (that helps). Newlyweds are carried on a throne to their wedding feast. Wedding fee: $1,000 plus 10 percent tax, which includes the cost of the feast.

Rates/Packages: $847 per couple per night for everything, including accommodations, activities, meals, all beverages (even unlimited champagne), stamps, excursions to neighboring islands, use of boats and water sports equipment, and all services

Payment/Credit Cards: Most major

Deposit: $1,000 due 7 days after booking. Balance due 30 days prior to your arrival. If you cancel, you can be rescheduled for another date within a 5-year period, but no refunds.

Government Taxes: 10 percent

Service Charges: Not necessary. If you wish, you can contribute to staff Christmas fund when you leave.

Entry Requirements for U.S. Citizens: Passport

The Wakaya Club

Location: Wakaya Island, set 30 miles off the main island of Viti Levu.

Romantic Features: Magnificent 5-mile-long private island with thirty-two beaches, seaside hammocks, and highly personalized service; picnics-for-two on hidden beaches.

When money is no object—but privacy is—the hideaway of choice is often Wakaya, where people such as actress Michelle Pfeiffer and Microsoft mogul Bill Gates have honeymooned.

Shaped like an emerald pendant, Wakaya is set in luminous turquoise seas off the southeast coast of Viti Levu, Fiji's principal island. Originally a copra (coconut oil) plantation, the 2,200-acre island opened as an exclusive resort in 1990. The island is owned by David Gilmour, a Canadian businessman, who wants visitors to feel like they are his personal guests. When Gilmour is on island, he loves chatting with people and often invites keen tennis players up to his clifftop private residence, Vale O (house in the clouds) for a match. Of course, there is also a Wimbledon-Tex surface court down at the resort, lighted for night play.

While Vatulele, Fiji's other celebrity sandbox, is for people who want to be seen, The Wakaya Club is for those who want to escape. With only eight *bures* (bungalows) accommodating a maximum of sixteen guests, fellow wayfarers disappear like a magician's white rabbit. You'll be astounded by the quiet, ruffled only by cooing doves or rustling palm fronds.

It's been said that "God is in the details," and the management of The Wakaya Club pays attention to the minutiae that turn a good vacation into a perfect one. Breakfasting on the large, oceanfront deck in the shade of a venerable dilo tree, you'll admire the trio of honey, jam, and marmalade pots from Portugal. The crisply pressed robes in the bathroom are by Natori. In fact, the resort seems to think of everything even before you realize you've forgotten to bring it. Straw hats and beach mats are available for your use; extra toothbrushes, razors, and a first-aid kit are tucked in the bathroom closet.

Each day poses delightful possibilities. Instead of a programmed list of daily activities, a friendly staff member approaches you at breakfast and asks, "What would you like to do today?" Your options might include snorkeling, hiking to some of the archaeological sites that dot the island, or just lolling along the beach. Scuba diving is excellent, with a 1,000-foot drop-off beyond the reef. Favorite scuba sites include Saxophone, a chimney that pops out of a wall at 70 feet into a traffic jam of manta rays and sharks. The club even offers a PADI diving certification course (course costs extra).

For lovers, a top choice is spending the day at a remote beach, accompanied by a picnic basket filled with goodies, a bottle of champagne, and a radio to arrange your transportation back to the resort when you tire of playing Fantasy Island. A favorite retreat—the aptly named Honeymoon Beach, which curves around a tranquil bay. (The resort has even arranged a luxury overnight camp-out for one couple here.)

Surrounded by green lawns and coconut palms, your accommodations are just steps away from the beach. The large, three-room wooden *bures* (living room, bedroom, bath) meld substantial, modern construction with traditional Fijian design, evidenced in the high ceilings and woven straw wall coverings. All accommodations have ceiling fans; several also feature air-conditioning. Decor is simple, with rattan furnishings and Indonesian touches, such as Balinese figurines and batik prints in the bathroom. Throughout the *bure,* glossy yaka wood is used, so smoothly polished and perfectly laid as to be nearly mirror-flat. However, the overall impression is that of immense comfort but not sumptuousness.

Enchantment awaits, however, in the private villas available for rent (currently three of the resort's residences). One of the most heavenly is Lawedua, named after an extinct bird that used to nest in island cliffs. During traditional Fijian ceremonies, its feathers were worn as a headdress by women with chiefly blood. This was the honeymoon abode for Michelle Pfeiffer, and also Bill Gates. Built of local stone interspersed with Balinese carvings, the villa features a huge, outdoor living room bulwarked by massive bamboo furniture. Adjacent to the main house, a thatch-roofed dining gazebo overlooks sea views so sweeping, you can actually discern the curve of the earth along the horizon. A path leads down to the private beach.

Yet another stone walkway winds to the bedroom, where an 18-foot-tall canopy tops a king-size bed swathed in embroidered linens. In the huge bathroom, there's a grottolike shower with a Balinese carving to hold your wash towels. Should you need more space, there's a second bedroom. Two bedrooms in a honeymoon cottage? "One couple brought their butler," a manager explained.

The marvelously attentive and personable staff live in a small village just a short drive from the club. You'll have many opportunities to become familiar with Fijian culture, from talking with the woodcarvers who craft various items for the resort, to joining in a traditional Fijian love feast, complete with a *yaqona* (kava or grog) ceremony and pig roasted in an underground oven. On Sundays, you're welcome to attend services in the trim, white-painted church—also a favorite locale for weddings.

What burnishes Wakaya's reputation even more is the sublime food. Wakaya's own organic gardens and farms would be the envy of the world's finest chef, producing everything from eggs to red ripe tomatoes, buttery avocados, and crisp baby salad greens. At breakfast, the fresh fruit might include tangy oranges and grapefruit plucked fresh from the trees. Every day there are different muffins hot from the oven—the papaya version is especially addictive. The three-course lunch might include a chilled carrot soup, vibrantly garnished with scallions, followed by a warm salad of freshly grilled tuna. You might not plan on dessert, but who can resist a banana split drizzled with butterscotch sauce and dusted with nuts and crystallized ginger? Dinner entrees might feature seafood pasta or local venison.

When the time comes for you to leave the island, the hotel staff will gather to sing "Isa Lei," the Fijian song of farewell. "O forget not when

you're far away, precious moments beside dear Fiji Isles." As the last ca-
dences fade in the air, you'll make up your minds to return—very soon—to
Wakaya.

Address/Phone: P.O. Box 15424, Suva, Fiji Islands; 679–440–128; fax:
    679–440–406
U.S. Reservations: (213) 468–9109
Owners/Managers: David Gilmour, owner; Robert Miller, managing
    director
Arrival/Departure: Transfers arranged
Distance from Nadi Airport: 45 minutes via the resort's private
    twin-engine 1992 Britten-Norman Islander aircraft
Distance from Nadi: 45 minutes
Accommodations: 8 *bures* (bungalows) as well as 3 privately owned villas
    in the rental pool
Best Rooms/Suites: Lawedua, a private, two-bedroom house set on the
    cliffs above a private beach
Amenities: Ceiling fans, air-conditioning (some), fully stocked wet bar, CD
    stereo, cotton bathrobes, hair dryer, Crabtree & Evelyn toiletries, use of
    straw hats
Electricity: 240 volts
Sports and Facilities: Tennis court; 9-hole golf course; guided hikes; water
    sports, including snorkeling, scuba diving, swimming, and glass-bottom
    boat excursions
Dress Code: Casual elegance
Weddings: Can be arranged. Many couples choose to marry in a beachside
    ceremony or at the nineteenth-century-style church in the island's tree-
    shaded village.
Rates/Packages: $875 per couple per night (3-night minimum stay); in-
    cludes all meals, alcoholic and nonalcoholic beverages, use of sporting
    facilities and equipment (including 2 one-tank dives a day for certified
    scuba divers). Lawedua is $1,450 per night. Packages: Stay 10 nights,
    pay for just 9 nights. Stay 14 nights, pay for just 12 nights.
Payment/Credit Cards: Most major
Deposit: A deposit of $1,000 is payable within 7 days of confirmation. The
    balance is due 30 days prior to arrival date and is nonrefundable. The
    deposit is refundable only up to 45 days prior to arrival date.
Government Taxes: 10 percent
Service Charges: Not included
Entry Requirements for U.S. Citizens: Passport

French Polynesia

Bora Bora Lagoon Resort

Location: Motu Toopua, a small island within the Bora Bora Lagoon.
Romantic Features: Tahitian-style *farés* (bungalows; pronounced fa-RAY; the Tahitian word for "home") built on stilts right over the lagoon; private island setting; magnificent views of the Bora Bora mountainscape; unusual adventures like shark-feeding expeditions.

A full moon rises over Mt. Otemanu, the crenellated peak that inspired the legends of Bali Hai. The moon's rays shimmer on the glassy lagoon like a king's ransom of silver. This is the vision that awaits when you step onto your *lanai* (terrace) at the Bora Bora Lagoon Resort, an exclusive enclave set on a private isle off Bora Bora. Many consider Bora Bora to be the loveliest island in French Polynesia, with its mountaintops soaring heavenward like the skyline of an emerald city. Here a necklace of barrier reef is clasped around a perfectly blue, perfectly clear lagoon.

The resort is located on Motu Toopua, an islet in the lagoon that's just five minutes by boat from Bora Bora's main town, Vaitape. There are no roads, no electricity (the hotel uses generators), no other businesses—just twelve acres of tropical gardens and views of the mountains, reefs, and fields. After arriving by launch at the hotel's long pier, you're taken to the main building, constructed of lava stone and bamboo, with local aito logs supporting the roof. Here, you're welcomed with a lei and refreshing drink of coconut water.

You'll stay in Tahitian-style *farés* (bungalows), with peaked roofs thatched with pandanus leaves. One wall is made up of louvered panels that you can slide open to the views and prevailing breezes. Each room offers a king-size bed and separate bath with a deep soaking tub and shower as well as a TV and VCR. The most romantic quarters are the over-water bungalows, built on stilts above the opalescent lagoon. A small stairway leads down to the water, so you can swim right from the deck.

Inside, the rooms reflect Polynesian chic, with tapa cloth hangings, coconut-shell inlays, and lovely floors of lustrous yucca wood streaked with a yellow and brown grain. Decorator fabrics come from French Polynesia, and intertwine tones of ocean turquoise and sunset red. The most unusual piece of furniture is the glass coffee table: The top slides back so you can feed morsels of bread to the multicolored fish that gather below . . . an unusual twist on a "floor" show. The underwater spectacle is even illuminated at night!

The so-called "beach" bungalows are actually located in the gardens. Although they have the exact same decor as the over-water accommodations, they lack the magic of the sea-moored *farés*.

The resort has three different restaurants. For formal dining, the Otemanu Room spotlights the prodigious talents of Ian Mancais, the enthusiastic young executive chef who has cooked at top hotels from Edinburgh to Tokyo. Although the written menu is seductive enough, Ian delights in asking diners, "Well, what do you feel like eating tonight?" He'll then whip up improvisational gourmet repasts of seafood pasta or stuffed leg of chicken with braised leeks. Twice a week the resort schedules a Tahitian feast, with roast suckling pig and a folkloric dance show.

Bora Bora Lagoon offers plenty of activities—and delicious ways of doing nothing at all. A quarter of a mile of white-sand beach stretches alongside the transparent waters, and there's a marvelous pool that flows right to the edge of the tiles—the largest swimming pool in French Polynesia. Practice your strokes on the two lighted tennis courts (racquets and balls are available if you didn't bring your own). At the fitness center, you'll find exercise machines and free weights. Learn to paddle an outrigger canoe, or opt for a massage in your own room or at the spa facility.

Feel adventurous? You can also choose from a roster of intriguing excursions (which cost extra) each day. Tops on your list should be a four-wheel-drive expedition around Bora Bora. Dauntless Land Rovers crash through jungle, revving up steep, rocky, muddy, pothole-wracked tracks to some dynamite scenic overlooks. For thrill seekers, there are the shark feeds. Wearing snorkel gear, you watch safely from the shallows as dive masters serve up chunks of raw fish to black-tip sharks, which circle just a jaw's breadth away. Other activities include helicopter tours and snorkel excursions.

Exciting as these excursions are, your most vivid memories will be of the spectacular scenery in Bora Bora.

Address/Phone: Moti Toopua; B.P. 175, Vaitape, Bora Bora, French Polynesia; 689–60–40–00; fax: 689–60–40–01

U.S. Reservations: Leading Hotels of the World, (800) 223–6800 or (212) 838–3110 in New York.

Owner/manager: Bernard Mercier, general manager

Arrival/Departure: From the moment you step off the airplane at Bora Bora Airport, you are welcomed with leis and whisked to the resort across the lagoon on a private motor launch.

Distance from Bora Bora Airport: 5 minutes

Distance from Vaitape: 5 minutes by boat

Accommodations: 50 over-water bungalows; 30 beach bungalows; 2 suites

Best Rooms/Suites: Over-water bungalows

Amenities: In-room safe, minibar, electric ceiling fan (air-conditioning is not needed), hair dryer, telephone, in-house video system, TV, double sinks, and in the over-water bungalows, an illuminated glass-top coffee table gives a private view of the marine life; daily laundry service

Electricity: 220 volts

Sports and Facilities: Two tennis courts, swimming pool, Tahitian outrigger canoes, glass-bottom boat, pedal boat, beach volleyball, snorkeling, windsurfing, sailing, fitness center. Deep-sea fishing and scuba diving can be arranged.

Dress Code: Tropically casual

Weddings: The resort can arrange an authentic Tahitian wedding, including Tahitian dress for the couple, a waterfront ceremony with Polynesian music and dance, photos, sunset cruise on a pirogue canoe, and a candlelight dinner for two. (The ceremony, however, is not legally recognized in the U.S.)

Rates/Packages: Beach bungalows, $520 per couple per night; over-water bungalows, $690; Beach suite, $760. Meal plans available: $85 per person per day for breakfast and dinner and $125 for all three meals. Honeymoon package for 4 days/3 nights, $2,505 per couple; includes accommodations in an over-water bungalow; floral greeting, champagne, and special gift upon arrival; American breakfast daily, a dinner for two with bottle of wine; special picnic lunch, shark-feeding excursion for two, and more.

Payment/Credit Cards: Most major

Deposit: Guarantee with credit card

Government Taxes: 8 percent

Service Charges: Not included; not encouraged

Entry Requirements for U.S. Citizens: Valid passport and outbound ticket; if you're staying more than 1 month, you may need a visa

Hotel Bora Bora

Location: On the southwestern coast of the island of Bora Bora, 150 miles northwest of Tahiti in the Leeward Society Islands.

Romantic Features: Over-water thatched bungalows; king-size beds covered with clouds of gauzy net.

Remember those pictures of thatched huts perched on stilts over turquoise blue water? This is it. Bora Bora, the Grace Kelly of islands, flawlessly beau-

Hotel Bora Bora, French Polynesia

tiful. Home to Hotel Bora Bora, a member of the prestigious Amanresorts group, this South Seas paradise appeals to sophisticates willing to go the extra mile to experience the exotic.

As your plane zooms in on this small island (only 4 miles long and 2½ miles wide), you'll spot palm-thatched bungalows half hidden in the greenery. Crystalline waters in blues, greens, and turquoise swirl around the white-fringed shoreline. Green volcanic peaks that run like a spine down the middle of the island soar toward the brilliant blue sky.

When you arrive, take off your watch, lie back, and soak in the scenery and seamless service. Many of those on the Polynesian staff have been working at the resort for over twenty years and truly know how to anticipate whatever it is you need.

Constructed of cedar, the individual bungalows and *farés* are spread over grounds that have had more than thirty years to grow lush and lovely. All have hand-tied, thatched pandanus (palm) roofs, private bars, radio/cassette players, and roomy tiled baths with freestanding, oval, wood-rimmed tubs and separate showers. Deluxe bungalows are located on the beach and have separate lounges and sundecks with steps leading to the water. Superior bungalows are also located on the beachfront and come with a small patio facing the sea and a hammock nearby. Bungalows have patios and hammocks but are set in the gardens.

For the most fun, opt for one of the bungalows over the water. Some are in the shallow lagoon waters; others are situated on a coral reef in a deeper section of the lagoon. Each of the over-water bungalows features an enormous room more than 750 square feet, a king-size, four-poster bed swathed in mosquito netting, sliding glass doors leading out to a deck with a pandanus shade overhang, and steps to a small platform, where you can sit on the edge and dangle your feet in the water. Floor-to-ceiling louvered panels allow the sea breezes to slide in, and you have a generous-sized sitting area and dressing area with loads of storage space.

Farés, which are located on the beach near the pool and gardens, are very roomy and come with a living room, a bedroom with a king-size, four-poster bed, en suite sitting room, bathroom, and large sundeck. Eight *farés* have private swimming pools enclosed in courtyards furnished with cedar lounges and comfortable cotton cushions; three have outdoor Jacuzzis set into sundecks.

You can eat at the Matira Terrace restaurant overlooking the lagoon or at the Pofai Beach Bar. Both have lofty thatched roofs and are open on all sides to great views and cooling sea breezes. By the time you realize that your dinner and drink tab is heading skyward like the volcanoes, you really won't care much; but be prepared. Meals are not included in the rates (unless you get the Honeymoon package, which gives you some breaks). Entrees can range from $15 upward; a reasonable bottle of wine, $25 and up.

You are entertained nightly by local musicians; a Tahitian dance show is held twice a week.

Much of the activities center on the water: picnics to deserted islands, outrigger canoe rides, sunset cruises and sailing. You'll find the snorkeling very good just offshore—the fish will eat bread right out of your hand. If you want to explore the colorful underwater world farther out, you can take one of the reef trips.

There is a scuba dive program for all levels of divers. Beginners can take a resort course or go all the way to certification. There are also catamaran sails, fishing excursions, island tours, jeep excursions, shark-feeding expeditions, and a library with enough books to fill any extra hours you may have.

A special package combines three nights in a *faré* at Hotel Bora Bora and a private yacht charter for three nights with full crew service aboard *Epicurien II,* a 65-foot luxury yacht.

If you want to experience something really wild, for $450 you can take part in the Warrior Ceremony, a colorful ritual performed by a Tahitian dance group leader with two Tahitian warriors standing in attendance, holding flaming torches. You drink champagne, nibble on canapés, and enjoy a mini–dance show before boarding an authentic Tahitian sailing canoe for a 45-minute sunset cruise.

Hotel Bora Bora is restrained, in harmony with its graceful surroundings and the gentle, graceful people who live and work here. It will take you very little time to shrug off the jet lag, sink your toes in the sand, and get into the rhythm of a world that moves at a pace you can absorb.

Address/Phone: Point Raititi, Bora Bora, French Polynesia; 689–60–44–60; fax 689–60–44–66

U.S. Reservations: Amanresorts, (800) 421–1490; fax (818) 710–0050

Owner/Manager: Monty Brown, manager

Arrival/Departure: Transfers from Bora Bora Airport are complimentary; VIP airport express services available on request

Distance from Bora Bora Airport: 30 minutes; flying time between Tahiti and Bora Bora is 45 minutes

Distance from Vaitape: 3.6 miles

Accommodations: 55 Polynesian style bungalows and *farés* set amid the gardens, on the beach, or over the lagoon

Best Rooms/Suites: Over-water bungalows numbers 118 to 128 or a *faré* with in-deck Jacuzzi or private pool.

Amenities: Ceiling fans, freestanding bathtubs, separate showers, hair dryers, minibars, coffee and tea facilities, radio/cassette players, personal safes, telephones (optional), toiletries, bathrobes, and slippers; *N.Y. Times* faxed daily

Electricity: 110/220 volts

Sports and Facilities: Complimentary activities include 2 tennis courts, snorkeling, outrigger paddles and sailing, canoes, billiards, table tennis, basketball, volleyball, and tennis; optional activities include jeep excursions, glass-bottom boat tours, sunset cruises, reef trips, deep-sea fishing, scuba diving, shark feeding, and sailing and hiking excursions.

Dress Code: Casual chic

Weddings: Can be arranged, but marriage may not be legally recognized in the United States

Rates/Packages: $395–$700 per couple per night for a bungalow; $600–$700 for a *faré;* honeymoon package for approximately $2,345 per couple includes roundtrip transfers from airport, 3 nights accommodations in a Lagoon Overwater bungalow, room tax, champagne and fruit, breakfasts, one candlelight dinner with wine served on the terrace of the bungalow, private sunset sail aboard an outrigger sailing canoe, and farewell gift.

Payment/Credit Cards: Most major

Deposit: Guarantee with credit card deposit within 7 days of acknowledgment from the central reservations office; should a reservation be cancelled within 7 days of arrival date or in the event of a no-show, the first night charge along with transfer costs will be charged to the credit card or deducted from the prepayment.

Government Taxes: 8 percent; included in honeymoon package
Service Charges: Not included; not encouraged
Entry Requirements for U.S. Citizens: Valid passport and outbound
   ticket; if you're staying more than one month, you may need a visa

Hotel Hana Iti

Location: A hilly, lush jungle peninsula on Huahine Iti, the smaller of the
two islands that make up Huahine and lie 60 miles southeast of Bora Bora
and 110 miles northeast of Tahiti.
Romantic Features: Cliff-hanging bungalows, each with an outdoor
Jacuzzi; glistening, white-sand beach; four-poster living tree-trunk beds.

Photographs are nearly always picture-perfect on Huahine, a lush, moun-
tainous hideaway that dozes in the sun about 100 miles away from the bet-
ter-known Society Islands such as Tahiti and Moorea. Just point your
camera, and you'll capture views of ancient *marae* (shrines), windswept
beaches, or the purple hulk of the neighboring island of Raiatea. No wonder local residents maintain, *"C'est l'île la plus belle, la plus sauvage"*—It's
the loveliest island—and the most unspoiled." The name of the island is
pronounced wa-HEE-nee by the French, WHO-ah-HEE-nay by the Polyne-
sians.

The island is scalloped with a series of bays, eddying in a symphony of
blues—one bay nearby is so polychrome that it is known as Gauguin's
palette. Here, at the end of a bumpy road, you'll find the mesmerizing retreat that is the Hana Iti Hotel. At one time, the property belonged to Spanish singer Julio Iglesias.

Imagine dwelling in a designer's treehouse, and you pretty much have
the picture of the *farés* (bungalows), each of which is completely different.
Some are cantilevered over the hillsides, others roost on stilts or up in the
gnarled boughs of trees. Roofs are thatched with pandandus (palms); living
tree trunks and limbs form supporting columns and beams, the leaves un-
furling right in your bedroom. Natural materials are used throughout: wood,
coral, and stone. No windows separate you from the views and trade winds
(so you do have to be prepared for visitations by harmless local fauna like
lizards).

Because accommodations are large and divided into separate sleeping
and living areas, you'll have plenty of room to spread out. The king-size
beds would be worthy of Tarzan and Jane, topped by canopies suspended
from the ceiling or moored on tree trunks. In the bathroom, a giant clam

shell serves as the wash basin. There's also an open-air shower and a Jacuzzi on your sheltered deck, where you can relax while admiring the montage of sea, mountains, and sky.

Embraced by two lines of cliffs, the resort occupies fifty-four acres of untrammeled tropical luxuriance, thick with fruit trees and flowers. Shuttle service will bring you down to the white-sand beach, which melts into a blaze-blue lagoon. The color contrast is so intense, you almost have to blink when you look at it. Next to a 75-foot waterfall that dances down the mountain is a freshwater swimming pool that rivals the sapphire sea.

Every evening, a Tahitian duo entertains in the bar. Weekly events also include performances of the Tahitian *tamure,* the rapid-fire dance accompanied by rhythmic drums. Dinner is served at the beachside restaurant, where choices might include scallops and shrimp in coconut sauce or filet of beef in a pepper and foie gras sauce.

The best way to get to know Huahine is on a four-wheel-drive tour that jounces along the rutted and muddy cross-island road, close-hemmed by giant ferns and vines. Look for the purau, a type of hibiscus blossom that lives only twenty-four hours, blooming yellow in the morning and turning red in the afternoon. If you scuba dive or snorkel, do as islanders recommend and rub the petals on your mask to prevent fogging. Also stop at Lake Fauna Nui—sacred to the island's royal families in olden days. Many stone *marae* are nearby, some of which may have been the sites of human sacrifice.

You'll pass many scenic overlooks as you drive around the island, but none will surpass the panoramas you'll enjoy from your very own *faré* at Hotel Hana Iti.

Address/Phone: B.P. 185, Fare, Huahine, French Polynesia; 689–68–85–05; fax: 689–68–85–04

U.S. Reservations: None

Owner/Manager: Tom Kurth, owner; Peter Eberhardt, general manager

Arrival/Departure: Transfers from airport arranged: $12 one-way

Distance from Huahine Airport: 20-minute drive

Distance from Fare: 20-minute drive

Accommodations: 22 *farés,* each completely unique

Best Rooms/Suites: There are wonderful *farés* practically hanging over the water's edge; some have trees growing up through them. Ask for descriptions and go with what turns you on.

Amenities: Minibar, outdoor Jacuzzi, toiletries, ceiling fans

Electricity: 220 volts

Sports and Facilities: Lovely beach, swimming pool, Jacuzzi, canoes, Hobie Cat, windsurfing, snorkeling; deep-sea fishing and horseback riding can be arranged at extra charge.

Dress Code: Tropical casual

Weddings: A traditional wedding ceremony may be arranged, but it may not be legally recognized in the U.S.

Rates/Packages: $695–$895 per couple per night for a *faré* (bungalow). Meal plans available: $92 per person per day for breakfast and dinner; $127 for all three meals.

Payment/Credit Cards: Most major

Deposit: Guarantee with credit card

Government Taxes: 8 percent

Service Charges: Not included except for meal plans, when both tax and service are included

Entry Requirements for U.S. Citizens: Passport and outgoing airline ticket

Indonesia

Amanwana

Location: On island of Moyo, east of Lombok and Bali.

Romantic Features: A hideaway close to nature; luxury tented "villas."

Ever thought of spending your honeymoon in a tent on some exotic, almost deserted South Pacific island? If so, then Amanwana, on the island of Moyo in Indonesia, may be your ticket to romance. There are only about 2,000 inhabitants on the entire 120-square-mile bit of land, and it's not exactly easy to reach. You need to get to Bali, take a plane, and then a boat, and after three hours, you should finally be pulling up to the jetty of the Amanwana resort. You'll have to look hard to see anything, for this little spot of heaven has been carefully placed in this dense junglelike forest—no trees were cut down during its construction, and all the work was done by hand.

Amanwana, which means "peaceful forest," is part of the upscale Amanresorts group, which has created unique, very special small vacation places in harmony with nature. Amanwana, the first in the resort company's hideaway category, is like going camping and having your cake, too. Its clever design combines the sense of camping in the wild with the luxuries of modern-day conveniences such as air-conditioning, king-size beds, and double tile vanities.

Set on an island that is a wildlife reserve, the spacious tented rooms are more luxurious than many resort hotel accommodations. The canvas ceiling swoops to a peak in the center of the room over the bed, which is enveloped in an umbrella of filmy netting falling from a high round crown. The canvas, which extends over an outside veranda, is actually roped and pegged to the ground. Here the similarity between this accommodation and the tent you slept in at summer camp ends. The floor of your room is polished teak, there is a generous-sized sitting area with two corner sofas covered in a natural, off-white fabric, and there are practical, well-designed, but simple tables and chairs as well as a desk.

Three sides of the tent are windows with off-white, cotton accordion shades, and there are beautiful straw mats on the floors. Native original sculpture, tapestries, and paintings decorate the off-white walls. The bathrooms are really an unexpected pleasure, boasting double vanities, beautiful twin mirrors in teakwood frames, teak louvered windows, a shower and toilet, plus baskets containing toiletries on the shelf. And the rooms are air-conditioned as well as cooled by ceiling fans.

The tents are randomly linked by paths that lead to the beach, the reception area, and dining pavilion. Located in a bungalow, the reception area has a library stocked with lots of books, and the decor is pure Indonesian, with hand-hewn wooden tables and stools and original wall hangings, carvings, and paintings.

The open-air pavilion, where you find the bar, restaurant, and lounge, is located under a soaring ceiling of woven bamboo. Views are of the sea; food is basic, fresh, and good with choices from both Western and Asian cultures; and dinner is by candlelight. In fact, since the lighting tends to be less than bright even in your rooms, you'll find the mood can readily be called seductive anywhere you are in camp after the sun goes down.

There is a teak sundeck perched on the edge of the shoreline with coral steps leading to the water. Lounges, which are sturdy and constructed of wood and have upholstered cushions, provide a great inducement for those who want to lie back and relax in the sun. You can also have a private dinner on the deck or on the beach.

Activities are centered on the crystal-clear turquoise sea and the land. A guided trek into the tropical forest takes you to a beautiful inland waterfall, where you can swim in the pools created by the cascading waters. Walk under the wide tamarind, banyan, and native teak trees; catch a glimpse of monkeys, deer, and wild boar.

Or head out to sea for a late afternoon sail and see the sun go down over the Flores Sea. Amanwana also has an outrigger canoe that can take you on a cruise of the area, stopping for a picnic on the beach along the way.

Scuba enthusiasts will love it here. The island is ringed with a wonderful coral reef, and a number of interesting dive sites are accessible right from the front of the camp as well as by boat. Beginner courses are $100; PADI International Certification and other instruction are also available. Keep in mind the rainy season is from December to March; the rest of the year is pretty dry.

For a real South Pacific experience, you might try combining a stay at Amanwana with two or three nights at one or more of the other Amanresorts. (Please see descriptions of Amanpuri and Amandari in this chapter.)

Address/Phone: Moyo Island, Indonesia; 62–371–22233; fax: 62–371–22288; Reservations, 62–361–771267; fax: 62–361–771266

U.S. Reservations: (800) 447–7462 or (800) 421–1490; (212) 223–2848 in New York or (818) 587–9650 in Los Angeles

Owner: Adrian Zecha, Amanresort Ltd.

Arrival/Departure: Transfers to Moyo Island are by a Merpati Airlines flight from Bali to Sumbawa (about 1 hour with a stop in Lombok); from there it's a 1-hour cruise on Amanwana's *Aman XI* motor yacht to the camp. Total round-trip fare from Bali, $150; Amanwana also has a helipad. *Please note:* There is a strict limit of 30 pounds of luggage per person, soft-sided preferred. Guests staying at any of Aman's three resorts in Bali prior to or after Amanwana will be provided with complimentary transfers to the airport.

Distance from Denpasar Airport, Bali: About 3 hours total travel time from door to door

Accommodations: 20 luxury tents with king-size beds and en suite bathrooms

Best Rooms/Suites: Open-front tents closest to the shoreline

Amenities: Hair dryer, toiletries, air-conditioning, ceiling fans, mosquito netting, twin vanities, minibar, veranda

Electricity: 220 volts

Sports and Facilities: Trekking excursions, boating, snorkeling, cruise excursions, sports fishing, massage; scuba diving can be arranged.

Dress Code: Smart casual

Weddings: Can be arranged

Rates/Packages: $450–$525 per tent per couple; includes all meals, water sports, and nonalcoholic beverages

Payment/Credit Cards: Most major

Deposit: Guarantee with credit card deposit within 7 days of acknowledgment from the Bali Central Reservations Office; should a reservation be cancelled within 7 days of arrival date or in the event of a no-show, the first night charge along with transfer costs will be charged to the credit card or deducted from the prepayment.

Government Taxes: 11 percent room tax
Service Charges: 10 percent
Entry Requirements for U.S. Citizens: Passport that is valid for duration
  of stay and ongoing or round-trip airline tickets. *Please note:* It is recommended that you start taking antimalaria medication (i.e. doxycycline) before you arrive.
Closed: January 15 to March 15

Amandari

Location: In Bali in the Indian Ocean, in the center of the Indonesian archipelago.
Romantic Features: Sunrise walk to the river; scent of frangipani; gamelon
concert at sunset; private garden pools; swimming in a pool that seems suspended in midair.

If you believe that the best things come in small packages, Amandari is just
further proof. You'll find this little jewel of a hotel perched dramatically on
a cliff overlooking the Ayung River Gorge, on the exquisite island of Bali.
Below are sweeping views of terraced rice paddies and tiny villages, palms
and orchids, a dreamscape to savor in luxury. Designed as a Balinese village, Amandari, one of the very special Amanresorts properties, has twenty-
nine garden suites, some with private pools and garden courtyards.
    What better place to go to celebrate your union than to Bali, which is
legendary for its beauty. The graceful, sarong-clad people sway as they
walk, balancing goods on their heads. The land is green and lush, with sin-
uous rice paddies, and the island is ringed by soft, white-sand beaches and
clear water.
    Traditional dancers greet you at the open-air lobby, with its thatched-
roof, templelike facade, floors of local marble, and carved teak furniture
made on the island. The adjacent library/lounge offers comfortable chairs
and a chance to learn about the surroundings and the gentle, artful Hindu
culture.
    The villages in the neighboring area each specialize in a different art
form: Ubud is known for painting; Mas, for woodcarving; Celuk, for gold
jewelry. The hotel can arrange to drive you around the island, where days
can be spent bargaining for art and soaking in the rich culture. Each village
also has its own distinctive dance, performed to the percussive music of the
gamelan. Visitors can enjoy watching a new presentation each night at the
open pavilions.

Dining here takes advantage of the views. The Verandah restaurant, overlooking the river, is dreamy with candlelight and soft music, and serves fine international and Indonesian cuisine. The lounge offers spectacular views; a poolside bar features light meals.

Activities include tennis, hikes into the gorge, biking in the villages, and rafting on the Ayung River. But the loveliest activity of all has to be swimming in one of the most beautiful pools in the world. Contoured in the shape of a rice terrace, the pool appears to meld into the valley beyond. With the reflection of the clouds spreading out over the water, it seems as if you are swimming right up to the edge of the gorge. At one end is a pavilion, where at sunset, the ringing sounds of the gamelan fills the air.

Suites are spectacular, some with private pools. Each is enclosed in its own garden courtyard and has a private entrance. Steep paths and stone steps lead to other bungalows and down to the river and the villages. Duplexes have spiral staircases that go up to the bedroom. All suites have polished marble floors, teak furnishings, four-poster beds with hand-painted canopies, and patios with sunken marble tubs hidden behind Balinese walls. Decorative sliding wall screens, creamy white walls accented by wood trim, and lovely paintings and sculpture further enhance the accommodations.

The high-pitched thatched roofs, oversized daybeds, elegant Asian furnishings accented with native art, flowers, glass walls overlooking the beauty of this island, and the sarongs provided to each guest to wear to temple ceremonies—all are wondrously romantic things.

Amandari, which means "place of peaceful spirits," is aptly named.

Address/Phone: Ubud, Bali, Indonesia; 62–361–975333; fax: 62–361–975–335

U.S. Reservations: (800) 447–7462 or (800) 421–1490; (212) 223–2848 in New York or (818) 587–9650 in Los Angeles

Owner/Manager: Adrian Zecha, Amanresorts Ltd.

Arrival/Departure: Complimentary transfers provided from airport

Distance from Bali Airport: 1 hour

Distance from Ubud: 5 minutes

Accommodations: 29 luxury suites enclosed in private courtyard, 6 with private pools; duplex suites have outdoor garden showers and queen-size beds; the Amandari suite is a 2-story bungalow with private pool and wonderful views of rice terraces and the valley

Best Rooms/Suites: Pool suites

Amenities: Hair dryer, toiletries, air-conditioning, ceiling fans, mosquito netting, twin vanities, minibar/refrigerator, garden patios, in-room safe,

radio, sunken marble tub; 24-hour room service
Electricity: 220 volts
Sports and Facilities: Swimming in main or private pool, rafting, trekking, biking, tennis court
Dress Code: Casual; shorts not allowed in temple areas of villages
Weddings: Can be arranged
Rates/Packages: $330–$770 per couple per night
Payment/Credit Cards: Most major
Deposit: Guarantee with credit card deposit within 7 days of acknowledgment from the Bali Central Reservations Office; should a reservation be cancelled within 7 days of arrival date or in the event of a no-show, the first night charge along with transfer costs will be charged to the credit card or deducted from the prepayment.
Government Taxes: 11 percent
Service Charges: 10 percent
Entry Requirements for U.S. Citizens: Passport

Puri Kamandalu Resort

Location: In the highlands of central Bali, just north of Ubud.
Romantic Features: Showering in a private walled Balinese shower under the stars; your own thatched pavilion overlooking emerald-green paddy fields and the Petanu River.

If you have decided to go all the way to exotic Bali for your honeymoon, consider including a stay at the Puri Kamandalu Resort. Granted it's not on the beach, but for those who want to really soak up Balinese culture, this little gem of a place, set on a tropical forested hillside with green padi fields spreading out below, would be an excellent choice. Enhanced by accommodations that have been designed to replicate a typical Balinese village, Puri Kamandalu is located very near Ubud, home of many gifted artists from Indonesia and other parts of the world, who come to live and work in this serene environment.

Just a short shuttle ride from the resort, you can visit this bustling little town and the artists and craftspeople who live and work in the village. You can also see some fine works by Balinese painters and sculptors at the newly opened Kamandalu Art Gallery, located right on the resort grounds.

At Puri Kamandalu, pavilion cottages with traditional thatched roofs hover just below the tall palms, which have been profusely planted on the hillside. Since the pavilions cling to the curved terraces of the hillside, you

Puri Kamandalu Resort, Indonesia

may find you have to walk many steps up (or down) a hill to get where you're going.

All pavilions and villas have garden showers, marble floors, modern baths with sunken marble tubs, and a *bale bengong* (sitting area). They come with modern amenities such as air-conditioning, minibar, TV, in-house movies, an audio system, in-room safe, and garden showers.

The simplest and smallest of the pavilions features an outdoor garden shower and *bale bengong* with views over the hills; the deluxe pavilions are more spacious, have better views, and outdoor Jacuzzis; the deluxe pavilions come with private sunbathing areas and pools and valley views; villas, designed in the typical thatched Lombok style *Sasak* (house) each contain a courtyard garden and two separate rooms, including a *bale bengong;* deluxe villas are more spacious versions of the smaller villa.

Many pavilions have king-beds that are richly decorated with Balinese canopies and headboards. Furniture is simple yet elegantly styled in wood with traditional Balinese fabric cushions. Ceilings are lofty and show the intricate underside of the thatched roofs.

Meals are served in the Angsoka Restaurant and highlight cuisine from Bali along with international specialties. There is also the Cempaka Bar and Lounge as well as a library bar with panoramic views of the rice terraces. Tea is served each afternoon, accompanied by the lilting sounds of a Balinese flute.

The resort has a large swimming pool, tennis courts, and hiking and jogging trails. If you feel adventurous, you can go whitewater rafting.

The Kamandalu Heritage Herbal Spa, a new addition to the property, offers health and beauty care treatments. Experience the soothing essences of selected *jamus,* herbal mixtures used in various treatments offered at the spa.

In its commitment to the local culture and people, Puri Kamandalu has provided a nearby village with clean water and an easy access to the hotel temple, which is built into the hills. Villagers come here to present their offerings to God. While you're staying at the resort, you see the villagers quietly going about their business, tending the rice fields and driving their ducks to the paddy to eat.

Sometimes in the distance, you may hear the music of a special festival or celebration. Puri Kamandalu is a tranquil place located in close proximity to authentic villages, not to be mistaken for the hub of Bali's tourist nightlife. The main pool may have a swim-up bar and you may have twenty-four-hour room service, but if you want discos and nightclubs, you'll have to go somewhere else. Here when the sun goes down, life slows. You relax; you enjoy.

Address/Phone: Jalan. Tegallalang, Banjar, Nagi, P.O. Box 77, Ubud Bali, Indonesia; 62–361–975–825 or 62–361–975–835; fax: 62–361–975–851

U.S. Reservations: (201) 902–7990; fax: (201) 902–7270

Owner/Manager: Eduard Hoogeweegen, general manager

Arrival/Departure: Guests are picked up from the airport; transfer to resort is complimentary; check-in is completed inside the room.

Distance from Bali Airport: 1-hour drive

Distance from Ubud: 1 mile

Accommodations: 50 thatched-roof pavilions and villas set in private walled enclosures; each is designed as a typical Balinese house, with *bale bengongs* (sitting areas) overlooking the rice paddies and hillside and outdoor showers; some have private pools and separate living rooms.

Best Rooms/Suites: Royal Villa

Amenities: Air-conditioning; in-room safe; minibar; I.D.D. telephone, audio system; satellite TV; toiletries; coffee and tea maker; hair dryer; garden showers, some with Jacuzzis and private pools; in-house movies

Electricity: 220 volts

Sports and Facilities: Large swimming pool and children's pool, tennis court, jogging track, hiking trails, nature walks; whitewater rafting can be arranged

Dress Code: Casual elegance

Weddings: A mock wedding in traditional rich red and gold Balinese costumes is part of the honeymoon package.

Rates/Packages: $175–$375 per room per night for a pavilion; $225–$1,750 for a villa, Honeymoon package, $985 per couple, including 4 days/3 nights in luxury one-bedroom pavilion, breakfasts either in your pavilion or in the Pudak restaurant, round-trip transfers, fruit basket and champagne, massage for two, candlelight dinner, sunset cruise, mock wedding in traditional Balinese costume, taxes, service charges, and late checkout.

Payment/Credit Cards: Most major

Deposit: Credit card

Government Taxes: Varies

Service Charges: 21 percent

Entry Requirements for U.S. Citizens: Proof of citizenship; passport best

Thailand

Amanpuri

Location: On the island of Phuket, off the southern coast of Thailand.
Romantic Features: Private treetop pavilions; serene island retreat.

In Sanskrit, *Amanpuri* means "place of peace." It is. No discos, no slot machines, no traffic noise. Amanpuri, the first of Adrian Zecha's elite Amanresorts, is a haven from the fast-paced world many of us live in. Once here, you'll have plenty of time to unwind and soak in the tranquility and beauty of Amanpuri. In fact, doing nothing in an exotic place is exactly what many come here for.

One thing for sure. You'll know you're in Thailand when you arrive in Amanpuri. Most of what has been built here has been created out of local materials made by local craftspeople.

The center roof of the Grand Sala, the centerpiece of Amanpuri, soars to 40 feet. Its multiple, pitched roofs and columns are reflected in the rectangular pool, which is filled to the brim with the clearest of water. The Grand Sala, simply yet elegantly decorated with live orchids and antique furniture, is where you are greeted when you arrive at Amanpuri. At that time a manager is assigned to look after you for the duration of your stay.

Built on three levels into the trees and tropical foliage of a former coconut plantation, forty pavilions are spread out over 20 acres. They stand on stilts over land and water, linked by elevated walkways. The design of the resort is refined with guest pavilions and the Grand Sala integrated into a harmonious whole. Steep-pitched roofs curve to a sharp peak like Buddhist temples, and buildings are constructed of wood accented by earthy, red-hued trim.

On the beach level, you'll find a well-equipped gym and treatment rooms where you can be pampered with massages, facials, and other soothing delights. The Grand Sala, a huge open-air reception area with a lounge and pool is found on the second level.

A lot of natural materials such as bamboo, stone, and teak are used throughout the resort. You'll find caned chairs, baskets, stone walls, and teak floors.

Pavilions are very spacious, containing 1,200 square feet including the bedroom, dressing area, bath and shower, outdoor *sala* (sitting area), and sundeck. Each bedroom is quietly elegant. Decor doesn't jump out and hit you with a resounding "wow." Rather it seduces with creamy, white walls;

floor-to-ceiling decorative wood panels; fibre rugs; carved furniture; soft, handwoven cottons and silks; pottery; plants; and Thai sculpture. Bathrooms are enormous, designed for two; closets have enough drawers to hold an entire winter wardrobe.

Although some rooms have good ocean views, most are located in the dense palm groves overlooking the gardens. When Amanpuri was built, the integrity of the land was respected.

The casual Terrace restaurant features fresh seafood and continental and Thai specialties daily; and surprise, there is also an Italian restaurant where you can dine by candlelight on the veranda overlooking the sea. Musicians will serenade you as the moon rises over the water. Service is seamless, gracious. If you prefer a quiet party for two in your pavilion, you can call on room service any hour.

You'll find a wide range of water sports activities on the beach, including sailing, windsurfing, Hobie Cats, and snorkeling. Amanpuri has an excellent marina and maintains a fleet of yachts, available for charter. Pack a picnic, your snorkeling gear and flippers, and explore some of the neighboring islands and bays close to the resort. Or climb aboard a restored classic Chinese junk for a sunset cruise.

Want to see some of the wonderful life beneath the sea? Check out the H2O Sportz operation, a full service PADI facility geared to scuba divers of all abilities. The resort course will give you a basic introduction to diving; for the more advanced and certified divers, there are trips to a number of world-class dive sites for exploring underwater caves and crevices as well as coral reefs and walls.

The resort has a library with a collection of more than 1,000 books and a gift shop where you can purchase a variety of Asian artifacts, including jewelry, textiles, pottery, and small sculptures.

It's a long way to this part of the world, so consider seeing both Thailand and Indonesia. Stay at Amanpuri in Thailand, Amandari in Indonesia, and/or Amanwana, a luxury "tented" island resort on the tiny island of Molo, near Bali. All are members of the Amanresorts group.

Address/Phone: Pansea Beach, Phuket Island, Thailand; 66–076–324–333; fax: 66–076–324–100 or 324–200

U.S. Reservations: (800) 447–7462 or (800) 421–1490; (212) 223–2848 in New York or (818) 587–9650 in Los Angeles

Owner/Manager: Adrian Zecha, Amanresort Ltd., owner; Anthony Lark, general manager

Arrival/Departure: Complimentary transfers provided from Phuket Airport; frequent air service from Bangkok daily (1-hour flight)

Distance from Phuket Airport: 12 miles (20 minutes)

Distance from Phuket Town: 10 miles

Accommodations: 40 pavilions, each with its own outdoor *sala* (sitting area); also 13 guest villa homes, with two, three, or four bedrooms

Best Rooms/Suites: Numbers 103 and 105, with ocean views

Amenities: Hair dryer, toiletries, air-conditioning, ceiling fans, mosquito netting, twin vanities, minibar/refrigerator, sundeck, in-room safe, stereo cassette system; 24-hour room service

Electricity: 220 volts

Sports and Facilities: 2 floodlit tennis courts, pool, gym, beach club, sailing, windsurfing, snorkeling, waterskiing, deep-sea fishing, scuba diving; golf nearby; island cruises

Dress Code: Smart casual

Weddings: Can be arranged

Rates/Packages: $257–$645 per couple per night (summer); $319–$855 (winter), including transfers.

Payment/Credit Cards: Most major

Deposit: Guarantee with credit card deposit within 7 days of acknowledgement from the Bali Central Reservations Office; should a reservation be cancelled within 7 days of arrival date or in the event of a no-show, the first night charge along with transfer costs will be charged to the credit card or deducted from the prepayment.

Government Taxes: 7.7 percent room tax

Service Charges: 10 percent

Entry Requirements for U.S. Citizens: Passport that is valid for duration of stay and ongoing or round-trip airline tickets. *Please note:* It is recommended that you start taking antimalaria medication (i.e., doxycycline) before you arrive.

Africa

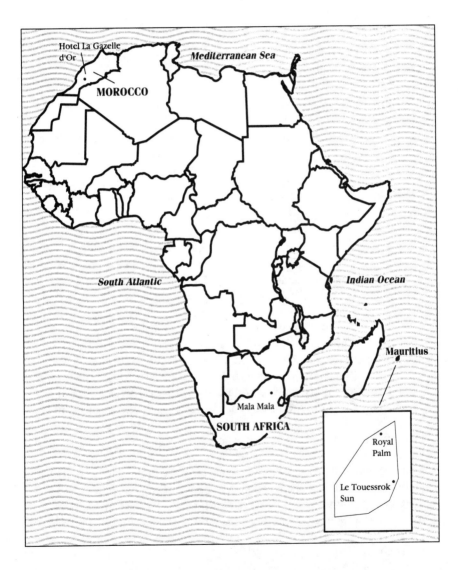

Hotel La Gazelle d'Or

MOROCCO

Mediterranean Sea

South Atlantic

Indian Ocean

Mauritius

Mala Mala

SOUTH AFRICA

Royal Palm

Le Touessrok
Sun

Mauritius

Royal Palm

Location: On the north coast of Mauritius, an island 500 miles east of Madagascar.
Romantic Features: Lush, beachfront setting; luxurious baths with Jacuzzis; private walkway to beach.

To reach Mauritius, you'll have to go almost halfway around the world to a tiny, coral-fringed island rising out of the Indian Ocean east of Madagascar. This exotic multicultural pearl was discovered long ago by the Europeans, but is relatively unknown to Americans. It's not uncommon to spend one or two weeks here and not meet anyone from the States. Known for its welcoming climate, spectacular white-sand beaches, and world-class resort facilities, this 720-square-mile island is a true tropical paradise.

If you want to splurge and join a handful of blue bloods and other jet-setters who head this way for their romantic rendezvous, try the Royal Palm. Discreet and classy, this little spot of heaven has been included in more than one well-respected list of the best romantic resorts in the world, including that of the English journalist, Garry Buchanan. Here you drink your champagne from Waterford crystal and sleep in a giant four-poster bed graced by a canopy of elegant beige and off-white fabric. The word "discreet" pops up a lot when people talk about the Royal Palm—you never know who will be lying under a coating of suntan oil on one of the luxurious pool lounges next to you. A princess? An industrial magnate? A movie star? Privacy is fiercely protected.

Located in the fashionable northwest corner of the island, the resort, which is the flagship of the Beachcomber Hotels group, sits amid a riot of bougainvillea, hibiscus, and lots of palms (naturally). The white-sand beach welcomes a gentle surf from the turquoise blue waters—a perfect place for those who love to sun and swim. Claim your very own palm tree and sit on a lounge under the waving fronds or head for one of the yellow-and-white umbrellas and let the waiters take your order for a tasty tropical brew. And there is only one word for the pool, which curves by the teak bar: elegant. A few low wicker chaises with plump cushions covered in pastels are placed around the tiled deck. And here and there is a beautiful little bridge to get you from one place to another.

Each of the sixty spacious rooms and four suites has its own balcony overlooking the sea, inviting you to sip a frosty cocktail as you watch the sun go down over the water. Undulating, straw-thatched roofs; stonework; elaborately carved teakwood; and native fabrics set against stark, white walls lend a quiet elegance to this intimate hideaway. The rooms are exquisitely furnished and come with king-size beds or two large single beds. Dark wicker chairs and stools with upholstered cushions as well as antique reproduction pieces and oriental rugs are part of the decor. The baths are very luxurious, and eight of the senior suites feature Jacuzzis. Suites each have a private staircase leading to the white-sand beach as well as a kitchenette, dining room, powder room, and, if requested, personal valet and kitchen service. Bouquets of fresh waxy red, pink, and white anthurium, a product of the island's nurseries, are artfully arranged and placed throughout your room.

Certainly you'd expect that guests staying in this palace of privilege would enjoy world-class cuisine, and they do. There are three restaurants overlooking the sea and beach and two more intimate dining rooms decorated in lacy, carved wood and original paintings and sculpture. European, Chinese, Indian, and Creole cuisine are featured.

It takes about twenty-four hours door-to-door to get here from the East Coast of the United States, so you might want to look forward to a massage or sauna on arrival. Then you can windsurf, sail, deep-sea fish, dance the night away at the night club, or just settle back into the cushions of one of the white wicker armchairs on the terrace and mentally drift away.

Should you want to venture outside the walls of the Royal Palm, you can either rent a car or go the whole route and take a discovery trip around the island in a private limousine. All these good things do not come cheap. But most sports are included in your room rate, except for big-game fishing, lagoon trawler fishing, scuba diving, trimaran cruising, and motorboat trips.

Mark Twain wrote, "You would gather that Mauritius was made first and heaven after and that heaven was copied after Mauritius."

Address/Phone: Royal Road, Grande Baie, Ile Maurice; 230–263–8353; fax: 230–263–8455
U.S. Reservations: Leading Hotels, (800) 223–6800
Owner/Manager: Jean-Pierre Chaumard, general manager
Arrival/Departure: The best way to get to Mauritius is to fly to London and then take Air Mauritius to the island. Allow 24 hours. Transfers can be arranged by private car or helicopter.
Distance from Mauritius Airport: 45 miles (1 hour)
Distance from Port Louis: 30 minutes
Accommodations: 66 rooms, 15 suites, and 1 Royal Suite, all with king-size or twin beds and private terrace

Best Rooms/Suites: Ask for ocean-view suites that have direct access to the beach.

Amenities: Hair dryer, air-conditioning, direct-dial telephones, television with video and 24-hour news channel, radio, minibar and in-room safe; suites have personal valet service, video player and library, 24-hour room service, and some have Jacuzzis. Laundry and dry-cleaning, beautician, sauna and massage services available.

Electricity: 220/240 volts

Sports and Facilities: 3 floodlit tennis courts, squash court, pool, snooker, table tennis, windsurfing, waterskiing; pedal or glass-bottom boating, snorkeling; golf nearby. Big-game fishing, scuba diving; trimaran cruising can be arranged.

Dress Code: Tropical elegance

Weddings: Can be arranged

Rates/Packages: 9,800–30,000 rupees per couple per night, including breakfast, tax, and service

Payment/Credit Cards: Most major (no personal checks)

Deposit: Guarantee with credit card

Government Taxes: Included

Service Charges: Included

Entry Requirements for U.S. Citizens: Valid passport

Le Touessrok Sun

Location: In Mauritius, off the coast of East Africa, 500 miles east of Madagascar.

Romantic Features: Four private beaches; sunset gondola cruise; candlelight dinner for two on the beach.

If you plan on an African safari for your honeymoon and want to wind up your vacation with a few days at an exotic island resort, check out Le Touessrok Sun in Mauritius. Built on a cluster of private islands just 100 yards offshore, it was chosen by Prince Andrew and Fergie as their hotel of residence when they came here just a few years ago. Mediterranean in feeling, the white, adobe-style, two-story buildings with flat and thatched roofs, and turquoise doors, the bridges trimmed with decorative woodcarvings and the narrow alleyways remind one of a small fishing village. Clouds of bougainvillea fall from balconies and over archways, and all rooms are either directly on the beach or overlook the magnificent lagoon.

The hotel has a private dock located beneath Les Papillotes Bar and

Le Touessrok Sun, Mauritius

Lounge, where pirogues (small boats) run regularly between the main resort area and the resort's private islands of Ile-aux-Cerfs and Ilot Mangenie.
Ile-aux-Cerfs, which is just a ten-minute boat ride across the lagoon, is an
idyllic island playground, where you can swim, sunbathe, or lounge in the
gardens. There is a free water sports center offering a whole list of activities. You can eat at the beachside barbecue grill or at La Chaumière, where
palm-thatched kiosks are half-hidden in the lush greenery. As you sit at
your treehouse table, you look out through the tall, thin Casuarina trees,
palms, and flowers to the beach just beyond.

Ilot Mangenie is your ultimate desert island hideaway, but with room
service. It is uninhabited and undeveloped, yet only a three-minute boat
ride away, and you can spend the day here exploring, sunning, and swimming. Just about the time when hunger pangs set in, you can dive into a
barbecue lunch, which is prepared and served by the staff between 12:30
and 2:30 P.M.

The whole place was upgraded and renovated in 1993, with $28 mil-
lion spent on the redo. A new group of thirty-seven junior suites were built
on Hibiscus Beach. From these suites, which snuggle right up to the water's
edge, you can lie in bed and gaze out at the water. Each of the resort's
rooms and suites is beautifully appointed and has a fully stocked minibar
and lounge with sliding doors opening onto a private terrace looking out to
the gardens and the sea.

The decor is an eclectic mix of Oriental, Asian, and European styles with lots of wicker, rattan, and Italian tile. Televisions are hidden in hand-carved Mauritius-made chests, bedspreads are brilliant-hued prints of bougainvillea and frangipani, and tables are topped with jade-green marble. Many accommodations come with large showers and enclosed toilet and bidet. In the redecoration, a number of original art pieces were commissioned to enhance the guest rooms as well as the public rooms.

There are two pools, one a shimmering, three-level beauty that appears to spill out into the ocean and has a floating bar, bandstand, and dance floor. There are three tennis courts, a sauna, massage rooms, and the use of a nine-hole golf course at the toney Le Ste. Geran, Sun's sister property, fifteen minutes away.

Le Touessrok's restaurants specialize in Mauritian food and offer a wide array of continental dishes as well. There is also an exchange dining program with Le St. Geran nearby. A discotheque is open nightly, and there is a casino in the vicinity.

Le Touessrok has often been called the Venice of the Tropics. Indeed, it has its own gondola available for sunset glides, and the resort is just about surrounded by water. Honeymooners are wooed with garlands of flowers, a welcome cocktail, champagne, fruit, and a free pareo and T-shirt.

It's a long way to this exotic Mauritian island, with its interesting mix of many cultures, but if you make the journey, Le Touessrok Sun is quite a find.

You might also consider booking a package combining a safari experience or Cape Town tour in South Africa with a beach vacation in Mauritius. Ask your travel agent about available packages. A stopover in London could also be included.

Address/Phone: Trou D'Eau Douce, Mauritius; 230–419–2451; fax: 230–419–2025. In the UK, fax: 441–491–576–194

U.S. Reservations: Sun International, (305) 891–2500, ext. 241. For packages, call SAA Costcutters, (800) 2-SAFARI.

Owners/Managers: Philippe Requin, general manager

Arrival/Departure: The best way to get to Mauritius is to fly to London and then take Air Mauritius to the island. Allow 24 hours. Transfers can be arranged.

Distance from Mauritius Airport: 27 miles (55 minutes)

Distance from Port Louis: 26 miles (50 minutes)

Accommodations: 200 rooms and suites; 130 located on a private island reached by a bridge

Best Rooms/Suites: Beachfront Hibiscus Suites or, for high rollers, The Royal Suite, a luxurious beachhouse with spectacular ocean views, spacious patio, dining room, living room, chandeliers, private courtyard, and Jacuzzi

Amenities: Air-conditioning, telephones, ceiling fans, radios, taped music, TV, minibars, balconies, 24-hour room service, in-room safes; some have walk-in closets, bathrobes, bidets.

Electricity: 220/240 volts

Sports and Facilities: 4 private beaches, 2 pools, volleyball court, 4 flood-lit tennis courts, sauna, massage, scuba diving, deep-sea fishing, sailing, snorkeling, windsurfing, waterskiing, parasailing, paddleboating, Hobie Cats, canoeing; golf nearby

Dress Code: Casually elegant

Weddings: Can be arranged—barefoot under a palm, in formal wear on the beach

Rates/Packages: Per person per night including accommodations, breakfast, and dinner: 6,595–23,295 rupees (Christmas); 4,115–12,995 rupees (winter); 4,475–21,895 rupees (fall); 3,650–17,995 rupees (summer) (highest rates are for Royal Suite). A 14-day package from SAA Costcutters, priced from $3,857 per person, visits South Africa and Mauritius and includes airfare, accommodations, transfers, Cape Town tour, game drive in Sun City, and 2-day tour in Mauritius.

Payment/Credit Cards: Most major

Deposit: Guarantee with credit card; cancellation fees apply according to season if not cancelled within time allowed.

Government Taxes: Included

Service Charges: Included

Entry Requirements for U.S. Citizens: Valid passport

Morocco

Hotel La Gazelle d'Or

Location: Ten minutes from Taroudant, a medieval walled city.

Romantic Features: Little stone villas in what was once the private hunting lodge of a French baron; lovely grounds fragrant with rose gardens and citrus orchards.

Having risen late, a couple called room service to ask until what time breakfast was served. The captain grandly responded, "Whenever you like. All we ask is that you finish breakfast before you have lunch."

That's the personal attention you can expect at La Gazelle d'Or, a hideaway just outside the medieval walled city of Taroudant. It's the kind of place where the maitre d' reserves your unfinished bottle of wine from the night before, and the attendant calls to ask if you'd care to swim before he covers the pool for the night.

Built in 1948, the enclave was the private hunting reserve of French Baron Jean Pellenc; it became a hotel in 1961. Formerly the baron's residence, the main building is opulently decorated with camel saddles, antique rifles with mother-of-pearl stocks, and magnificent mosaics, most notably the gilt-trimmed floor of the Zodiac Room.

The resort encompasses twenty-five acres of tropical gardens, which cast the intoxicating fragrances of rose and citrus onto the breezes. There are just thirty stone cottages, draped with bowers of bougainvillea and overlooking orange groves, gardens, and the Atlas Mountains.

Cottages face a broad, emerald lawn shaded by palms, cedars, and olive trees and bordered by beds of roses. You'll find the same profusion of roses gathered into bouquets in your room—vivid arrangements of alabaster, pink, coral, and crimson. Cottages are large, each with an entrance foyer leading to a separate bedroom and bathroom. Furnishings capture the romance of the Arabian Nights, with blue and white terrazzo floors, mosaic tables, and filigreed plasterwork over the bed. A corner fireplace adds to the romantic ambience. The bathrobes for your use are thick and heavy—it seems as if they weigh nearly ten pounds.

La Gazelle d'Or is a place for utter relaxation and sensual pleasure—the hardest thing you might have to do is brush bougainvillea blossoms off your chairs on the terrace.

Your day might begin with a jog through the citrus groves and alleys of roses. Then order breakfast, which will be brought to your private terrace by a white-robed attendant. The ample continental repast includes a large glass of fresh-squeezed orange juice (from the hotel's own trees) and a platter of ripe nectarines, grapes, and melon. In the basket of breads, you'll find croissants, rolls, and *pain au chocolat,* the filling still warm from the oven. You'll probably make friends with some of the resident cats, who drop by not just to mooch extra milk but also to appeal to your sense of largess—they are especially fond of the crisp corners of the croissants.

Read and sun by the magnificent large pool, lined with blue tiles and shaded by ancient olive trees. Then play tennis or go horseback riding on one of the fine Arabians, trotting through the Souss valley, where doves skim along the breezes.

If you can tear yourself away from this peaceful oasis, tour nearby Taroudant, a walled city with ramparts dating back to the twelfth century. A city of 35,000 inhabitants, it is nonetheless an exotic desert outpost, the street thronging with horse-drawn buggies and Berber women draped in black. Visit the market, where vendors sell amber, musk, kohl, and huge piles of fragrant spices looking like they were poured from a child's sand pail. The hotel can arrange excursions to the waterfalls at Amagour or the beaches near Imouzer.

Dinner is served in a circular, tented dining room that recalls the tales of Scheherazade. In this delicious, five-course repast, portions are sized just right, providing a parade of exquisite tastes without leaving you overly stuffed. You might start with a shrimp bisque enlivened by ripe tomatoes, or fish soufflé, brought to the table at the peak of its crescendo. For entrees, choices can include a chicken fricassee or tagine of lamb with okra— the meat is so tender, it flakes off the bone. Desserts are heavenly, like the lemon tart, heady with citrus flavor.

After dinner, head to the adjoining salon, where mint tea is served with a flourish by gentlemen who pour from a metal pot held several feet above the tiny glass cups. Enhancing the magic, manager Adam Stevenson plays tunes ranging from Gershwin to Rachmaninov on the piano.

"We have found our Paradise," one honeymoon couple inscribed in the hotel guest book. All who sojourn at La Gazelle d'Or are sure to agree.

Address/Phone: BP 60, Taroudant, Morocco; 212–8–85–2039, fax: 212–8–85–2737

U.S. Reservations: None; contact the hotel directly.

Owner/Manager: G. Angelides, general manager

Arrival/Departure: Transfers can be arranged at a cost of about $60 each way.

Distance from Agadir Airport: 48 miles (1 hour)

Distance from Taroudant: 5 minutes; 45 minutes from Agadir

Accommodations: 30 cottages

Best Rooms/Suites: Junior suites

Amenities: Ceiling fans (some), hair dryer, minibar, toiletries, bathrobes; TV in lounge

Electricity: 110/220 volts

Sports and Facilities: Large heated swimming pool, 2 tennis courts, riding stables, croquet, *hammam* (traditional steam bath), massage and beauty center

Dress Code: Casual elegance

Weddings: The resort does not arrange weddings for U.S. citizens. However, there is a Christian church in the town of Taroudant where you can be married. La Gazelle d'Or will provide assistance.

Rates/Packages: $365 per couple per night for a cottage; $471 per couple per night for a junior suite; $801 per couple per night for a large suite;

rates include continental breakfast and dinner. There is no special honeymoon package; a perk package for an additional charge (about
$150) includes flowers, fruit, champagne, Moroccan pastries, and up-
grade to junior suite.

Payment/Credit Cards: Most major

Deposit: Normally, a deposit of 30 percent is expected except during peak
periods, such as Christmas, when full prepayment is requested. Cancel
10 days prior to arrival date for full refund.

Government Taxes: Included

Service Charge: Included in rate; gratuities at discretion of guests

Entry Requirements for U.S. Citizens: Valid passport

South Africa

Mala Mala

Location: Mala Mala is one of six safari lodge camps located on the Rattray
Reserves, a private, 45,000-acre-game preserve adjacent to the Kruger National Park, in the northeastern part of the country.

Romantic Features: Moonlight safaris; thatched *rondavels* overlooking
Sand River.

At Mala Mala, your wake-up call comes about 5:30 A.M., just in time to watch
the moon set into the shelter of the distant hills over the Sand River. After a
cup of tea or coffee in the lodge, you climb into an open Land Rover, and
with a ranger-driver and armed tracker aboard, head into the bush for a
magic morning of game viewing. You may see a mother cheetah sitting
under a tree with her four cubs lazing about in a heap around her, or you
may pick up the trail of a lioness loping along, her tail swaying back and
forth. You'll get close to giraffes and elephants, warthogs, kudu, and water-
bucks. Later, back at the lodge, you'll chow down on a lavish breakfast.

Coming to Mala Mala and not participating in the early morning and
late evening game safaris would be like visiting the Tuileries and passing
over the flowers. Everywhere you go in this amazing camp, you are re-
minded that you are in the heart of the largest tract of privately owned big-
game territory in South Africa. Walk around the grounds in the evening,
and you hear the cries and calls of the animals stirring; the sounds of their
nighttime activities of roaming, eating, and mating.

Rooms at Mala Mala are in spacious, ochre-colored *rondavels* (bungalows), which sit on a knoll overlooking the Sand River, where animals come daily to drink. The rooms are remarkably luxurious for the bush. They come with "his" and "her" bathrooms; comfortable, oversized Posturepedic twin beds; and high thatched ceilings. Norma Rattray, who oversees the designs of the interiors, says, "Just because you come to camp doesn't mean you have to be uncomfortable." Large window walls give you wonderful views of the river, and rooms are furnished with attractive rattan furniture and nature prints.

Afternoons at camp are spent as the animals spend them: leisurely. You can take a nap, swim in the pool, or sip a cool drink under the shade of a tree.

Night drives begin in late afternoon while the sun is still hot, but beware; once the sun goes down, it cools off rapidly, especially in the winter. Then you'll need some warm clothing—think "layered look." As it gets dark, the rangers slowly drive the Land Rovers into the bush. The tracker holds a spotlight, which would seem to intrude on the animals' privacy and to frighten them. It doesn't. Over the years, the animals have become accustomed to the light and the sounds of the vehicles' engines and accept these things as just part of their world.

The light finds a lion and her two cubs finishing their meal of impala. Later the Land Rover slowly rolls off the path into the center of a large buffalo herd. A large, mud-caked bull shakes his thick horns as he grazes—just three feet away from the Rover's passengers. The motor is turned off, and you can hear the animals rustle through the low bush and the night sounds all around. Behind the buffalo, acacia trees are silhouetted by a full, white moon hanging in the African sky.

Back at the lodge, there is an air-conditioned dining room where meals are served. Dinner can really be fun on the nights you eat in a reed enclosed *boma*, a traditional South African round open-air area. You sit in a large circle with everyone facing a log fire blazing in the center of the area. Your meal includes beautifully prepared fresh local fruits and vegetables and game meats such as venison and impala. After dinner, dancing and entertainment is provided by the staff under the starry South African skies.

There is a cozy bar where people gather in the evenings after the game drives to compare their sightings. It's always a challenge to see if you qualify for the prestigious "Big Five Club": more than three-quarters of Mala Mala's guests achieve membership in the club after spotting lion, leopard, rhino, elephant, and buffalo. Rangers join in exchanging tales of animals they have known, such as Mafunyane, an old elephant with tusks so long they reached the ground. Mala Mala's rangers are highly trained and qualified; most have university degrees in areas like ecology or zoology, and all have an intimate understanding of animals and their relationship to their environment.

The Buffalo Lounge is just what you'd imagine it would be: casual, walls decorated with animal heads and skins; native artwork; and a high, vaulted, wood and thatch ceiling. The lounge opens onto an expansive veranda, a good place to watch the rhinos and other animals coming for a drink in the river below. It's also a great place to relax at the end of the day with a glass of fine South African wine. Mala Mala has an excellent and extensive collection of tasty regional wines.

The romance of Mala Mala is a heady concoction of exotic safari experiences, warm knowledgeable people, exceptional accommodations, and brilliant African skies.

Address/Phone: Mala Mala Game Reserves, Box 2575, Randburg 2125, South Africa; 27–789–2677; fax: 27–886–4382; fax to camp: 21–1311–65686

U.S. Reservations: None; contact Mala Mala directly.

Owner/Manager: Michael Rattray, owner/managing director; Angus Sholto-Douglas, camp manager

Arrival/Departure: Rattray Reserves offers direct flights from Johannesburg into the Mala Mala airstrip in chartered pressurized King Air aircraft daily. You can also fly from Johannesburg to Skukuza Airport where you will be met by rangers from the Mala Mala camp.

Distance from Skukuza Airport: 25 miles (½ hour); 1 hour, 10–minute flight from Jan Smuts Airport in Johannesburg to Skukuza

Distance from Skukuza: 25 miles

Accommodations: 25 twin *rondavels* (bungalows) plus the Sable Suite, which accommodates 16 guests and has its own dining room, lounge, bar, *boma* (see description, p. 313), swimming pool, and viewing deck.

Best Rooms/Suites: Ask for end suites overlooking the river

Amenities: Air-conditioning, electric shaver plug, PABX telephone/intercom, extra large twin beds; ice service

Electricity: 220 volts

Sports and Facilities: Wild game viewing, swimming, hiking

Dress Code: Bushveld casual, but a sweater may be required at anytime; during winter months (May to September) very warm clothes, including a windbreaker are essential.

Weddings: Not usually

Rates/Packages: From $520 per person per night, includes twin *rondavel* accommodations, all meals, snacks, teas, game drives, walking safaris, laundry, and transfers from local airports.

Payment/Credit Cards: Most major

Deposit: 1-night deposit required to secure accommodations; balance due 14 days prior to arrival. Cancellation fees apply as follows: 5 percent, 90 days prior to arrival; 25 percent, 21 days prior; 50 percent, 7 days prior; 100 percent, 24 hours or less prior. Special policies for high season periods.

Government Taxes: Included
Service Charges: Included
Entry Rrequirements for U.S. Citizens: Passport and return or onward ticket required. Check whether visa is necessary

INDEXES
Alphabetical Index to Honeymoon Resorts

Seaside Resorts

Resorts with Tennis

Resorts with Golf on Premises
(*Note:* Many other resorts offer golf nearby)

Resorts with Horseback Riding

In-City/Town Hotels

Resorts with Area Skiing

Adventure/Safari Lodges and Resorts

Resorts with Private Pools

Resorts with Fireplaces

About the Author

Katharine D. Dyson is a freelance writer who specializes in travel. For this book, her work has taken her around the world researching and writing about the best honeymoon spots. Her articles have appeared in many newspapers and magazines, including *Modern Bride, Golfweek, Specialty Travel Index,* and *Jax Fax Travel Marketing.* She writes a weekly travel column, *Travel Savvy,* for several Fairfield County, Connecticut, newspapers and publishes a consumer newsletter of the same name.

Also of Interest from The Globe Pequot Press

100 Best Resorts of the Caribbean $18.95
  Find your own version of paradise

Recommended Island Inns $12.95
  Over 160 inn and guest house accommodations

Sailboat Chartering $13.95
  International guide for hiring a sailboat

*The 1996 Berlitz Complete Guide To Cruising
and Cruise Ships* $21.95
  230 ships have been rated for your cruising pleasure

Caribbean Ports of Call $19.95
  29 ports of call for the cruise passenger

Eastern Caribbean Ports of Call $17.95
  57 ports of call from Puerto Rico to Aruba

Travel Smarts $12.95
  Getting the most for your travel dollar

Available from your bookstore or directly from the publisher. For a free catalogue or to place an order, call toll free, 24 hours a day, 1-800-243-0495, or write to The Globe Pequot Press, P.O. Box 833, Old Saybrook, Connecticut 06475-0833.